I0310206

THE GATHERING OF INTENTIONS

This image appears thanks to the courtesy of the Himalayan Art Resources (www.himalayanart.org). The nineteenth-century painting depicts the buddha Vajrapāṇi's original preaching of the Buddhist tantras, and the *Gathering of Intentions* in particular, atop Mount Malaya on the island of Laṅka. Surrounding Vajrapāṇi are the five excellent ones (*dam pa lnga*) who are receiving his teaching. Led by Rāvaṇa (Blo gros thabs ldan), king of the *rākṣasa* demons, each of the five represents a different class of beings: gods, *nāgas*, *yakṣas*, *rākṣasas*, and humans, with the latter represented by Licchavi Vimalakīrti. Rāvaṇa sits at Vajrapāṇi's proper right, while the god Brahmā is at his left. Beneath and to the proper left of Vajrapāṇi sits a sixth figure: that of King Dza. As explained in chapter 1, King Dza is not counted among the five excellent ones receiving the teaching atop Malaya. At the end of Vajrapāṇi's sermon, however, Rāvaṇa, who inscribes the buddha's words in melted beryl on golden pages, places the resulting tantra within a casket and hides it the sky. Through the blessings of this "symbolic transmission of the conquerors," at the same moment, King Dza receives the same casket as it descends out of the sky onto the roof of his palace, as depicted directly above the king, thus inaugurating the "hearing transmission of persons" and thence all the lineages of tantric Buddhism. The comprehensiveness of Vajrapāṇi's teaching is represented by six volumes, embodying the six classes of tantras from Kriyā to Atiyoga, seen descending from the sky at the top of the painting. The lower three classes, of Kriyā, Ubhayā, and Yoga, each descend on a light ray to a specific Indian locale: Vāraṇasī, the Blazing Mountain (Me ri 'bar ba), and the Craving Wood (*Sred tshal*), respectively, while the destinations of the higher three are left unnamed. In the painting's lower half sit five Tibetan teachers, all important figures in the history of the Nyingma School. From left to right, they are: Nyak Lotsawa Yeshé Zhönu, Zurché Śākya Jungné, Longchenpa, Terdak Lingpa, and Nupchen Sangyé Yeshé.

THE GATHERING OF INTENTIONS

A History of a Tibetan Tantra

Jacob P. Dalton

Columbia University Press New York

Columbia University Press
Publishers Since 1893
New York Chichester, West Sussex
cup.columbia.edu
Copyright © 2016 Columbia University Press
Paperback edition, 2022
All rights reserved

Library of Congress Cataloging-in-Publication Data

Names: Dalton, Jacob Paul, author.
Title: The gathering of intentions : a history of a Tibetan Tantra / Jacob P. Dalton.
Description: New York : Columbia University Press, 2016. | Includes bibliographical references and index.
Identifiers: LCCN 2015018086| ISBN 9780231176002 (cloth) | ISBN 9780231176019 (pbk.) | ISBN 9780231541176 (electronic)
Subjects: LCSH: Dgongs pa 'dus pa'i mdo. | Rñiṅ-ma-pa (Sect)—Rituals. | Spiritual life—Rñiṅ-ma-pa (Sect)
Classification: LCC BQ7662.4 .D35 2016 | DDC 294.3/438--dc23
LC record available at http://lccn.loc.gov/2015018086

Cover design: Noah Arlow
Cover image: Simon Dack Archive/Alamy

CONTENTS

Preface *vii*
Introduction *xiii*

1. Origins: Myth and History 1

2. The *Gathering of Intentions* in Early Tibetan Tantra 30

3. The Spoken Teachings 48

4. The Rise of the Sutra Initiation 65

5. Dorjé Drak and the Formation of a New Lineage 78

6. The Mindröling Tradition 97

7. Returns to the Origin 114

Appendix: The Four Root Tantras of Anuyoga *133*
Notes *149*
Glossary *211*
Bibliography *223*
Index *239*

PREFACE

My research on this project began in the spring of 1997. While staying at Namdröling monastery in south India, I began to work my way through the *Gathering of Intentions*, with the help of Nupchen Sangyé Yeshé's late ninth-century commentary, the *Armor Against Darkness*. By the time I returned to the United States, I was confused but also captivated by the vast and mysterious unexplored territory I had glimpsed. Over the next year and a half, I assembled a small library of everything written on the *Gathering of Intentions* that I could find. Finally, in October 1998, I was ready to return to India and my research proper. On the advice of Gene Smith, I decided to begin with Pema Trinlé's collection of biographies of the lamas belonging to the *Gathering of Intentions* lineage.

In the winter of 1998–99, while still reading through this collection under the supervision of Khenpo Chöwang at the Namgyal Institute of Tibetology in Gangtok, Sikkim, I learned that the current head of the Nyingma School, Penor Rinpoche, was in town, at the behest of the Sikkimese royal family. This was fortunate, as I was having an extraordinarily hard time locating anyone experienced in the *Gathering of Intentions* with whom I could study, and I had heard that Penor Rinpoche was the last living holder of the complete lineage, having received its initiations, the reading transmission, and the explanations. (I later learned that Thubzang Rinpoche of Pelyul monastery in eastern Tibet also held the lineage.)

On his final morning before leaving Gangtok, Penor Rinpoche granted me an audience in his hotel room, with many members of the local government present. I prostrated three times and in my halting Tibetan explained my predicament. I was quickly reprimanded that I should not have been reading the text in the first place without having received the initiation. When I asked if Penor Rinpoche would grant me that initiation, he told me that he would be in the United States the following summer and I should meet him there.

It just so happened that I was back for a brief visit that summer. One day, while staying with friends in upstate New York, I learned that Penor Rinpoche had just opened a new center only a few hours away and was visiting there at that very time. On a hot afternoon, up a small, dusty road, I found Penor Rinpoche sitting alone in an upstairs room in an isolated farmhouse that was otherwise silent and strewn with slumbering monks. After prostrating three times, I reminded Penor Rinpoche of our meeting in Gangtok and that he had instructed me to come find him here, in the United States. Again I requested the initiation. This time he responded, somewhat more kindly, that the following October he would be at his monastery in south India, and that I should come see him there. I thanked him and drove away.

Returning to India, I made sure to arrive at Namdröling monastery, located in the Tibetan settlement of Bylakuppe, a few hours from Mysore, at the proper time. The Dalai Lama had just left, having helped Penor Rinpoche with the consecration of his grand new temple, and Penor Rinpoche was preparing to leave for Singapore. I gained entrance to his room, and after prostrating three times, reminded him of our first meeting in Gangtok and how he had told me to come see him in the United States the following summer. Then I reminded him of our second meeting in the isolated farmhouse and how he had told me to come see him here, in Bylakuppe, in October. Again I asked him for the initiation. This time he responded with exasperation, telling me to go and wait in the monastery's guesthouse until summoned.

I waited for four days. One morning I awoke to find the monastery bustling with preparations for an initiation ceremony that was to begin later that day. I went in to see Rinpoche and asked if this had anything to do with the request I had made. It did indeed. He impressed upon me the seriousness of the event, that he had postponed his trip to

Singapore just for this, and that I should not take this initiation in order to become famous. Certainly, he said, I should not publish any photos of the elaborate sand mandala that had been constructed for the event and hidden behind silk brocade curtains. Sufficiently cowed, I crept out of the room.

Around three thousand people attended the ceremony. For three full days, Penor Rinpoche granted the hundreds of initiations for all nine vehicles of the Nyingma School's teachings. At the end, as the blessings were being distributed while Penor Rinpoche sat upon his throne in meditation, a hard rain fell. Finally, as Rinpoche raised himself up to leave, the rains stopped as suddenly as they had begun, leaving the monastery grounds cleansed and cool.

Over the months that followed, in Bodhgaya and Kathmandu, I read through the various writings by Katok Dampa Déshek, paying particular attention to his influential *Outline of the Vehicles* and his *Summary*, a detailed outline of the entire *Gathering of Intentions* that itself fills about 146 folio sides. Meanwhile, I still had not found anyone who knew the *Gathering of Intentions* apart from Penor Rinpoche, who obviously could not afford the time to read with the likes of me. Finally, Khenpo Pema Sherab, the abbot of Penor Rinpoche's Namdröling monastery, agreed to help me, even though he himself had never read the text. For four months in the spring of 2000, we sat together for two or three hours every day in his room at Shuksep nunnery in Dharamsala, picking our way through the more important parts of the tantra. I used my translation of Dampa Déshek's *Summary* to determine which sections to read. To supplement his own vast knowledge, Khenpo used both of the extant word-by-word commentaries (*tshig 'grel*)—Nupchen Sangyé Yeshé's late ninth-century commentary, the *Armor Against Darkness*, and Khenpo Nüden's massive early twentieth-century subcommentary.

It was from Khenpo Pema Sherab that I first learned of a Spoken Teachings festival held annually at Namdröling. I was thrilled to hear that the *Gathering of Intentions* plays a central role in the ten days of ceremonies, so much so that the event is called the festival of the Gathered Great Assembly, this being the name of the *Gathering of Intentions'* main mandala. Immediately upon finishing my work with Khenpo in early June, I returned to south India to observe the performance of this festival. As the activities reached their climax, I experienced my first significant breakthrough regarding how to conceptualize this tradition that I had now been studying for nearly two years. As I watched, the entire Nyingma pantheon was symbolically returned to its collective origin in the Gathered Great Assembly mandala. I perceived this as a defining moment for the Nyingma School. The grandeur of the event led me to expand my view of what I had been studying. For the first time, I began to sense the extent of the *Gathering of Intentions*' influence upon the history and the identity of the Nyingma School.

For the rest of that summer I continued reading on my own, working through Lochen Dharmaśrī's late seventeenth-century *General Exposition*, a history of the Sutra Initiation (Mdo dbang) tradition. This is certainly the richest source for information about the *Gathering of Intentions*' shifting influences. It answered some crucial questions and bore out many of my evolving theories. In particular, Dharmaśrī's discussions of what he and his brother, Terdak Lingpa, had accomplished at Mindröling monastery with their late seventeenth-century reformulation of the *Gathering of Intentions*' ritual system confirmed the new insights I had gained during the festival in June. The *General Exposition* led me in turn to Dharmaśrī's initiation ritual manual, the shortest of all such manuals, which I had already seen in action during the initiation I had received from Penor Rinpoche. As I plodded through this work's ritual forms, I compared it to the much longer manual by Pema Trinlé, the author of the lineage biographies I had read earlier.

In October 2000, I returned to the United States and established myself in Cambridge, Massachusetts, where I had access to the incomparable library and generous advice of Gene Smith at his new Tibetan Buddhist Resource Center (TBRC). During my time away, two different editions of a new and greatly expanded Spoken Teachings collection had been published. One edition had just arrived at TBRC, while the other was held by David Germano at the University of Virginia. Both editions included additional long manuals for the performance of the *Gathering of Intentions* initiation, texts that had been lost in the Chinese invasion. The quantity of new materials was a mixed blessing. Suddenly I had a lot more work to do, but it was a timely opportunity to fill a huge gap in my knowledge—all three manuals dated from between the fourteenth and sixteenth centuries, a period about which I still knew next to nothing. In late November, thanks to the hospitality of David Germano, I traveled to Virginia to examine a couple of relatively short works that were included in that edition of the Spoken Teachings but missing in the TBRC edition. (All of the texts have since been gathered together in a further, authoritative 133-volume edition that was published in 2009.) I spent the rest of the winter studying the newly discovered ritual manuals at TBRC. Finally, in March 2001, I began writing, though with an extended detour into the background materials necessary to place Pema Trinlé's seventeenth-century writings in their proper political context.

In May, I traveled to eastern Tibet to observe the Spoken Teachings festival as it was performed at Pelyul monastery, just south of Degé on the Yangtze river. While there, I met the exceptionally learned Tupzang Rinpoche; finally, at the end of my researches, I had found someone well acquainted with the *Gathering of Intentions* system. As I explored the monastery grounds, I saw that he had ordered murals from the *Gathering of Intentions*' central myths to be painted on the walls of the main temples. In a series of meetings, I confirmed with him some of my interpretations of the *Gathering of Intentions* and its legacies, while he recounted its history during the nineteenth and twentieth centuries.

In the spring of 2002, as I was at last completing what would become the first draft of the present book, I was contacted by Khenpo Pema Sherap. He asked if I could send him scans of the initiation manuals that had so recently appeared in the new *Greatly Expanded Spoken Teachings* collection. Of course, I obliged and some months later heard that Penor Rinpoché had granted a large number of his students the Sutra Initiation in accordance with the Katok tradition for the first time since leaving Tibet. Thanks to the digital revolution, the Sutra Initiation tradition now has a chance of survival. Had these technological advances come ten years earlier, however, I might never have had many of the adventures or the invigorating meetings and conversations with such wonderful people that I did.

Those who most directly helped me with the research and writing that went into this book include Kyapjé Drüpwang Pema Norbu Rinpoche and Khenpo Pema Sherap of Namdröling monastery in south India, Khenpo Chöwang of Gangtok, Sikkim, and Tulku Tupzang Rinpoche of Pelyul monastery in eastern Tibet, as well as Donald Lopez and Gene Smith. To all of these generous teachers, I owe my profound gratitude. This project was also made possible thanks to a Fulbright-Hays Fellowship from the U.S. Department of Education that funded much of my original research, and to a Charles A. Ryskamp Fellowship from the American Council of Learned Societies as well as a UC President's Faculty Research Fellowship in the Humanities from the Humanities Research Institute at the University of California, both of which gave me the time to finish this project during the academic year 2011–12. I also want to thank José Cabezon, Bryan Cuevas, and Christian Wedemeyer for their valuable feedback. Finally, I thank all of my other teachers, colleagues, friends, and family who made the production of this volume not only possible but a great pleasure.

INTRODUCTION

The Spoken Teachings provide the structure and the treasures the ornaments.

(*bka' ma khob 'bubs gter ma zur rgyan*)

—a well-known Nyingmapa saying

As anyone encountering Tibetan Buddhism for the first time will soon discover, the panoply of tantric ritual systems can be overwhelming. Tibetan culture has been shaped by some of the most elaborate and esoteric ritual systems in the world. Already in early medieval India, the tantras had introduced into Buddhism a plethora of ritual practices, but only in Tibet were so many of them preserved, transmitted through countless lineages, and interwoven to produce still further systems. Given the complexity of the situation, where should the interested student begin? What are the historical relationships among these many varied tantric systems? Between the *Guhyasamāja* and the **Guhyagarbha*?[1] Between the *Cakrasaṃvara* and the *Hevajra*? Between the revelations of Jikmé Lingpa's *Seminal Heart of the Great Expanse* and those of Chogyur Lingpa's *New Treasure of Choling*? And, for that matter, what is the relationship between tantric treasure revelations and the canonical tantras in the first place? How do ritual practices correlate to the canonical tantras upon which they are supposedly based? Which parts of all this are originally Indian and which Tibetan? Why are there so many methods, each enshrined in its own manual or *sādhana*, for performing a single rite? What are the histories behind the various esoteric classes of tantric practice? Where did all of this come from? None of these fundamental questions has yet been answered.

In part, Western scholars' own historical prejudices have not helped the situation. As is now well documented, the Protestant Reformation and the Enlightenment inspired many Western scholars of the nineteenth and twentieth centuries to downplay Tibetan Buddhism's ritual side in favor of its "higher," more philosophical elements, or even to dismiss tantric ritual outright as priestly hocus-pocus.[2] Still today, a surprising number of scholars working on early Indian or Chinese Buddhism continue to see Tibet, and especially its bewildering rites, in a somewhat dismissive light. Such prejudices, of course, are often reflections of our own ignorance more than of Tibetan Buddhism and its rituals themselves.

Nor do Tibetans always help. Many lamas are extraordinarily generous with their time and knowledge, but others can be rather proprietary when it comes to the particulars of their rituals. This may be understandable, as foreign scholars often ignore the tradition's own values, ask the wrong kinds of questions, or are eager to historicize certain unassailable truths. In addition, there is the secrecy in which tantric ritual has been shrouded throughout its history, an esotericism that is still maintained for a variety of reasons. Mystery and the element of surprise can be spiritually powerful, and in a tradition that is suspicious of conceptuality and its detrimental effects on meditation, care must be taken not to dampen the practitioner's experiences. Considerable too are the economic effects of secrecy. Proprietary expertise in a given ritual system can be a marker of a Tibetan Buddhist teacher's authority and is therefore not readily given away. Over the centuries, some Tibetans have struggled hard to maintain control over certain tantric lineages.

But beyond all of this, teachings on a given ritual system, even when offered openly, can themselves obscure as much as reveal that system's *history*; these teachings are construed as eternal, after all, their forms written into the very fabric of the universe. Despite the long-standing Buddhist insistence on the impermanence of all things, the Buddhist tantras are widely held to be temporal manifestations of enormous ur-tantras that are held eternally in the heavens. To subject tantric ritual to a critical historical gaze is sometimes to work at odds with such deeply held beliefs.

For all of these reasons, the study of Tibetan tantra is a daunting task, yet it is also an important one. For centuries, tantric ritual has ensured the endurance of Tibetan culture. When Genghis Khan and his descendents swept across central Asia, they are purported to have supported Tibet's lamas in exchange for regular performances of powerful tantric rites. Even today, Tibetan lamas and their esoteric rituals continue to attract wealthy patrons from around the world, from New York and Hollywood to Taiwan and Beijing. Indeed, it may not be going too far to say that tantric Buddhism has provided the primary language through which Tibetans have articulated their culture. It has shaped the language of Tibet's art, its politics, and its very identity. Without some sense of this ritual world, the modern student of Tibet cannot grasp the full import of fundamental events. When the Dalai Lama and the Paṇchen Lama meet, it is not just a carefully scripted meeting of two dignitaries; it is a ritualized encounter between Avalokiteśvara, the bodhisattva of compassion, and Amitabha, the father of the Lotus buddha family; it is the eighth-century king Trisong Detsen prostrating to the tantric master Padmasambhava; it is Dromtön requesting initiation from Jowo Atiśa in the eleventh century. If we are ever to understand this rich and layered culture, we must come to terms with its ritual universe and intricate ritual histories.

This book takes a small step in that direction by tracing the vicissitudes of a single ritual system—that of the *Gathering of Intentions Sutra* (*Dgongs pa 'dus pa'i mdo*)—from its ninth-century origins to the present day. The *Gathering of Intentions* (as it will be called here) is often referred to as the fundamental "root tantra" of the Anuyoga class of teachings belonging to the Nyingma ("Ancient") school of Tibetan Buddhism.[3] Its odyssey offers unique insights into the history of Tibet, and the Nyingma School in particular.

The study is divided into seven chapters, each of which focuses on another reworking of the *Gathering of Intentions*' ritual tradition. They proceed chronologically and thereby depict a tantric system in constant negotiation with the events of Tibetan history. Each chapter presents an encounter, perhaps even a confrontation, between the original root text—the *Gathering of Intentions* itself—and the latest political or religious concerns. Each Tibetan author wrote his new commentary or ritual manual to negotiate a perceived gap between the original tantra and the lived tradition. The shifting relationships between past and present, between the enduring structures of Tibetan religion and the changing conditions of history, therefore constitute the central theme of this study. Which parts of a given tradition remain fixed and which parts are available for adaptation? As a tantra enters a new phase in its history, does it remain the same text? Or has it in some way died out, become obsolete? Such questions are raised in each chapter, as the *Gathering of Intentions* is reborn again and again, taking new forms generation after generation, amid the dominant paradigms of Tibetan history.

THE PLACE OF THIS STUDY WITHIN THE FIELD OF TIBETAN STUDIES

The Nyingma School is often regarded as a disparate grouping of wild-eyed antinomian visionaries, lone hermits meditating in caves, or at most, lay village lamas working as local priests in small communities. Such images are juxtaposed to those of the other three New (*Gsar ma*) schools—the Kagyu, Sakya, and Geluk—which, according to stereotype, comprise strictly disciplined Buddhist monks ensconced in great hierarchical institutions where lofty scholarship and large-scale state rituals are the primary focus. Such stereotypes have exercised a significant effect on Western scholarship. As long ago as 1895, in his seminal work on Tibetan religions, L. Austine Waddell described a variety of what he saw as "monster outgrowths" within Tibetan "Lamaism," with the Geluk School at one end, being "the purest and most powerful of all,"[4] and the Nyingma School at the other, exhibiting "a greater laxity in living than any other sect of Lāmas."[5] Sixty years later, in another major survey of Tibetan Buddhism, this dim view of the Nyingma School persisted. Helmut Hoffman described the school, which traces its roots back to the arrival in Tibet of the Indian master Padmasambhava, as a "Padmaist religion" that deviated so far from Buddhism into tantric excess that it required repeated purges by the followers of the reformist New Schools.[6] More recently, however, as Tibetan Studies has come into its own as a legitimate field, the popularity of the Nyingma School has improved dramatically. In 1993, Geoffrey Samuel turned the earlier prejudices on their head by removing the negative judgments that accompanied them. Noting the damage already done by such views throughout "popular texts on the history of religion,"[7] Samuel placed "the Nyingmapa yogin in his or her mountain hermitage" on an equal footing with "the Gelukpa scholar with his *geshé* diploma."[8] Despite his rehabilitation of the Nyingmapa, however, Samuel maintained the common characterization of the school as "shamanic," as opposed to the "clerical" Geluk School. "The most 'shamanic,'" he writes, "and least centralized and hierarchical of these [Tibetan Buddhist] orders are the Nyingmapa."[9] To be a Nyingmapa means, according to Samuel, to be tantric, nonmonastic, to act primarily through "analogy and metaphor," and *not* to be engaged in scholarship, textual analysis, and centralized monasticism.[10]

Like all stereotypes, such characterizations are not without their truths. They have persisted in part because they mirror our own familiar dichotomies of the mystic versus the scholar, the ecstatic versus the rational, the profligate versus the celibate, but they are not entirely Western constructions. Tibetans themselves have long espoused similar views, portraying the Nyingmapa as mindlessly absorbed in meditation and the Gelukpa as obsessed with scholarship. Indeed, the Nyingmapa and the Gelukpa often see themselves in similar terms. The problem is that the stereotype also conceals much. Many of the Nyingma School's most significant characteristics are occluded by its standard portrayals. The present study is a history of the Nyingma School as seen through a single ritual system, and the picture that emerges stands in stark opposition to the one so often presented. The *Gathering of Intentions* is without doubt a thoroughly "tantric" work, yet counter to the suppositions of some, every time it is reworked in some new commentary or ritual manual, the purpose is precisely to bring greater centralization and hierarchization to the Nyingma School. The writings on the *Gathering of Intentions* are rigorous works of scholarship and textual analysis, even as they delve deeply into the mysterious realms of tantric myth and ritual. The school revealed in these pages is intimately involved in highly complex and carefully constructed hierarchies, its practitioners often housed in large monastic institutions.

Admittedly, this is partly a reflection of the institutional nature of the *Gathering of Intentions* in particular.[11] This text is fundamental to the so-called Spoken Teachings (*bka' ma*), a class of tantras that are traditionally juxtaposed to the Treasure Teachings (*gter ma*), the revelatory writings that began to emerge in the eleventh century and went on to take the Nyingma School by storm; today the vast majority of rituals performed by the Nyingmapa have their roots in treasure revelation. Notwithstanding the popularity of the Treasure Teachings, the Spoken Teachings have long formed the canonical backbone of the Nyingma School. Today's practitioners can choose from any number of treasure-based ritual systems, which share in common the ritual structures in the Spoken Teachings. The Spoken Teachings are thus foundational, and as a central text, the *Gathering of Intentions* represents an especially institutional aspect of the Nyingma School. Nonetheless, the current popularity and the fascinating origins of the Treasure Teachings have brought them considerable scholarly attention, while the Spoken Teachings have only recently begun to receive the notice they deserve.[12]

SUMMARY OF CONTENTS

Almost all Tibetan canonical works—sutras and tantras—are supposed to have been translated from Sanskritic originals. The *Gathering of Intentions* represents a rare exception, for it purports to have been translated into Tibetan from Burushaski (Tib. *Bru sha skad*), a linguistically exotic language spoken today in just one remote valley in Kashmir. Given internal evidence, there may be some limited truth to the *Gathering of Intentions*' claim, but the bulk of its pages were more likely composed directly in Tibetan. This probably occurred around the middle of the ninth century, at the beginning of Tibet's "age of fragmentation" (*sil bu'i dus*), a period of social disintegration that saw the gradual collapse of the Pugyel empire that had ruled Tibet and much of Central Asia from the seventh through the ninth centuries.[13]

The *Gathering of Intentions*' original purpose was to provide Tibetans with a comprehensive system for organizing all of the Buddhist teachings—and especially the tantric teachings—that had so far arrived in Tibet. It wove together many of the day's most popular myths, doxographical schemes, rituals, and doctrines into a single, elaborate structure. In constructing their comprehensive system, its authors deployed a range of strategies, perhaps most importantly a scheme of nine "vehicles" (i.e., methods for traversing the Buddhist path to enlightenment) that gathered all the Buddhist teachings into a single organizational hierarchy. The *Gathering of Intentions*' initiation ceremony, whereby the disciple was ritually inducted into the mandala and taught its secret rites, could grant initiation into some or all of the nine levels of the teachings. The mandala palace had nine stories, one for each vehicle, with spaces for all the deities relevant to that vehicle to dwell.[14] The *Gathering of Intentions*' Gathered Great Assembly Mandala thus provided room for all nine vehicles of its doxographic scheme. Its authors included the exoteric teachings of the sutras, but their attentions were clearly focused on the esoteric tantras, and particularly the three highest vehicles, Mahāyoga, Anuyoga, and Atiyoga. They developed new tantric equivalents for some of the best known exoteric doctrines of the Buddhist sutras—ten tantric levels (*bhūmi*) through which the practitioner must ascend, five "yogas" corresponding to the five paths of the Mahāyāna sutras, and so on. The result was a massive work, meant to encompass no less than the entirety of the Buddhist dharma.

Chapter 1 of the present study begins at the beginning, with the *Gathering of Intentions*' presentations of tantric myth and its own mythic origins. The authors integrated the two principal myths that had emerged in India to explain the origins of the Buddhist tantras—that of King Dza (sometimes called Indrabhūti), who supposedly first received the tantras through a series of visions atop his palace, and that of the demon Rudra's subjugation by the buddhas, a violent act that required the extreme methods taught only in the tantras. The *Gathering of Intentions* combined these two narratives through a creative reading that would be formative for later Tibetans' approaches to both myth and ritual, at least within the Nyingma School. According to this reading, the tantric teachings always appear in the world on multiple levels at once. Every time, the tantras' "way of arising" (*byung tshul*) unfolds on three planes simultaneously—that of the primordial buddha who dwells beyond all concepts, that of pure beings who play out symbolic patterns through mythic activities, and that of worldly beings who communicate through ordinary language. Of particular significance is the second, symbolic level, for within this realm of unresolved paradoxes and multiple interpretations, Buddhists may glimpse the primordial patterns that structure their tantric practice. The chapter ends with a reading of this intermediary level according to which the tantric ritualist, on the symbolic plane, replays the multiple mythic narratives of the *Gathering of Intentions*' origins through her every reading and ritual performance.

Chapter 2 turns to the early Tibetan master Nupchen Sangyé Yeshé's late ninth-century work, the *Armor Against Darkness* (*Mun pa'i go cha*), and looks at how early Tibetans understood the *Gathering of Intentions* and its place within the larger world of tantric Buddhist ritual. At the time, the three classes of Mahāyoga, Anuyoga, and Atiyoga tantras were highly popular. Nupchen's writings make clear that he, at least, did not understand the *Gathering of Intentions* as a tantra of Anuyoga alone. Later Tibetan exegetes would come to classify it as such, but Nupchen saw it as encompassing all three classes. His commentary thus provides valuable insights into early Tibetan tantric Buddhism when it was still very much a tradition in the making.

Chapter 3 moves to the eleventh and twelfth centuries to take up the issue of canon formation in Tibet, focusing on the *Gathering of Intentions*-related materials written by Dampa Deshek (1122–1192), an early disciple of the influential Zur clan and founder of Katok monastery. This was a period of intense competition among the various Buddhist communities emerging at the time. Each group sought to ensure its survival by codifying and securing exclusive control over its own set of teachings; the same pressures were likely behind the very creation of the Nyingma School as such.[15] The *Gathering of Intentions* came under attack from Tibetans who accused it of being a Tibetan forgery, and not at all the Indic (or even Burushaski) work it claimed to be. Those who defended the work—the Zur clan and its spiritual descendents in particular—responded by canonizing it within a wider triad of tantras. They recast the *Gathering of Intentions* as a uniquely "Anuyoga" work that functioned alongside two other tantras of the Mahāyoga and Atiyoga classes, respectively. In this way, the *Gathering of Intentions* was at once downgraded, pigeonholed, and enshrined at the canonical heart of the Nyingma School.

In the fourteenth and fifteenth centuries, the *Gathering of Intentions*' *apparent* influence continued to wane. Chapter 4, on initiation, traces this decline through a series of ritual manuals written for the performance of the initiation ceremony. As mentioned above, the *Gathering of Intentions*' initiation structure is unusually elaborate, as it grants initiation into any or all of nine vehicles. In the fourteenth and fifteenth centuries, three major initiation ritual manuals were composed, each reflecting the lessening influence of the *Gathering of Intentions* to little more than a sacred placeholder within the Nyingma School. The chapter is technically dense, but for good reason: the development of tantric ritual is inherently complex, sometimes intentionally so, but it is also the language within which many aspects of Tibetan history and politics unfold. In order to gain an appreciation of the kinds of subtle shifts and competitions at stake, it is necessary to delve into this world and reckon with its complexities.

Chapters 5 and 6 examine the *Gathering of Intentions*' role in the tumultuous political events of the seventeenth century. In 1642, the Fifth Dalai Lama gained control of Tibet and began consolidating the early modern Tibetan state. The *Gathering of Intentions* became a kind of pawn in the politics of the day. With the Dalai Lama's support, large new Nyingma monasteries began to spring up throughout central and eastern Tibet. The first of these was Dorjé Drak, founded just outside Lhasa in 1632. The power of Dorjé Drak grew swiftly, thanks to the combined efforts of the Fifth Dalai Lama, his regent successor, and the monastery's second head, Pema Trinlé (1641–1717). All three figures were politically astute, and all recognized the benefits of making the *Gathering of Intentions* a jewel in the crown of Dorjé Drak. To install it there, however, a new third lineage had to be created, to wrest control of the *Gathering of Intentions* away from Katok monastery and the inheritors of the Zur system in central Tibet, both longtime enemies of the Dalai Lama and Pema Trinlé. Chapter 5 therefore turns to the writings of Pema Trinlé, and in particular his collection of biographies of the past masters of the *Gathering of Intentions*' "Sutra Initiation" lineage. Through this work, Pema Trinlé sought to construct a new lineage that would put his monastery at the heart of the Nyingma School. The chapter examines his motivations and exposes the deep involvements of Nyingmapa religious masters in the politics of this formative period in Tibet's history.

Chapter 6 turns to another set of *Gathering of Intentions*-based innovations that played perhaps an even greater role in the politics of the seventeenth century. These occurred at Mindröling monastery, located just across the river from Dorjé Drak. Mindröling's founder, Terdak Lingpa (1646–1714), together with his brother, Lochen Dharmaśrī (1654–1717), embarked on a mission to unite the Nyingma School through rigorous historical investigation and the creation of new, large-scale ritual performances. Their strategies closely mirrored the Dalai Lama's own use of public festivals in his construction of the nascent Tibetan state, and their efforts marked a turning point in the identity of the Nyingma School. Late into their lives, they worked assiduously to export their new vision, inviting lamas from all over Tibet to grand festivals at their monastery, during which they would transmit their new ritual systems.

Finally, chapter 7 examines the tensions between conservation and modernization in the nineteenth and early twentieth centuries. In the mid-nineteenth century, an elaborate new Spoken Teachings festival (*bka' ma'i sgrub mchog*) was created at Pelyul monastery in eastern Tibet. Within a few years, all the largest "mother" monasteries in Kham had adopted the festival, and today it is perhaps the largest uniquely Nyingma event to be observed on an annual basis at almost all of the school's major monasteries, both within Tibet and in exile. In this form, the *Gathering of Intentions* has been preserved into the modern day, yet the tantra itself plays an incongruous role. On the one hand, it defines the ritual space for, and thus the basic structure of, the entire festival; on the other hand, its own rituals are strangely absent from the proceedings. This incongruity reflects the tensions inherent in canonization and preservation. The chapter concludes with an account of the remarkable events of the twentieth century, a series of adventures that included the magical rediscovery of a long-lost text, the self-conscious reenactment of the *Gathering of Intentions*' mythic origins atop a remote mountain in eastern Tibet, and the fateful smuggling of a manuscript across the world's highest mountain range. Each is another tale of preservation, another example of how Tibetans struggled to maintain their religious traditions in the face of possible extinction.

Today, the *Gathering of Intentions* and its commentaries are almost never read and its rites are rarely performed, yet its organizational strategies, especially its nine vehicles schema and its elaborate mythologies, continue to be highly influential from behind the scenes. In a sense, the *Gathering of Intentions*' gradual demise was written into its nature, made inevitable by its very success. Back in the ninth and tenth centuries, the *Gathering of Intentions* was meant to provide Tibetans with an elaborate system for organizing all the doctrines and practices that were flooding in from India. In this it succeeded, but after its systems had been widely adopted (in the eleventh and twelfth centuries), the *Gathering of Intentions* itself, as a read text, began to fade away. Its purpose had been achieved. Its innovations and structures had become so ubiquitous as to disappear from sight. Today, the *Gathering of Intentions* continues to be fundamental to the identity of the Nyingma School, but its structures are so familiar to the Nyingmapa that they are usually overlooked. To look for them is like the eye looking for the eye, to use a traditional Buddhist metaphor. And in this sense, the *Gathering of Intentions*' influence functions very much on the symbolic level, beyond the ken of ordinary beings involved in routine religious practices. Few, if any see or read the tantra itself, yet they repeat its mythic patterns daily, patterns that continue to work on an invisible plane, providing the structures and the shared archetypes that Tibetans of the Nyingma School inhabit.

THE GATHERING OF INTENTIONS

1

ORIGINS

MYTH AND HISTORY

The *Gathering of Intentions* stands astride multiple worlds. Termed a sutra, an *āgama* (Tib. *lung*), and a tantra, it is said to have been translated into Tibetan by an international team of scholars working in Nepal and Brusha, both ancient Himalayan kingdoms located along the Indo-Tibetan border. It is considered the fundamental tantra of the Anuyoga class, a category of Buddhist tantras that lies between the more familiar classes of Mahāyoga and Atiyoga that comprise the Nyingma School's tantric system. But perhaps most important for its enduring influence within Tibet, the *Gathering of Intentions* constitutes a powerful mythic bridge between the abstract heights of the ultimate *dharmakāya* buddha (i.e., awakening in the formless form of utter emptiness) and the all-too-human world that we inhabit. It is at once a nondual reflection of buddhahood wordlessly communicated beyond all time, and a transcript of an elaborate teaching that has been passed down from master to disciple for some eleven centuries. In affording a passage between the buddhas and ourselves, the *Gathering of Intentions* and its mythic narratives allow the ultimate to manifest within the conventional, and conversely, modern-day Tibetans to trace their practices back to the original buddha, Samantabhadra himself.

From early on, the authors of the Buddhist tantras were intensely interested in the mechanics of emanation: How do the buddhas move from undifferentiated meditative absorption into their compassionately emanated worldly forms? In the earliest tantras, this was not just some matter of abstract theorizing; it had practical consequences, for once the inner workings of the buddhas' emanations were laid bare, they could be reformulated as ritual processes and reenacted by tantric practitioners. Another Buddhist tantra, the famous *Sarvatathāgata-tattvasaṃgraha*, for example, describes a series of five stages through which all buddhas and tantric ritualists alike must pass in order to arise as the fully efficacious *tathāgata*, Vajradhātu seated atop Mount Meru at the center of the universe.[1] Here, at the origin of all enlightened activity, myth and ritual are inextricable.

But such mythic accounts of emanational processes not only provided models for tantric ritual practice, they also revealed the very origins out of which the tantric teachings emerged. Thus the above-cited *Sarvatathāgata-tattvasaṃgraha*, in narrating the Buddha's progress through the five stages by which he manifested complete enlightenment, is also telling the tale of its own appearance in this world. This was, after all, the originary moment when the heads of the five buddha families introduced Buddha Śākyamuni to the teachings of the *Sarvatathāgata-tattvasaṃgraha* and its central Vajradhātu mandala. Thus the early tantric interest in the mechanics of emanation was also driven by a need to legitimate new scriptures, to explain their origins, and to tie them to the historical Buddha Śākyamuni.

An assortment of tantric origin myths may be found. The *Purification of All Negative Rebirths*, for instance, tells how the Buddha first preached that tantra in the heavens, to save a god named Vimalaprabhā who had died and subsequently plunged into the hells. But that story remained tied to that particular tantra. Over time, two other narratives emerged as the principal tantric origin myths.[2] One told of how the tantras were first received in this world by King Indrabhūti, the legendary ruler of Oḍḍiyāna in northwestern India. In some versions, the king's name differed (he might be King Dza from Bengal, or King Sucandra of the mythical realm of Śambhala), but the basic story remained the same: a great Buddhist king receives a tantra from an emanated buddha and thereby inaugurates a new lineage of tantric teachings on earth. Alongside this myth grew a second, even more influential narrative in which the tantras were originally taught in order to tame the terrible demon Rudra, sometimes Maheśvara, whose power had grown to an otherwise unruly extent. The buddhas emanate for this purpose, enact the violent subjugation of Rudra, and teach him the tantra in question.[3]

The *Gathering of Intentions* is unusual for weaving extensive versions of both these origin myths into a single narrative. It does so by introducing a system of three transmissions (*brgyud pa gsum*), three levels on which its teachings emanate into the world. This triadic structure has exerted considerable influence upon Tibet's Nyingma School. The extent of its impact becomes clear when one reads any modern-day presentation of the school's history; it will almost certainly open with a discussion of these three transmissions and King Dza's original reception of the tantras.[4] Origins, myth, emanation: the weave of these three ideas within the *Gathering of Intentions* forms the focus of this first chapter. We begin, then, at the beginning, with the origins of this obscure tantra, first in history, then in myth.

HISTORICAL ORIGINS

One often begins a Tibetan text by turning not to its first page but to its last, where lies the colophon. In the *Gathering of Intentions* it reads: "In the district of Brusha, the Indian scholar Dharmabodhi and [the master of] the great tradition, Dhanarakṣita, as well as the principal editor, the translator Che Tsengye, translated and edited [the *Gathering of Intentions*] from Burushaski into Tibetan."[5] Unfortunately, all three of the figures named—Dharmabodhi, Dhanarakṣita, and Che Tsenkyé—are rather obscure. To date their supposed translation, one must turn instead to a related and better-known figure.

The great Tibetan exegete Nupchen Sangyé Yeshé lived through Tibet's "age of fragmentation," a kind of "dark age" in Tibetan history that stretched from around the mid-ninth to the late tenth century.[6] During these years, Nupchen composed several influential texts, most famously his *Lamp for the Eyes in Contemplation*, an extended discussion of nonconceptuality in sutric and tantric Buddhism.[7] By far his longest work, however, is his two-volume commentary on the *Gathering of Intentions*, titled *Armor Against Darkness*. This remarkable work stands out as one of the longest Buddhist treatises to be composed by a

Tibetan prior to the eleventh century. Nupchen seems to have written it around the turn of the tenth century, and it is said that he studied directly under the *Gathering of Intentions*' three translators, especially the Tibetan Che Tsenkyé. Given this, it would seem that the *Gathering of Intentions* was translated—if "translated" is the right term—not long before Nupchen penned his commentary, i.e., around the mid-ninth century.[8]

The question remains, however, whether the *Gathering of Intentions* really was ever "translated" in the normal sense. Certainly today the work exists only in Tibetan, and no mention of it appears in any definitively Indian texts. The colophon's claim that it was translated from the obscure language of Burushaski rather than from Sanskrit is remarkable; no such claim is made of any other text in the Tibetan Buddhist canon. Indeed, precious little is even known about the kingdom of Brusha.[9] Burushaski has received some attention from linguists, as it is developmentally distinct from other languages in the region.[10] Once upon a time, it enjoyed considerable popularity around Gilgit, but at some point its speakers were forced to move into the much smaller area where they are found today, the Hunza Valley and its environs.[11] Knowledge about the people of Brusha in their Buddhist days has been obscured by their later conversion to Islam, and by a paucity of documents dating from the period. However, they continue to sing a version of the Tibetan Gesar epic in Burushaski; there, at least, their ancient connections to Tibet may still be remembered.[12]

Among Tibetan sources, the *Old Tibetan Annals*, an ancient record of the Tibetan empire discovered near Dunhuang, mention Brusha in the context of a Tibetan military expedition to the region that took place around 737/8 C.E.[13] The campaign was successful and shifted control of the area from Chinese into Tibetan hands. In 740, Tibet's sovereignty was further secured through marriage, and Tibetans maintained control of the region for another decade, until, after several attempts, the Chinese finally dislodged them. Even so, Tibetans seem "to have held on to some of their positions in the Pamirs until later in the [ninth] century,"[14] when the Tibetan empire collapsed.[15] That occurred following the death of the Tibetan king Wui Dumten (a.k.a. Lang Darma) and inaugurated the so-called age of fragmentation, a period of economic collapse and political chaos. The imperial government was divided and the Buddhist monasteries of Tibet closed. If the *Gathering of Intentions* was "translated" around 850 C.E., it would have been at the beginning of this period of imperial decline. One twelfth-century author, to whom we will return later, even suggests that the *Gathering of Intentions*' translation had to take place outside of Tibet precisely because of all the internal political turmoil,[16] and Buddhism does seem to have fared better in Brusha during this time.[17] On this point, at least, we are given no reason to doubt that the *Gathering of Intentions* might have originated there.

Nonetheless, the possibility remains that the *Gathering of Intentions* was composed directly in Tibetan and that no Burushaski original ever existed. In the eleventh century, both the princely monk Podrang Zhiwa Ö and the translator Gö Khukpa Lhetsé leveled claims that the *Gathering of Intentions* was apocryphal and actually written by the ninth-century Tibetan Dorjé Pelgyi Drakpa.[18] There is some evidence that such was not entirely the case, at least for a few parts of the work.[19]

In his cursory study of the *Gathering of Intentions*' famous Rudra-taming myth, R. A. Stein observes that "the Tibetan translation is awkward, often confused," and made worse by Burushaski words left untranslated.[20] A couple of explanations may be offered for this. The words may have been retained to lend legitimacy to the document. Stein goes on to observe that similar practices are seen in early Bön works, where untranslated Zhang-zhung terms commonly appear, and that both Burushaski and Zhang-zhung were, after all, sacred languages for the early Bönpo. It is unlikely, however, that Brusha would already have had such "sacred" associations for Tibetan *Buddhists* as early as the mid-ninth century, when the *Gathering of Intentions* was "translated."[21]

Nor does Stein's theory explain why the untranslated Burushaski appears in only a few chapters. The *Gathering of Intentions* is a long work of seventy-five chapters, twelve of which (chs. 20–31) are devoted to the core myth of the buddhas' subjugation of Rudra. These chapters are peppered with untranslated Burushaski, but outside of this myth, not a single Burushaski word occurs. This may be interpreted in two ways. It could be that the Rudra narrative was all that the translators managed to complete before they were forced to move their operation from Brusha. In such a (somewhat unlikely) scenario, they would have translated the rest of the *Gathering of Intentions* elsewhere, where Burushaski was not the local lingua franca or they were able to consult instead a Sanskritic version. This idea would at least be consistent with the tradition's own claims that a Sanskrit original did exist. It would also square with a story found in several later sources that recounts how the translators were forced by antagonistic Brusha locals to abandon their efforts mid-project and were able to complete their translation only some years later, after moving their operation to Nepal.[22] Unfortunately, there are several problems with this ideal picture. First, it raises the question of why the translators would have passed over the first nineteen chapters to begin their translation with the Rudra myth in Brusha. Second, even if they had moved their project to a new location, one might expect that at least the occasional Burushaski word still would have crept in. Third, no claim has ever been made that any part of the *Gathering of Intentions* was translated directly from Sanskrit, and had such a claim been possible, it probably would have been made.

A more likely explanation is that the Rudra myth represents the original core of the *Gathering of Intentions*, not just thematically but compositionally. That is to say, first the Rudra myth was translated from Burushaski, and then the rest of the *Gathering of Intentions* was constructed—in Tibetan—around the resulting narrative. That some part, at least, really was translated from Burushaski would help to explain the colophon's claim for the text as a whole, which is otherwise rather anomalous and arbitrary.

One problem with this hypothesis remains to be addressed: if the Rudra myth represents an earlier textual stratum translated from Burushaski, why does it contain so many references to the larger doctrinal and ritual systems discussed elsewhere in the *Gathering of Intentions*? The myth must have been rewritten, at least somewhat, to conform to the larger tantric system being elaborated in the rest of the tantra. And this prompts a closer examination of how these interpolated technical sections match up with the parts containing untranslated Burushaski.

First, the Burushaski stops after chapter 27. This is significant given that the remaining chapters, 28 to 31, are almost entirely devoted to the initiation ritual granted to Rudra and his horde following their subjugation, an elaborate ceremony specific to the *Gathering of Intentions'* ritual tradition. Similarly, at the beginning of the myth, there is no Burushaski before chapter 25, except for chapter 22. Again this makes some sense, as the Burushaski-free chapters 20 and 21 describe Rudra's past lives and his followers' wrong views, respectively, and both descriptions are presented in technical terms that are set forth elsewhere, in later chapters.[23] Then chapter 22, where Burushaski does appear, is straightforward mythic narrative, after which, again, chapters 23 and 24 describe the processes by which the deities emanate to tame Rudra. In short, the chapters break down as follows:

20–21: Technical doctrine, no Burushaski.
22: Plot narration, Burushaski present.
23–24: Technical doctrine, no Burushaski.
25–27: Plot narration, Burushaski present.[24]
28–31: Technical doctrine, no Burushaski.

All this suggests that most of the *Gathering of Intentions* was composed directly in Tibetan, though around an original core of the narrative sections of the Rudra myth that were translated from Burushaski.[25]

Despite this theory, it is still possible that the larger ritual system upon which the *Gathering of Intentions* was based itself may have been Indian, at least in part. A number of Indian scholars were supposedly involved in the wider literary and ritual milieu surrounding the *Gathering of Intentions*; this raises the question, how many Indians need to be involved in a tantra's composition for it to be "Indian"? And conversely, how many Tibetans need to be involved for a tantra to be "apocryphal"? And then, to complicate matters still further, there are other tantras extant in Tibetan that partake of the same (rather unusual) ritual system,[26] which makes it conceivable that a genuinely Indic ritual system might have been behind the composition of the *Gathering of Intentions*.

We are thus presented with a picture of Indians and Tibetans collaborating on a work "written for export" directly in Tibetan. Such a "gray text" is a clear alternative to the usual black-and-white categories of "authentic" (Indian) and "apocryphal" (Tibetan) that the later tradition employed. Ronald Davidson, who first introduced the concept of such "gray texts," observes that "they are apocryphal in the sense that they are not what they represent themselves to be, but then very few Indian Buddhist scriptures or other compositions actually are precisely what they are represented to be. Conversely, these new works are authentic in that they demonstrate the method of continual composition under the specific circumstances of Buddhist insight embedded in both a time and a place."[27] In other words, the authors of such works may have considered them authentic in that they were revealed texts, expressions of or inspired by real Buddhist insight. By the time of the *Gathering of Intentions*' composition, such inspired or visionary modes of writing may already have been part of a long and venerable history. Since in its earliest days, writes Paul Harrison, the Mahāyāna may have involved "a convergence of meditation and textual transmission," in which "the specific circumstances of the real world combine with visions in deep states of meditation or dream to transform received oral tradition into a new kind of Buddhism . . . the creative recasting of material already accepted as authentic *buddhavacana*."[28] Some centuries later, the tantras would have taken this visionary trend a step further, when they introduced more systematic ritual practices for encountering buddhas and, perhaps more crucially, transforming oneself into a buddha—practices that blurred even further the lines between human and divine authorship. And as Buddhism began to move from India into the Tibetan cultural milieu, such creative approaches to textual transmission would have facilitated still more recastings of the authentic word of the Buddha.

Thus in his seventeenth-century *General Exposition* and its ritual traditions, the Tibetan scholar Lochen Dharmaśrī recounts a presumably earlier story that suggests precisely such an inspired sense of translation:

> During the translation, a nonhuman, holding [in one hand] a *pāṭala*-colored flower of the gods who are beyond this Jambudvipa world and [in the other hand] a chariot wheel, came and said, "To whom are you listening?"
>
> The scholars replied, "We are listening to the noble Vajrasattva."

> Then that being, scattering flowers and circumambulating three times with great respect, venerated them with an elephantlike [i.e., stolidly faithful] conduct, without any doubts. He said, "*Jina rāja*!" and then withdrew.
>
> The scholars were amazed at this and proclaimed, "Surely excellent good qualities will arise in plenty!" At the Fragrant Mountain there dwells an elephant earth protector [spirit] who is an emanation of a bodhisattva. Hereafter this [apparition] will recognized to be a manifestation of that [spirit].[29]

Unfortunately, Dharmaśrī does not provide the source of this story. Nonetheless, the tale may have grown, in part at least, out of concerns of the translators or of the later Tibetan lineage holders about the legitimacy of their "translation." Their solution was to look not to a Sanskrit (or even a Burushaski) original for authority, but straight to Vajrasattva himself and their own visionary experiences. The story certainly reflects a loose sense of "translation" that allowed for considerable creative innovation.

Whatever the circumstances of its translation, the *Gathering of Intentions*' authors were clearly educated and well acquainted with Buddhist scripture. The Rudra myth alone reflects familiarity with a wide range of Buddhist narrative literature. It follows the classic structure of the *avadāna* stories, with a narrator buddha, a past life story, and the present story.[30] It employs narrative refrains such as "at the time of that age" (*de'i tshe de'i dus na*), seen also throughout the *avadāna*s, and its narratives are carefully constructed out of well-known narrative incidents. As in the *Sudāya-jātaka* (preserved today only in Chinese, but well represented in early northern Indian Buddhist art), for example, chapter 20 relates how local villagers abandon the baby Rudra in a cemetery upon his dead mother's breast, from which the infant then nourishes himself. The authors were similarly aware of other tantric sources. Chapter 21's account of the nine mistaken views produced by Rudra is also found (with some variations) in the *Sarvabuddhasamāyoga*, another important early Buddhist tantra, while the Rudra myth's overall narrative represents a skillful weave of earlier renditions of the taming myth with the *Gathering of Intentions*' own complex tantric system.[31]

MYTHIC ORIGINS: THE KING DZA MYTH

Whatever modern scholarship may tell us about the historical origins of the *Gathering of Intentions*, the tantra itself gives quite another story. According to the tantra's own framing narrative, its teachings were first delivered by the buddha Vajrapāṇi to five bodhisattvas, all of whom had gathered atop Mount Malaya on the island of Laṅka. It was a momentous occasion, for it marked the mythical advent of tantric Buddhism in this world, the original transmission of not only the *Gathering of Intentions* but also the Buddhist tantras as a whole.

In India, the Buddhist tantras began appearing in the seventh century. They marked a discernable shift in Buddhist thought and practice. Wu Hsing, a Chinese pilgrim who died in northern India in 685 C.E., bears firsthand witness to the shift in a letter he sent back to China: "Nowadays, there is what seems a novelty, the doctrine of *mantra* (or *dhāraṇi*), that is in great favor throughout the entire country."[32] The tantras and their powerful rituals were clearly something new, and they required fresh narratives to explain and justify their origins. The two principal narratives that emerged in the seventh and eighth centuries to accomplish this end—the legend of King Dza/Indrabhūti and that of Rudra/Maheśvara's subjugation—describe the origins of the tantras, how the tantric teachings first came into the world. Both were highly influential in the later Tibetan tradition, and both are found in elaborate forms in the *Gathering of Intentions*, where they are synthesized into a comprehensive mythological system. Here we turn first to the legend of King Dza.

A number of Buddhist tantras tell of a legendary king who was the first human to receive the tantric teachings. In the tantras followed within the Tibetan New (Gsar ma) schools, the king's name is usually Indrabhūti, and he is placed in either Bengal (Za hor) or Oḍḍiyāna.[33] The fourteenth-century Tibetan historian Butön reports on the earliest known instance of the myth. According to him, the legend appeared in a work known as the **Śrī-saṃvarodaya-uttaratantra* (*Dpal sdom pa'i 'byung ba'i rgyud phyi ma*), in which the Buddha is said to have uttered the following prophecy:

> 112 years[34] after I have gone from here an excellent essence of the teachings, one that is already known in the three heavens, will be revealed by Vajrapāṇi, through compassionately adapted blessings, to King Tsa on the mountain called Śrī in the southeast of Jambudvīpa.[35]

Butön goes on to explain how, in accordance with the Buddha's prophecy, Vajrapāṇi subsequently appeared to King Tsa (or Dza) at the appointed moment to teach the *Sarvatathāgata-tattvasaṃgraha* for the first time in this world.[36]

Followers of the Nyingma tradition have generally preferred the name King Dza. Dza was well known in early Tibet, when he was already being put to a variety of uses. His name appears in a couple of early manuscripts from Dunhuang, including Pelliot tibétain 840, where King Tsa is identified with the famous late eighth-century Tibetan King Trisong Detsen.[37] IOL Tib J 340 similarly contains a prophecy extracted from the *Mañjuśrīmūlakalpa Tantra* that is rendered as if it were a reference to Tibet.[38] Despite the king's popularity in early Tibet, however, the *Gathering of Intentions*' telling is one of the few pre-tenth-century narratives to have survived. Here, the king's full name is Kuñjara (*Ku nydza ra*),[39] and he is placed in eastern India.[40] By the thirteenth century, the resulting version of the myth had become the *locus classicus* for later Nyingmapa retellings.[41]

Another ancient narrative shares certain aspects in common with the King Dza legend. The tale of the early Tibetan king Lhato Tori is an important part of Tibet Buddhism's prehistory. Although the story's general outlines may have been known by the tenth century, the full narrative appears first in works of the eleventh and twelfth centuries, such as the *Sayings of Wa* and the *Pillar Testament*.[42] According to the story, five generations before the great king Songtsen Gampo, King Lhato Tori, while standing on the roof of his palace, received Tibet's first Buddhist texts as they descended out of the sky in a golden casket.

We have already seen that several texts preserved at Dunhuang applied the tantric myth of King Dza to the later, eighth-century king, Trisong Detsen. Perhaps in a similar way, the various Dza myths circulating in early Tibet may have inspired the Lhato Tori legend as well. Both the Dza and Lhato Tori narratives tell of a new Buddhist teaching's arrival into the world, its descent from the sky in a casket, and its reception by a great king. A further parallel is that, in many versions, the king is unable to make sense of the new teachings he receives. In Jñānamitra's commentary and many texts following it, Indrabhūti requires the assistance of the wild tantric siddha Kukkura, or "Dog Man" (surely meant to emphasize the importance of the king-*tāntrika* relationship), while Lhato Tori's sutra is said to have sat unread for five generations before his people could understand its significance.

Certainly there are significant differences between the two legends; the Lhato Tori legend makes no mention of the seven dreams that accompanied Dza's reception.[43] Similarly, some early versions of the Dza/Indrabhūti myth place the Indian king on a holy mountain rather than atop his palace roof. Over time, however, the two stories were occasionally conflated. The twelfth-century *Pillar Testament* and those later sources that followed its account, such as the influential *Collected Precepts on Maṇi*, forged an explicit connection between King Dza and Lhato Tori. Accordingly, Lhato Tori's reception of the Buddhist teachings was the direct result of King Dza's own reception in India:

> The king [Dza] built [a *stūpa*] accordingly, and a form of Vajrasattva appeared in the sky and *poti* [books] rained down. He placed the volumes and a crystal four-terraced *stūpa* inside a precious basket and attached it to the top of the victory banner [that crowned the *stūpa*]. Having made extensive offerings to the *stūpa*, he performed the consecration, at which time the *ḍāka*s and *ḍākinīs* caused the winds of gnosis to swirl up and carry away the volumes and the *stūpa*, up into the sky until they disappeared. At that time an emanation of noble Vajrapāṇi, Lhato Tori Nyentsen, was residing within the Yumbu Lhakhang palace. Just as he was paying homage to his father and mother, the music of various instruments resounded in the sky. A circular multicolored rainbow appeared, from the middle of which a five-colored light ray emerged [and entered] into the royal treasury. Upon the tip of that light ray there appeared a basket made from the five precious substances, and when the king opened it, he found within a crystal four-terraced *stūpa* and a volume of golden pages written in melted beryl. When the king saw what was inside, he could not

even recognize whether it was Buddhist or Bön. Utterly amazed, he named it simply "The Secret Sacredness."[44]

Here the two legends of King Dza and Lhato Tori are woven into a single narrative. For some, at least, the parallels between the legends were apparent enough that they were best understood as part of a single karmic continuum, two aspects of the same karmic event. Through the power of King Dza's momentous act, the tantras appeared in the world, and simultaneously, Buddhism arrived in Tibet. In many ways, this kind of syncretic mythological thinking is an extension of multilayered interpretations seen in the *Gathering of Intentions* itself.

In order to understand the *Gathering of Intentions*' treatment of the King Dza myth, one needs some sense of the tantra's overall narrative structure. The *Gathering of Intentions* may be divided into two parts, what later exegetes called the *root tantra* and the *explanatory tantra*, corresponding to the first two chapters and the remaining seventy-three, respectively.[45] Each has its own narrative setting. The root tantra unfolds at the scene of Śākyamuni's *parinirvāṇa*, i.e., his deathbed, where King Dza appears among the Buddha's disciples gathered there. At the king's request, the Buddha prophesies that he will return in 112 years to teach the tantric teachings of Secret Mantra atop the peak of Mount Malaya in Laṅka. The "explanatory tantra" then shifts the narrative to the five excellent ones (*dam pa lnga*), named in the Buddha's deathbed prophecy as the future recipients of the tantric teachings, who assemble at the appointed time and pray for Śākyamuni to fulfill his promise. The Buddha responds by emanating in the form of Vajrapāṇi and descending onto the peak of Mount Malaya. There he teaches the "the substance of the tantra" (*rgyud kyi don*),[46] which comprises chapters 6 to 75 and thus the bulk of the text's 617 pages. The King Dza myth therefore not only formed a crucial part of the *Gathering of Intentions*' content; it was fundamental to the work's entire narrative structure.

How exactly King Dza figures in all this remains unexplained. The *Gathering of Intentions*' first chapter describes how its teachings are conveyed primordially by means of the "thought transmission of the conquerors" (*rgyal ba dgongs brgyud*). In this way, the *Gathering of Intentions*, as "the essence of Secret Mantra, the mirror of all phenomena," is transmitted wordlessly and simultaneously across all three buddha bodies—within the nondual *dharmakāya*, and within the *sambhogakāya* (the buddha's blissful body of clear light) in each of the buddha fields of the five buddha families (*tathāgata*, *vajra*, *ratna*, *padma*, and *karma*). In each of these fields, the ruling buddha reveals the clear light mandala of mind at the peak of a mountain to a million bodhisattvas who understand it completely and effortlessly. Simultaneously too, the same thought transmission of the conquerors unfolds within the *nirmāṇakāya*, in Śākyamuni's buddha field, as Vajrapāṇi (here the tantric form of Śākyamuni) instantly reveals the clear light mandala of mind while likewise revealing it in the various parallel worlds of the gods, demons, ghosts, animals, hell beings, and *nāgas*. Thus ends the tantra's description of the thought transmission of the conquerors.

Chapter 2 takes us to Śākyamuni's deathbed. Having decided to pass away, the Buddha orders Maudgalyāyana to summon his disciples. All assemble but for the five excellent ones, who remain happily absorbed in "the great meditation on mantra" (*sngags gi bsam gtan chen po*) within which the Buddha is known to be birthless and deathless. The Buddha from his deathbed informs his assembled disciples that he is soon to die and instructs them to present their final questions. At this point King Dza makes his entrance:

> Then he who was the king of the *vidyādharas* gathered in that assembly, the one called Kuñjara, arose from his seat. With a lion-like gaze he regarded the teacher's face and offered these words: "You are the very nature of the sky. You are utterly without passing away and not passing away. However, adapting to the ways of the world, you are passing away, by which you mean to discipline completely [your followers]. You shine as the lamp of the world. Having cleansed all the darkened mandalas in all the worlds of the gods and humans, you have illuminated the mandala of mind. You have arranged in stages the three vehicles that lead to the attainment of enlightenment through the practice of the levels and the liberations.[47]
>
> "Yet you have not set forth the supreme means which with equanimity neither accepts nor rejects and does not seek enlightenment elsewhere, the immeasureable definitive great

vehicle. If you do not formulate into instructions and precepts the third utterance[48] that is the intention of the conqueror, how will an awareness of certainty be established in those of little intelligence who are obscured by ignorance?

"How are these three vehicles for liberation to be compiled? On what [basis]? And by whom? After [you,] the sun that lights the world, set, who will light the lamp? And who will prevent the threat of enemies bent on destroying the teachings?"[49]

To the first of the latter five questions, the Buddha answers that the teachings of Secret Mantra will arise in twelve ways. He then lists these "twelve ways of arising" (*byung tshul bcu gnyis*) by which Secret Mantra will always appear in the world in every aeon. The *Gathering of Intentions*' commentators emphasize repeatedly that there are, of course, far more ways Secret Mantra arises in the world, in the sense that the tantras are taught in all sorts of contexts, but that these twelve are being taught here for heuristic purposes. Each way of arising is then discussed in detail in the *Gathering of Intentions*, with each addressed through a certain number of chapters. Taken as a whole, then, the twelve provide the structure for the entire tantra.[50]

In addressing King Dza's next two questions (On what basis and by whom will Secret Mantra be taught?), the Buddha explains that his teachings will always be present and their meaning should be decided through discussion and practice. Finally, in answer to the two remaining questions (Who will light the lamp, and who will prevent the threat of enemies bent on destroying the teachings?), the Buddha draws King Dza closer: "O Vidyādhara, brother of the dharma, listen well. The lighter of the lamp, as well as the previously prophesied heroes of embodied beings, will arise and will clarify [the teaching] and refute any errors."[51]

The Buddha proceeds to bestow upon King Dza a prophecy that the king himself, along with five other "heroes," i.e., the five excellent ones, will be the lighters of the lamp and will teach the highest vehicles. Nupchen's *Armor Against Darkness* elaborates on the prophecy as follows:

Summoning Kuñjara forward, [the Buddha] instructed him. Mantra would be taught after the teacher's body would pass

> away, but the teachings of Secret Mantra would arise because of this prophecy, made [by the Buddha] before his body's passing, that the Secret Mantra would appear in the future. Vajrapāṇi would appear to the five excellent *vidyādharas*, those heroes of lesser beings. He would teach them, and they in turn would activate the teaching in their respective realms, spreading and clarifying it. They would refute and prevent, once and for all, any enemies.[52]

The five heroes named in the prophecy are precisely those above-mentioned five "excellent ones" who remain happily meditating even as the Buddha is pronouncing his last testament. Each represents a different race of beings: Vimalakīrti for the humans, the king of the *nāgas*, Brahmā for the gods, Ulkāmukha of the *yakṣas*, and most importantly the ten-headed *rākśasa* demon, Rāvaṇa, the Lord of Laṅka.[53]

The actual wording of the Buddha's prophecy appears only later in the *Gathering of Intentions*. In chapter 43 are some crucial elements of the myth, including six prophecies, each made by a certain buddha in a particular aeon, and each describing how the Secret Mantra will originate in that aeon. Taken together, the prophecies drive home the point that Secret Mantra is an exceedingly rare teaching that appears only once every few aeons but always according to the same basic structures. In each of these aeons, a buddha prophesies that the Secret Mantra (here called specifically the *Gathering of the Intentions of All* [*Kun gi dgongs pa 'dus pa nyid*], a clear reference to the *Gathering of Intentions*)[54] will be taught sometime after he dies, when he returns in the form of Vajrapāṇi. In our own aeon, the prophecy is made by Śākyamuni in these words:

> In accordance with the great prophecies made by all [the buddhas], 112 years after I have ceased to appear in this [world], to a worthy noble of the human realm named King Dza, who lives in the eastern direction of the world [i.e., east of Bodhgāya], there will appear first dreams and then the excellent essence of the teaching already renowned in the three heavens. At the ferocious peak, Vajrapāṇi will appear to the Lord of Laṅka, a friendly bodhisattva in the inferior body [of a demon], and others.[55]

The next chapters (3 through 5) are brief and transitional and move to a new narrative setting (Tib. *gleng gzhi*; Skt. *nidāna*).[56] Chapter 3 explains how in the years that followed the Buddha's death, the world descended into confusion. People were filled with longing for the Buddha, until finally after 112 years, the five excellent ones arose from their meditations to discover that the Buddha had died and the world had plunged into misery:

> Having marvelously and involuntarily wept, they each clairvoyantly perceived all. Through acts of magic they all gathered upon the thunderbolt peak of Mount Malaya on the ocean island of the realm of Laṅka. Thus gathered together, the whole assembly in unison let out a wail of extreme desperation.[57]

In chapter 4, this cry of yearning is heard by the buddhas, who rouse Śākyamuni and send him as Vajrapāṇi to fulfill his own prophecy upon the peak called "Ferocious," otherwise known as Mount Malaya, on the island of Laṅka. Chapter 5 then describes his arrival, followed by the five excellent ones' request for the teachings of Secret Mantra.

Chapter 6 inaugurates the "substance of the tantra," which also corresponds to the "symbolic transmission of *vidyādharas*" (*rig 'dzin brda brgyud*), the second of the three transmissions with which this discussion began.[58] The symbolic transmission is somewhat coarser than the ultrarefined, nondual thought transmission of the conquerors described in the *Gathering of Intentions*' first chapter. Here, the Buddha responds to the longings of the five excellent ones by explaining that everyone is already enlightened, that the teaching is present everywhere, and that those who long for the Buddha are ignorant and creating problems needlessly.

This succinct teaching is enough to enlighten the five excellent ones, who, after all, already understood this. But as chapter 7 opens, one of the five, the Lord of Laṅka, asks a question. He points out that the Buddha had prophesied to King Kuñjara *twelve* ways of arising, but the condensed teaching he just gave represents only one. This provokes the second way of arising, and the *Gathering of Intentions*' remaining chapters (8 through 75) are taught by Vajrapāṇi to the Lord of Laṅka. All five excellent ones continue to be present, but the Lord of

Laṅka (a.k.a. the demon king Rāvaṇa) is the Buddha's primary interlocutor for the remainder of the tantra.

The *Gathering of Intentions* itself never explains exactly what King Dza is doing during this teaching atop Mount Malaya. This may be because the Dza myth was already so well known from other, earlier Yoga and Mahāyoga tantric writings. The details are implicit, however, in the wording of the Buddha's prophecy, translated above, that a series of dreams will precede the king's reception of the tantras. For the complete story, the seventeenth-century exegete Lochen Dharmaśrī turns to a no-longer-extant commentary, the *Ornamental Appearance of Wisdom: A Commentary on the Sūtra.*[59] According to this work, the teaching atop Mount Malaya ends with the Lord of Laṅka committing Vajrapāṇi's teachings to writing. Thus for the first time in this aeon, the *Gathering of Intentions* was written down. The Lord of Laṅka puts beryl ink to golden paper, and upon finishing his manuscript, he hides it in the sky before him. At that same moment, "through the blessings of the dharma wheel having been turned at Mount Malaya,"[60] King Dza has a series of seven dreams. In the fifth dream, he receives a tantric text: "From a sun disc blazing with light rays appeared a casket containing volumes with golden pages beautifully inscribed with melted beryl ink."[61] The conclusion is obvious: according to this tradition, King Dza receives the *Gathering of Intentions* just as its compiler, the Lord of Laṅka atop Mount Malaya, sends it into the sky. In the years following his dreams, King Dza expands his visionary text (the *Gathering of Intentions*) into all the various tantras that are then taught separately from that point forward.

In chapter 36, the *Gathering of Intentions* further explains that King Dza's reception and redaction of the tantras in this way inaugurated the third of the three transmissions, the "hearing transmission of persons" (*gang zag snyan brgyud*), just as the perfect, undifferentiated teaching described at the beginning of chapter 1 constituted the "thought transmission of the conquerors" and Vajrapāṇi's imparting of the *Gathering of Intentions* atop Mount Malaya was the "symbolic transmission of *vidyādharas*." King Dza's inauguration of the hearing transmission of persons is thus empowered by the symbolic transmission that occurred on the mountain, which is itself empowered by the thought transmission's nondual turnings of the wheel within the *dharmakāya*, the *sambhogakāya* buddha fields, and the manifold worlds of our *nirmāṇakāya* universe. Presented in this way, the King Dza narrative is woven into a larger, multilayered mythological system that allowed later Tibetans to trace their tantric lineages through the hearing transmission of persons back to the original Indian King Dza, then from him through the symbolic transmission of *vidyādharas* back to the original teaching atop Mount Malaya, and thereby too to the nondual teaching of the primordial *dharmakāya*. In this elaborated form, the King Dza myth would become a foundational myth for the entire Nyingma School.[62]

MYTHIC ORIGINS: THE RUDRA MYTH

The *Gathering of Intentions* also became the *locus classicus* for the Nyingma School's Rudra myth.[63] And again, the myth's narrative was woven deeply into the fabric of the tantra. The Rudra-taming myth describes the buddhas' battle with the demon Rudra, which culminates in their killing the demon, then reviving him as a worldly god bound by powerful oaths to protect the Buddhist teachings. From the seventh century, renditions of this basic narrative served to explain the origins of the tantras. For early Buddhist *tāntrikas*, the myth justified the tantras' teachings on compassionate violence as a path to buddhahood in particular, as it explains how the extraordinary violence of tantric Buddhism was necessitated by Rudra's rise to power. Rudra (sometimes called Maheśvara), in this narrative, was a terrible demon that long ago grew to threaten all of Buddhism and plunged the universe into unthinkable suffering. Such a powerful manifestation of demonic ignorance could not be tamed by the ordinary, pacific methods of the buddhas, and so more of the violent rites of the tantras were taught. The myth thus describes how, for the first time in this aeon, the wrathful buddhas of tantric Buddhism were sent forth to subjugate Rudra and thereby to introduce the tantras into the world.

Despite its widespread influence in later Tibet, the *Gathering of Intentions*' rendition of the Rudra-subjugation narrative was not the earliest of its kind. Demon-taming myths have a long history in India, and the figure of Rudra has long been associated with violence. In the *Ṛgveda*, Rudra was already a terrible deity who dwelled on the margins of society and stole away cattle and children. As one Vedic scholar writes, "Fiery power, ascetic frenzy, mobility on the wind, the garment of red are already in the late *Ṛgveda* (e.g., 10:136) associated with the outsider god, Rudra, the fierce resident of the mountain wilderness. Later Vedic texts stress his isolation from the prescribed shares of sacrifices, regarding him always with awe."[64] In the somewhat later Vedic texts, beginning with the *Yajurveda*, a distinction begins to emerge between the deity's benign aspect, as Śiva, and his malevolent aspect, as Rudra. The earlier *Ṛgveda* combined both aspects in the figure of Rudra, though his dangerous side was certainly primary, like the "beneficent rains loosened by the storm."[65] Later, however, the Indian god Śiva began to merge with the Aryan Rudra and take on his less fearsome attributes. This amalgamation process became pronounced in the *Atharvaveda*, "which represents a transitional stage between the conception of Rudra in the *Ṛgveda* and the systematic philosophy of Śaivism in the *Śvetāśvatara Upaniṣad*."[66] The latter work was crucial to the development of the Śiva-Rudra cult. It was the principal text to establish the use of Śiva as a name for Rudra, and it promoted Rudra as a mountain god, an image that may have continued to resonate in the Buddhist taming myths (though the notion of Mount Kailāśa as Śiva's residence did not arise until the *Purāṇas*).[67]

Within Buddhist literature, Rudra-subjugation tales were apparently popular from at least the early fifth century.[68] Despite such antecedents, most Western scholars trace the origin of the myth in its tantric Buddhist form to chapter 6 of the influential seventh-century Yoga tantra, the *Sarvatathāgata-tattvasaṃgraha*. In this version, it is Maheśvara who is tamed[69] by Vajrapāṇi upon Mount Sumeru. Some decades later, the new Mahāyoga tantras of the eighth century elaborated on the myth still further, introducing intensely violent descriptions of the buddha's treatment of Maheśvara.[70] The trend was successful, and it continued in the later versions of the myth, including the *Gathering of Intentions*.

In the *Gathering of Intentions*' account, the scene of the subjugation is not Mount Sumeru but Mount Malaya, on the island of Laṅka.[71] This shift was almost certainly influenced by the *Laṅkāvatāra Sūtra*, which is similarly taught to Rāvaṇa atop Mount Malaya in Laṅka.[72] Despite the dominance of Theravadin Buddhism in Sri Lanka today, in the eighth and ninth centuries the island was an important place for tantric Buddhists.[73] Laṅka and its inhabitants evoked in the minds of Buddhists across India images of demons and mythic subjugations, and the *Gathering of Intentions*' Rudra-taming myth should be seen against this background of wider mythic associations. Even the legend of the Buddhist Singha people conquering Laṅka, told in both the *Dīpavaṃsa* (late fourth century C.E.) and the *Mahāvaṃsa* (sixth century C.E.), bears certain resemblances to our own Rudra myth. There, Vijaya the Singha leader arrives in Laṅka on the day of the Buddha's birth to find the island overrun by *yakṣa* demons. He defeats the *yakṣa* king by first seducing his queen, Kuveṇī, and following his victory raises five of his own Singha companions to the rank of minister, establishing five colonies on the island bearing their names. Étienne Lamotte dates Vijaya's reign to 486–448 B.C.E. and suggests that the legend is "a distant echo of the struggle between the native Veḍḍa [who apparently belonged to the same race as the pre-Dravidians] and the Aryan settlers."[74]

There are certainly some curious parallels between these legends and the Rudra myth: the seduction of the demon's wife that renders him vulnerable, the flying descent upon the mountain to tame the *yakṣa* king in need of conversion, the sacred mountain itself. And it is not inconceivable that the *Gathering of Intentions*' authors knew of these legends; they were famous enough to be repeated by two Chinese travelers, Fa-Hsiang and Hsuan-Tsang, in the latter's case, when he passed through the region of Kashmir, not far from the kingdom of Brusha.[75] Here again, it seems that the *Gathering of Intentions*' authors referenced themes from a wide range of Buddhist literature, the *Laṅkāvatāra*, the *Rāmayāṇa*, and more, in constructing their narratives.

The details of the Rudra myth's narrative itself have been published elsewhere.[76] For present purposes, I focus on the various doctrinal teachings that are woven into the fabric of the narrative. As already observed, a number of doctrinal elements elaborated upon elsewhere in the *Gathering of Intentions* were probably added to the myth's original (Burushaski?) core narrative, presumably at the time of the tantra's composition. These elements constitute a carefully constructed hierarchical cosmology within which the narrative unfolds, a scheme that completes the mythic universe sketched out by the King Dza myth and its system of three transmissions.

The Rudra myth's narrative arc follows the hapless future demon through countless previous births up to his lifetime in this world as Rudra. His gradual rise to power, which culminates when he becomes the most powerful mundane (*laukika*) god in the universe, begins at the very nadir of existence, in the Avīci hell. Rudra-to-be is tortured incessantly for eighty thousand lifetimes and is freed from this realm only thanks to his karmic connection to an earlier Buddhist teacher, Invincible Youth, who has since become identical with Vajrasattva. Thus freed, Rudra moves up to the only slightly less torturous Extremely Hot Hell for another eighty thousand lifetimes, then on up through a series of lesser hells for several billion more lifetimes. "Finally," we read, "the aeons at the destruction of the universe came—the aeons of famine, of plague, and of war—and he took rebirth in those. The devastations of those aeons emptied the worlds of everything. Yet even when all others had been destroyed, [the future Rudra] continued to take rebirth."[77] The apocalyptic aeons of famine, plague, and war are discussed elsewhere in the *Gathering of Intentions*. Chapter 44 explains that these are the three "outer" aeons that occur at the end of the universe. They last for three years, three months, and three days, respectively, as time speeds up to the vanishing point in the final "inner" aeons of fire, water, wind, and space. And they are themselves manifestations of the buddhas' teachings:

> Some sentient beings are full of desire and tortured with lust. Some sentient beings are extraordinarily ignorant and dense. Some sentient beings are exceedingly angry and savagely wicked. For such beings, the three poisons have ripened in these ways and there is no helping them. In order to sever the karmic continua of their evil actions by revealing to them the characteristic of impermanence, however, the magical display manifests. . . . The aeon in which samsara and nirvana are devoid of sustenance [i.e., the aeon of famine] severs the continua of those desirous with lust. The aeon of ignorant endurance [i.e., of plagues that, through their unendurable sufferings, render their victims senseless] severs the karmic continua of mind and intellect. The aeon of efficacious weaponry severs all the existents [of self] and the existents [of others]. [Following those,]

> the aeon of the fires of insight incinerates all the existents of the afflictions. The aeon of the waters of calm abiding washes all the impurities of the afflictions. The aeon of unimpeded winds completely shakes loose all the objects of knowledge. And the aeon of the space of wisdom evacuates all the aging and decay of signs. When those of evil actions have their continua suddenly severed [by these means], they are suddenly liberated from the lower realms.[78]

The last seven aeons of the universe are thereby framed as Buddhist vehicles to enlightenment. They represent the buddhas' final effort to save, through extreme suffering, those who are so stubborn as not to have been liberated before this late date. All this is exactly what Rudra-to-be undergoes at the end of his extended sojourn in the hells. Unfortunately, he is so deeply engrossed in the three poisons of desire, hatred, and ignorance that he remains unaffected: "Even when all others had been destroyed, he continued to take rebirth." Following the formation of a new universe, he gradually rises up the rungs on the ladder of rebirth, taking the form of one terrible demon or another, until he is finally born in our world on the island of Laṅka.

Now within the span of a single lifetime, Rudra continues his ascent through the *Gathering of Intentions*' cosmic hierarchy. He begins by conquering the representatives of the vehicle of gods and humans (*lha mi'i theg pa*). From his natal charnel ground, he first defeats Rāvaṇa, the Lord of Laṅka and king of the demons (the same Rāvaṇa who received the *Gathering of Intentions*, a point to which we shall return shortly), and thereby extends his power across the entire island of Laṅka. Rudra's celebrations are short-lived, however, for he soon hears about Mahākaruṇā, the leader of the gods. In a fury, Rudra sweeps down upon Mahākaruṇā's abode, kills him with his vile powers, and flings the pieces of the dead deity's corpse across the world, creating the eight sacred sites of the tantras. This gives Rudra immediate control over the entire Indian pantheon, from Indra, Brahmā, and Viṣṇu to the kings of the four directions.

Now the ruler of the entire mundane universe, Rudra resumes his upward march and is finally confronted with the followers of the Buddha. He first defeats the *śrāvaka*s, represented by monks, "those little children," as he calls them, "those slaves to slinging their robes over their shoulders."[79] Next he faces down Hayagrīva: "You too, Neck Boy!" he shouts. "You must also happily promise [to perform my austerities]," whereupon Hayagrīva retreats. While the referent of Hayagrīva's emanation here remains only implied, he might be understood to represent either the exoteric teachings of the Mahāyāna or perhaps those plus the outer tantras.

Finally, Rudra reaches the highest three vehicles of Secret Mantra, those of Mahāyoga, Anuyoga, and Atiyoga, with their four activities of pacification, enhancement, coercion, and violence.[80] Thus the culmination of the narrative may be seen as a mythic presentation of the nine vehicles of the Buddhist teachings, as they are presented in chapter 44 of the *Gathering of Intentions*. The activities of pacification and enhancement are enacted in chapter 25 by Śākyamuni and Hayagrīva, respectively. Both fail, and finally the buddhas send forth Vajrakumāra Bhurkuṃkūṭa to coerce into bed Rudra's queen and the women in his demonic horde, followed by the wrathful Vajra-Heruka to kill and liberate Rudra himself.

Following Rudra's violent purification and resurrection, the myth's two closing chapters describe the initiation ceremony that the *heruka* performs for Rudra and his horde. In a certain sense, this can be seen as a continuation of Rudra's ascent from the hells, for the initiations he receives raise him through increasingly subtle levels of realization. And woven into the narrative description of the initiation is another of the *Gathering of Intentions*' doctrinal systems: the five yogas.[81] These are a tantric reinterpretation of the five paths of exoteric Mahāyāna doctrine. Throughout the *Gathering of Intentions*, they are associated with a new set of ten levels, which also mirror the standard set in the nontantric Buddhist literature.[82] Like the "common" five paths and ten levels, these new "uncommon" sets mark the tantric practitioner's progress on the path toward buddhahood. The early commentator Nupchen Sangyé Yeshé explains that "The uncommon come only on the path of Secret Mantra, though they do not contradict the teaching on the common stages."[83] On the other hand, he says that these uncommon yogas and levels bring the practitioner to a higher state than the common five paths and ten levels of the bodhisattva vehicle, which cannot purify the very subtlest obscurations. The *Gathering of Intentions*' fifteenth chapter says that the five heads of the five buddha families attained enlightenment by ascending through the common levels, after which they rested for a number of aeons before traversing the uncommon levels of the inner tantras. They accomplished the first five, a later commentator explains, for their own welfare and the second set for the welfare of others, in order to manifest the tantric teachings.[84] Furthermore, the highest three levels, which correspond to the fifth path, are only attained via the vehicles of Mahāyoga, Anuyoga, and Atiyoga respectively.[85]

The initiation ceremony performed for Rudra and his followers is described in some detail. The mythic event is significant, for every subsequent performance of the *Gathering of Intentions*' initiation ceremony would be, in a sense, a reenactment of it.[86] The Sutra Initiation (*mdo dbang*), as it came to be known, would become a crucial element in the *Gathering of Intentions*' systematization of tantric Buddhism, alongside its mythological schemes and its nine vehicles. Indeed, the Sutra Initiation ritual, perhaps more clearly than any other aspect of the *Gathering of Intentions*, reflects the extent of the work's vision for its grand tantric system.

The initiations are divided into two parts, the precedent initiations (*sngon byung*) and the subsequent initiations (*rjes 'jug*). The precedent initiations are those that took place in the buddha fields in timeless time, while the subsequent initiations are the ordinary ones received by latter-day humans. The former are described in chapter 13 in order to engender faith in the *Gathering of Intentions*' initiation system.[87] Nupchen states that these initiations were also what the prince Siddhārtha received at the moment of his awakening.[88]

At the center of the initiation ceremony stands (sometimes literally a construction of) the main mandala for the *Gathering of Intentions*' tantric system. The Gathered Great Assembly (*Tshogs chen 'dus pa*) is a highly unusual mandala, for it has nine stories, corresponding to the nine vehicles.[89] Disciples may be led upward through the mandala as far as their abilities warrant, culminating in the highest teachings in the Buddhist world, those of Atiyoga.[90] The mandala is therefore woven, if indirectly, into the Rudra-subjugation myth. In the myth's closing scene, at the end of the initiation ceremony, Rudra and his followers take vows to remain as the protectors to this mandala. Thus every major aspect of the *Gathering of Intentions*' tantric system may be seen reflected in the Rudra myth's narrative.

READING TANTRIC MYTH: THE PARTICIPATORY READER

The King Dza myth and the Rudra myth represent two visions of a single event, two ways of arising of the same tantra. The prayers and longings of King Dza and the five excellent ones for the Buddha to return give rise to Secret Mantra in this world; Rudra's terrible reign provokes the same. Both narratives describe Vajrapāṇi's original transmission of Secret Mantra atop Mount Malaya on the island of Laṅka. But surely this is a contradiction: two myths in the same text describing the same event? Did the *Gathering of Intentions*' authors ignore or overlook this glaring inconsistency? Or did they understand their myths in a way that allowed the two narratives to coexist? The latter was probably the case, for Nupchen, who studied directly under the work's translators-cum-authors, calls attention to precisely this (apparent) contradition:

> The teaching of Secret Mantra by the Lord of the Guhyakas [i.e., Vajrapāṇi] consists of both the explanation [of the whole *Gathering of Intentions*] to the assembly [that included Rāvaṇa] gathered at the peak of Mount Malaya and Rudra's descent onto Mount Malaya.
>
> Someone might say in objection, "If these [two myths of King Dza and Rudra] occur at one time, then there should only be eleven ways of arising [i.e., instead of the twelve originally prophesied by Śākyamuni]; there would be no need to tell how a single teaching occurred at two times." And if [to this you were to reply that] this is not so, that these are separate [events], then you must be saying that the Secret Mantra was arising at the same time in two [different places]. And if *that* is not the case, then you are saying that both events arose at the same time on Mount Malaya, and that would be contradictory.[91]

In other words, how could these two events happen at the same moment in the same place? Nupchen was clearly aware of the potential clash between the *Gathering of Intentions*' mythic claims and the conventional requirements of time and space, yet with complete confidence he draws the reader's attention right to the point. His understanding of tantric myth (or, in more emic terms, the symbolic transmission of *vidyādharas*) apparently allowed for a single event to be described in two altogether different narratives.

Nupchen's discussion of this issue actually appears in the context of a particularly strange moment in the Rudra myth. Chapter 26 opens with a meeting of the buddhas on what to do about Rudra. Suddenly the myth's narrator, Vajrapāṇi, breaks the flow of the story by calling out to the listener, Rāvaṇa (the head of the five excellent *vidyādharas* who first received the tantra atop Mount Malaya): "Lord of Lanka! In the time of that temporality, I was one of those assembled in that very meeting. For the sake of fully awakening everyone into alertness, I thoroughly questioned a bodhisattva named Armor of Exhortation, Capable Intelligence, who was also present in that meeting."[92]

From elsewhere we know that the bodhisattva Capable Intelligence is none other than Rāvaṇa himself, the Lord of Lanka. This means that here, in the midst of Vajrapāṇi telling Rāvaṇa and the other excellent ones the tale of Rudra's subjugation, he describes a scene in which they themselves—Vajrapāṇi and Rāvaṇa—both played a role. In a sense, then, the scene mirrors the larger setting of the tantra as a whole, in which Vajrapāṇi is teaching the Lord of Lanka atop Mount Malaya. Vajrapāṇi is speaking to Rāvaṇa about a time when Vajrapāṇi spoke to Rāvaṇa.

It is significant too that this conversation constitutes the last moment before the buddhas' violent activities begin. Immediately following this scene, the orders are given and the emanations sent forth. Thus Vajrapāṇi's conversation with Rāvaṇa marks the decisive moment out of which this "way of arising," of Rudra's subjugation, unfolds. Just as Vajrapāṇi and the Lord of Lanka are the key players in the original preaching of the *Gathering of Intentions* atop Mount Malaya, they are also responsible for enacting the teachings of Secret Mantra for the subjugation of Rudra. "This means," Nupchen explains, "that throughout samsara without beginning and without end, whenever the Secret [Mantra] arises, the names proclaimed are always those of the Lord of the Guhyakas [i.e., Vajrapāṇi] and Armor of Exhortation Capable Intelligence [i.e., Rāvaṇa]."[93] Here, mythic narrative is repeating within mythic narrative, a reprise that stresses the enduring nature of these fundamental narrative structures within which Secret Mantra will always arise.

It is within this context that Nupchen raises the paradoxical question about the timing of the myths of Rudra's taming and of King Dza and the teaching atop Mount Malaya, *and*, for that matter, of Vajrapāṇi and Rāvaṇa's discussion at the buddhas' meeting. How could these all be occurring in the same place at the same time? "There is no contradiction,"[94] Nupchen writes. "Those [teachings of Secret Mantra] are being expressed throughout time without beginning and without end. Out of those, how Rudra was tamed at some time in the past, how the secret [teaching] arose [atop Mount Malaya], and how this particular discussion [between Vajrapāṇi and Rāvaṇa within the buddhas' meeting] happened are all being related as a story [even right now], and are thus arising at this present moment too; they are [all] taking place at once."[95]

Here Nupchen addresses those readers who might question the idea that Secret Mantra (and the *Gathering of Intentions*, more specifically) arises in multiple ways at the same time and in the same place. He begins by reminding them that there have been, are, and will be countless appearances of Secret Mantra in the world. Every time the *Gathering of Intentions* (and, by extension, any Buddhist tantra held to be contained within it) is taught, it is a "way of arising." He then points out that all three scenarios in question—the Rudra-taming myth, the King Dza myth (which involves Vajrapāṇi teaching the *Gathering of Intentions* to Rāvaṇa atop Mount Malaya), and "this particular discussion" between Vajrapāṇi and Rāvaṇa in the buddhas' meeting—are arising *right now*, that is, in the present moment of reading the tantra. (Remember that Nupchen is communicating through his commentary on the *Gathering of Intentions* and is therefore assuming that his reader is in the process of reading the tantra.) In other words, through this present act of reading, and as one considers these mythic scenarios, all three are arising in the mind of the reader. All three scenes are being played out at the same time and in the same place.

Nupchen's explanation thereby shifts the reader's attention from the multilayered fictions of the mythic events to herself. The reader no longer stands outside these mythic narratives; she is suddenly implicated within them, bringing them to life through her reading. In this sense, every reading is itself another way of arising, another instance of the *Gathering of Intentions* manifesting in the world. The reader plays an active role through her imaginative reenactments of the narratives. One might even suggest that, by reading the *Gathering of Intentions*' narrative accounts of its original transmissions, the reader becomes an actor in those same myths herself. Such is the power of the *Gathering of Intentions*: simply by reading it—simply by conceiving of it—one is inscribed within it. On another interpretive register, the reader is at the peak of Mount Malaya, simultaneously seated at the feet of Vajrapāṇi and included among Rudra's horde, being violently subjugated.

In this way, both the King Dza and Rudra myths describe an archetypal structure that is always present when the *Gathering of Intentions* is taught. On some level, Vajrapāṇi is eternally teaching it to the demonic Lord of Lanka atop Mount Malaya.[96] Whenever the *Gathering of Intentions* is transmitted, the same fundamental narrative is reenacted.

The *Gathering of Intentions*' mythic system was remarkably successful. Its elaborate narratives and extraordinary mythic vision may not have spread throughout India, but they remain ubiquitous within the Nyingma School of Tibetan Buddhism. Indeed, they are foundational to the Nyingmapas' self-understanding. Yet today this influential work goes almost entirely unread, and its lineage is in danger of dying out. The *Gathering of Intentions*' paradoxical mix of success and failure can only be understood through an examination of its complex vicissitudes over the past thousand years. We have seen how the *Gathering of Intentions*' myths placed it at the center of a tantric universe. Over the ensuing centuries, its influence spread forth from this center and pervaded the imaginative world of the Nyingma School. But this spread was also a diffusion. As we turn to the evolution of the *Gathering of Intentions* in Tibet, the manner of this dissipation will become clearer.

2

THE *GATHERING OF INTENTIONS* IN EARLY TIBETAN TANTRA

When the tantras first arrived in Tibet, Tibetans were slow to compose full-blown commentaries on these esoteric works. In accordance with the texts' rhetoric of secrecy and transgression, the imperial court prohibited their translation and circulation. Even after the empire's gradual collapse in the late ninth century, early Tibetan tantric authors mostly limited themselves to scattered notes, short instructional texts, and ritual manuals. The few early Tibetans to write longer commentaries stand out as conspicuous exceptions to the rule, and above all of them stands Nupchen Sangyé Yeshé, the great protector of tantric Buddhism during Tibet's age of fragmentation.[1] Born around 844 C.E. in Drak,[2] in a valley south of Lhasa, Nupchen is said to have begun his study of Buddhism at nine years old under a visiting Nepalese scholar named Vasudhāra. Four years later, at Vasudhāra's invitation, Nupchen made his first trip to Nepal and thence to India. According to our earliest biographical source, the *Great Seal of Nup*, Nupchen's authority derived from his seven trips to India and Nepal, where he met some of the top tantric Buddhist masters of the mid-to-late ninth century. Recognized repeatedly as a prodigy, he eventually studied directly under the "translators" of the *Gathering of Intentions* and returned to central Tibet a master of the tantras in his own right.

Nupchen flourished after the fragmentation of the Tibetan imperial line that began around 842 C.E. His decision, so unusual for an early

Tibetan, to compose an extensive 1,340-folio tantric commentary was likely facilitated by his learning and authority, but also perhaps by the loosening of imperial limits on such writings. Later followers of the Nyingma School would portray Nupchen as the principal Tibetan guardian of Buddhism, and tantric Buddhism in particular, following the empire's collapse.[3] His commentary, titled the *Armor Against Darkness*, is by far his longest work. That he chose to focus his considerable scholarly attention on the *Gathering of Intentions*, a tantra that was relatively unknown in India, may be a testament to the charisma of his teachers or to the relative ignorance of early Tibetan Buddhists, but it may also be a reflection of the creative ferment of the times; which of the innumerable emerging tantras would go on to enjoy long-standing international success and which would soon die out may have been difficult to predict.

Today, hundreds of tantric ritual texts—both of the revealed (Treasure) and authored (Spoken Teachings) varieties—are attributed to Nupchen, many bearing on the wrathful practices of Yamāntaka, the slayer of the Lord of Death. But Nupchen's two major compositions are somewhat less ritually focused. Far better known to contemporary scholars than *Armor Against Darkness* is his *Lamp for the Eyes in Contemplation*. Over 250 folio sides in length, the *Lamp* is almost entirely concerned with questions of doctrine, and specifically the differences—vis-à-vis nonconceptuality—between the gradual and the immediate approaches to enlightenment, typified by Indian and Chinese forms of Buddhism, respectively, as well as the tantric teachings of Mahāyoga and Atiyoga, or the Great Perfection (Rdzogs chen).[4]

The *Armor Against Darkness*, Nupchen's commentary on the *Gathering of Intentions*, is also doctrinal in content, at least compared to other early tantric writings, which tend to focus on ritual. Generally speaking, its readings do not strain to reinterpret its root text, as do many later commentaries in their attempts to bring their objects of study up to date. In other words, Nupchen's interpretive agenda is generally in line with that of the tantra's authors themselves, a fact that may support the idea that Nupchen really did study directly under the tantra's translators/authors. This chapter examines how Nupchen understood the *Gathering of Intentions* and its place within the larger development of tantric Buddhism in the ninth century.

NINE VEHICLES FOR TRAVELING THE PATH TO ENLIGHTENMENT

As noted in chapter 1, the *Gathering of Intentions* describes a doxographic system that classifies the Buddhist teachings into nine categories:

1. Śrāvaka
2. Pratyekabuddha
3. Bodhisattva
4. Kriyā-tantra
5. Ubhaya-tantra
6. Yoga-tantra
7. Mahāyoga-tantra
8. Anuyoga-tantra
9. Atiyoga-tantra

This ninefold scheme will be recognized by anyone familiar with the doctrinal system of the Nyingma School, for which the *Gathering of Intentions* would become the *locus classicus*. Similar ninefold schemes appear in a variety of early Tibetan documents from Dunhuang and elsewhere,[5] but it was the *Gathering of Intentions*' particular rendition that was propagated by the early Zur in the eleventh and twelfth centuries, whence it became normative for the entire school.

The *Gathering of Intentions* presents its nine vehicles system in the forty-fourth chapter. It sets the scheme within three larger vehicles that function together to comprise an entire cosmology of Buddhist soteriology. The first is the vehicle of the "continuous wheel" (*'khor lo rgyun*), teachings directed at those beings particularly attached to the desire realm. It employs the forces of nature to tame their constant desire for momentary pleasures. Thus, through the compassion of the buddhas, the tantra explains, the natural world provides three gifts that satisfy their needs so that they can progress toward enlightenment: birth, sustenance, and support.[6]

The second of the three larger vehicles is that of the "magical display manifesting" (*cho 'phrul mngon par 'byung ba*), which arises for the most obstinate of disciples who are extremely difficult to tame. This is the vehicle of the apocalyptic aeons discussed in chapter 1, a series of soteriological interventions designed to sever the karmic continuums of those most intensely engrossed in the three poisons of desire, ignorance, and anger. The crescendo of sufferings experienced during these aeons is supposed to cause many of these benighted beings to reflect upon and feel regret for their earlier misdeeds, and thereby to reach enlightenment.

The last of the three larger vehicles is the "vehicle for ascertaining the ultimate" (*don dam nges pa'i theg pa*), which includes the system of nine (sub)vehicles. The *Gathering of Intentions* arranges them into three groups of three, so that the "vehicle that extracts the source [of suffering]" includes the exoteric vehicles of the Śrāvakas, Pratyekabuddhas, and Bodhisattvas. The "vehicle of awareness through asceticism" contains the outward Kriyā, Ubhaya, and Yoga tantras. And the "vehicle with powerful methods" has the three inward classes of Mahāyoga, Anuyoga, and Atiyoga.[7] The actual names of all nine classes do not appear in the tantra's discussion itself, nor are they explicitly termed "vehicles" there. The tantra's description of each does, however, make clear enough what was intended, and Nupchen's commentary on the passage makes the names explicit.[8]

Modern-day followers of the Nyingma School see the *Gathering of Intentions* as a tantra of the Anuyoga class. This has long been the case, probably since the early Zurs formulated the "triad of sutra, tantra, and mind" (*mdo rgyud sems gsum*), corresponding to the classes of Anuyoga, Mahāyoga, and Atiyoga, as the core of their tantric canon in the eleventh or twelfth century.[9] The *Gathering of Intentions* itself, however, shows no sign of having been conceived of in this way.[10] At one point, Nupchen states that the *Gathering of Intentions* comprises all nine vehicles of the Buddhist teachings—"the nine vehicles themselves may be mastered through this single tantra"[11]—and as we shall see in chapter 4, its elaborate initiation system does provide initiation into all nine, one by one. But the authors seem to have seen their composition foremost as a work of "Secret Mantra," by which they meant all of the three highest vehicles—Mahāyoga, Anuyoga, and Atiyoga. The *Gathering of Intentions*' presentation of these three classes conveys a sense of how its authors, and Nupchen following them, understood their composition.

MAHĀYOGA

The historical significance of the category "Mahāyoga" may not be fully appreciated by contemporary students of Tibetan Buddhism. Today it has been relegated to a class of Nyingma tantras that emphasize the generation stage of tantric practice, but historically Mahāyoga was an extraordinarily long-lived and influential label that, between the eighth and twelfth centuries, referred to those tantras at the cutting edge of Buddhist ritual development. Toward the end of this period, followers of Tibet's New (Gsar ma) schools began to use the term "Unexcelled" (Tib. *rnal 'byor bla na med pa*; Skt. *yoganiruttara*) instead.[12] Nonetheless, as late as the thirteenth century, even the great scholar (and anti-Nyingma polemicist) Sakya Paṇḍita (1182–1251) recognized the significance of Mahāyoga when he wrote, "In the Secret Mantra of the New Schools, the superiority of Mahāyoga rests in the fact that there is no class of tantras superior to it. Nor is there is any object of meditation higher than Mahāyoga."[13]

The eighth to the twelfth centuries also marked the most creative time in the development of tantric ritual. Given the widespread use of "Mahāyoga" throughout this fast-changing period, it is difficult to pin down exactly what the term meant. Its uses in eighth-century India may have differed greatly from those in eleventh-century Tibet. And even within a given period and geographic region, the term's significance still could vary dramatically from one tantric exegete to another. A recent scholarly review of the definitions offered just in the tenth-century Tibetan manuscripts from Dunhuang, for example, reveals a wide variety of interests and interpretations.[14]

However, historically the category of Mahāyoga was created to distinguish certain tantras from the somewhat earlier category of Yoga tantras.[15] Where the Yoga tantras offer elaborate methods for imaginatively generating oneself as the buddha himself, the Mahāyoga tantras tend to focus more on what one does after becoming that buddha. Certainly the Yoga tantras exhibit an interest in reenacting the enlightened activities of the buddhas, but the Mahāyoga tantras speak far more from an enlightened perspective, out of a space beyond the dualisms of self and other, good and evil, pure and impure. From this transcendent Mahāyoga standpoint, everything is already perfected, so effortful action is no longer required. Social taboos are mere convention, so that from the perspective of emptiness, practicing sexual union with low-caste women is inherently pure. Moral laws are relative, so killing is ethically acceptable. Given its emphasis on being a buddha, Mahāyoga ritual from early on was divided into an initial "generation stage" (*utpattikrama*), roughly corresponding to the earlier Yoga tantra-style generations of oneself as a buddha, and a subsequent "perfection stage" (*niṣpannakrama* or *utpannakrama*), in which one performs the activities of an enlightened buddha. The latter would typically involve engagement in ritualized sexual union (real or imagined), and within this context of the perfection stage, the most significant tantric ritual innovations unfolded between the ninth and eleventh centuries.[16]

Such was the world that the *Gathering of Intentions* inhabited. However, its authors saw it as a work not just of Mahāyoga but of Anuyoga and Atiyoga as well. What might such distinctions have meant? To gain a better sense of how the *Gathering of Intentions* fit within the fast-changing tantric trends of its day, we may look to what Nupchen Sangyé Yeshé writes about Mahāyoga in his *Armor Against Darkness*:

> Mahāyoga is the system of techniques for generation [of oneself as a deity]. One attains an experience of the coemergent wisdom that realizes both means and wisdom—in view and in action—as free of appearance and emptiness, whereupon feces, urine, [blood,][17] the *bodhicitta* of the superior dew [i.e., semen], and the five *māṃsa*, mixed with other things, are the five desirable objects, the five things with which to practice, and the five meats. The natures of those [substances] have always been thusness, essentially free from extremes [of good vs. bad, etc.], because of which they are buddhas, no different than the five families. Therefore, [in Mahāyoga,] one practices without adopting or rejecting, deliberately practicing with those [substances]. By doing that, and by cultivating the gradual generation of the deity's mandala within a state of thusness, one becomes a buddha in that very assembly of realized substances, that is, in the resulting mandala. One attains the level of perfect great dynamism.[18]

Within a state of realizing nonduality, then, one offers, eats, and otherwise practices with the five profane substances (feces, urine, and so on). From the perspective of emptiness, one sees them as desireable objects and recognizes their essentially pure, awakened nature, and through that realization, in combination with cultivating the generation-stage practices for imagining oneself as a buddha at the center of a mandala that is inseparable from those substances, one achieves buddhahood.

All this is pretty standard for Mahāyoga, with profane substances as pure when seen from the perspective of a buddha, but there is one significant difference: in the *Gathering of Intentions*, Mahāyoga is primarily limited to the generation stage. The usual rhetoric about the perfection of all phenomena is present, but it is not applied to the practice of the subsequent perfection stage. This shift was a direct result of the *Gathering of Intentions*' scheme of nine vehicles. Normally at this time, Mahāyoga included the generation and perfection stages, as well as (occasionally) a third and final stage of "great perfection" (*rdzogs pa chen po*).[19] Here, however, by limiting Mahāyoga to the generation stage, the *Gathering of Intentions* preserves the remaining stages of perfection and great perfection for its corresponding categories of Anuyoga and Atiyoga. The *Gathering of Intentions*, in other words, encompasses all three stages that were typical of Mahāyoga, but divides them into three distinct vehicles.

ANUYOGA

The *Gathering of Intentions*' authors, and Nupchen following them, saw their composition as a work of "Secret Mantra," by which they meant the three classes of "inner tantras," Mahāyoga, Anuyoga, and Atiyoga. Nonetheless, beginning around the eleventh or twelfth century, followers of the Nyingma School classified the *Gathering of Intentions* as a work of Anuyoga alone. Nupchen's writings themselves reflect no particular interest in the category, so why did this happen?[20] In a certain sense, it seems, the *Gathering of Intentions* fell victim to the success of its own nine vehicles system. It promoted the two vehicles of Anuyoga and Atiyoga above and beyond Mahāyoga (although of course, it was not completely unique in doing so). Around the mid-ninth century (the probable time of its composition), the distinctions among the vehicles—and indeed, the very definition of a vehicle per se—were still unclear. Even as the *Gathering of Intentions* divided the three Mahāyoga ritual stages of generation, perfection, and great perfection into separate vehicles, it was still possible for a single text to encompass all three. Mahāyoga, Anuyoga, and Atiyoga were discrete, yet still in some sense united as one. Over the next two centuries, as the *Gathering of Intentions* and the nine-vehicle scheme took hold within the Nyingma School, these three classes solidified and became increasingly canonized as distinct categories. At first, they functioned primarily as doctrinal and ritual categories, but by the eleventh and twelfth centuries they were being used to organize the textual tradition of the Nyingma School. It was no longer possible for a single work to encompass all three classes, for that would defeat their very purpose qua *textual* categories. The *Gathering of Intentions* had to be relegated to one of its own vehicles. It could not be a work of Mahāyoga, as it included clear discussions of the perfection stage that, according to its own definitions, did not belong in a truly Mahāyoga text. Yet it could no longer be a work of Atiyoga, as the latter had developed into its own distinct and increasingly elaborate vehicle with specific metaphors, rhetoric, and practices. Awkward as it may have been, only Anuyoga remained as a real possibility. Such a classification could explain why the work included discussions of the (still rudimentary) perfection stage, and the *Gathering of Intentions*' discussions of Atiyoga could be dismissed as a kind of transitional Anuyoga interpretation. The *Gathering of Intentions*' Sutra Initiation ceremony granted initiation, after all, into all nine vehicles, even those exoteric vehicles for which no initiations are required. Clearly, this was a tantric take on the Śrāvaka vehicle, the Pratyekabuddha vehicle, and so forth, so why not read its discussions of the Great Perfection in the same way, as a tantric (or Anuyoga) take on Atiyoga?

What, then, does the *Gathering of Intentions* say about Anuyoga, the class to which it would eventually be limited? The clearest exposition of the vehicle as a whole comes in chapter 44, immediately following the above-cited discussion of Mahāyoga:

> Regarding Anuyoga, the system for practicing the techniques of perfection: One realizes the objective in which all the phenomena

> of samsara and nirvana are illuminated, without fluctuations in degree, as the son, the *bodhicitta*, the great bliss, just as it is. At that time, the *dharmadhātu* is utterly without any activity, or even any basis for perception. Sheer awareness is illuminated in the likeness of an unestablished essence whereby everything is realized as essentially nondual, and therefore all phenomena are known in their thusness to be distinct yet perfect and are illuminated through the three times as the identity (*bdag nyid*) of all the phenomena of causality. For this reason there is not the slightest gradual development of the mandala, nor any reliance on deliberate practice.[21]

Several points can be gleaned from this passage, foremost that Anuyoga is associated with the perfection phase. The ritual context is thus one of sexual union, within which all phenomena are realized as "the son, the *bodhicitta*, the great bliss." Here, "the son" likely refers to the son mandala that is produced by the male and female practitioners (the father and the mother) at the point of union. This is identified with the bodhicitta, i.e., the drop of semen that is produced. Within this state of nondual bliss, the mandala appears "just as it is," "without fluctuations in degree," "utterly without action," and without "the slightest gradual development." This is unlike Nupchen's description of Mahāyoga, in which one cultivates "the gradual development of the deity's mandala." In Anuyoga, the mandala is not constructed through painstaking effort but appears in a flash, "like a fish leaping out of the water."[22]

The above description does lack one piece that is critical to later formulations of the perfection stage: any mention of the subtle body practices involving the channels, winds, and seminal drops. By the late ninth century, Indian practitioners of the perfection stage would become increasingly concerned with these manipulations of subtle bodily energies, but here they are conspicuously absent. In fact, these practices appear to be absent from the entire *Gathering of Intentions*. Perhaps the best potential evidence of them in the tantra appears at the beginning of the fifty-fifth chapter. The chapter is narrated within a new setting, that of the "secret body," which is introduced as follows:

> In this way the blessed Lord of the Supreme Secret rested for an instant in the secret place called Padmāvatī, the supreme secret palace of the womb of emanations that is transformed by the *uṣṇīṣa* wheel. At that time, countless excellent beings' doubts regarding the supreme secret of suchness were cut, entirely melted away, and finished within that melting. Having cut their doubts, he arose once more.[23]

In his subcommentary to Nupchen's *Armor Against Darkness*, the early twentieth-century Khenpo Nüden reads this passage through the lens of later "treatises on [sexual] union," interpreting it in terms of the four joys of the *Hevajra Tantra* and the melting of the essential drops within the energy channels (*rtsa gnas*).[24] Taken on its own terms, however, the passage does not clearly refer to such technical processes. It may be describing a far simpler perfection-stage sexual practice through which conceptuality is dissolved ("melted") within the bliss of union.[25]

A perfection stage involving sexual union but no (or at least relatively minimal) "channels and winds" (*rtsa rlung*) is typical of late eighth- and early ninth-century tantric sources.[26] These kinds of instructions are seen in the Tibetan documents discovered at Dunhuang, which seem to reflect the state of tantric Buddhist ritual in India around the end of the eighth century, in early Mahāyoga tantras such as the *Guhyasamāja* and the **Guhyagarbha*. During this developmental period, sexual union was performed in order to generate a state of nonconceptual, nondual bliss and culminated in the production of a drop of sanctified semen (*bodhicitta*) that was then bestowed as a supreme sacrament upon oneself.[27] In the same way, the *Gathering of Intentions*' Sutra Initiation system grants a series of initiations that conclude with a secret initiation (*guhyābhiṣeka*) in which the guru bestows a sacramental drop of sexual fluids upon the initiate.[28] None of this, however, involves the techniques of the famous chakras, channels, and psychophysical energies of the subtle body.

In his later writings, however, Nupchen makes occasional reference to subtle body techniques. In his early tenth-century *Lamp for the Eyes in Contemplation*, he describes a rite that sounds very much like later inner heat (*gtum mo*) practices: "Cultivating that at the top of the head, one arouses the activities of the different individual methods for thought or the karmic fires and winds, that is, one milks the sky cow, the gnostic nectar descends, and bliss is produced."[29] Given the presence of such passages in Nupchen's later writings, it is quite possible that subtle-body practices were being taught orally in connection with the early transmission of the *Gathering of Intentions*. Nonetheless, concrete written evidence of such teachings is largely absent.

ATIYOGA

The above-cited fifty-fifth chapter, taught within the buddha's "secret body," stands at the doctrinal heart of the *Gathering of Intentions*. Its importance is reflected in the title of Nupchen's commentary, the *Armor Against Darkness*, which may have been derived, in part at least, from the chapter's closing line: "The explanation herein of the aspect of darkness [i.e., of ignorance] should be regarded as an armor to be worn [against it]."[30] The chapter is also the longest in the tantra. According to Nupchen, it constitutes an elaborate presentation of the ninth and highest of the nine vehicles, that of Atiyoga, or the Great Perfection. Before examining Nupchen's commentary on the chapter, however, we should begin with his summary of the vehicle in chapter 44:

> Regarding the system in which all is perfected as the great identity (*bdag nyid chen po*) by means of the system of Atiyoga: . . . Dualistic phenomena are illuminated within the naturally and spontaneously present state that is primordially beyond cleansing or establishing. There is absolutely no comprehension of any tenets system for evaluating things. Merely by not positing, considering, or analyzing any ideas at all, the meaning of suchness comes to be seen without seeing. In the *Great Sky of Vajrasattva* it is said: "Freed by liberation through nonaction, effortless self-arising wisdom displays the path of freedom from liberation."[31] Thus sheerly through not practicing the activities of evaluating things and seeking meanings, one is said to be, as a mere designation, "liberated," because the phenomena binding one are not perceived [in the first place]. For that reason, there is no mental basis at all within the nonduality of space and wisdom that is

> essentially devoid of objects, so apart from just the mind, there is nothing to understand. Someone might object, "Well then, if there is never anything to understand, how can phenomena become suchness?' [Answer:] When one knows that there is nothing whatsoever to know, then, as a linguistic designation for having realized without realizing and seen without seeing, one is said to have "realized." This is learning without learning. Whoever achieves the goal of embracing what has been explained with this kind of indwelling confidence does not gain accomplishment through hardships of the three doors (i.e., of the body, speech, and mind).[32]

Such language is fairly typical of early Great Perfection accounts, which commonly employ apophatic language recommending nonaction and paradoxical phrases promoting "realizing without realizing" and "seeing without seeing." The point is to emphasize the dangers of making conscious efforts toward the realization of awakening. "One cannot gain definitive understanding [of the Great Perfection]," Nupchen writes, "through complex intellectual inference. The enlightened essence is [realized] quickly, so it is not arrived at through effortful progress."[33] Rhetorically, at least, such accounts claim to have transcended the ritual concerns of Mahāyoga and Anuyoga. In the words of David Germano, "The Great Perfection thus originates on the periphery of the vast discursive terrain of the Mahāyoga. . . . A vacuum is created in this landscape through the systematic expulsion of every standard tantric principle. Just as in Dignāga's theory of language where meaning derives from exclusion (*apoha*), it creates itself through denial, rejection, and negation, resulting in a space with nothing at all."[34] Even as early exponents of the Great Perfection defined their tradition in opposition to Mahāyoga, however, their arguments were shot through with tantric language. Thus the Great Perfection meditator is told repeatedly that there is no generation stage, there is no perfection stage, there are no tantric vows (*samaya*), and so on.

Despite such language, the question remains: How are we to understand early Great Perfection *practice*? What did its adherents *do*? Analyses of the earliest materials reveal a variety of approaches. Some have suggested that the Great Perfection referred to "a kind of technique-free 'natural' immersion in a nonconceptual state."[35] For others, it provided an interpretive "framework" within which tantric deity yoga was to be performed as usual.[36] For still others, it may have described the nonconceptual state engendered through ingesting a sacramental drop of sexual fluids that was administered at the culmination of the perfection stage.[37] In fact, the early Great Perfection was probably understood in all of these ways, and still others, by various people in different contexts. Right from its earliest days, the Great Perfection appears to have inspired a broad range of interpretations and practices.

For further insights into how Nupchen and the authors of the *Gathering of Intentions* viewed the practice of the Great Perfection around the end of the ninth century, we may turn to Nupchen's commentary on chapters 54 through 56 of the *Gathering of Intentions*. He begins by distinguishing a gradual and an immediate approach to Great Perfection meditation, presenting them as sequential, with the practitioner starting with the gradual meditations in order to "understand the meaning" of Secret Mantra and only afterward engaging in the immediate approach.[38]

Not surprisingly, the discussion of the gradual approach provides more concrete detail. In this context, the *Gathering of Intentions* reads, "One who seeks the path to ascertaining the middle should maintain solitude in an isolated place and, with an intellect that examines by means of the two valid cognitions [of direct perception and inference], sever conceptualization."[39] Thus one should enter retreat, study and reflect upon the Buddhist teachings, then cut all conceptual thinking and maintain that state for as long as possible. Nupchen describes how this might be accomplished in the following words:

> When the time comes for those seeking the golden result to meditate, they should bind the constantly engaging mental [consciousness] to the pillar of wakefulness and attention. Then [too], in a similar way, they should catch the afflicted mind (*kliṣṭa-manas*) consciousness and its illusory mentations. Without engaging at all in the dispersal of the doors of the five collected [physical sense consciousnesses] toward their objects even, one enslaves the elements, the sense bases, and the aggregates of subject-object conceptualization to a state of nonperception

(*mi dmigs pa*). Then the good qualities of the great equality foundation (*ālaya*), the spontaneously accomplishing reality, will come to be illuminated. And thereby, those yogins who cultivate in accordance with their various texts will become identical with the result, completely perfect buddhahood.[40]

Nupchen here recommends a meditative withdrawal from the senses and thinking, and even from the subtly dualistic activities of the afflicted mind, whereby the pure foundation (Tib. *kun gzhi*; Skt. *ālaya*) will eventually be revealed. (Elsewhere, Nupchen clarifies that such a withdrawal does not imply that the foundation exists apart from the senses and so forth. "By taking [the foundation] as an object," he writes, "it will not be found throughout the three times. Rather, it abides as all the objects of samsara.")[41] Here, and throughout his discussions of the Great Perfection in chapters 54 to 56, Nupchen draws upon the Vijñānavāda language of the eight consciousnesses: the foundation consciousness (*ālayavijñāna*), the afflicted mind (*kliṣṭamanas*), the mental consciousness (*manovijñāna*), and the consciousnesses of the five physical senses. Nonetheless, he is careful to distinguish his own perspective: "Those who are undeveloped with regard to the purpose, such as the Vijñanavādins," he writes, "assert the nature of this foundation to be 'like this.'"[42] Followers of the Vijñānavāda, in other words, reify their foundation consciousness in ways that those of Atiyoga do not.

Nupchen's characterization of the Vijñānavādins here is a bit of a caricature, for many are quite explicit that the foundation consciousness cannot be objectified. In his *Bodhisattvabhūmi*, for instance, Asaṅga warns that the foundation consciousness is "momentary regarding its object, and even though it arises continuously in a stream of instants, it is not singular."[43] Thus most early Vijñānavādins preferred to see the foundation consciousness as a set of subliminal mentational processes not phenomenologically available to the subject as a distinct entity. Despite Nupchen's criticism of the Vijñānavādins, moreover, he couches his entire discussion of Atiyoga meditation very much in their language. He uses the eight consciousnesses both descriptively, as a conceptual scheme for explaining how conceptuality arises, and prescriptively, in order to teach how the meditator should recognize the foundation and thereby avoid falling into ignorance and conceptuality.

He labels his ultimate unborn state a "foundation," and he defines it vis-à-vis the "mundane" foundation consciousness.

The foundation of Atiyoga, he insists, eludes objectification and is therefore purer and subtler than the more mundane foundation consciousness of the Vijñānavādins. It is the "genuine foundation of unification" (*sbyor ba don gyi kun gzhi*) that unifies all samsara and nirvana, because it is "both the cause for all thoroughly afflicted phenomena to appear and the basis for their purification. . . . It is not just some general conglomeration [as is the foundation consciousness], like some straw hut or a house, which appears due to each person's negative aspects. It is from the beginning naturally without any arisen essence. Unmade by any creator, it is clear light, reality, free from causes and conditions: the unborn state."[44] Nupchen's genuine foundation of unification is specific to Secret Mantra and beyond the ordinary sutra-based foundation consciousness. To meditate without mental engagement upon this genuine foundation is the very essence of Atiyoga.[45]

In cultivating such a state, Nupchen goes on to explain, a number of problems can arise. These can be of three kinds: conceptualizations, mental waverings, and obscurations (*rtog pa, g.yeng ba, sgrib pa*), listed in order of increasing subtlety and each subdivided in turn. Of conceptualizations, for example, there are five kinds: conceptual thoughts, signs, movements, [bodily] sensations, and [mental] feelings (*rtog pa, mtshan ma, rgyu ba, tshor ba, byung tshor*). And each of these may be still further subdivided into their coarse and subtle variations. "The resulting ten [conceptualizations]," writes Nupchen, "are obstructing demons that do not allow reality to be seen."[46] Each of these kinds of problems is further explained as leading to a specific type of rebirth. Conceptual thoughts, the first subset of conceptualizations, for example, will lead to rebirth in the three lower realms; signs lead to rebirth as a human; and so on, up to rebirth as a god in the formless realms.[47]

Following the *Gathering of Intentions*' lead, Nupchen prescribes a cure for each of these problems in the form of an analytic meditation on the causes driving it. Thus, he explains, "by understanding conceptualization itself, which depends on causes, to be apparent but unestablished, conceptual thought is purified, whereby one does not fall into the three negative rebirths. 'From what [cause] does that conceptual thought arise? It arises from signs.' By analyzing the cause from which that conceptual thought spreads forth, one comes to understand that it arises from objective signs" [i.e., from the next and slightly subtler form of "conceptualizations"].[48] Thus an examination of the causes of conceptual thought (the first sort of conceptualization) reveals the next sort, signs. The meditations continue, with each prescribed cure—the comprehension of that particular problem's immediate cause—implying and leading the yogin on to the next problem.

In this way, the problems—conceptualizations, mental waverings, and obscurations—and their respective causes demarcate a graduated path to awakening that culminates in the level of Atiyoga proper. Here at the pinnacle, Nupchen continues,

> one cultivates the purpose of not holding on to the nature of reality, which is free from all extreme positions that view the two truths as divisible, or as "like *this*." One leaves the body and mind relaxed and open, totally natural. Without any tightness emerging for any purpose, merely without separating, nor slipping from equanimity, one rests with an easy mind and without thinking of anything at all. Persevere in that for longer and longer periods.[49]

This, explains one twelfth-century commentator, represents the very "essence" of the practice.[50]

As the durations of the meditation periods extend, Nupchen explains, five signs that one is nearing the end may arise, namely, "heat, omens, magical displays, clairvoyance, and omniscient wisdom." These "will come without one doing anything to generate them as ends to be achieved,"[51] and they apparently reflect a kind of progression. Nupchen describes them through the metaphor of the sun rising: "The heat is like the illumination [that is revealed] as the darkness clears. The omens are like dawn breaking. The magical displays are like the sun shining in an utterly clear sky. Clairvoyance is like seeing throughout the entire realm. And [wisdom] is like the risen sun by which all things are pervaded and illuminated."[52] At last, one comes to possess the eye of knowledge, "and is able to proclaim, teach, and pour forth profound principles through the dynamism of one's reason, without having studied in words."[53] Eventually, then, the signs of one's realization collapse into the clear light of wisdom and the teachings flow effortlessly.

Despite the attention Nupchen pays here to these five meditative signs of accomplishment, elsewhere in the same commentary he emphasizes that such visions are not part of the *method* of the Great Perfection. "One great person of today is [held to be] 'the foundation of the dharma,'" he complains. "But this person thinks that in Atiyoga there is a need for perception (*dmigs pa*). He claims that one gains liberation through pith instructions that teach methods involving having perceptions. It is clear that he has not attained confidence in the meaning of thusness. That blind man is like one who wishes to open the lock to a treasury with the horn of a wild yak."[54] It is one thing for visions to appear unintentionally, as incidental signs of one's realization, but quite another to use them as a method to achieve enlightenment. It is unclear precisely what kind of methods Nupchen refers to, but little more than a century later, the visionary practices of the Great Perfection's Seminal Heart traditions were being put into writing. It is possible that in Nupchen's late ninth-century commentary we may see the beginnings of such practices. In any case, Nupchen took a more conservative approach and condemned all such innovations.

Nupchen's discussions of the early Great Perfection provide rare insights into the origins of this tradition. The teachings outlined here belong to Nupchen's gradual approach, but even so they reveal a meditation system that is surprisingly nontantric and in many ways typical of standard exoteric Buddhist meditation, with abstract concentrative states framed by Yogācāra doctrine that produce visionary signs that eventually give way to enlightenment. However, Nupchen insists that such techniques are unique to the tantras. Indeed, that the *Gathering of Intentions*' teachings are narrated within the setting of a "secret body" that is generated by the buddha through sexual union immediately marks them as secret and tantric. In discussing the significance of this setting, Nupchen writes, "The illumination of suchness within awareness is not an object [of meditation] in other vehicles. It is a teaching intended as an object for Secret Mantra, that speaks of the secret meaning just as it is."[55] As already observed, the early Great Perfection was defined as much *by* the intricate ritual systems of tantric Buddhism as *against* them, and Nupchen's *Armor Against Darkness* reflects this.[56] Even as Nupchen describes a relatively simple nonconceptual meditation, he embeds it within a thoroughly tantric narrative frame. For him, the Great Perfection is still very much part of Secret Mantra, one aspect of the tantric triad of Mahāyoga, Anuyoga, and Atiyoga.

The *Gathering of Intentions* and Nupchen's *Armor Against Darkness* reflect a transitional period in the development of tantric Buddhism, when ritual practice and its exegesis were still very much in flux. The definition of a tantric vehicle remained highly unclear, as did the significance of key terms such as "Mahāyoga," "Anuyoga," and "Atiyoga." Earlier eighth-century Indian authors had introduced the lower classes of Kriyā and Yoga for the purpose of distinguishing different kinds of tantras,[57] but in Nupchen's commentary, the tantric vehicles are unmoored from such concrete bibliographic referents. Instead, Nupchen seems to have viewed the vehicles as ascending stages of Buddhist practice. As we shall see in the next chapter, during the Later Dispensation period, members of the Zur clan would tie the *Gathering of Intentions*' tantric vehicles back to specific texts. But in the late ninth century, Nupchen was striving to have his *Gathering of Intentions* transcend such particularized categories, to float above and yet encompass all other Buddhist tantras.

The hubris of such a project may have been precisely what brought down the *Gathering of Intentions* in the end. Its authors' and Nupchen's grand vision of a tantra to end all tantras came too soon. They did not recognize the extent to which tantric ritual was still growing. The perfection stage had yet to spell out the techniques of the subtle body, and Atiyoga was not yet a full-fledged vehicle complete with its own corpus of tantras and ritual systems. By the eleventh and twelfth centuries, all this changed. Tibetans became enamored of the new subtle body practices that were flooding in from India, and of the revolutionary new visionary techniques of the *Kālacakra* and, on the Nyingma side, Atiyoga. Still, for its day, the *Gathering of Intentions* represented the cutting edge.

3

THE SPOKEN TEACHINGS

THE EARLY ZUR TRADITION AND THE FORMATION OF THE SPOKEN TEACHINGS

In the year 1002 C.E., one Śākya Jungné was born into the Zur clan in Yardzong, in the eastern Tibetan region of Kham. The youth ordained under Gongpa Rabsel (953–1035), the famous *vinaya* master from Amdo, to the north. He spent his first years studying under his grandfather, then departed for central Tibet. There he went to Yarlung, the ancient seat of the Pugyel dynasty just south of Lhasa, where he practiced the rites of the Kriyā tantras. Before long, however, all the rules and obligatory procedures of these lower tantras drove him onward, farther west to Tsang province, where he received the teachings that would become the focus of his life's work—instructions on the Great Perfection and the higher tantras of the **Guhyagarbha* and the *Gathering of Intentions*. Over the decades that followed, Śākya Jungné, or Zurché (Zur the Elder), became renowned for his expertise in the tantras. He drew great numbers of followers and established a series of small temples in Upper Nyang, in the area around his new seat at Ukpalung (The Valley of the Owls). Following his death, Zurché's activities were continued by his younger relative, Zurchung (Zur the Younger) Sherap Drakpa (1014–1074), and then in turn by Zurchung's son, Zur Śākya Sengé (1074–1134), also known as Dropukpa. These three are credited with founding the early Zur tradition. As the saying goes, "Zurpoche Śākya Jungné inaugurated the tradition, Zurchung Sherap Drak institutionalized it, and Zur Śākya Sengé spread and extended it. Thus they are called the three Zur patriarchs."[1]

The early Zur tradition that took root in the eleventh and twelfth centuries was fundamental to the burgeoning Nyingma School. The three patriarchs codified a textual corpus that came to be shared across the entire school. They were conservative in their selections, relative to some of their Nyingmapa contemporaries, yet for precisely that reason, the canon that resulted was able to serve as a common foundation. The Zurs oversaw the compilation and systematization of many of the most basic Nyingma teachings to have emerged unscathed from the political fragmentation of the tenth century. Three tantras in particular—the *Gathering of Intentions Sutra*, the **Guhyagarbha Tantra*, and the *All-Creating King*—were gathered as the so-called "triad of sutra, tantra, and mind" (*mdo rgyud sems gsum*). The Zurs established these scriptures as the "root tantras" of the classes of Anuyoga, Mahāyoga, and Atiyoga, respectively, and in doing so, they may have been the first to classify the *Gathering of Intentions* as an Anuyoga tantra. As we have seen in chapter 2, the *Gathering of Intentions*' authors saw their work as spanning all three classes, but in the eleventh century with the early Zurs, it came to be categorized as a work of Anuyoga alone. This was at once a demotion and a promotion, for the *Gathering of Intentions* was also forever positioned as a crown jewel in the larger canonical system of the Nyingma School.

The Zurs' tradition of sutra, tantra, and mind, along with their related tantras, commentaries, and ritual manuals, would eventually come to be known collectively as the "Spoken Teachings" (*bka' ma*). Just when this exact term began to be used remains unclear, but at least one early source suggests that already during the lifetime of Zurché, the tradition began to be called the "Zur Spoken Class" (*bka' sde zur ba*).[2] In any case, within the Nyingma School, the Spoken Teachings came to be presented in juxtaposition to the Treasure Teachings (*Gter ma*) that were revealed from the eleventh century onward. As Tibetans emerged from the tenth century and the age of fragmentation, they expressed a marked nostalgia for the halcyon days of the Pugyel empire. They valued highly any religious objects dating from that early period and saw them as imbued with a certain romanticism and sacrality. Many such objects had been hidden away for safekeeping following the closure of the monasteries in the mid-ninth century and were now being unearthed, as temples were reopened and institutional support for the study of Buddhism returned. Among the material treasures were Buddhist texts written or translated by the legendary figures of the imperial period. As Ronald Davidson, in his history of the Tibetan "renaissance" period, has observed, "There can be little doubt that the phenomenon of treasure texts (Terma) is closely connected with the material remains of the Tibetan imperium, the artifacts and hoards of precious materials that flowed into the imperial sites as tribute and booty during the two centuries of Tibetan adventurism and that remained after its fall."[3] Such yellowed manuscripts, and the images they conjured, likely provided at least part of the inspiration for the more visionary treasures that were revealed from the eleventh century on.

Treasure revelation provided the Nyingmapa of the later dispensation period with a highly adaptive scriptural space into which they could incorporate the latest tantric developments arriving from India, even while maintaining their sectarian identity as followers of the early (*snga dar*) translations. By channeling the great masters of Tibet's imperial past, treasure revealers of later centuries could introduce new readings and ritual systems into their school. Their revelations were supposed to be not new compositions but rediscovered treasures that had been authored by famous masters of the glorious past, then concealed within either the reincarnating unconscious minds of their disciples or the Tibetan landscape itself. There the treasures would remain until the appointed occasion of their discovery. In this sense the revealers were not authors but tantric mystics who had been karmically preordained by the earlier masters to be in the right place at the right time in order to make the prophesied discovery.[4]

The Spoken Teachings of the Zur were different. Like the treasure texts, they were supposed to have been translated during the early imperial period, but unlike them, they were never hidden away and rediscovered. Rather, they were purported to have been taught and practiced continuously, passed down from master to disciple in lineages that survived the age of fragmentation, to descend fully intact into the hands of Zurché. Of course, what Zurché actually received were the raw materials, disparate texts that he and his descendents worked into a coherent Spoken Teachings corpus. The *Gathering of Intentions*, the **Guhyagarbha*, the Great Perfection tantras of the Mind Class (*sems sde*),[5] and other tantras came to him through multiple lineages, from nearly eighty different teachers, but with Zurché they were carefully systematized: "He distinguished the root tantras and explanatory tantras, organized the root texts and their commentaries, combined the tantras and their *sādhanas*, and put into writing the *sādhanas* and ritual manuals. Then he spread extensively the teachings on their theory and practice."[6]

In formulating their canon, the early Zurs followed a fairly conservative path, ignoring the treasure texts and resisting new interpretations of their key works.[7] In doing so, they may have followed in the footsteps of their lineal predecessor; Nupchen Sangyé Yeshé himself seems to have resisted certain new developments within Great Perfection thought. The Zurs' own conservatism is seen clearly in a disagreement over how to interpret the **Guhyagarbha Tantra*. Later Nyingmapa came to distinguish two lines of thought on this issue—"the way of the Zur" and "the way of Rong[zom] and Long[chenpa]." The former represented a conservative reading of the **Guhyagarbha* from a strictly Mahāyoga standpoint, the latter a more gnostic interpretation of the same work through the lens of the Great Perfection tradition.[8]

Despite the Zurs' exegetical conservatism, their successes soon made them targets for early critics of the Nyingma School. Zurché and Zurchung were both accused of composing misleading and apocryphal works in eleventh-century polemical writings,[9] and Zurchung in particular became embroiled in multiple disputes with his New School contemporaries.[10] Such disagreements were not unusual in the eleventh and twelfth centuries, which saw a marked upsurge in sectarianism and religious competition. As a second wave of Indian Buddhist teachings arrived in Tibet, new tantras replete with the latest ritual techniques offered those who controlled them unprecedented power and prestige. Tibetans seeking access to the secrets of a given tantric ritual system could pay extraordinary prices to those who held exclusive rights over that system. Hagiographic sources depict Tibetans vying over particular teachings and resorting to slander, bribery, or even violence to achieve their aims.[11] Against this backdrop the early Zurs formulated their Nyingma tradition, and their adherence (conservative as it was) to the tantric systems of the earlier translation period was condemned by many of their rivals. All three of their central tantras—the *Gathering of Intentions*, the **Guhyagarbha*, and the *All-Creating King*—were suspected of being apocryphal Tibetan compositions. Although the *All-Creating King*, a compilation of early Great Perfection texts packaged as a translated Indian tantra, was clearly a Tibetan creation, a Sanskrit original of the **Guhyagarbha* was eventually discovered, disproving its critics' accusations, and the *Gathering of Intentions*, as we have seen, was likely a "gray text," produced jointly by Indians and Tibetans for a Tibetan audience.[12]

Unfortunately, almost no writings by the early Zurs are currently available, so our knowledge of their activities must be deduced from other materials—later commentaries and hagiographies.[13] In any case, it is clear that the *Gathering of Intentions* played a key role in their codification of the Spoken Teachings. When Zurché established his seat at Ukpalung, for example, he is said to have had the *Gathering of Intentions*' mandala painted on the front wall of the main temple.[14] For a clearer picture of the sutra's role in the codification of the Spoken Teachings, however, we must turn to the writings of one of the most famous inheritors of the early Zur tradition: Katok Dampa Deshek.

KATOK DAMPA DESHEK (1122–1192)

Dampa Deshek was the founder of Katok monastery in eastern Tibet, and he used the *Gathering of Intentions* and the Zurs' Spoken Teachings to organize his new institution's monastic curriculum. Of all the extant literature on the *Gathering of Intentions*, Dampa's writings are the most systematic. They consist of outlines, structural analyses, doxographies, and clarifications of difficult points. In their form and content, Dampa's works shed considerable light on both the early Zur treatment of the *Gathering of Intentions* and its function in the early Katok tradition.

Dampa was born Gewa Pel, in eastern Tibet in the water tiger year of 1122. His father was a tantric specialist named Tsangpa Peldrak[15] of the Ga clan, and his mother was Tsangmo Rinchen Gyen; apparently both were from the central Tibetan region of Tsang. Gewa Pel had three brothers and one sister.[16] At nine years of age, he went to live with the famous Kagyupa master Pakmo Drüpa at the island monastery of Pelgyi Chökhor. There, he took the bodhisattva vow and studied various topics, with particular emphasis on Mahāyāna works such as the *Samādhirāja*, *Saṃdhinirmocana*, *Laṅkāvatāra*, and *Aṣṭasāhasrikā*. He also received some tantric initiations and instructions, most notably for the deity Cakrasaṃvara.[17] Already in their teens, Dampa and his brother had tantric abilities that involved them in the politics of the region. During this time, "Together with Lama Pakmo Drüpa, through direct violent intervention, [Dampa] decisively 'liberated' [i.e., killed with black magic] an enemy of the teachings, the king of Minyag."[18]

As he continued his education, Dampa turned increasingly to the tantras, studying under Jampa Namdak for several years before finally leaving Kham for central Tibet at age nineteen. There he received teachings from the greatest masters of his time, including the *Path and Result* and *Hevajra* from Sönam Tsemo and the *Cakrasaṃvara* from both Ra Lotsawa's direct disciple, Kam Lotsawa, and Rechungpa. At twenty-four he took ordination under the Nyingmapa, Jangchup Sengé, receiving the name Sherap Sengé. Soon after this he met Dzamtön Drowé Gönpo, a close disciple of Zur Śākya Sengé (a.k.a. Dropukpa, the third of the three Zur patriarchs). Dampa stayed with this master for nearly ten years, during which he immersed himself in the Spoken Teachings, including the *Gathering of Intentions*.[19] At this time, it is said, his fame began to spread.[20]

At the age of twenty-nine, Dampa is said to have received a prophecy from Dzamtön that would change the course of his life. In this rather generic prophecy, Dzamtön told him that he could take one of two paths. If he went into solitary retreat, he would attain the highest level of enlightenment. If he returned to his birthplace in Kham and established a monastery in a place called Katok, he would benefit many beings. Dampa chose the latter path and soon left his teacher to make his way back east. His journey included a long stay at the newly established seat of the first Karmapa, Düsum Khyenpa. While there, Dampa received the principal Kagyu teachings and, according to his biographers, quickly became an important disciple of the Karmapa.[21] His relationship with this major figure of Tibetan history was surely helped by the fact that they both hailed from the same region of eastern Tibet, and that Dampa had already studied with Pakmo Drüpa. Together, these three lamas, traveling back and forth between their native Kham and central Tibet, were responsible for an unprecedented influx of Buddhism into eastern Tibet during the twelfth century.

Dampa spent his mid-thirties traveling around Kham, acting as the court priest for local kings and ordaining hundreds of Buddhist monks. Eventually he gained the favor of a Horpo chieftain named Pön Gelu, who sent some hundred Horpo orphans (*kha lhags*) to be ordained by Dampa and agreed to sponsor the construction of a temple. With Gelu's backing, Dampa founded Katok in his thirty-eighth year, in 1159. Before he could begin construction, he had to subdue the local deity, who initially resisted his spiritual incursions, and he is said to have deployed the rites of Cakrasaṃvara that he had received from his Kagyupa teachers.[22] The central temple completed, he filled its statues with relics, the nature of which provides some idea of how Dampa positioned Katok vis-à-vis the larger Tibetan Buddhist tradition of his day. He is said to have included scriptures penned by Padmasambhava and Vimalamitra that were found at Samyé, Dropukpa's robe, a tooth of Zurché, Atiśa's hat, Nupchen's dagger (*rked phur*), and other more generic items, including ninety volumes of the word of the Buddha (*buddhavacana*) written with golden ink.[23] Despite his Kagyu connections, then, Dampa's Katok tradition appears to have been focused on his Nyingma lineages right from the start, in particular those passing through the Nup and Zur lines.

One of the first major monasteries in the region, Katok seems to have enjoyed immediate success. Within two years, 1,000 monks were living nearby, and a summer college (*bshad grwa*) and winter meditation center (*sgom grwa*) were founded. Apparently linked to the establishment of these new institutes, around the same time a large ceremony was performed for the *Gathering of Intentions* tradition (*shin tu gsang ba 'dus pa mdo'i sgrub chen*).[24] Thus right from the beginning, the *Gathering of Intentions* played a central role in the establishment of the Katok institution. During this period, Dampa composed the works relevant to the present study.[25]

DAMPA'S TREATMENT OF THE *GATHERING OF INTENTIONS*

Dampa's five extant works on the *Gathering of Intentions* are relatively short compared to the tantra itself and Nupchen's extensive commentary:[26]

1. *Brief Structural Analysis of the Sutra* (7 folio sides)
2. *Dawning of the Sun of Good Explanation: A Structural Analysis of the* Gathering of Intentions (47 folio sides)
3. *Summary of the* Gathering of Intentions (146 folio sides)
4. *Key for Opening the Vajra Lock: An Explanation of the Difficult Points in the* Gathering of Intentions (72 folio sides)
5. *Outline of the Vehicles* (32 pages)

In each of these five texts, Dampa works to consolidate the various notes, ritual works, and commentaries that had proliferated over the previous two and a half centuries. In doing so, he draws heavily upon the Zur tradition that he inherited from his teacher, Dzamtön.

At the end of his longer *Structural Analysis* (*yang khog dbub*; no. 2 above), Dampa traces what he considers to be the authoritative lineage out of the tangle of early *Gathering of Intentions* transmissions. During the eleventh and twelfth centuries, a lineal connection to an Indian master was of particular importance, and there was a growing interest among Tibetans in constructing lineages tying themselves and their teachings back to India. Such a connection was relatively easy to prove for those following the New Schools' tantric systems, which had arrived from India only recently, but for adherents of the old tantras, whose ties to India had weathered the age of fragmentation, proof was more difficult. The increasing concern with lineage construction mirrored precisely what was taking place among Chinese Buddhists to the east. As Griffith Foulk writes, "It was in the late tenth and eleventh centuries . . . that the concept of the *ch'an-tsung* [lineage] first gained widespread acceptance in China and first had a major impact on the organization and operation of the Buddhist monastic institution."[27] Foulk goes on to explain that these Chinese lineages were "intrinsically historical. That is to say, the very idea of the *ch'an-tsung* entailed a consciousness of history, and the means by which the idea was spread was the publication of quasi-historical records." All of this could also be said of Tibetan Buddhism during the same period. It was crucial for Dampa, and the Zurs before him, to establish an unbroken lineage leading back to India, and he did so by writing a "quasi-historical record" of the *Gathering of Intentions*' past.

Dampa begins with the legendary King Dza. He recounts the king's seven miraculous dreams and how the buddha Vajrapāṇi appears before him to grant initiation and explain the tantras. Eventually, King Dza teaches everything to his son, Indrabodhi, from whom the teaching passes to Nāgabodhi, to Guhyabodhi, and then to the dog king, Kukkurāja.[28] The latter teaches Rolang Dewa (a.k.a. Garap Dorjé), an important figure in the Great Perfection tradition, who is usually considered the first human recipient of the Atiyoga teachings. From Garap Dorjé, Dampa traces the lineage through the king of Zahor, Prabhāhasti, to the threesome of Śākya Sengé, *Śākya Mudrā, and Śākya Prabhā. Śākya Sengé teaches Dhanarakṣita, after whom it passes through the small circle of Indian, Nepalese, and Tibetan teachers discussed in chapter 1 and finally to Nupchen Sangyé Yeshé.

In Tibet, Dampa tells us, the *Gathering of Intentions* remains under the control of the Nup clan, passing from Nupchen to Nup Yönten Gyatso and then to his son, Nup Yeshé Gyatso. From there, two separate lines emerge, converging again only in the person of Zur Śākya Sengé, the last of the three Zur patriarchs. The first line constitutes the main Zur lineage received by Zurché,[29] while the second passes through the Marpa clan of Lhodrak.[30] The former focuses on Nupchen's "great commentary," the *Armor Against Darkness*, while the latter focuses on a competing and no longer extant commentary ascribed to King Dza himself, the *Prophetic Commentary*.

These were not the only significant texts to appear prior to Dampa Deshek's time. In his *Brief Structural Analysis*, Dampa lists a number of shorter works that had also surfaced. He distinguishes two kinds of commentaries: theoretical works on the tantra as a whole and practical works addressing specific sections of the tantra. Dampa then divides the general theoretical works into four genres and provides examples for each.[31] Turning to those that address more specific topics,

Dampa cites a list from the *Prophetic Commentary* of eight main topics in the *Gathering of Intentions*—view, practices, the mandala, inititations, vows, accomplishment, activities, *samādhi*—then uses these topics to organize the remaining literature into eight groups.[32] According to these, Dampa was aware of at least seventy-six texts of lengths varying from short sets of notes and oral instructions to two volumes. Given the relative obscurity of the *Gathering of Intentions* tradition today, it is remarkable how widely it spread in the tenth and eleventh centuries. By the mid-twelfth century, the tradition had become so complex that, if it were to be widely taught at Katok, it needed to be categorized and organized, and this is precisely what Dampa does in his *Brief Structural Analysis.*

In his slightly longer *Dawning of the Sun*, Dampa continues organizing the tradition but focuses less on the various systems of commentary than on the doctrinal content of the *Gathering of Intentions.* On the whole, he does not add much to what Nupchen had laid out two and a half centuries earlier, but he provides a more convenient summary of the major doctrinal terms, from the nine vehicles to the variously numbered sets of yogas, the three doors, six tantras, four sutras, and three roots, the twelve ways of arising, and the three transmissions; all are presented in a manageable outline format. Such a work would have lent itself to the pedagogical concerns of Dampa's new monastic curriculum. Through works like this, Dampa sought to provide his students with a manageable introduction to the complexities of the *Gathering of Intentions.*

Perhaps the most useful of Dampa's works is his *Summary of the* Gathering of Intentions, which he attributes to his teacher, Lharjé Mar (possibly the same person as Dzamtön).[33] This work consists of a detailed outline of the *Gathering of Intentions* in its entirety. Its 144 folio sides help the reader access the otherwise unwieldy sutra and retrieve whatever information is required. Recognizing its significance, Khenpo Nüden, writing in the early twentieth century, used the *Summary of the* Gathering of Intentions to structure his own four-volume subcommentary.

The fourth extant text by Dampa is his *Key for Opening the Vajra Lock.* In this work, he moves through the *Gathering of Intentions*, stopping at each point of possible difficulty. Again, on many points he does not add much to Nupchen's commentary, but he expresses some of his own concerns, and for the most part they are scholastic in nature. He gives considerable attention to explaining the ten tantric levels and the corresponding yogas, visualizations, and signs of accomplishment. He also works to integrate the different commentarial traditions, in particular the *Armor Against Darkness* and the *Prophetic Commentary*.

Dampa's solutions to his various "difficult points" also reveal whom he regarded as his principal authorities. He cites two authors foremost: Jowo Lharjé and Lharjé Yangkhyé. The former is probably Zurché,[34] while Lharjé Yangkhyé was one of Zurchung's four "pillar" students, named as the one most specialized in the *Gathering of Intentions*.[35] Whenever possible, however, it is the word of Zur Śākya Sengé/Dropukpa, the third of the three Zur patriarchs, that decides any disagreements, and in this way Dampa saw himself as a direct inheritor of the early Zur tradition.

The codification of the Spoken Teachings may have begun with Zurché, but many important lineages were not gathered into one stream until Dropukpa. Regarding the *Gathering of Intentions* system, one major commentary, the *Prophetic Commentary*, was transmitted outside the Zur clan until Dropukpa received it from Shangpa. Then, writes Gö Lotsawa in his *Blue Annals*, "from that time on the Lineage of the [*Gathering of Intentions*] mDo was handed down through the Lineage of the Māyā (sGyu-'phrul)."[36]

A continuation of the early Zur project to unify the systems of the *Gathering of Intentions Sūtra* with the **Guhyagarbha Tantra* and the Great Perfection Mind Class may be observed in Dampa's works. In this respect, perhaps the most interesting is one that has only recently resurfaced. In his *Outline of the Vehicles*, Dampa used the *Gathering of Intentions*' nine vehicles scheme to organize the Spoken Teachings as a whole, but he was careful also to harmonize the scheme with the **Guhyagarbha*'s own distinct doxographical system. Although these two tantras certainly grew out of the same matrix of eighth- and ninth-century Indian Mahāyoga developments, some key differences between their contents had to be reconciled before they could work together as a single system. Dampa was forced to perform a hermeneutical balancing act, to bring the texts of his received canon into line with each other to form a single, coherent Spoken Teachings system.

The Zurs' reputation had been built on their conservation of the old tantras and their conservative readings of those works, and in Dampa's *Outline of the Vehicles* we see a delicate maneuvering of the tantras in order to maintain the doctrinal unity of his canon.

Dampa opens his *Outline of Vehicles* by tracing the *Gathering of Intentions*' presentation of the Buddhist vehicles. As he turns to the classic system of nine vehicles, he first distinguishes two general types of views: the incidental and those of the Buddhist vehicles (*zhar las byung dang theg pa*). The incidental views appear to be the mistaken, non-Buddhist positions that arise inevitably alongside the correct ones.[37] The *Gathering of Intentions* divides them into two kinds: those of no understanding at all (*mi shes*) and those of misunderstanding (*log shes*). The first, no understanding, is further subdivided into the hedonists (*phyal ba*) and the materialists (*rgyang 'phen pa*). Both types are utterly fixated on samsaric concerns, the former because they are ignorant of karma and therefore indulge in whatever pleases them, the latter because they do not care--they may have heard teachings on karma, but think only of this present lifetime. Hence both have "no understanding." The second kind of worldly views, involving misunderstanding, is also subdivided into two: the nihilists (*mu stug pa*) and the eternalists (*mu stegs pa*). The latter is then further subdivided to include the standard Hindu views and those mistaken views that can arise through the reification of a particular Buddhist view. Thus there is a mistaken Śrāvaka view, a mistaken Pratyekabuddha view, and so on up to a mistaken Atiyoga view.

In the midst of presenting these heterodox views, however, Dampa suddenly introduces another scheme, from the **Guhyagarbha Tantra*. The **Guhyagarbha* played an important role in the early dispensation of tantric Buddhism in Tibet. Like the *Gathering of Intentions*, though on a somewhat smaller scale, it sought to systematize the numerous tantric deities proliferating during the eighth century into a large mandala of one hundred peaceful and wrathful deities. In later centuries, the **Guhyagarbha* became the most heavily studied tantra in the Nyingma School, and its pantheon populated many later treasure texts, the *Tibetan Book of the Dead* being a particularly well-known example.[38] It was also central to the Zurs' Spoken Teachings. The *Gathering of Intentions*' authors were likely well aware of the earlier **Guhyagarbha*, as their mandala, myths, and doctrines all built upon it, yet their own system went beyond it, and the two works differed on many points. Most conspicuous was the difference between their respective doxographical schemes, particularly awkward for Dampa, who sought to systematize the Spoken Teachings within a unified curriculum that could be taught at Katok's new monastic college.

Dampa is forced to draw attention to the discrepancy because the terminology used in the *Gathering of Intentions*' presentation so obviously recalls that used in the **Guhyagarbha*'s own thirteenth chapter. He cites the latter's famous passage as follows: "Also, the **Guhyagarbha Tantra* lists, 'Those who are of no understanding and of misunderstanding, those of partial understanding, those with misunderstanding of the genuine, and those of discipline, the intention, the secret, the natural, the secret meaning.'"[39]

Dampa then offers his explanation of the passage, interpreting each term and its corresponding Buddhist or non-Buddhist vehicles by resorting to the *Gathering of Intentions*' sixty-eighth chapter, which shares some of the same terminology.[40] From his perspective, the two systems are easily exchangeable, and he makes precisely this equivalence explicit at the end of his discussion: "Therefore," he concludes, the foregoing nine vehicles of the *Gathering of Intentions*, "are just like the passage in the [**Guhyagarbha*] tantra."[41] However, it is somewhat unclear precisely how Dampa lines up the two systems. How does he read the nine vehicles onto the terms "partial understanding, misunderstanding of the genuine, discipline, the intention, the secret, the natural, the secret meaning"? Unfortunately, none of his extant writings tells us. To get an idea of how he might have resolved this issue, we may turn to the **Guhyagarbha* commentary of his direct disciple, Dorjé Gyeltsen (1137–1227).

First, however, we should review how the **Guhyagarbha* passage was understood by other exegetes, for only against this backdrop will the unusual nature of Dampa's presentation be apparent. The famous passage is unanimously read as a doxography, with most commentators parsing it as follows:[42]

1. no understanding:
    hedonists
    materialists

2. misunderstanding:
   nihilists
   eternalists
3. partial understanding:
   Śrāvaka
   Pratyekabuddha
4. misunderstanding of the genuine:
   Madhyamika
   Cittamātra
5. discipline:
   Kriyā-tantra
   Ubhaya-tantra
6. intention: Yoga-tantra
7. secret: Mahāyoga
8. natural secret meaning: Atiyoga

For the most part, this scheme agrees with the influential and early *Parkhap *Guhyagarbha* commentary attributed to the eighth-century Indian master Vilāsavajra, though there are some differences. First, under those of no understanding, Vilāsavajra describes the hedonists but makes no mention of the materialists.[43] Second, he places Cittamātra under those of partial understanding. Third, and most importantly for our purposes, in his treatment of the tantric vehicles he writes,

> [Regarding] "those of discipline, the intention, the secret, and the natural secret meaning," while certainly a correct teaching, those who, through their practice, control the three doors [perform] Kriyā. Those practitioners who perform primarily the inner yogas [of intention practice] Yoga. By abiding in the uncommon view and practice, one is "secret." Then, even though one abides in the natural fruition of the two inner [yogas] and of all things, there is Atiyoga, which is taught as merely the obscurations of the various stages of craving after imputations.[44]

One may safely assume that Vilāsavajra meant "the secret" to correspond to Mahāyoga. This means that, according to this reading, one who achieves the fruition of the two inner yogas (of the Yoga and

Mahāyoga tantras) experiences ordinary obscurations as Atiyoga. In other words, the "natural secret meaning" corresponds to Atiyoga. Despite certain differences between Vilāsavajra's reading and the later ones charted above, all agree that "the secret" refers to Mahāyoga, and "the natural secret meaning" to Atiyoga. However, Vilāsavajra does not see the category of Anuyoga anywhere in the *Guhyagarbha* system; indeed, he does not even mention the vehicle. Some later commentators incorporate Anuyoga by including it with either Mahāyoga, under "the secret," or with Atiyoga, under "the natural secret meaning,"[45] but none affords Anuyoga its own category.[46] In this way, then, the *Guhyagarbha* does not square with the *Gathering of Intentions*' nine-vehicle scheme and appears to have been unaware of the Mahā-Anu-Ati triad that was so central to the Zurs' Spoken Teaching canon.

Dampa and the Zurs before him were concerned to create a single cohesive system out of the Spoken Teachings. That the doxographical schemes of their two central tantras did not fit together was unacceptable. How did they bring them into agreement? We catch a glimpse of the answer in the *Guhyagarbha* commentary of Dorjé Gyeltsen, second throne holder of Katok and immediate successor to Dampa Deshek:

> Regarding "the natural, the secret meaning," the suchness of things abides primordially in the fruition of *the natural*, in the indivisibility of the three truths explained above, yet within the aspects of space and wisdom one realizes in an instant that which has been obscured by the various stages of craving after imputations [i.e., by the lower vehicles]—this is Anuyoga. And when the sheer *meaning*, just as it is, is illuminated, without even a moment, as the direct perception of intrinsic awareness—this is Atiyoga.[47]

The natural, then, refers to Anuyoga, or more specifically to the primordial state of suchness within which Anuyoga occurs, while the secret meaning corresponds to Atiyoga. Dorjé Gyeltsen thus divides "the natural, the secret meaning," which all other commentators read as a single unit, into two, thereby creating an extra category for Anuyoga. In offering this creative interpretation, Dorjé Gyeltsen likely follows the example of his teacher, Dampa. In concluding his work, he explains that "This was written in accordance with the teachings of my lama."[48] And the colophon continues: "This thorough explanation of the glorious **Guhyagarbha* represents a marvelous commentarial tradition that was taught and put into writing by he who resides on the eleventh level of complete radiance, the dharma lord Tsangtön Dorjé Gyeltsen, in accordance with the explanations of the unmistaken hearing lineage and pith instructions transmitted by Pema Gyalpo to the great lama of Katok in the east, Dampa Deshek."[49]

This unusual approach appears to have become common in the Katok exegetical tradition, for it is seen still in the fifteenth-century writings of Katokpa Yeshé Gyeltsen (b. 1395). In his commentary on Dampa's *Outline of the Vehicles*, Yeshé Gyeltsen explains: "'Those of the secret' primarily perform the profound view and the transgressive practices, so they are of Mahāyoga. 'Those of the natural' are free of contriving and altering, i.e., Anuyoga. 'Those of the secret meaning' are those of Atiyoga."[50] Here again, Yeshé Gyeltsen splits the final element, "those of the natural, the secret meaning," to add a ninth vehicle and provide Anuyoga (and thus the *Gathering of Intentions*) its own place within the doxographical system of **Guhyagarbha.*

Dampa thereby carefully negotiated a common ground between the variant doxographies of the **Guhyagarbha* and the *Gathering of Intentions*. The close attention he gave to such detailed exegetical issues reflects the significance of the wider Zur project to formulate the Spoken Teachings as a coherent canon. The *Outline of the Vehicles* effectively treads the narrow path between creative reinterpretation and conservative maintenance of the tradition, a path made all the more perilous by the competitive atmosphere of eleventh- and twelfth-century Tibet. Through his careful readings, Dampa smoothed over the gaps between the doxographical schemes of the *Gathering of Intentions* and the **Guhyagarbha*, a hermeneutical feat that gave his students an impression of a natural canon, a timeless set of teachings beyond the vagaries of ordinary humans. Having merged its key texts into a coherent whole, Dampa was free to make the Zurs' Spoken Teachings the centerpiece of his new monastic curriculum in eastern Tibet.

Thanks in part to Dampa's painstaking work, the Nyingma tradition of Katok was firmly established in eastern Tibet. Following the example of the Zur tradition in Ukpalung, the monks of Katok engaged in regular scholastic study of the Spoken Teachings, and the tradition continued for centuries to come.[51] As late as the sixteenth century, the famous Kagyupa master Pawo Tsuklak Trengwa testified to the continuing importance of the Spoken Teachings at Katok: "They propagated all of the (teachings of) mantra and dialectics and in particular the main teaching of the triad of Sutra, Illusion, and Mind abide here."[52] Alongside the Zurs' central Tibetan seat of Ukpalung, Katok had become the home of the Spoken Teachings, and it remains the preeminent center in Tibet.

In Dampa's writings we catch a glimpse of canon in the making. The early Zurs forged the Spoken Teachings, and their spiritual descendents were, to a large extent, responsible for the subsequent compilation of the *Collected Tantras of the Ancients*, the "extracanonical" canon of the Nyingma School.[53] While the founding of the Nyingma School may not be attributable to any one person or group, the early Zurs were key players in the process. The founders of the other Tibetan Buddhist schools that emerged during the same historical period introduced new specific tantras or secret teachings; the Zurs' authority lay less in any cutting-edge ritual or doctrinal innovation than in their codification of a canon that could be shared across the entire Nyingma School. Even the revealed texts of the treasure tradition, against which the Spoken Teachings were defined, relied directly on the categories, doctrines, and pantheons of the Spoken Teachings.[54]

The scholar of religion J. Z. Smith has written that "The only formal element that is lacking to transform a catalog into a *canon* is the element of closure: that the list be held to be complete. This formal requirement generates a corollary. Where there is a canon, it is possible to predict the *necessary* occurrence of a hermeneute, of an interpreter whose task it is continually to extend the domain of the closed canon over everything that is known or everything that exists *without* altering the canon in the process."[55] The exegetical moves seen here bear witness to Smith's observations. The formulation of the Spoken Teachings drove Dampa's careful efforts to plug the holes and smooth over the cracks in his canonical edifice. The early Zur catalogs of the eighteen Mahāyoga tantras, the five Anuyoga sutras, and the eighteen Pith Instructions of Atiyoga were being closed. Their historical differences were being effaced as they were moved into the realm of the eternal dharma.

4

THE RISE OF THE SUTRA INITIATION

Tantric initiations (and even a single initiation ceremony) can serve multiple purposes. For the dedicated few, they open a door to future practice, but for most they simply represent an opportunity to receive blessings and generate merit. For the tantric professional, initiation can effect a transmission of the lineage, a passing of religious authority from master to disciple. For the spiritual materialist, an initiation may be something to collect and thereafter be trotted out as badge of pious honor. Initiation is thus a formal ceremony, a polysemic floating signifier, the ritual significances of which are often not understood by and perhaps even irrelevant for most participants.

Parallels exist elsewhere in the tradition—other cases in which the contents of the Buddha's teachings have faded in significance in favor of a more formal, ritualized role. Today, for example, no Tibetan Buddhist community is complete without a set of the Kangyur, the canonical collection of the Buddha's teachings. Nearly every monastery has one, each volume carefully wrapped in brocade and arranged in a central shrine room, often behind glass. Monks and pilgrims visit it to make offerings and prostrate before it, or to take turns stooping into the small space beneath its shelves to receive the blessings that eternally descend from the hallowed tomes. But few, if any read it. The Kangyur is necessary for its sanctifying presence, but its contents are rarely considered. On special occasions, the 108 volumes might be taken down and distributed among the monks to be read aloud, not in chorus but in cacophony, each monk reciting his portion at the top of his lungs. The merit generated by such ceremonies may be boundless, but the semantic meanings of the texts are largely irrelevant.[1] In the past, some Tibetans read the sutras and tantras for their content—when they first translated them, at least, and in some cases for several centuries afterward.[2] Gradually, though, they mostly stopped. Exceptions exist, but today's Tibetan Buddhists prefer their own Tibetan-authored scholastic handbooks—their monastic debate manuals (*yig cha*), presentations of tenets (*grub mtha'*), and ground-and-path summaries (*sa lam*). The Buddhist canon's function, like that of the tantric initiation ceremony, has become less about content than about its formal and ritual place within the tradition.

The *Gathering of Intentions* initiation ceremony is one of the most complex in the Nyingma arsenal.[3] After the twelfth century, it became the single most important aspect of the tantra, so that by the fourteenth century, the entire system came to be referred to as the Sutra Initiation tradition. In this light, it is significant that such a large portion of the extant *Gathering of Intentions*-related materials dating from the thirteenth to sixteenth centuries consists of manuals for the performance of the initiation ceremony. This chapter analyzes the ritual structure of the Sutra Initiation and how it was altered in each successive manual to reflect better the wider concerns of the day. Particular attention will be paid to certain changes made to the initiation ceremony during the fourteenth and fifteenth centuries, alterations that reflected a gradual emptying of content and formalization of the tradition. Less and less were Nyingmapa masters reading and commenting upon the *Gathering of Intentions* itself. More and more, they were treating it as a kind of sepulchre, a sacred placeholder whose contents were no longer living but that still had to be worshiped and maintained for its place in the Nyingma canon.

SUCCESSES AND FAILURES OF THE *GATHERING OF INTENTIONS*

In the years after Dampa Deshek, the gradual codification of the Nyingma School continued, and by the fifteenth century the fundamentals of the school's identity were more or less set. The canonical collections were closed (with the *Gathering of Intentions* inside); the Indian and early Tibetan portions of most lineages were fixed. Back in the ninth century, the *Gathering of Intentions*' authors had sought to organize all of tantric Buddhism through their sophisticated weave of myth, doctrine, doxography, and ritual. At that time, the tantra's various organizational strategies had worked together as relative equals, each playing its role within the system as a whole. Gradually, however, many of the elements that had made the *Gathering of Intentions* unique spread widely and became part of the shared mythic and doxographical background common to all Nyingma tantric systems. They were so successful that they took on a life of their own and thrived independently from the tantra itself. Every treasure cycle had its own origin myth and its own version of the Rudra-taming myth, with its own particular deity playing the central role. Similarly, the nine vehicles doxographical scheme that had put the *Gathering of Intentions* at the heart of the Zur and Katok traditions became so ubiquitous within the Nyingma School that its foundation began to be forgotten. The Zurs' and Dampa Deshek's efforts to integrate and canonize the Spoken Teachings had succeeded. The *Gathering of Intentions*' King Dza and Rudra-taming myths and its nine vehicles had become so basic to the Nyingma School that they were now seen as primordial principles that had always structured the Buddhist teachings. How could concepts so fundamental to the very structure of the eternal dharma have come from just one text?[4]

In other ways too, the *Gathering of Intentions* was fading into obscurity. The absence of an Indic original could not have helped in the contentious environment of the eleventh to fourteenth centuries, and the discovery of a Sanskrit **Guhyagarbha* in the early thirteenth century would have helped to elevate that Mahāyoga root tantra above the *Gathering of Intentions* in the eyes of some Tibetan critics of the Nyingma School.[5] But the decline of the *Gathering of Intentions* should really be seen in terms of its changing role within the school. In the arena of Atiyoga, an array of innovative new practices had emerged; the treasure revelations and the sophisticated visionary systems of the Seminal Heart are just two examples. At the same time, in Mahāyoga, the new subtle body (*rtsa rlung*) and other perfection-stage practices were enjoying widespread popularity and were even being read back into the early Mahāyoga tantras.[6] New materials relating to the *Guhyasamāja Tantra* had arrived from India and new commentaries on the **Guhyagarbha* had been composed in Tibet, all of which made explicit reference to the subtle body practices of the perfection stage. Such developments left the category of Anuyoga, whose original *raison d'être* had been the perfection stage, increasingly superfluous. With the perfection stage seen in all Yoganiruttara tantras, even in those of the early Mahāyoga class, Anuyoga no longer warranted its own vehicle. This was unfortunate for the *Gathering of Intentions*, which had been labeled as the root tantra for Anuyoga, in spite of its own claims to encompass all nine vehicles. The category was being eaten away from both sides, losing its claim over the highest tantric teachings to further developments in Atiyoga and its role as the centerpiece of Anuyoga to retrospective readings within Mahāyoga.

By the fourteenth century, all these factors combined to leave the *Gathering of Intentions* in a much-diminished state, yet its place within the Spoken Teachings and the Nyingma canon remained unassailable. Less and less were its doctrines studied or its *sādhana*s performed, yet its symbolic role continued to be crucial to the identity of the Nyingma School. The *Gathering of Intentions*' lineage therefore had to be maintained, and toward this end, its unique and complex initiation ceremony remained vital. From around the fourteenth century, the Sutra Initiation ceremony became central to the *Gathering of Intentions*' history. Even as fewer Tibetans read the *Gathering of Intentions* itself, the Sutra Initiation's ritual forms continued to be deployed and even expanded within the Zur and Katok traditions.

THE SUTRA INITIATION SYSTEM

Chapter 3 traced the *Gathering of Intentions*' lineage through the third of the three Zur patriarchs, Zur Śākya Sengé (Dropukpa), whose student, Dzamtön, taught Dampa Deshek, the founder of Katok monastery. In central Tibet, however, another line continued, passing through another of Dropukpa's students, one Gartön Zungé. Around the same time, a second family began to play a crucial role in the lineage. The Len clan maintained extremely close ties with the better-known Zurs, such that the *Gathering of Intentions*' central Tibetan lineage was held between the two families for over four hundred years.[7] The Len's control of the *Gathering of Intentions* culminated in the person of Lentön Sönam Gönpo (active late thirteenth to early fourteenth century), who remains one of the most famous of the clan, probably thanks in large part to his prolific writings. Foremost among these was his *Len Manual*,[8] which came to represent the so-called Len System (*Glan lugs*) of the *Gathering of Intentions*' Sutra Initiation tradition. Len Sönam Gönpo passed his line on to Drölmawa Drotön Samdrup Dorjé (1294–1375),[9] who transmitted his, in turn, to Zurham Śākya Jungné. Concurrently, a notable shift occurred in the initiation ritual's structure. An immediate disciple of Zurham, one Nyelwa Delek, composed a new initiation manual called the *Jewel Rosary* around the end of the fourteenth century.[10] It quickly became the authoritative manual throughout central Tibet and served as the basis for the next few manuals to emerge.[11] The next to appear was the late fifteenth-century *River of Honey*, by Moktön Dorjé Pelzangpo of the Katok tradition.[12] Thus in the fourteenth and fifteenth centuries, three major manuals were written for the performance of the initiation ceremony: the *Len Manual*, the *Jewel Rosary*, and the *River of Honey*. Each altered the Sutra Initiation ceremony in significant ways, and the changes reflected the *Gathering of Intentions*' diminishing influence within the Nyingma School.

Most initiations serve to introduce the disciples into a tantric mandala derived from a certain tantra that, in turn, belongs to a particular class of tantras. One might, for example, be initated into the Vajradhātu mandala of the *Sarvatathāgata-tattvasaṃgraha Tantra*, which is classed as a Yoga tantra. The *Gathering of Intentions*' initiation system is highly unusual in that it initiates the disciple into a series of progressively higher vehicles, starting from the this-worldly vehicle of gods and humans and culminating with Atiyoga.[13] Since early on, this series of initiations was divided into four "initiation streams" (*dbang gi chu bo*). These four streams correspond to the nine vehicles so that the "outer initiation stream of tantra" covers the first six vehicles up through Yoga tantra, the "inner initiation stream of arising" grants initiation into Mahāyoga, the "accomplishment initiation stream of renown" into Anuyoga, and the "secret initiation stream of perfection" into Atiyoga.[14]

At the center of the initiation ceremony stands the *Gathering of Intentions* mandala, called the Gathered Great Assembly. The mandala palace is unusual for having nine stories, each corresponding to one of the nine vehicles.[15] The initiates are ritually led up through each level, finally reaching the top of the mandala palace, where they receive initiation into the highest vehicle of Atiyoga. The Gathered Great Assembly mandala is also unusual for having two layers at its center, representing the central buddha in his peaceful and the wrathful aspects, Samantabhadra and Mahottara Heruka (Tib. Che mchog he ru ka). This whole state of affairs is further complicated by the fact that two distinct mandalas of the Gathered Great Assembly were actually used in Tibet, an uncommon and a common one.[16]

The basic structure of the initiation ritual is traditionally credited to Déwa Seldzé, also known as Selwé Gyen (*Prakāśālaṃkāra).[17] This Indian master did not write a single comprehensive ritual manual, but a number of shorter works that are said to have been later assembled by Nupchen as a collection of eighteen texts.[18] Even in these earliest materials, two distinct systems were represented. Lochen Dharmaśrī, the great historian of the Sutra Initiation tradition who wrote around the turn of the eighteenth century, referred to them as the "tantra system" (*rgyud lugs*) and the "pith instructions system" (*man ngag lugs*).[19] The former is the more abbreviated of the two, in which the disciple is empowered into the nine levels of the Gathered Great Assembly mandala (either the common or the uncommon form). The pith instructions system is more elaborate, as it grants initiation into the "fully complete sutra" (*mdo yongs rdzogs kyi dbang*). Here, the disciple is led into separate mandalas corresponding to the various vehicles, with the common mandala of the Gathered Great Assembly used for the Mahāyoga section and the uncommon mandala used for the Anuyoga. Thus, for example, the famous Vajradhātu mandala might be used for the Yoga tantra initiations, a mandala with Śākyamuni at the center for the Śrāvaka initiations, and so on. These other mandalas are called the "branch mandalas" (*yan lag gi dkyil 'khor*), while the Gathered Great Assembly mandala is known as the "root mandala" (*rtsa ba'i dkyil 'khor*). This means that in the pith instructions system the disciple might be led through the vehicles twice—once through the branch mandalas, then again through the nine levels of the root mandala.

ZURHAM ŚĀKYA JUNGNÉ AND THE PROLIFERATION OF BRANCHES

After the Indian Déwa Seldzé and Nupchen's early writings, we have nothing else on the initiation ritual until well into the fourteenth century. This is not to say nothing was written during the intervening years, but no texts are extant, and none appears to have been of significant length. Writings on the initiation that date earlier appear to consist of short lists or notes on the ritual's performance, not unlike the kinds of texts attributed to Déwa Seldzé and Nupchen.[20]

Dating from around the turn of the fourteenth century, Lentön Sönam Gönpo's *Len Manual* marked a turning point in the *Gathering of Intentions*' history, a shift toward an ever more elaborate initiation rite.[21] The *Len Manual* provides our best comprehensive picture of the so-called Sutra Initiation before the pivotal figure of Zurham Śākya Jungné. It seems that the early tradition, from Déwa Seldzé and Nupchen through the early Zur and Len clans, tended to follow the simpler tantra system that used only the Gathered Great Assembly mandala.[22] Even when practitioners did adopt the pith instruction system, with its branch mandalas for individual vehicles, they did so in an abbreviated form compared to what came later, when a much expanded pith instructions system became the norm. The turning point came after Drölmawa, with his student Zurham Śākya Jungné and the manual entitled the *Jewel Rosary* by Zurham's student, Nyelwa Delek.[23]

Before this manual, all the Sutra Initiation traditions, including the *Len Manual*, followed a pith instructions system that used only two branch mandalas for the initiations into the first six vehicles, from that of gods and humans through Yoga tantra. But the *Jewel Rosary* and all the manuals after it added many more branch mandalas, using one (or more) for every one of the first six vehicles. Dharmaśrī explains the shift as follows:

> Earlier, before Drölmawa and his son, in the ritual traditions of the Len and [Dro]pukpa, each of the branch mandalas for Yoga and below were not performed. Then [Zurham's] initiation manual granted [the initiations] on the basis of an arrangement of

> certain sections of the Len system, but Zurham distinguished the forty-three enumerated vows and other details for the root [*Gathering of Intentions*] sutra and the branch mandalas. Nyelwa Delek then composed his ritual arrangements in accordance with that tradition. Those who grant initiation using that manual, thinking of it as the ritual tradition of Zurham, have labeled it the "Zur system."[24]

In expanding the pith instructions system in this way, Nyelwa Delek was following the tradition of his own teacher, Zurham. This is indicated in a passage in the *Biographies for the Sutra Initiation Lineage*, where Pema Trinlé explains that "the ritual arrangements of Nyelwa Delek, a direct disciple of Zurham . . . were written in accordance with the teachings of Zurham himself."[25]

The two branch mandalas used in the earlier *Len Manual* are the Vajravidāraṇā for the Kriyā vehicle and the famous Vajradhātu mandala for Yoga. That these were the only branch mandalas used for the "fully complete" Sutra Initiation of the pith instructions system appears to have been the norm throughout the early tradition. Even Déwa Seldzé's *Consecration Ritual Notes* says, "Next, the outer tantra vehicles: erect the mandalas of the twenty-one in three families and the Vajradhātu."[26] Once these two mandalas had been constructed, the first of the four "streams" of Sutra Initiations, "the outer initiation stream of tantra," was to be granted, consisting of 10 "branch" initiations, or 108 "coarse branch" initiations. These would effect initiation into the Kriyā and Yoga tantra mandalas. After that, for the three remaining streams of the inner tantras (Mahā-, Anu-, and Atiyoga), there were two options. First, one could use the common Gathered Great Assembly mandala for the second stream of eleven initiations into Mahāyoga, followed by the uncommon root mandala for the third stream of thirteen Anuyoga initiations.[27] No separate mandala would be required for the final two Atiyoga initiations, which, insofar as they can be said to require a mandala at all, continued to use the uncommon root mandala. The second option available to someone following the *Len Manual* was to use only one of these two root mandalas for all three streams of Mahāyoga, Anuyoga, and Atiyoga initiations. (This is the option described in the *Consecration Ritual Notes*.) Thus the

Len system included both choices seen in the scattered notes attributed to Déwa Seldzé.

Until the fourteenth century, this was the system followed in most Sutra Initiation ceremonies. Then Zurham complicated the ritual considerably by introducing branch mandalas for *each* of the first six vehicles, even the nontantric ones. To make matters worse, multiple mandalas were used for each vehicle. He had nine mandalas for the gods and humans initiations, five for the Śrāvaka, and so on, for a total of forty-three. According to this "Zur System," one would receive the respective initiations for each of these mandalas one vehicle at a time through Yoga tantra. Then, for the Mahāyoga, Anuyoga, and Atiyoga initiations, Zurham appears to have followed the second option outlined above, deploying only a single root mandala.

Zurham further altered the ritual structure by moving the ten outer initiations of the first stream (gods and humans through Yoga) so that they were no longer granted into their respective branch mandalas but into the single root mandala, along with the other three streams of Mahā-, Anu-, and Atiyoga. Thus, after the disciple was inducted into each of the branch mandalas, the root mandala would be constructed and all four streams of initiations for all nine vehicles would be granted, repeating, in effect, the initiations for the first six vehicles.

So what did all this mean from a larger perspective? Zurham added numerous branch mandalas and confined the four streams, which constituted the heart of the Sutra Initiation, to the root mandala. This addition and simultaneous contraction functioned to limit the *Gathering of Intentions* and place it within a larger ritual scheme. It reduced the tantra's symbolic standing vis-à-vis the other vehicles. In this regard, Zurham's modifications reflected the *Gathering of Intentions*' waning influence within the Nyingma School. His insertion of more branch mandalas allowed each of the first six vehicles greater ritual independence from the Gathered Great Assembly mandala by lifting each to a more equal footing relative to the Anuyoga vehicle. No longer could one be initiated into the *Vajradhātu* mandala by means of the ten outer initiations of the first stream. In this sense, the *Gathering of Intentions* had been exiled from its own ritual. Zurham kept the larger structure of the fully complete Sutra Initiation but restricted the root *Gathering of Intentions* to the vehicle of Anuyoga. That he elected to follow the second of the Len system's two options, constructing just one mandala for all three inner tantric vehicles, further allowed him to suggest that the Mahāyoga and Atiyoga initiations were not Mahāyoga and Atiyoga proper, but Anuyoga takes on them.

According to Zurham's system, then, the nine vehicles into which the disciple is initiated during the Anuyoga section of the fully complete initiation ceremony were to be understood merely as an Anuyoga view of these vehicles, not the actual vehicles themselves. Through his manipulations of the rites, Zurham brought the symbolic structure of the Sutra Initiation ceremony into line with the historical reality of the *Gathering of Intentions'* diminished position within the Nyingma School. Given the innovations in Nyingma tantric practice over the preceding three centuries, the *Gathering of Intentions* could no longer be said to embrace all the vehicles.

Even so, Zurham did not go so far as to introduce separate branch mandalas for Mahāyoga and Atiyoga. The root mandala was still allowed to include all three of the highest vehicles, Anuyoga as well as Mahāyoga and Atiyoga (though these were now understood to be Anu-Mahā and Anu-Ati). Soon, however, even these would be taken away.

THE KATOK SYSTEM

About one hundred years after Zurham's student, Nyelwa Delek, wrote his *Jewel Rosary*, another manual was composed, at Katok monastery in Kham. The *River of Honey* was written in the late fifteenth century by Moktön Dorjé Pelzangpo, a student of Yeshé Gyeltsen, the last of the original thirteen generations of Katok masters and the author of a commentary on Dampa Deshek's *Outline of the Vehicles*. Together, Moktön and his teacher seem to have initiated the most significant revival of the *Gathering of Intentions* at Katok after Dampa's original groundbreaking work.

The *River of Honey* is the most elaborate of all the Sutra Initiation systems. As we will see in chapter 5, its extraordinary complexity became a target for criticism in the seventeenth century. In constructing his new initiation ceremony, Moktön took Zurham and Nyelwa Delek's already complicated *Jewel Rosary* and added still more branch mandalas, plus their attendant initiations. Specifically, he added separate mandalas for the Mahāyoga and Atiyoga sections. Following the Yoga initiations into the Vajradhātu mandala, he inserted the peaceful and wrathful Māyājāla mandalas and the eighteen initiations of benefit, ability, and profundity (*phan nus zab dbang bco brgyad*) that comprise the complete initiations of the **Guhyagarbha Tantra*. Then he had the four streams of Sutra Initiations into the Gathered Great Assembly mandala, and finally the eighteen Mind Class Meanings of *A* (*sems sde a don*) initiations for Atiyoga. The twentieth-century scholar Khenpo Jamyang provides a succinct summary:

> Taking pieces of the Len tradition's initiation ritual manual as his base, [Moktön] ornamented it with the practice tradition of Gö Tsikungpa and the ritual arrangements of Drotön Pelden Drak.[28] He also added the teachings particular to the peaceful and wrathful deities of the *Māyājāla* and the eighteen mind class meanings of *A*. Thus it is known as "the River of Honey initiation manual for the triad of Sutra, Illusory [Net], and Mind [Class]."[29] It is also called the "Kham system of Sutra Initiation." The initiations of the fifteen common accomplishment substances [for the *Māyājāla*], that had been excluded in the ritual arrangements of Nelwa [Delek], appear in this [manual], and the teaching of the three profound initiations of the peaceful *Māyājāla*, that were excluded during the intermediate period in central Tibet, are also included in this Katok system. Thus it was enhanced. Moreover, the initiation streams of the eighteen mind class meanings of *A* were incorporated into this work, whereby it became a means of great benefit for the continuity of the teachings.[30]

The Katokpa's reputation for expertise in the Spoken Teachings originated with Dampa Deshek, who worked to weave the *Gathering of Intentions* into the larger cloth of the Spoken Teachings canon and its triad of Sutra, Illusion, and Mind. Moktön's new manual can be seen as an extension of the same project. There, the Sutra Initiation became a massive ceremony for granting initiation into not just the *Gathering of Intentions*' Gathered Great Assembly but also the entire Spoken Teachings canon. Under the early Zurs' and Dampa's guidance, the *Gathering of Intentions* came to provide the mythic and doctrinal structure for the Spoken Teachings writ large. Now, under Moktön's own contributions, it provided a ritual structure too—an initiation ceremony encompassing every one of the nine vehicles, each with its own set of mandalas.[31]

Here we see the Sutra Initiation in its most elaborate and comprehensive form. Yet strangely, at the same moment, the *diminishment* of the *Gathering of Intentions*' role within its own initiation ceremony, a process begun in the fourteenth century by Zurham, was also complete. The four streams of the *Gathering of Intentions*' initiation were now restricted to the single vehicle of Anuyoga. The tantra had forfeited all control over its own initiation structure and become subservient to its own creation.

The *Gathering of Intentions*' changing role within the Nyingma School was mirrored in the various iterations of the Sutra Initiation's ritual structure that were produced in the fourteenth and fifteenth centuries. As the *Gathering of Intentions*' influence waned, so did its role within its own initiation ceremony. By the fifteenth century and Moktön's *River of Honey*, the Sutra Initiation's entire series of 831 initiations, which used to wield authority over all nine of the Buddhist vehicles to enlightenment, was now squeezed into the single vehicle of Anuyoga.

Chapter 3 showed how by the twelfth century the *Gathering of Intentions* had become a centerpiece of the Nyingma canon, but what exactly this meant continued to change over the centuries that followed. The texts included in the Spoken Teachings remained relatively stable, but how they were understood in relation to one another was an open question. In this sense, the Spoken Teachings canon was not simply a vacuous space, an empty repository within which texts could be collected. It had a shape, an internal structure that was constantly being remade by Tibetans motivated by a variety of shifting concerns. How the canon functioned within the Nyingma School and, conversely, how the school and its followers shaped the canon were vital questions.

After the twelfth century, the *Gathering of Intentions*' role was increasingly that of an iconic presence rather than an active system of study and practice. It continued to be worshiped as a kind of sepulchre through its initiation ritual, transmitted as a crucial symbol within the Nyingma School. But the tomb itself was rarely opened; the text's contents themselves were rarely studied. The next chapter examines how the *Gathering of Intentions*, without ever being opened, became the subject of a powerful struggle in the seventeenth century.

5

DORJÉ DRAK AND THE FORMATION OF A NEW LINEAGE

Lineage is crucial to Tibetan identity. One may be born into an ancestral line (or two), receive novice vows from one teacher, be ordained by another, study philosophy in one monastic tradition, live in another, receive initiations from any number of tantric masters, and even be the incarnation of several figures of the past. Many lineages can act upon a single individual, inspiring and shaping his or her identity from multiple angles. But lineage is not only constitutive; it is itself constituted. It operates in a reciprocal relationship with its present-day holders, at once shaping and being shaped by them. A lama who reads himself into a lineage dons its mantle and also, in doing so, alters it. A lineage and the authority it bestows depend very much on its perceived givenness, yet it does not simply exist to be discovered; it is *created*. A lineage is woven out of numerous threads of transmissions in the past. It is simply one feasible line traced through a tangle, starting at some point in the past and ending in the present. Lineage thus pretends to be destiny but is (at least in part) narrative.

Here then is another aspect of the familiar tensions between tantric myth, or ritual, and history. In each chapter thus far, we have witnessed an author, deeply involved in the eternal truths of the *Gathering of Intentions*, in careful negotiation with the events of Tibetan history. This chapter explores the efforts of Pema Trinlé (1641–1717), second throneholder of Dorjé Drak monastery, to construct a new Sutra Initiation lineage that would, he hoped, replace two earlier lines. The seventeenth century marked a pivotal time in the history of Tibet. During these years, the modern Tibetan government of the Dalai Lamas rose to the fore, and the *Gathering of Intentions*-related materials from the period reveal a tradition intertwined with the politics of the day. While Mongol and Tibetan armies battled on the field, another war was being waged in the realm of religious lineage, between the great masters of the Nyingma School. In Pema Trinlé's writings, his nation's politics were being translated into the language of prophecy and ritual.

PEMA TRINLÉ'S NEW LINEAGE

After the fifteenth century, the next significant reworking of the Sutra Initiation tradition occurs in the works of Pema Trinlé. His predecessor, Ngagi Wangpo (1580–1639), had founded Dorjé Drak monastery, the home of the Northern Treasures (*Byang gter*), but it was Pema Trinlé who turned the new monastery into a major Nyingma institution. Toward this end, he worked to establish a new Sutra Initiation lineage there.[1]

The Northern Treasures community (also known as the Evam Chokar) traced its roots to the revealer of the Northern Treasures, Gödemchen (1337–1408). The community seems to have formed around the influential master Ngari Paṇchen Pema Wangyel (1487–1542), whose younger brother, Lekden Dudjom Dorjé (b. 1512),[2] was recognized as Gödemchen's reincarnation. Under the charismatic leadership of these two brothers, the Northern Treasures was the primary focus of the early community, but the Spoken Teachings were also carefully nurtured. Following the brothers' deaths, however, the community allowed its Spoken Teachings lineage to fade.[3] This is not surprising, for during this period the Evam Chokar (Evam Dharma Encampment) was forced to wander homeless through Tibet, fleeing persecution by Tibet's rulers, who were then based in the western province of Tsang. Only in 1632, when Ngagi Wangpo brought these peregrinations to an end and the Evam Chokar finally took root at Dorjé Drak, could the lost Spoken Teachings lineage finally be restored.

As seen in chapter 3, the Nyingma School's Spoken Teachings are defined vis-à-vis the treasure revelations that began to appear in the eleventh century. In the centuries that followed, it seems that the Spoken Teachings—and the *Gathering of Intentions* in particular—were found primarily in the larger monastic institutions and were of less interest to Nyingmapa lamas working at the village level. The history of the Evam Chokar community confirms such a view. For smaller communities, or those centered upon a single charismatic teacher, the *Gathering of Intentions*' complex rituals were neither feasible nor necessary, but for major Nyingma institutions, the *Gathering of Intentions* was crucial. Pema Trinlé strove hard to create a Sutra Initiation tradition at Dorjé Drak monastery by composing two major works—a massive (three-volume) new ritual manual and a collection of biographies of the masters of the *Gathering of Intentions* lineage. A central purpose of the latter work in particular was to justify Pema Trinlé's new lineage.[4]

Pema Trinlé begins by following the usual path from Nupchen Sangyé Yeshé, through the early Zurs, up to Drölmawa Drotön Samdrup Dorjé (1294–1375), teacher to Zurham. From Drölmawa, however, three different lineages diverge: the one favored by Pema Trinlé that passes to Zurham; another that passes through Zurham's sister, Zurmo Gendün Bum; and one that passes through Drölmawa's son, Drölchen Sangyé Rinchen Gyeltsen Pelzangpo (b. 1350). Pema Trinlé mentions the existence of the other two but traces only the first.[5] He even makes the bold claim that "During the later period, Zurham was the exclusive lord of the Zur system of the Sutra Initiation. Nowadays this is our line of practice."[6] As we have seen, Zurham oversaw the introduction of a host of new branch mandalas to the *Gathering of Intentions* initiation ceremony, and his innovations were preserved in the *Jewel Rosary*, the manual written by his close disciple, Nyelwa Delek. Given Pema Trinlé's emphasis on Zurham's place in his lineage, he held the *Jewel Rosary* in high regard and made much of how he used it as the "root manual" for his own work.

Oddly, however, Pema Trinlé does not trace his main lineage from Zurham to Nyelwa Delek. Instead, and rather awkwardly, he says that Zurham transmitted his line to Langdro Tülku Tsewang Gyelpo, who then passed it to the lineage holder, Lekpa Pelzang. Neither of these two figures seems very important, but that is not the point, for the latter transmitted the teaching to Jamyang Rinchen Gyeltsen, a great master and the father of Ngari Paṇchen and Lekden Dorjé, the founders of the Northern Treasures community. In their efforts to establish their Northern Treasures tradition, this family trio appears to have had some interest in the *Gathering of Intentions*: handwritten notes attributed to Ngari Paṇchen and his father were used by Pema Trinlé in writing his own ritual manual, and the father was recognized as an emanation of the main protector of the *Gathering of Intentions*, Black Excellence.[7]

The two brothers both are said to have bestowed their lineage on Kyitön Tsering Wangpo, Lekden Dorjé granting him the initiation at Samdruptsé, the palace of the Tsang rulers of Tibet. From Kyitön it passed to Lhachen Dreshongpa Chögyel Dorjé (1602–1677). He spent his youth at the ancient headquarters of the Zur clan, Ukpalung, and studied under many teachers, most notably the sixth Zhamarpa (1584–1630) and Gongra Lochen Zhenpen Dorjé (1594–1654).[8] Dreshongpa received the Sutra Initiation three times, first from Gongra Lochen, then from Dzokchenpa Namkha Drukdra (himself a Northern Treasures master). Then came the main transmission that interested Pema Trinlé, the one from Kyitön that stemmed from Lekden Dorjé. Dreshongpa received this initiation later in life, when Kyitön returned to Samdruptsé palace, the site of his own initiation, to grant it. Finally, he passed the lineage *in private* to Menlungpa Lochok Dorjé (1607–1671), the teacher of Pema Trinlé.[9] Apparently the secrecy of this penultimate transmission caused some to doubt its facticity, for Pema Trinlé defends it in writing:

> Nowadays certain parties gossip in secret whispers that "The master Dre[shong] Rinpoché did not really grant the Sutra Initiation to the pervasive lord, the great Menlungpa." This is nothing but a conspiracy. This has been claimed even in my own presence. There are indeed many marginal characters who would harm our great teachers with insulting accusations, but thanks to Jamyang Khyentsé Wangchuk and his nephews, as well as the great omniscient Conqueror [i.e., the fifth Dalai Lama], it has been stated time and again that the *vidyādhara* lord [Lekden Dorjé]'s lineage remains definitely unbroken. Therefore, whosoever casts

aspersions as these people do, rejecting the dharma and speaking against all those excellent masters, will cause many obstructions to be accumulated. Such benighted beings are objects for pity. The great lama Dreshongpa did not transgress even the slightest of his three vows and was completely pure in his conduct and vows.[10]

Pema Trinlé here defends the legitimacy of a specific transmission of the *Gathering of Intentions* teachings, from Dreshongpa to Menlungpa, that was key to the lineage he was trying to reconstruct. Apparently there was some doubt as to whether it had ever actually occurred. But who were the "marginal characters" who doubted Pema Trinlé's lineage, and why was he so interested in setting them straight?

OUT WITH THE OLD, IN WITH THE NEW: PEMA TRINLÉ'S RELOCATION OF AUTHORITY

Pema Trinlé's teacher, Menlungpa, the recipient of the questioned transmission, also transmitted the Sutra Initiation to the Fifth Dalai Lama, Ngawang Losang Gyatso (1617–1682), even receiving the honorary title of *ti-shih* from the great leader. So Pema Trinlé and the Great Fifth shared similar lineage concerns. But their relationship went far beyond this; Pema Trinlé first took ordination from the Dalai Lama, received teachings from him, and shared with him many other Nyingmapa teachers. And the Fifth Dalai Lama took a particularly keen interest in Pema Trinlé's work on the *Gathering of Intentions* tradition. The extent of his influence is clear from the following story, which may be pieced together from both Pema Trinlé's ritual manual and his collection of lineage biographies.

Pema Trinlé writes that before he received the Sutra Initiation, the Dalai Lama himself had already gotten it from Menlungpa. After that, he writes, "the omniscient master of speech, Losang Gyatso [the Fifth Dalai Lama] instructed the pervasive lord of the ocean of mandalas [Menlungpa]: 'Please grant the initiation that is the supreme crown of the golden teachings and explain the ritual arrangements [to Pema Trinlé].'"[11] Pema Trinlé goes on to describe his unusual experiences during the initiation ceremony that resulted from the Dalai Lama's request:

> Having arranged a certain date, in my twenty-fourth year, that pervasive lord of the one hundred [peaceful and wrathful] families, Menlungpa, was invited to my home, Tupten Dorjé Drak. On the very day he arrived, he began by granting the Vajrapāṇi initiation. Then, granting it step by step, when he reached the level of the Gathered Great Assembly [i.e., the *Gathering of Intentions*' main mandala], that excellent lord put on the costume—the secret robe, the flat hat, and so forth—and took hold of the vajra and bell, the white mustard seeds, and the far-reaching lasso to expel any hindrances. After that, making a vajra leap, the soles of his feet left a series of various blazing vajra marks [wherever he stepped]. Proclaiming, "Hūṃ! Hūṃ!" and with a posture and a look of ferocity, he even caused one person who was unable to endure his incredible splendor to faint. Faith and devotion were born [in me]; I felt as if this very same holy lama were the real vajra anger of the blessed one. When he flapped his thunderous wings, he made himself be seen as the actual deity, though only to those suitable. Then my comprehension increased still further in its faith; I attained a firm certainty that everything he did was perfect, and however he acted was not separate from wisdom's display. During the initiation of the *vidyādhara* lama of the Great Assembly, even though I did not abide in his actual lineage, he [included me] in the marvelous lineage, sending the two nephews of Jamyang Khyentsé [Wangchuk] out [of the room].[12]

This last sentence marks a crucial point, for it draws attention to Pema Trinlé's ambiguous place in the Sutra Initiation lineage. According to traditional criteria, as the head of the Evam Chokar, he would not normally have been in a position to inherit Menlungpa's Sutra Initiation lineage, but here Menlungpa is said to have made special arrangements during the initiation ceremony to establish Pema Trinlé as an authoritative lineage holder. Pema Trinlé is careful to emphasize this moment in his account, and he goes on to describe the extent of Menlungpa's transmission as follows:

> Thanks to that lord's great kindness toward me, even though that supreme lama of the *Gathering of All [Knowledge]* root text,

that majestic ruler of karma, did not have anyone helping the three doors [of his body, speech, and mind], I saw the blessings and signs again and again. Certainty, faith and devotion were born from the depths [of my being]. The presence [of the deity] rested at the top of my head. He wrote in tiny letters, "secret name: Karma Wangdruk Tsel," and when he told me, while granting the initiations, I was struck with tears.[13] Seeing the presence [of the deity], again I wept many tears and felt I could bear no more. In that way the fully complete initiation of the Great Gathering, together with the entrustment of the *[Gathering of Intentions] Sutra* protectors, was granted in full.

He gave me the secret name Dorjé Dudjom Tsel. During the seal of entrustment, he spoke of the metaphor of planting the tiniest seed of the *nyagrodha* [fig] tree, by means of which all directions come to be pervaded by the fruits and the twigs of the great tree of paradise. "You must spread the tiny seed of this Sutra Initiation of this old man widely and perform it extensively," he told me. I took this to heart. I offered him vows that I would listen, reflect, cultivate, teach, study, and perform widely this aspect of the dharma. Then that supreme lama too became happy.

When I reached the age of twenty-five, there arrived a letter from the great conqueror Vajradhara [Zur Chöying Dorjé] that I should compose a ritual arrangement. Accordingly, I wrote one. However, because I had not completed my studies, I had many doubts and felt unhappy with what I had written. Therefore, when I was twenty-six, once again the pervasive lord Menlungpa was invited to my home. He thoroughly granted the ripening initiation into the mandala of the peaceful and wrathful deities of the *Māyājāla* and gave detailed instructions on the rites for the Sutra Initiation, including even the dancing postures for the site ritual.[14]

Pema Trinlé dwells at length here on his visions, his tears, and his private conversations with Menlungpa. His autobiographical account attests to the strength of his connection to the lineage. This was not just some formal affair, an empty ritual performance devoid of faith, feeling, and religious experience. This was a complete transmission, and Menlungpa is said to have recognized the depth of his disciple's attainment explicitly, entrusting the lineage to his care and teaching him all the necessary minor rites.

With the Dalai Lama's encouragement, Menlungpa was going to great lengths to transmit every detail of the Sutra Initiation to Pema Trinlé. And the pressure from the Dalai Lama upon both Menlungpa and Pema Trinlé was unrelenting:

> In accordance with the order that had already come from the presence of the Supreme Conqueror [Dalai Lama], he [Menlungpa] told me, "Before this old man reaches the fifth path [i.e., dies], you absolutely must compose a convenient explanation of the ritual arrangements of the Sutra Initiation and make a capable restoration of this good casket of the precious Spoken Teachings."
>
> Ordered as I was by these two excellent lamas, in the following year I wrote only the [concluding] expressions of reverence, for I became stuck for a long time in the torpor of indifference and in the comfort of being distracted by pointless diversions. Then in my thirty-third year, 1673, I wrote a ritual manual for the initiations of the three Vajrakīlas of the Northern Treasures. [At that time,] I came again into the presence of the Supreme Conqueror, and he offered encouragement, once more with head respectfully bowed, offering the flower of his words together with a good gift of *suvarṇa* [gold]. In 1675 I wrote only about 100 pages, up to the mundane [initiation for] gods and humans. Then as before, due to distractions and my years of retreat, I abandoned my writing. Finally, when I was thirty-nine years old, after the great gathering for the Buddha's birthday in 1679, I wrote the sections from the Śrāvaka initiation onward, and in the last month of autumn of that year, during the eighth month, . . . it was completed.[15]

The Fifth Dalai Lama's relationship with Dorjé Drak had begun well before Pema Trinlé's birth, with the monastery's founder (and Pema Trinlé's previous incarnation), Ngagi Wangpo (1580–1639). Perhaps most significantly, the Great Fifth and Ngagi Wangpo had been first cousins; the Dalai Lama's mother, Künga Lhamdzé, princess of Yardrok, was a younger sister of Ngagi Wangpo's own mother, Yidzin Wangmo, princess of Taktsé. Given their close familial relations, it is not surprising that the Fifth Dalai Lama received his first major ceremonial blessing from Ngagi Wangpo,[16] and throughout his life, he took an active interest in building up his cousin's Dorjé Drak monastery. His support is acknowledged in the opening stanzas of Pema Trinlé's new initiation ritual manual, which recount how the Dalai Lama commissioned the work: "The gentle protector and omniscient lama, Ngawang Lozang Gyatso, told me, 'In order to hold and kindly protect beings and future generations so that they will be unafraid as they teach, debate, and write, you should expertly compose a properly arranged path that blends all the scattered ritual manuals for the initiation that is the jeweled staircase of the *Gathering of Intentions* initiations, the highest point for the lone travelers on the many varied paths."[17] Thus Pema Trinlé had been given his task: to gather all the scattered traditions of the Sutra Initiation into a new, authoritative system.

But why did the Dalai Lama commission this work? Prior to Pema Trinlé, there were two other active Sutra Initiation lineages, so we return to the three-way split in the *Gathering of Intentions* lineage that took place after Drölmawa, back in the fourteenth century. Pema Trinlé's line, which he traces in his biographical collection, passed from Drölmawa through Zurham, but there were two others, passing through Zurham's sister and Drölmawa's son, respectively. Within two generations, the lineage of Zurmo, the sister, moved to eastern Tibet, where it breathed new life into the Katok tradition.[18] By the seventeenth century, Katok's initiation liturgy was one of the foremost in Tibet, called either the Katok or the Kham System. The other lineage stemming from Drölmawa was that of his son, Drölchen Sangyé Rinchen. This one remained in central Tibet, and its members followed the same ritual manual that Pema Trinlé took as his own source—the *Jewel Rosary*, by Zurham's student Nyelwa Delek.[19]

Both lineages, of the sister and the son, predated the one traced by Pema Trinlé. Both had long since been recognized in earlier materials—Zurmo's in the *River of Honey* and Drölchen's in the writings of Sokdokpa Lodrö Gyeltsen (1552–1624). Before Pema Trinlé, Dorjé Drak did not have its own Sutra Initiation lineage.[20] The earlier Evam Chokar community had been led by the great Northern Treasures masters Tashi Topgyel (the rebirth of Ngari Paṇchen) and his son Ngagi

Wangpo (the rebirth of Lekden Dorjé), but neither could be included in Pema Trinlé's Sutra Initiation lineage biographies, because, quite simply, they had been uninterested in or unable to uphold the tradition. This may have been partly because the Sutra Initiation had become so elaborate that its performance required settled communities with enough people and resources to perform the complex rites. During the late sixteenth and early seventeenth centuries, the Evam Chokar community fulfilled none of these requirements. Only later, with the protection and sponsorship of the Fifth Dalai Lama, was the community able to construct its own Sutra Initiation tradition. The colophon to Pema Trinlé's lineage biographies supports such an interpretation, stating that the third Yolmo Tülku Tendzin Norbu[21] had already asked Pema Trinlé's previous incarnation (and the founder of Dorjé Drak), Ngagi Wangpo, to construct a new Sutra Initiation system appropriate to the burgeoning Dorjé Drak tradition.[22] But the project would not only provide a place for the revitalized Northern Treasures tradition at the table of the Spoken Teachings; it would also exclude others. Dési Sangyé Gyatso, the regent of the Fifth Dalai Lama, tells us that the Yolmo Tülku's recommendation was made "in order to cleanse what had become a polluted teaching."[23] The Desi's claim follows some verses that make explicit who was responsible for this pollution:[24]

> With a mind to help others who are [lost] in the caverns of
>   Yudruk's deceitful lies,
> the intention to guide many was established. In the well of
>   broken continuity,
> the confused and ultimately lifeless manuals
> that spread through the upper, lower, and middle regions are
>   unlike this one.
> Because of them, the long tradition of the secret, whose flames
>   to the highest heavens
> once reached, has now become mere sparks in a heap of ash.[25]

This somewhat obscure verse is helpfully explained, beginning with a reference to the anti-Nyingmapa polemical tracts of the eleventh to fourteenth centuries:

> After Nupchen, the three yogas spread widely, but many persons, basing themselves on various *Broadsides* (*'byams yig*) by Gö [Khukpa], Chak [Lotsawa], [Drikung] Peldzin [Nyi'ö Zangpo], and others, became caught in the trap of rejecting the dharma. With the passage of time, they gradually became confused as a result of taking the countless petty sectarian judgments (*grub mtha'*) as the dharma. Furthermore, there is reason to doubt whether the [*Gathering of Intentions*] lineage was continuous from Yudruk Dorjé's teachings. And too, in [those traditions that] spread in Kham, the ritual tradition became an impure teaching through [confusing] the subtle with the coarse.[26]

Here two groups are blamed for the supposed pollution of the *Gathering of Intentions* tradition: the lineage passing through Yudruk Dorjé and that of the Kham System. Yudruk Dorjé is accused of lies and deceit and breaking the lineage, while those following the Kham System are faulted for spreading their confusing and overly complicated ritual manual throughout Tibet. These two groups correspond precisely to the two main lineages—of Drölmawa's son and Zurham's sister—that preexisted Pema Trinlé's project. Yudruk Dorjé was the teacher of Sokdokpa, in whose writings the central Tibetan lineage of the son is described, and the purportedly complicated Kham System certainly refers to Katok Moktön's ritual manual, the *River of Honey*. Both of these groups, we are told, had so corrupted their lineages as to warrant their expulsion from the Sutra Initiation tradition by Pema Trinlé's faction. One is left suspecting there may be more to the story.

NYINGMAPA POLITICS IN THE SEVENTEENTH CENTURY

The seventeenth century marked a turning point in Tibetan history, when the Fifth Dalai Lama and his Mongol allies established the Ganden Podrang government that would remain in power until the Chinese invasion of the 1950s. During the civil war that brought this about, the Dalai Lama's faction deposed the previous rulers of Tibet, a line of secular rulers who had ruled since 1565 from the Samdruptsé palace in the western province of Tsang. These kings had inherited a long-standing enmity between their Rinpungpa predecessors and the burgeoning Geluk School centered around Lhasa. Matters worsened in 1578, when the Gelukpa abbot of Drepung monastery, Sönam Gyatso (1543–1588), traveled to Mongolia and succeeded in converting the Tumed leader Altan Khan (1507–1582) to Buddhism, receiving in return the previously unknown honorary title of "Dalai Lama."[27] Over the following decades, the Mongols' interest in the fortunes of the Geluk School only increased, straining their relations with the Tsang court. In 1621, they established a small army near Lhasa to protect their Gelukpa allies, and finally in 1640 (the year of Pema Trinlé's birth), the new Mongol leader Gushi Khan invaded the eastern region of Kham, capturing it after a yearlong fight. The eastern Tibetans were deemed "partisans of the royal government,"[28] which made them natural enemies of the Gelukpa and their Mongol supporters. The following year, 1642, Gushi Khan led his troops against central Tibet, deposed the Tsang king at Samdruptsé, and enthroned the Fifth Dalai Lama as king of all Tibet. Broadly speaking, then, on one side were the Tsang kings and the kings of Kham, and on the other side the Dalai Lama's Geluk School, based in Ü and supported by the Mongols.

This much is relatively well known. Somewhat less studied, however, is the Nyingmapa role in these events that were so crucial to the history of Tibet. A common stereotype of the Nyingma School imagines it very much outside of large-scale Tibetan politics, but closer examination reveals a markedly different picture, particularly during this period, that goes a long way to explain the motivations behind Pema Trinlé's reconstruction of the Sutra Initiation lineage. The early nineteenth-century historical work by Guru Tashi offers a good place to start. It states that, despite being some of the most influential Nyingmapa of their day, the threesome of "Nang, Sok, and Gong" were roundly despised by the Fifth Dalai Lama.[29] Throughout his own writings, the Fifth Dalai Lama focuses particularly on the "Nang," or the "Nangtsé chieftain," as he disparagingly refers to him. This was none other than the famous treasure revealer Zhikpo Lingpa (1524–1583), a title the Dalai Lama claims he did not deserve: "The title of Zhikpo Lingpa [prophesied] in the *Chronicles* [of Orgyen Lingpa]," the Dalai Lama insists, "may have been *claimed* by this aspirant, but in the *General Prophecy* of Ratna [Lingpa], it says, 'The revealer of the profound treasures from Khyüngchenri and Kharchu also has the secret name Zhikpo Lingpa.' Therefore please do not be drawn into doubt."[30]

The Nang-Sok-Gong trio actually constitute a short lineage. Zhikpo Lingpa was Sokdokpa's main teacher, and (as in the Sutra Initiation's son lineage described above) Sokdokpa taught Gongra Lochen. As we have seen, Pema Trinlé, in the colophons to his two works on the *Gathering of Intentions*, names a fourth figure, Yudruk Dorjé, as the source of corruptions in the Sutra Initiation lineage, and he was the Sutra Initiation teacher of Sokdokpa. That all of the Dalai Lama's Nyingmapa enemies came from the same small circle should give us pause. Who were these three, and why did the Fifth Dalai Lama dislike them so? All worked closely with the Tsang kings against the Mongol invaders. The middle member of the Dalai Lama's detestable trio, Sokdokpa (lit. "the Mongol Repeller"), was even named for his expertise in large-scale war rites for repelling the Mongol armies. His *History of How the Mongols Were Repelled* describes in detail his repeated ritual performances on behalf of the Tsang court, often with the support of his teacher Zhikpo Lingpa's blessings and prophecies.[31] The Nyingmapa masters targeted by the Dalai Lama, then, were powerful allies of the Tsang kings. As treasure revealers and ritual specialists, they provided the prophecies and the war magic required for the Tsang kings' military ventures. In this way, the Nyingmapa of the sixteenth and seventeenth centuries were deeply enmeshed in the politics of the day. While Mongol and Tibetan armies battled on the field, another war was being waged in the parallel realm of prophecy and black magic, between the great masters of the Nyingma School.

All this lurked in the background of Pema Trinlé's project to remake the Sutra Initiation lineage, but yet another related element was at play: that of clan lines and family feuds. As the new head of the Evam Chokar, Pema Trinlé inherited his community's long history of political conflicts. The Northern Treasures were first revealed in the fourteenth century, but the Evam Chokar community itself was only established a century or two later, during the lifetime of Ngari Paṇchen and his brother Lekden Dorjé, the reincarnation of Gödemchen. Following Ngari Paṇchen's death in 1542, the community fell to the younger brother. More a charismatic visionary than a politician, Lekden Dorjé appears to have been less successful without his brother's guidance.

It was "during the time of Rikdzin II, Lekden Je, who was the second Gödemchen, and of Tashi Topgyel Wangpö De,"[32] suggests Dudjom Rinpoché, that the troubles began for the Evam Chokar. The Fifth Dalai Lama similarly indicates that Lekden Je became something of a lightning rod:

> There was an official prophecy that [Sangyé Lingpa's] *Collected Intentions of the Guru* would be distorted [by those] following the *vidyādhara* Gödemchen. Nangtsé's [i.e., Zhikpo Lingpa's] faction identified Lekden Dorjé [as the distorter] and proclaimed it widely. Thanks to them, many less fortunate people were plunged into doubt. But this was like the heretics who said the *tathāgata* was in love with a brahmin girl, or the evil ministers who claimed the master Padmasambhava tried to poison the king.[33]

The precise nature of Lekden Dorjé's troubles remains obscure, but they may have been related to his search for Ngari Paṇchen's reincarnation. Ultimately he selected a prince from the wealthy Jangpa family named Tashi Topgyel Wangpö De (1550–1603),[34] but it seems his choice was not without complications. The Fifth Dalai Lama devotes several pages to defending Lekden Dorjé's decision against conflicting views. After citing several prophecies regarding Ngari Paṇchen's rebirth, he explains how they predicted five incarnations of the early Tibetan king Trisong Detsen, of whom Ngari Paṇchen was the third (the emanation of the mind). The fourth emanation, "the emanation of the good qualities, would be the king of dharma, Wangpö De. If the conditions were right, he would be born in a dog or a dragon year into the royal family of Minyak Tsashing."[35] Sure enough, the Jangpa family traced its roots to the Minyak region of eastern Tibet, so the Dalai Lama was clearly supporting Lekden Dorjé's choice.[36]

The issues around Lekden Dorjé's selection remain unclear. Most likely, another faction had backed another competing candidate. The Fifth Dalai Lama's account suggests one possible explanation:

> Without understanding this [prophecy], many biased fools said that the Jang Lord had made incorrect prayers, so [Ngari Paṇchen] took rebirth as the son of the Tsang ruler. If the important

> virtuous deeds of the King of Tsang, Karma Tenkyong Wangpo, are analyzed, he was an excellent being for the most part. However, he did not practice the secret mantra of the Nyingma [School] as his main doctrinal system. What is more, the tiny bit of practice in the cycles of the Nyingma traditions that he did practice was exclusively of the Nangtsé chieftain's [i.e., Zhikpo Lingpa's] faction. He could not even do the preparatory rites for a revelation; forget about him being a treasure revealer! And even if he could reveal [a treasure], it seems he did not have the [appropriate] belief or interest, so the predispositions of this great dharma king would not have been awakened. This is proven by all scriptures and reasoning. Some following the talk of fools then cite some fabricated prophecy that this great being's teachings were [for this reason] defeated in the end [i.e., by the king's son, whom they uphold as the rightful heir]. But this is just a mirror that clearly reveals themselves.[37]

In other words, the competing candidate for Ngari Paṇchen's reincarnation may have been none other than the son of the Tsang king.[38] By recognizing Ngari Paṇchen's reincarnation within their own family, the Tsangpa court sought to bolster its reputation by gaining control of this prestigious line of Northern Treasures masters and the Evam Chokar community. Ultimately their efforts failed, not least, according to the Dalai Lama, due to their family's weak connections to Nyingma ritual practice.

Whatever Lekden Dorjé's troubles may have been, the real conflict did not erupt until some years later. Ngari Paṇchen's reincarnation, Tashi Topgyel, grew up under the tutelage of some of the greatest masters of his day, in a royal house at the height of its powers. But the halcyon days of his youth ended in his thirtieth year, when the Jangpa house ran afoul of the Tsangpa king, Zhingshakpa Tseten Dorjé, who forcibly expelled both Tashi Topgyel and his brother Namkha Gyeltsen from their ancestral home. The two brothers sought refuge in Ü province, at Chongyé, a choice that is notable for several reasons, not least because the Fifth Dalai Lama would be born into the same Chongyé household some thirty-seven years later. It was during this period (c. 1580) that Tashi Topgyel's son, Ngagi Wangpo, was born; his mother was Yidzin Wangmo, the princess of the hospitable Chongyé family (and sister to the Great Fifth's mother).[39]

Tashi Topgyel was now living in exile. Written insults were exchanged, and the situation continued to escalate. In Dudjom Rinpoché's words:

> After Zhingshakpa [i.e., the Tsangpa ruler] consolidated his power, he had a disagreement with the Jang Lord, Tashi Topgyel. Along with Jangpa Namkha Gyeltsen, he exiled Tashi Topgyel. The Tsangpa [ruler] said with self-satisfaction, "You, the so-called 'Powerful One' ('Top'), are [now nothing but] a powerless Khampa.[40] I banish you into the city of the hungry ghosts." To which Tashi Topgyel replied, "You, the so-called 'Field' ('Zhing'), in whom the ten fields [of an appropriate victim for violent "liberation"] are complete, I hereby send into the mouth of Rāhula," and by applying the rites of Rāhula, he killed Zhingshakpa. It seems the reason for the short duration of the Tsangpa family and its regime may even be attributed to this [incident].[41]

From his new base at Chongyé, Tashi Topgyel appears to have mounted a magical attack against his persecutors, and before long, the offending king was dead.

The Fifth Dalai Lama begins his own discussion of the incident by pointing to a prophecy in Ngari Paṇchen's revelations: "In the southeastern direction of the world, the demoness Sharp-and-Fast Blackness will give birth to nine sons and rule the world. In particular, in this snowy land of Tibet, as the fortieth year in the future approaches, nine emanated demons and nine evil ministers . . . will drag all beings into oppression."[42] Zhingshakpa had nine sons who helped their father establish control over Tibet, as the Dalai Lama takes care to point out before continuing with his story:

> Foremost among those nine children was Künpang Lhawang Dorjé. This son and his Zhingshakpa father concocted an accusation against the Northern [Treasures] followers, including Namkha Gyeltsen [i.e., Tashi Topgyel's brother] and others. Then they cast terrible aspersions against this same great *vidyādhara*, expelling

> him into the [central] Ü region and otherwise carrying on. On this account, [Tashi Topgyel] understood that these horrible ones were disciples who first required subjugation by wrathful means and only then acceptance as students. While residing at Chongyé and Drikung, he performed many violent spells, including those of Mañjuśrī Yamāntaka and the Razor of the All-Pervading Rāhula, by means of which, before long, his enemies were led into the tent of the lord of death. In his powers and abilities he was unmatched by any other.[43]

Following this confrontation, Tashi Topgyel turned his attention increasingly to his religious responsibilities, excavating treasures and composing ritual manuals for his community of Northern Treasures devotees. Such was the environment within which his son, Ngagi Wangpo, grew up. The Fifth Dalai Lama's biography describes the father and son's adventures as they traveled during these years, many involving fights with supporters of the Tsang king and the "Nangtsé faction."

We now have some idea why Pema Trinlé, as the rebirth of the son, Ngagi Wangpo, might have had his own reasons for distrusting the central Tibetan Sutra Initiation lineage controlled at that time by Gongra Lochen, inheritor to Yudruk Dorjé and Sokdokpa. What remains to be considered is why he also held the Katok System in such low regard. Once more, the Dalai Lama's writings provide a clue. In the years that Ngagi Wangpo spent wandering homeless at his father's side, they visited eastern Tibet and propagated the Northern Treasures widely.[44] Later, following Tashi Topgyel's death, Ngagi Wangpo returned to Kham and visited Katok monastery. It was not an entirely successful visit:

> Then they came to Katok monastery, which is like the source of the Nyingma teachings of secret mantra in Kham. All the monks and laity of that region paid extensive reverence and made material offerings of gold, silver, turquoise, horses, armor, and tea. In accordance with each individual's abilities, he extensively enacted the welfare of beings by means of the excellent dharma, through initiations, oral transmissions, and pith instructions.

> However, some holders of the lineage of the Nangtsé chieftain who had evil motivations created dissent, so that the public performance of a great accomplishment ceremony for the eight protectors and other events could not take place. When the father, the dharma king Tashi Topgyel, had visited [earlier], the Katokpas had said they needed a tea offering for the three roots. He [Tashi Topgyel] had offered from his heart the *Teaching the Path of Goodness*, which is a text by the great *vidyādhara* Ngari Pa[ṇdita], and established it there. Though [the Katokpas] regularly recited it, they did not understand that this was a text by the *vidyādhara* lord. Later, one Tsangpa Rapjampa, who was great in good qualities and wisdom but a direct disciple of the Nangtsé chieftain, recognized the recitation and changed [the title] to *Teaching the Path of [Lang] Darma.*[45] For this reason, [Tashi Topgyel] became enraged and destroyed both Tsangpa Rapjampa and that thief of many horses and mules, Wönpo Tsegyel. By performing the "Whirlwind of the Black Sun and Moon," he caused Wönpo Tsegyel to die suddenly. Meanwhile, Tsangpa Rapjampa had a disagreement with his patrons and [ended up] wandering through three provinces, being ousted from one place to another, until finally he was afflicted by a powerful demonic plague and passed into the next world.[46]

Within Katok, then, both of the central Tibetan Nyingmapa factions were represented. While some made generous offerings and received teachings from the two Northern Treasures masters, others who were followers of Zhikpo Lingpa saw Ngagi Wangpo and his father as corrupting influences. Once again, the dispute ended in a display of violent ritual. Given such a history, it is not surprising that Pema Trinlé, the immediate reincarnation of Ngagi Wangpo, might have inherited a mixed opinion of Katok and allowed it to color his new Sutra Initiation ritual manual. The Katok system, as represented by its massive three-volume *River of Honey* manual, was the yardstick against which he measured his own. He began by calling theirs the "common" system and his own the "uncommon system of the Zur."[47] Then he littered his work with innumerable asides on the many ways his manual was better than the *River of Honey*. The criticisms are varied, but they often fit with the larger theme described in the colophon, that the Katok System was overcomplicated. Early on, for example, he writes,

> The [*River of Honey*] manual of Katok Dor[je] [Pel]zang indeed seems to have a very great and wonderful framework and elaborations, but at the point [in the ritual] for blessing and protecting the ground, the king's pole [*torma* offering], the purification of the [three] doors, the violator Matran[ka Rudra], and so forth are all already included [and there is no reason to include them again], so right from the beginning, it is overly complicated and there is too much to do.[48]

Pema Trinlé's new Sutra Initiation lineage highlighted members of his own Northern Treasures lineage while excising the supposedly corrupt lines of Katok and "the Nangtsé faction." Two parallel forces drove him: his benefactor, the Fifth Dalai Lama, and his own community's history of persecution at the hands of the Tsang kings and their Nyingmapa associates. Pema Trinlé's *Gathering of Intentions* project was deeply enmeshed in the politics of the seventeenth century, in a complex weave of the state and the personal. While the Dalai Lama sought to consolidate his government and his hold on the Nyingma School, Pema Trinlé worked with the ghosts of his spiritual forebears—Lekden Dorjé, Tashi Topgyel, and Ngagi Wangpo. From Lekden Dorjé's controversial recognition of his brother's reincarnation to Tashi Topgyel's eviction from his family home to Ngagi Wangpo's quarrel at Katok, Pema Trinlé's new lineage reflected the concerns of his lineal ancestors.

Despite his best efforts, traces of the earlier lineages still show through the inevitable gaps in his account. The Nang-Zhik-Gong clique was so influential within the *Gathering of Intentions* tradition of the period that Pema Trinlé could not avoid using some of them in his own lineage. He was forced to admit that Gongra Lochen transmitted the lineage to his own teacher, Menlungpa, as well as to his teacher before him, Dreshongpa.[49] Like all lineages, his is thus a construction, but it had to be fashioned out of preexisting elements, accepted historical "facts" that limited its shape and scope.

6

THE MINDRÖLING TRADITION

If Pema Trinlé's writings on the Sutra Initiation tradition reflect the interests of the Fifth Dalai Lama, the only slightly later Mindröling tradition shows more the influence of the Great Fifth's famous regent, Désí Sangyé Gyatso (1653–1705). In 1681, Sangyé Gyatso completed his *Pure Crystal Mirror: Guidelines for Clarifying Regulations and Prohibitions in Twenty-One [Chapters]*. In this work, the new regent sought to systematize the burgeoning bureaucracy of the Ganden Podrang, and over the next twenty years he composed many other texts similarly aimed at classifying and arranging Tibetan political life around the Dalai Lama government. Through encyclopedic lists, detailed descriptions, and elaborately choreographed ceremonies, he developed an intricately ordered vision of Tibet that incorporated its inhabitants and even its landscape and put them all in service of his government. This was an intensely symbolic project. For example, Sangyé Gyatso had the relics of many past Buddhist masters brought from monasteries throughout Tibet to the Potala and placed in the Fifth Dalai Lama's reliquary stupa. In the words of the scholar Kurtis Schaeffer, "Just as philosophical positions are arranged hierarchically in a treatise on tenets, the relics of other schools' masters, including those taken from such places as Rinpung, were subsumed within the greater structure of the Dalai Lama's stupa, both physically and symbolically."[1] In this and many other ways, Sangyé Gyatso oversaw a broad bureaucratization of the Ganden Podrang, and even of Tibet more generally, with the Dalai Lama at its head.

A similar symbolic and bureaucratic trend may be detected in the Sutra Initiation tradition that emerged from Mindröling around the end of the seventeenth century. Whereas the Dorjé Drak Rikdzin Pema Trinlé had sought to expunge his enemies from the Sutra Initiation lineage and supplant their ritual texts with his own, Terdak Lingpa Rikdzin Gyurmé Dorjé (1646–1714) and his brother Lochen Dharmaśrī (1654–1717) forged a more inclusive system that provided places for everyone. Together, the brothers remade the Spoken Teachings from the bottom up. They combined extensive historical research with creative innovation to provide a new ritual platform that could be shared across the Nyingma School. Their careful typologies of ritual texts, compartmentalization of ritual procedures, and unprecedented emphasis on public performance produced a Sutra Initiation tradition that in many ways mirrored Sangyé Gyatso's political project.

RELIGIOUS CEREMONY AS POLITICAL STRATEGY

In September 1691, over three hundred of the most renowned masters of the Nyingma School gathered at the recently founded monastery of Mindröling in central Tibet. Sacramental feasts, religious dances, and elaborate ceremonies were performed over eleven days. All those present received the initiations and instructions for a comprehensive new ritual system that drew together the various traditions related to the *Gathering of Intentions*. This event marked a turning point in the history of the Nyingma School. It was the culmination of the efforts of the two charismatic brothers to reshape their tradition by unifying the scattered local lineages under large monastic institutions. Twenty-five years later, these teachers would be dead, their monastery destroyed in a violent religious persecution. Yet today the identity of the Nyingma School is still defined in large part by the regular observance of the same community rituals first performed at this gathering.

Around the same time that Pema Trinlé was completing his new Sutra Initiation manual, Terdak Lingpa was founding the great monastery of Mindröling, directly across the Tsangpo river from Dorjé Drak. Like Pema Trinlé, Terdak Lingpa received generous support from the Fifth Dalai Lama and his new government. The two simultaneously burgeoning Nyingma centers thus shared much in common, but there were some significant differences between the attitudes of their respective founders, at least in their treatments of the Sutra Initiation tradition. Pema Trinlé took a more exclusionary course, perhaps reflecting the decades of persecution his Northern Treasures forbears had experienced, and quite unlike the one taken by the brothers at Mindröling; their larger movement sought to strengthen the Nyingma teachings across all of central and eastern Tibet. Ultimately, both monasteries were successful, and the results of their distinct strategies can be seen to this day in the contours of the Nyingma School. Dorjé Drak enjoys a reputation for its exceptionally strong Northern Treasures system, which has remained intact since its fourteenth-century inception, while the Mindröling tradition, less associated with any one cycle of teachings, pervades the ritual fabric of nearly every major Nyingma monastery.

The Mindröling brothers implemented their inclusive approach through several interlocking strategies: in-depth historical research, the systematization of the Spoken Teachings canon, and the creation of new, large-scale public rituals. They formulated ornate ceremonies to be performed over periods of days before large public audiences, and Mindröling soon became known for its extensive rituals and elaborate dances by large numbers of monks. The popularity and scale of these new ceremonies helped to establish Mindröling at the heart of the Nyingma School.

Terdak Lingpa's use of public ritual shared much in common with the contemporaneous activities of the Fifth Dalai Lama and perhaps even more with the efforts of Dési Sangyé Gyatso. While Terdak Lingpa worked at Mindröling, in Lhasa, Sangyé Gyatso built his new Tibetan state, and one of his principal strategies was to establish annual festivals and public rituals, intricately scripted in detail and inclusive in scope. Some of the ceremonies were new creations, but others had their roots in earlier times. The origins of the Great Prayer Festival (*smon lam chen mo*), for example, may be traced to 1409 and the activities of Tsongkhapa (1357–1419), the founder of the Geluk School. While the festival, which was held annually as part of Lhasa's extensive New Year ceremonies, was a politically significant event even then, the

Fifth Dalai Lama and his regent remade it as a—possibly *the*—high point in the state ritual calendar. Such ceremonies were highly elaborate and had to be performed in exact accordance with prescribed forms. Officials were required to be present, with no excuses, and even the seating arrangements were strictly ordered, with a set number of seat cushions corresponding to each office.[2] Here too, the Dalai Lama and his regent may have been following earlier regimes. The fourteenth-century government of Tai Situ Jangchup Gyeltsen (1302–1364) in particular emphasized the importance of precedence and court etiquette at state events.[3]

The Great Prayer Festival and ceremonies like it continued to be central to the authority of the Ganden Podrang government right into the twentieth century. The British diplomat Hugh Richardson, who lived in Lhasa for some eight years between 1936 and 1950, witnessed the annual ceremonies and offered the following observations:

> The origin of most of the ceremonies lies in the remote past, but they have been rearranged and elaborated at different times, especially in the seventeenth century during the rule of the Great Fifth Dalai Lama and his equally great regent Sangyé Gyatso when they were put into what was very much their latest form with the clear intention of enhancing the grandeur of the new regime . . . and the prestige and stability of the position of the Dalai Lama and the Gelukpa, Yellow Hat, church.[4]

The Fifth Dalai Lama and Dési Sangyé Gyatso's new ceremonies brought together (even if by force) all competing political factions beneath the banner of the Ganden Podrang. Everyone was guaranteed a place at the table, as long as they remained seated and followed the proper ceremonial procedures.

Just as the nation of Tibet was gathered and symbolically arranged through these new public ceremonies, so too was the Nyingma School united by the new Mindröling rituals. The scale of Terdak Lingpa and Lochen Dharmaśrī's work was similarly large, and although this study focuses on the *Gathering of Intentions*' role in their project, many other elements were also crucial. Terdak Lingpa's own treasure revelations relating to the bodhisattva Avalokiteśvara served as the basis for the popular Maṇi Rimdu festival and thus similarly contributed to the Mindröling project.[5] And in some cases, the connections between Mindröling and the Tibetan state are even clearer than in the Sutra Initiation tradition. The central deity in the Maṇi Rimdu is closely related to the Ṣaḍakṣarī form of the bodhisattva Avalokiteśvara, of which the Dalai Lama is supposed to be an incarnation,[6] so the Mindröling festival served in part to promote the new cult of the Dalai Lamas.

THE SPOKEN TEACHINGS OF MINDRÖLING

Today, our principal source for information on the Spoken Teachings is the *Expanded Spoken Teachings of the Nyingma School*, a fifty-eight-volume collection compiled by Dudjom Rinpoché during the 1980s.[7] The collection "expands" upon an earlier edition compiled by Dzokchen Gyelsé Zhenpen Tayé (1800–1855), which was based, in turn, upon the original Mindröling compilation. The collection reflects a strong focus on ritual manuals. The whole is arranged by tantric ritual system, with separate sections for *Buddhasamāyoga*, *Vajrakīlaya*, **Guhyagarbha*, and so on. The contents of these sections are then quite regular; each contains a minimum of three kinds of manuals—a *sādhana* for accomplishing oneself as the deity, a *maṇḍala vidhi* for constructing the relevant mandala, and an *abhiṣeka vidhi* for performing the initiation ceremony—and nearly every one was composed by Terdak Lingpa, Lochen Dharmaśrī, or Terdak Lingpa's son, Rinchen Namgyal (1694–1758).[8] The ritual manuals are tightly interwoven, with references to one another and to further ancillary manuals. These appear at the end of the ritual collection, and they are almost all products of the early Mindröling tradition.[9] Being ancillary, they describe the lesser components necessary for most ritual procedures: laying the lines of the mandala, consecration rites, *torma* offerings, and so forth. In short, the modern Spoken Teachings collection still reflects the early Mindröling project to regularize the ritual systems of the entire tradition.

The Mindröling brothers (and especially Lochen Dharmaśrī) directed considerable attention to the Spoken Teachings in general and the *Gathering of Intentions* in particular. In his modern history of the Nyingma School, Dudjom Rinpoché writes: "In order that the teaching might endure for a long time, Lochen Dharmaśrī composed the texts making up his eighteen-volume *Collected Works*, beginning with his unprecedented writings on the intentional meaning of the *[Gathering of Intentions Sutra]* and the *Magical Net*."[10] Five of the volumes are devoted to the *Gathering of Intentions,* and Dharmaśrī's writings focus almost exclusively on ritual issues.[11] To support his new ritual tradition, however, he published a comprehensive study of its history, the *General Exposition*. Dharmaśrī conducted an extensive review of the *Gathering of Intentions*' history, excavating the long-buried foundations of this influential text so that they might serve as the basis for his new system. By digging beneath the layers of Nyingmapa infighting that had accreted over the fifteenth, sixteenth, and seventeenth centuries, he uncovered a much earlier shared historical base on which all Nyingmapa could find common ground.

Pema Trinlé refused to accept Katok's additions to the initiation ritual and chose instead to base his own manual on the earlier *Jewel Rosary* and the handwritten notes he inherited from his Northern Treasures predecessors, Jamyang Rinchen Gyeltsen and Ngari Paṇchen. According to Pema Trinlé, the Katok tradition's *River of Honey* was overly complicated, and though he pointed to all sorts of offenses in the manual, worst of all were the new initiations Moktön had added for the stages of Mahāyoga and Atiyoga. Further exacerbating these tensions were those within central Tibet, between Pema Trinlé (and the Fifth Dalai Lama) on one side and the Nang-Sok-Gong faction on the other.

Such was the contentious state of affairs that faced Lochen Dharmaśrī as he embarked on his project. In order to unite the opposing factions within their school, he and his brother first made sure to gather teachings from all three major lineages—Pema Trinlé, Katok, and the Gongra faction. The first they received directly from Pema Trinlé, and the latter two from their father, Sangdak Trinlé Lhündrup (1611–1662). With all three lineages under his belt, Dharmaśrī could now claim the authority to proceed with his historical excavation of the Sutra Initiation.

Dharmaśrī's approach to history reflects the beginning of a shift in the Nyingma School. Between the twelfth and sixteenth centuries, Nyingmapa writing on the Sutra Initiation turned away from the original canonical tantras to focus on differences between more recent ritual practices. There was a similar change in the arena of lineage, where the early sections of the Nyingmapa lineages became fixed at a certain point, agreed on by all, which freed post-fourteenth-century authors to focus on the legitimacy of more recent transmissions. Now, at the end of the seventeenth century, the Mindröling project to reform the Sutra Initiation tradition involved a return to the past, and thus it set a precedent for the remarkable Nyingma renaissance that was to unfold over the following two centuries. Scholars have pointed to "the antiquarian and archaeological interest" of late eighteenth-century Nyingmapa scholars such as Jikmé Lingpa, or Tsewang Norbu, who was "not content simply to repeat what he found in secondary sources considered authoritative by the Tibetan tradition . . . [he] sought to go back to the original."[12] Such high valuation of historical research was characteristic of many Nyingmapa thinkers of the eighteenth and nineteenth centuries, and what occurred at Mindröling at the end of the seventeenth century may have set an early example for them.

Dharmaśrī's genius lay not only in his ability to comprehend the details of all the initiation traditions but also in his discernment of the wider structural issues at stake. Unlike any before him, Dharmaśrī was able to step back from the specific manuals to reflect on the overall framework of the ritual and make explicit the historical foundations for his new system. In his *General Exposition*, he distinguished, with some historical rigor, two ritual formats that had existed in the Sutra Initiation tradition since the beginning, calling them the "tantra system" and the "pith instructions system" (both were introduced in chapter 4). The importance of this distinction to Dharmaśrī's larger project is suggested by the full title of his own initiation manual: the *Vajra Staircase: An Initiation Ritual Manual That Unifies the Systems of Tantra and Pith Instructions* (*Rgyud dang man ngag gi lugs gcig tu dril ba'i dbang chog rdo rje'i them skas*). Dharmaśrī devotes many pages of the *General Exposition* to delineating the precise roles of these two systems throughout the history of the Sutra Initiation tradition. In this way, he was able to undercut the various disagreements that had grown up around the *Gathering of Intentions*' initiation ritual.

Dharmaśrī opens his "exposition" with an extended review of the Nyingma lineages, first for the *Gathering of Intentions*, then for each of the other eight non-Anuyoga vehicles. The last lineage he traces is that of Atiyoga, the origin of which he attributes to Garap Dorjé. Dharmaśrī notes that the Anuyoga lineage, which originated with the teaching of the *Gathering of Intentions* atop Mount Malaya and, concurrently, with King Dza, also passed through Garap Dorjé. This leads him to the question of how the individual lineages of the nine vehicles are related to the single lineage of the complete Sutra Initiation, which includes all nine vehicles. Is the Sutra Initiation merely the sum of the latter or something else? Not surprisingly, this question bred significant confusion among early Tibetan Buddhists:

> Most of the later mantrins who dwelled here [in Tibet] believed that [the initiations] included within the fully complete *[Gathering of Intentions] Sutra* must be [the same as] the initiations for the nine vehicles themselves, and since that is the case, the [fully complete initiation] must have included a collection of the eight [other] vehicles' own liturgies, which must have been fashioned into a single general liturgy. By that reasoning, it made sense that [the initiations from this system] were also transmitted within the lineages of all the other eight vehicles and could be transmitted individually.[13]

In contrast, Dharmaśrī asserts that even though Garap Dorjé held all nine vehicles and their lineages, the full "practice tradition" (*phyag bzhes*) of the Sutra Inititation did not begin until Déwa Seldzé, the author of the first Sutra Initiation ritual manuals. Thus Dharmaśrī makes a crucial distinction between when the individual lineages of all nine vehicles met for the first time in a single person, Garap Dorjé, and when they first were gathered into the fully complete Sutra Initiation by Déwa Seldzé. This is key to the discussion that follows:

> It must be held that only with [Garap Dorjé] did both of the tantra systems—that of the root *Gathering of Intentions* [first taught atop Mount Malaya] and those of the fully complete four streams [i.e., each with its own initiations]—begin to be transmitted together as a single river.[14] And with regard to the *practice tradition* in which the initiations of the fully complete *[Gathering of Intentions] Sutra* are granted, we must say that they [were first] granted on the basis of the eighteen various texts (the *Las tho* and

> so forth) by the great master Déwa Seldzé, because in the individual lineages explained above [that were subsequently gathered into] the fully complete *[Gathering of Intentions] Sutra*, Déwa Seldzé does not appear. Therefore the [individual] teachings connected to the branch mandalas for the stream of arising [i.e., for the *Gathering of Intentions*' Mahāyoga initiations] and below originated separately, without [originally] being connected to the general scripture [of the *Gathering of Intentions*]. It seems this [lineage that originated with Déwa Seldzé] was the single transmission system that Ācārya Dharmarāja granted to Nupchen.[15]

In short, Dharmaśrī has the tantra system, within which is included the "root" *Gathering of Intentions* itself, first appearing atop Mount Malaya and with King Dza. Garap Dorjé was then the first human to hold the individual lineages for all nine vehicles and therefore also the first to hold all the parts theoretically necessary for the pith instructions system, or the "fully complete Sutra Initiation." He did not, however, conceive of the latter. First Déwa Seldzé created the *practice tradition* of the pith instructions system. Through this kind of careful research and analysis, Dharmaśrī exposed and then reinforced the historical foundations of the *Gathering of Intentions*' ritual system. He could now be sure that the new system he built would stand for centuries to come, made strong by the authority it gained through his rigorous excavations.

THE MINDRÖLING SUTRA INITIATION

In his new ritual manual, Dharmaśrī weaves together the two systems he had so carefully outlined in his historical work. Given his interest in the tradition's early history, he might have simply returned to the original procedures set down in Déwa Seldzé's notes. Instead, although he does consult them, Dharmaśrī strives to balance these early forms against the concerns of his Nyingmapa contemporaries, explicitly adopting certain innovations and rejecting others. He calls attention to the sincerity of his diplomatic efforts by repeatedly referencing his "strategy of adoption and rejection" (*'dor len bya tshul*).[16]

Dharmaśrī's "rolled into one" (*gcig tu dril ba*) system opens with sixteen preliminary initiations into a Vajrapāṇi mandala.[17] Then the branch mandalas are assembled for each of the first six vehicles, per Zurham's system, and the "outer stream" of ten initiations is granted along with the deity initiations specific to each vehicle. (The outer stream is the first of the Sutra Initiation system's four streams and corresponds to the first six vehicles.) Thus in his pith instructions system, Dharmaśrī adopts Zurham's additional branch mandalas but rejects his idea that the Sutra Initiation's ten outer stream initiations should be postponed and granted into the Gathered Great Assembly mandala during the higher vehicles of Mahā-Anu-Ati. In this way, Dharmaśrī strikes a balance. On the one hand, he concedes that each of the six lower vehicles needs its own mandala and cannot be truly represented by the Gathered Great Assembly mandala alone. On the other hand, he acknowledges that these initiations are being performed, after all, as part of the Sutra Initiation system, and for this reason the ten outer stream initiations must be applied at this point in order to keep the branch mandalas under the ritual umbrella of that system. To apply them later in the Gathered Great Assembly, as Zurham did, would reduce the first six vehicles to mere appendages to the main ritual, preparatory rites not a necessary in the Sutra Initiation system.

This was a completely novel approach. Déwa Seldzé (and the *Len Manual* that followed him) similarly granted the ten outer stream initiations into the branch mandalas, but he had used just two branch mandalas (the Vajravidāraṇā and the Vajradhātu) and granted the ten initiations all at once, after both of those mandalas had been built. For Dharmaśrī to follow this scheme now, while deploying all of Zurham's forty-three branch mandalas, would mean postponing the outer stream of initiations until much later in the ritual (after all forty-three had been constructed) and thereby weakening the connection between the branch mandalas and their respective Sutra Initiations. Recognizing this, Dharmaśrī carefully divided the outer stream's 108 coarse branch initiations (which comprise the ten outer initiations) into their corresponding vehicles. He then wove each of the resulting sets into its proper ritual place, positioning each immediately prior to the deity initiations for its respective branch mandalas.

To take just one example, the first of the ten outer stream initiations is traditionally subdivided into twenty coarse branch initiations.

Dharmaśrī took the first eleven of these to be for the first vehicle of gods and humans. After the first vehicle is introduced and its branch mandalas are arranged, its eleven coarse branch initiations are granted, followed by the appropriate deity initiations. The same basic structure is then observed for each of the first six vehicles.[18]

In this way, Dharmaśrī initiates the student into the branch mandalas by means of the outer stream initiations in accordance with the pith instructions system. Next he orders the construction of the common Gathered Great Assembly mandala, and the ten outer initiations are granted all over again, this time according to the tantra system. As Dharmaśrī explains, this repetition is necessary because the two systems' outer initiations are different in both number and way they are granted.[19] Elsewhere, Dharmaśrī adds that the branch mandalas are more appropriate for lesser disciples who require training in the first six vehicles, whereas the same initiations into the root mandala are more suitable for people who have already attained these levels of realization:

> It is further said regarding the two ways of granting, by the tantra and the pith instructions systems, that for those extraordinarily worthy ones who, being inherently qualified, already have faith in the profound meaning, the thirty-six initiations that perfect the four streams are granted into the mandala of the root sutra. And for those worthy ones who only can become qualified through training and have faith in the elaborated+, the system of the fully complete sutra, distinguishing the individual branch mandalas, is granted by means of distinguishing between the 801 coarse branches of the thirty-six root sutra initiations, within which all the vehicles are gathered.[20]

Here Dharmaśrī takes care to distinguish between two types of potential initiates: the specialist and the general public. In composing his new Sutra Initiation manual, he intends a public performance before an unrestricted audience, and in this, his manual is unlike earlier ones. Repeatedly, he simplifies parts of the ritual, lowering the overall level to the lowest common denominator, and as he proceeds up to the higher initiations, the trend becomes increasingly pronounced.

Following the outer initiations, the eleven inner and the thirteen accomplishment initiations are granted into the same common root mandala.[21] Dharmaśrī explains why this is okay:

> When [the initiation is] being performed for a group, the vast majority will be neither ripened [through practice] nor educated. Therefore, since little harm will come of it, the construction of the uncommon root mandala of the Gathered Great Assembly, the mandala of the Supreme Secret Charnel Grounds, may be disregarded. Instead, the 115 branches are to be distinguished within the thirteen roots of the accomplishment initiation stream of renown and granted into the same mandala from the inner initiations, i.e., the common root mandala.[22]

In earlier manuals, there were two Gathered Great Assembly mandalas, a common and an uncommon one. The former was used for the "inner" Mahāyoga initiations and the latter for the "accomplishment" Anuyoga initiations. On this point, Dharmaśrī decides to simplify the situation by using the common mandala for both sets of initiations. He does this because he expects that "the vast majority" of those receiving the initiation will not have attained the high level of realization needed to benefit fully from the Anuyoga initiations. Most will be there just for the blessings, for "merely aspiration or study," as he writes elsewhere,[23] and for this reason, it does not matter if one abbreviates the ritual, even if it means less benefit for the rare expert in the crowd.

The latter possibility prompts Dharmaśrī, in his section on the final, secret initiation stream of perfection (also performed according to the tantra system),[24] to direct the presiding lama to separate out the select few experts in the crowd and grant them the highest initiations in private, after the main ceremony is over. "Afterward," Dharmaśrī writes, "it is possible that some extraordinary students who are working on the perfection stage might be present. If so, in order to care for them, one can take them aside and perform the rites for granting the pith instructions system, the initiation method of the fully complete *[Gathering of Intentions] Sutra.*"[25]

Such passages fit with the wider Mindröling project to reformulate the Nyingma School through public ritual performance at major monasteries. The primary purpose of the new Mindröling Sutra Initiation was no longer to initiate a small group of disciples into the *Gathering of Intentions*' mandala, but to reinforce a sense of community on a much larger scale. The ceremony was now a public performance foremost. In this sense, its focus had shifted from the participants to the observers. How it was perceived as a public spectacle was now crucial to its function within the Nyingma School.

The new Mindröling Sutra Initiation ritual reflected this goal in one other way: Dharmaśrī further increased the splendor of the performance by dividing what had been one huge ritual manual into a number of shorter, distinct works. Thus he composed separate texts on how to construct the mandala, the ritual cards (*tsakli*), the musical arrangements, and so on. In doing so, Dharmaśrī extended the strategy already at work in the Mindröling Spoken Teachings collection overall: the arrangement of interwoven sets of principal and ancillary manuals. By delegating the ritual responsibilities in this way, Dharmaśrī facilitated a larger performance that was easier to assemble. The different groups of monks had only to master their own particular responsibilities, but when combined, they could create a spectacle of unprecedented grandeur.

In increasing the size and splendor of the ceremony, Dharmaśrī had to be careful not to overwhelm his audience, so he also made it far shorter than the earlier versions, only three full days instead of ten or more. Unlike the Katok initiation system, which packed in every detail it could, Dharmaśrī's was relatively efficient in its grandeur. This desire for brevity may also explain, in part, why the additional Mahāyoga and Atiyoga initiations introduced by Moktön in his Katok manual, the *River of Honey*, were conspicuously missing from the Mindröling version. The case for including them was weakened by the absence of a precedent in Déwa Seldzé's early notes. Dharmaśrī explains in the following passage:

> In that same text [by Yungtön] it says, "According to some who do not understand our methods, . . . these [Atiyoga] introductions are not discussed in any of the tantras, commentaries, or pith instructions of Anuyoga whatsoever, so these [Atiyoga initiations] should be known as the mere wishful thinking of people

> with no practice tradition for the four streams of initiation." Such [criticisms] may be valid in terms of how in the Kham tradition [of Katok], the initiations of the Eighteen Mind Class Meanings of "A" were added. However, in the Len tradition there are explicit and implicit texts, and these [critics] appear to have made the mistake of assuming the ritual arrangements without first discovering the hidden texts.[26]

Dharmaśrī goes on to cite the presentation of the Atiyoga initiations in Déwa Seldzé's *Amazing Practice Manual for Guiding* as proof that Atiyoga initiations of some sort existed in the *Sūtra* tradition from the beginning. Yet he clearly felt that Katok Moktön's addition of the eighteen Mind Class meanings of "A" was vulnerable to criticism, as there was no precedent for it in the early tradition. Perhaps he felt the same way about Moktön's other major addition, of the eighteen *Māyājāla* initiations, for which there was also no precedent.

Dharmaśrī completed his new manual in the autumn of 1704 and his accompanying historical study, the *General Exposition*, in December 1710.[27] In his writings, Dharmaśrī consistently defers to Terdak Lingpa. He insists that his own writings on the *Gathering of Intentions* "should be perceived as supplements" to two earlier works composed by his elder brother, Terdak Lingpa, namely a *sādhana* (the *Mdo rtsa ba'i sgrub thabs dngos grub char 'bebs*) and a mandala ritual (*Dkyil chog dri med 'od 'phreng*). Dharmaśrī's new manual may therefore have followed a ritual format that had already been developed by his elder brother. Before putting his brother's new initiation ritual into writing, Dharmaśrī received it on three occasions. These were major events, with many important lamas from all over Tibet in attendance. The first was the ceremony mentioned at the beginning of this chapter, which took place in September 1691. Dharmaśrī describes it in the following words:

> Once there gathered together we who normally live at Mindröling—a congregation headed by [Terdak Lingpa's] supreme son . . . , Pema Gyurmé Gyatso[28]—together with other realized ones assembled there only temporarily such as Treho Tülku, Rapjampa Chakpa Chöpel, the lamas of Pelri Densawa and Powo, three hundred in all. To all of us, in accordance with a [new]

> system in which the earlier and later classifications of the root and branch mandalas, those of Lharjé Gar, of Len, and so forth, were all brought into a single tradition of ritual practice . . . [according to that system] for eleven days, from the seventh to the eighteenth of September, 1691, were bestowed the ripened and developed fulfillments of the complete four rivers of the *Gathering of Intentions*, based on a mandala of colored powders, together with the seal of entrustment, the flanking explanatory instructions, and the related ritual sequence of the great accomplishment. Thus signs were displayed and the welfare of beings was immensely and continuously enacted.[29]

The precise relationship between this 1691 initiation system and that described in Dharmaśrī's manual, completed some fifteen years later, remains unclear. However, the picture sketched here, of a ritual system that unified all the earlier traditions, appears to refer to some early prototype for the later "rolled into one" system.

Terdak Lingpa granted the Sutra Initiation twice more before Dharmaśrī wrote his manual. Neither time is described in any detail, but Dharmaśrī does list some of the more imporant lamas who received it.[30] It is clear both from the length of these lists and the geographical spread of the toponyms that Mindröling functioned as a font from which the new Sutra Initiation system spread to all corners of Tibet. The inclusive nature of the Mindröling Sutra Initiation combined with the charisma of its creators to draw lamas from all the Nyingma monasteries, old and new. These events were not simply initiations, they were workshops, to which the major Nyingmapa lamas of the day came to receive and learn the latest rituals. By the time of Terdak Lingpa's death in 1714, his version of the Sutra Initiation tradition was becoming the standard throughout the Nyingma School.

The Mindröling Sutra Initiation writings reflect the epistemic changes that Tibet was undergoing around the turn of the eighteenth century. Through their comprehensive system of interlocking manuals, the Mindröling brothers sought to organize Nyingma monasticism under a single ritual banner. But this project was also part of a larger change in ritual emphasis that was taking place. The Spoken Teachings manuals mirror the rise of public ritual performance and elaborate state ceremony throughout central Tibet. These large-scale events lent symbolic support to the Tibetan state, as public displays of the state's grandeur. As such, they emphasized less the transmission of the lineage or the realization of the presiding lama and more the elaborate spectacle of the performance itself. The structure of the Mindröling Sutra Initiation materials and of the Spoken Teachings collection generally suggests that this shift involved what might be termed a "professionalization" of ritual performance. The public events were not only larger; they took on a different form, as evidenced by the proliferation of shorter, specialized ritual manuals. Too complex to be run by a single master, the intricately prescribed ceremonies were made possible through delegations of power to a concert of experts—specialists in dance, in offering rites, in shrine construction, in building *torma*, and so on. Even the observers were made part of the performance, in some cases through their required presence and intricate seating arrangements. Everyone had his own well-defined role at these prescribed occasions, and thereby too within the larger Tibetan state.

This shift in state ritual should be understood too in light of the concurrent bureaucratization of secular and religious society that was taking place. Such events created individuals who both participated in and themselves embodied the power relations of the state. Not only did the ritual expert perform the ritual, but as a sanctioned specialist, he also embodied and reproduced the system of hierarchical relationships that were supported and defined by the state. Thus the Mindröling Spoken Teachings manuals suggest a change in ritual practice that occurred both at the level of high performance and at the level of individually articulated power dynamics. The Tibetan state rose to power in the seventeenth and early eighteenth centuries on the back of religious symbolism and public ceremony. Through ritual performance, the new Dalai Lama government tied itself to Tibet's patron deities and kings of the past. But the power of these rituals not only lay in the past; it also functioned very much in the present, organizing and reinforcing the bureaucratic structures of the state and its major monastic institutions. The importance of ceremony in this crucial period leaves ritual manuals in a unique position to provide illuminating insights into the inner workings of Tibetan political power. The manuals can thus teach us much about the meticulous rituals of power that accompanied the new Dalai Lama regime.

But Mindröling also effected a major shift within the Nyingma School. Fast becoming united as never before, the school enjoyed lavish support from the new Dalai Lama government. In the lifetimes of Terdak Lingpa and Lochen Dharmaśrī, nearly all the major Nyingma monasteries in central and eastern Tibet were founded. The efforts of these two brothers changed the face of the Nyingma School forever, and the trends they set in motion continued to unfold over the next two centuries. After Mindröling, the Nyingmapa became increasingly focused on their monastic institutions and large public rituals.

Three years after Terdak Lingpa's death, tensions between the Dzungar Mongols and the Chinese erupted into war.[31] Late in the year 1717, the Dzungar Mongols invaded central Tibet, bringing with them a terrible bout of sectarian violence. Many within the ruling Geluk School had long expressed displeasure at the rising fortunes of the Nyingma School, and the Dzungars gave vent to these rumblings with the zeal of the recently converted. The Dzungar soldiers executed Lochen Dharmaśrī, as well as the new Mindröling throne holder, Padma Gyurmé Gyatso, and Pema Trinlé.[32] Almost overnight, decades of work at the new Nyingma monasteries in central Tibet was undone, as libraries were burned and temples looted.

Yet none of this could stem the flood of these masters' wider project. Following the Dzungars' departure, both Dorjé Drak and Mindröling were restored with the help of Tibet's new leader, Polhané Sönam Topgye (1689–1747), and their former relations with the Dalai Lamas resumed.[33] But even without Polhané's restoration of the physical place, Mindröling's rituals were assured of success. Long before the Dzungar invasion, Terdak Lingpa had guaranteed his new system's spread by convening large assemblies of Nyingma lamas like the one in 1691. The ceremonies he transmitted at these gatherings formed the ritual backbone of the new Nyingma monasteries to the east. The arrival of Mindröling's rituals in eastern Tibet was crucial to the future identity of the Nyingma School, for it was there that they really took root, at the large new monasteries throughout Kham and Amdo. These were the site of the next major development in the history of the *Gathering of Intentions*.

7

RETURNS TO THE ORIGIN

In 1959, the Fourteenth Dalai Lama fled Lhasa and the Chinese People's Liberation Army into exile. That same year, Khenpo Khyentsé Lodrö, a.k.a. Khenpo Nüden, gathered some of the most promising young lamas of Pelyul monastery in eastern Tibet for several months of intensive teachings on the *Gathering of Intentions*. They retreated to a small house that had been built just for the occasion, atop a mountain above their home monastery. The location and the number of students were no accident. In the minds of the participants, this isolated peak was a second Mount Malaya, a reflection of the mythic mountain of Laṅka, atop which the *Gathering of Intentions* was originally taught. In the original myth, the buddha Vajrapāṇi descended upon the peak to teach five excellent *vidyādharas*, and just so, Khenpo Nüden selected five young masters of the Nyingma School. According to the myth, the five earlier disciples represented the five "races" of beings: the *nāgas*, the gods, the *yākṣasa* demons, and the humans, and they were led by the king of the *rākṣasas*, Rāvaṇa, the Lord of Laṅka. Just so, the five Tibetan students were led by the third Pema Norbu Rinpoché (1932–2009), the future head of the Nyingma School in exile.

Pema Norbu would leave Tibet later that year. Of the three hundred Tibetans that accompanied him, only thirty would survive. This, then, was an eleventh-hour effort to revive and preserve the fading tradition of the *Gathering of Intentions* and its ninth-century commentary, the

Armor Against Darkness. Their strategy was well supported by the *Gathering of Intentions*' own theory of mythic origins and the three transmissions. As seen in chapter 1, early Tibetans understood the mythic narrative of the *Gathering of Intentions*' origins to describe a kind of archetypal event, a primordial teaching that is reenacted, at the symbolic level, each time the tantra is taught. Now, in 1959, as Chinese control was growing ever tighter, these six Tibetans made a conscious effort to return to this source and remake their tradition once more.

From its origins in the ninth century to today, the *Gathering of Intentions* has repeatedly emerged, or been excavated, to be reworked toward new ends that better reflect the concerns of the day. In this sense, the *Gathering of Intentions* has long served as a touchstone, a fundamental source to which the Nyingmapa have returned to remake their tradition. Each time, its adherents sought to negotiate between their ancient ritual traditions and new events in Tibetan history. Each time, the same tensions were perceptible, between sameness and difference, between the prescriptive nature of religion and the performative. And each time, this gap was papered over by new texts composed for that purpose. In this sense, each new emanation of the *Gathering of Intentions* was formed by the gap that opened between the past tradition and the present needs. It was shaped from both sides. This final chapter turns to Tibetans' twentieth-century attempts to preserve the *Gathering of Intentions*, efforts that once again spanned the divide between past and present.

THE HOMOGENIZATION OF THE NYINGMA SCHOOL

By the nineteenth century, Nupchen's ancient commentary, the *Armor Against Darkness*, had been lost, and the Sutra Initiation tradition was refashioned once more, this time as an annual festival dedicated to the system's central mandala, the Gathered Great Assembly. The festival continued Mindröling's earlier focus on public performance but was no longer even ostensibly related to the *Gathering of Intentions*' initiation rites and continued lineal transmissions; now the festivities were little more than an elaborate nod to this ancient tradition's original role in the formation of the Nyingma School. The *Gathering of Intentions* and its elaborate history were ritually condensed into its Gathered Great Assembly mandala and granted an iconic place at the heart of the Nyingma School. In this way, the new festival fit within a broader trend of the late eighteenth and nineteenth centuries, primarily in the eastern region of Kham.

Thanks to the Fifth Dalai Lama's support, a number of large Nyingma monasteries were founded in the area around Degé.[1] In the eighteenth and nineteenth centuries, the town of Degé and its environs grew into a major center of Tibetan Buddhism, a kind of cultural counterweight to Lhasa and the central Tibetan Geluk state. Kham's geographically peripheral position, at the border between Tibet and China, allowed it to thrive with considerable autonomy throughout the nineteenth century and even to develop a short-lived independence movement in the 1860s.[2] The region also witnessed the rise of the so-called "nonsectarian movement" (*ris med*) that facilitated a period of remarkable exchange between the followers of all non-Geluk religious schools, the Nyingma, Sakya, and Kagyu, as well as Bon. At the heart of this trend labored two close associates: Jamyang Khyentsé Wangpo (1820–1892) and Jamgön Kongtrül Lodrö Tayé (1813–1899). Together, these luminaries oversaw the compilation of authoritative new anthologies of each school's literature.[3] The countless Nyingma revelations and ritual methods that had proliferated over the centuries were now neatly encapsulated and preserved for easy and efficient transmission en masse.

These two masters' collaborations had far-reaching effects on the Nyingma School that in many ways echoed the earlier projects at Mindröling but were amplified by the growth of the large new Nyingma monasteries in the east. Building on the efforts of Mindröling and others, they forged a solid institutional structure. Even in the poetic realm of Dzokchen nonconceptuality, which traditionally resisted scholastics, in the words of Gene Smith, "certain Nyingmapa gurus perceived a need to formulate Dzokchen and, especially, the *Nyingtik* methodology into a system if these profound teachings were to benefit the scholastically oriented."[4] Nyingmapa philosophy grew increasingly systematic and was taught at new monastic colleges. Freshly revealed treasure cycles, the eighteenth-century *Seminal Essence of the Great Expanse* foremost, spread quickly and were adopted by whole swaths of Nyingmapa masters, no matter what their individual lineal affiliations or where they worked. This was a systematization of the entire school, from its lowest teachings to its highest, and also a paring down. The huge new anthologies preserved many Nyingma ritual systems but pushed others into obscurity. Those that were excluded were condemned to the trash bin of history,[5] and even those that were included would ultimately fall into disuse, as their initiations, reading transmissions, and explanations were now transmitted as a set rather than individually. The trend toward homogenization that had started at Mindröling reached its culmination at the monasteries around Degé, at Dzokchen, Katok, Pelyul, and their nearby affiliates.

In fact, Jamyang Khyentsé and Jamgön Kongtrül built not just on the project at Mindröling but also on the efforts of several other earlier masters, Nyingmapa who had already worked hard to standardize the monasteries of Kham. The Mindröling brothers, in seeking to institutionalize their Nyingma School, had turned to the Spoken Teachings. At the end of the eighteenth century, their project was picked up in the east by the third Dzokchen Rinpoché, Ati Tenpé Gyeltsen (c. 1759–1792), and Katok Getsé Mahāpaṇḍita (1761–1829). After lengthy discussions about how key aspects of the Spoken Teachings had not been properly sustained in Kham, these two masters set in motion a project to reestablish them at their respective monasteries. In 1791, they invited a party of monks from Mindröling in central Tibet to come to Degé and teach the rituals of the thirteen principal mandalas of the Spoken Teachings in all their detail.[6] With the financial support of the Degé court, the event was a great success, and the monks proceeded to Katok, Getsé's base, to repeat the entire transmission there.

In his autobiography, Getsé makes it explicit that he looked to Mindröling as his model for reviving the Spoken Teachings. The inspiration originated from there too:

> During the intermediate period [of the sixteenth and seventeenth centuries], the Katok teachings waxed and waned. Subsequently the Mindröling brothers became concerned and revived the teachings of the triad of Sutra, Illusion, and Mind. I am emulating their rekindling of the embers of the teachings. I explain that [the Spoken Teachings] constitute our ancestral dharma, yet

> nobody understands [them]. The central pillar of the Nyingma tenet system is this triad of yogas.[7]

Despite Katok's long history of involvements with the Spoken Teachings, dating back to the twelfth century and its founder, Dampa Deshek, the Mindröling tradition now reigned supreme. Getsé's aim was to provide an institutional structure not just for his own monastery but for the entire Nyingma School, to unite its followers around the "central pillar" of the elaborate rituals of the Spoken Teachings. As at Mindröling previously, this was a concerted effort to reform the whole school, to shift its focus away from the local level toward the traditions of elite monasticism. Those who did not worship the Spoken Teachings, he explained, were no better than ignorant village priests.[8]

From Katok and Dzokchen, the newly arrived Spoken Teachings spread throughout eastern Tibet. While Getsé carried his gospel to other monasteries, famous Nyingmapa teachers from across the region descended on Katok to study the texts (particularly the **Guhyagarbha Tantra*) and learn the relevant rites. In 1794, Getsé initiated another project: to compile a new edition of the *Collected Tantras of the Ancients*, which included the *Gathering of Intentions* and the other root tantras of the Spoken Teachings class. The result went on to become the most well-regarded and widely distributed collection of its kind, capped by what was perhaps Getsé's most famous single work, his historical index to the edition.

From Dzokchen monastery too, the newly arrived Spoken Teachings spread forth. Getsé's early partner, the third Dzokchen Rinpoché, died the year after he oversaw the Mindröling monks' visit to Degé, but in 1845, Dzokchen Gyelsé Zhenpen Tayé (1800–1855) carved the first woodblock edition of the collected Spoken Teachings.[9] Dzokchen Gyelsé, himself a recognized reincarnation of Terdak Lingpa (the elder of the Mindröling brothers), is said to have based his ten-volume edition on earlier manuscripts brought to Kham from Mindröling.[10] Meanwhile, the Spoken Teachings made their way to Pelyul. In his history of Pelyul monastery, Tsering Lama Jampel Zangpo writes that, following the Mindröling monks' visit to Degé, the third Dzokchen Rinpoché, before his imminent death,

> gave the transmissions at Dzokchen monastery. This was particularly important to the great masters of this time because the original source of the Nyingmapa tradition is the *kama* [Spoken Teachings] lineage. Later still, Gyatrül Rinpoché invited Khenpo Dorjé Rabten (Jamgon Khontrul's nephew) of Dzokchen monastery to come to the Palyul monastery to pass on all of the newly acquired transmission. The Khenpo came and taught all aspects of *sadhana* practice in great depth, including chanting, musical instrumentation, lama dancing and so forth.[11]

The Pelyul lama who implemented all this was Gyatrül Pema Dongak Tendzin (1830–1891). He was probably also behind yet another edition of the Spoken Teachings—the Pelyul edition—that expanded upon Dzokchen Gyelsé's earlier collection and appeared around this time.[12]

This same Gyatrül Rinpoché initiated a new annual festival. Dudjom Rinpoché writes:

> Inspired by both Jamgön Khyentsé Wangpo and the great treasure-finder Chogyur Lingpa, Gyaltrul Pema Do-nga Tendzin instituted, at that very seat [of Pelyul], the annual attainment and worship of the twenty-seven great mandalas of the transmitted precepts [i.e., the Spoken Teachings] of the Ancient Translation School, which are all those of which the continuous initiation and transmission exists at present.[13]

Gyatrül Rinpoché inaugurated his festival on a grand scale, using the ritual arrangements he had received from Mindröling. A sense of the extent of his undertaking may be gained from the following later account: "Gyatrül Rinpoché prepared all of the materials used for these *sadhana* mandalas from the very best substance, scepters, *Dhyani* Buddha crown ornaments, costumes for the wrathful lama dances and sixteen offering goddesses' dance, hats, cloaks, head ornaments, hand implements, bone ornaments, musical instruments and others. Even the king of Degé offered the crops from a large fertile field to help cover the expenses."[14] The festival soon spread to other monasteries throughout Kham. Its annual performance guaranteed that the Spoken Teachings would be recognized regularly across the Nyingma

School. It marked the culmination of the project, begun three hundred years earlier at Mindröling, to reshape the Nyingma School into a unified institution by means of large-scale monastic ceremony.

THE GATHERED GREAT ASSEMBLY FESTIVAL

The Spoken Teachings "festival" (*sgrub mchod*)[15] that was started by Gyatrül Rinpoché is the last remaining trace of the *Gathering of Intentions* in today's Nyingma School. It is held annually at all the major Nyingmapa monasteries in Kham. The festival revolves around the central mandala of the Gathered Great Assembly. At its crescendo, all the blessings from all the deities of the Spoken Teachings are ritually channeled into the body of the presiding lama, who embodies the primordial buddha at the center of the Gathered Great Assembly, then redistributed among the assembled crowd. Watching this ritual being performed, one cannot help but see it as a defining moment for the Nyingma School.

Each of the observing monasteries holds the festival on the same date every year, though the date differs from one monastery to the next. At Pelyul, it takes place from the fifth to the fifteenth day of the fourth Tibetan month, and it is performed simultaneously at Pelyul's branch monastery in exile, Namdroling monastery in Bylakuppe, South India.[16] This is a highly significant date, as it culminates in *saka dawa*, the annual Tibetan celebration of the Buddha Śākyamuni's birth, awakening, and *parinirvāṇa*.

In brief, the festival's proceedings unfold as follows. The first day is devoted to the site ritual (*sa chog*) and the root dance (*rtsa 'chams*). Both are performed to prepare the ritual space for the rest of the festival. The site ritual is common to all such festivals, while the root dance derives from the *Māyājāla* ritual system—the morning dances from its peaceful sections and the afternoon dances from the wrathful. Day 2 brings the mandala drawing rituals (*'bri chog*) and the preparatory practices (*sta gon*) for the various mandalas. Under ideal circumstances, if the festival is performed in full, a mandala is required for each of the thirteen principal deities of the Spoken Teachings. Unfortunately, owing to the limited resources of most Tibetan monasteries nowadays, only some of the more important mandalas are usually practiced. The

Gathered Great Assembly mandala is constructed in the monastery's main temple, and usually one or two other mandalas in each of the other temples. On day 3, the mandalas are constructed using colored sands, and on day 4, the offering cakes are sculpted for each mandala shrine before the deities are invited into the mandalas that evening. First thing in the morning of day 5, the recitations of the ritual manuals (*cho ga*) begin, with an assembly of monks assigned to each of the mandalas. These continue nonstop for three days, until day 8, when the offering dances (*gar 'chams*), based on the *Buddhasamāyoga* system of the Spoken Teachings, are performed. On day 9 come the wrathful dances (*khro bo 'chams*), in which the subjugation of Rudra is reenacted, complete with an effigy of the hapless demon being chopped to pieces. Like the root dances on the festival's opening day, these dances derive from the *Māyājāla* system.

Finally, on day 10, an elaborate fire offering is performed in the morning, followed by the grand finale—the distribution of the blessings (*dngos sgrub len*). In fact, four fire offerings are performed simultaneously, one for each of the tantric ritual activities. The fire offering for pacification is drawn from the ritual procedures of the peaceful *Māyājāla*, for enhancement from the Gathered Great Assembly, for coercion from Yangdak, and for violence from the wrathful *Māyājāla*.

After lunch, the blessing ceremony is performed. A particularly large number from the lay community attends this, amid a festive atmosphere. Marking the culmination of the entire ten days, the ceremony unfolds in the main hall, where the Gathered Great Assembly mandala still stands. In the middle of the hall are many long tables, laden with mountains of food. The team that has been accomplishing the Gathered Great Assembly is seated as usual, and the rest of the hall is filled with other monks, nuns, and laity. One at a time, each of the other halls containing the other mandalas empties out as each team proceeds to the main hall. The team enters ceremoniously in single file, bearing incense and all the blessed objects from their mandala shrine. They progress up the aisle to the *vajrācārya*, seated on his throne, and empower him with each object before the next team enters and does the same.

Without seeing this ceremony, one can only imagine the impression it gives. In the central cathedral of Penor Rinpoché, the head of the Nyingma School, for ten days, every sort of ritual is performed on as grand a scale as possible. Then the products of each temple's efforts are presented to the lead *vajrācārya*. This figure, usually the top *tülku* living at the monastery, has over the preceding days established himself as the primordial buddha, Samantabhadra/Mahottara Heruka, atop the nine-storied Gathered Great Assembly mandala. Within this state, he receives the blessings, one by one, from each of the other deities of the Spoken Teachings. By the time all the blessings from the entire tradition have been channeled into this single figure, the atmosphere is pregnant with energy.

This is dissolved only gradually, as the monks and then the laity receive the blessings. The mountain of food is distributed to all assembled, and the people eventually disperse. After the hubbub dies down, as evening falls, a brief butter lamp offering is performed in the same main hall. The next morning, the mandalas are disassembled, and the sands together with the sacrificial cakes are carried down to the river to be returned to the *nāga* spirits living there.

The annual Spoken Teachings festival is a uniquely Nyingma event shared by all the school's major monasteries. In its fullest form, it involves all the mandalas of the Spoken Teachings in a ritual celebration and acknowledgment of the school's origins, and in this way it reinforces the institutional identity of the Nyingma School. The festival builds over ten days to a crescendo, when all the groups enter the main hall and reunite within the central deity of the Gathered Great Assembly mandala. It constitutes a return to the source, a reaffirmation of what binds the school together. It is a family reunion.[17]

In this way, the entire festival centers on the Gathered Great Assembly mandala. To anyone not knowing the history of the *Gathering of Intentions*, this obscure mandala's presence at the heart of such a significant festival might seem odd. This is, after all, a tradition that is no longer studied, a mandala that appears almost nowhere else in today's Nyingma ritual and educational programs. One might expect instead the *Māyājāla* mandala, which is still used and studied in a number of arenas. And this apparent incongruity—in a certain sense, a disjunction between ritual form and content—is compounded: for each of the rites, from the dances to the fire offerings, the *Gathering of Intentions* is repeatedly passed over for the *Māyājāla* or another of the better-known ritual systems of the Spoken Teachings. If the *Gathering of Intentions* is so central to this festival, why are *its* ritual forms not preferable? The short answer is that its own rituals have faded from use, and the other systems are simply more popular. Therefore, it must be operating in some other way.

When the *Gathering of Intentions* arrived in Tibet at the turn of the tenth century, it provided a set of strategies for organizing the Buddhist teachings in their entirety. Other tantras arriving at the time focused on a specific deity, such as Śrī Heruka, Vajrakīlaya, Yamāntaka, or Hayagrīva, each with its own mandala and its own ritual system. The *Gathering of Intentions* stood out for its breadth, as it integrated these other tantras into a comprehensive vision of tantric Buddhism. It encouraged Tibetans to step back from the closed systems of their personal deities and gain a larger perspective. In this sense, the *Gathering of Intentions* operated through a different dimension from most other tantras. Rather than limiting itself to a single mandala, for example, it provided a space that all the other mandalas could inhabit. (The nine levels of the Gathered Great Assembly mandala are a particularly clear representation of this additional dimension.) The result was an intricately structured palace, with nine stories, three interpretive levels (via the three transmissions discussed in chapter 1), and separate entrances for everyone.

The *Gathering of Intentions*' early vision continues to inform the Spoken Teachings festival, opening and defining the ritual space. Insofar as the *Gathering of Intentions*' own rituals are not used, it is not present in the ordinary ways. Each of the other tantric systems is effective for its particular purpose, whether preparing the site (Vajrakīlaya), making offerings (Buddhasamāyoga), "liberating" Rudra (the wrathful Māyājāla), or overpowering obstacles (Yangdak). But the Gathered Great Assembly works in the background. From its position in the main hall, it is the source from which all these activities emanate, the center around which they orbit, and at the festival's climax, the summit to which they all return. In the festival, as in early Tibet, the *Gathering of Intentions* and its mandala provide the ritual architecture within which the other tantric systems operate.

REVIVING THE *ARMOR AGAINST DARKNESS*

The final chapter in the history of the *Gathering of Intentions* begins in 1919. On the fifth day of the ninth Tibetan month, Katok Situ Chökyi Gyatso (1880–1925) arrived at the Geluk monastery of Tashi Lhünpo.[18] On one of his first evenings there, a strange thing happened.[19] As darkness was falling, an old woman entered the encampment of Katok Situ's party, just outside the monastic complex. She asked to see the lama, claiming that she had an important message for him. She entered his tent and was heard conversing with Katok Situ in a foreign tongue that no one else could understand. Several times, she pointed toward the monastery. Katok Situ later told his followers that this woman was none other than Ekajaṭī, the grand protectress of the Nyingma School, and that she had instructed him with a prophecy[20] to go first thing next morning to the monastery's main library. The next day, as he entered the library and began to look around, he noticed a light shining upon a dusty old manuscript in the corner.[21] The lama turned to the librarian and asked him to fetch that particular book. To Katok Situ's amazement, it was the long-lost *Gathering of Intentions* commentary by Nupchen Sangyé Yeshé, the *Armor Against Darkness*.

This ancient text had been missing for up to two hundred years, possibly ever since the libraries at Mindröling and Dorjé Drak were destroyed in 1718.[22] Before the Dzungar invasion, the first Paṇchen Lama, Lozang Chökyi Gyeltsen (1570–1662), who had been a supporter of the Nyingma traditions, had received the *Gathering of Intentions*' Sutra Initiation from Terdak Lingpa's father, Sangdak Trinlé Lhündrup. At that time, he is said also to have obtained a copy of the *Armor Against Darkness* for his own studies.[23] Shortly after this, the Paṇchen Lama died, and his library at Tashi Lhünpo was sealed, with Nupchen's commentary inside. There it stayed, unrecognized by its Gelukpa caretakers, until its discovery in 1919 by Katok Situ.

Situ Rinpoché pleaded with the librarian to let him have the text. Only after considerable hesitation did the librarian allow it to be smuggled out, and only on the condition that Situ replace it with some other book, wrapped up in the original cloth and shelved in the same place. Over the years that followed, Situ Rinpoché, ever on the lookout for rare books, supplemented his discovery with several sets of early notes on the initiation ritual that he found at Daklha Gampo and other places.[24]

When Situ arrived back at Katok, his discovery generated a flurry of activity throughout the thriving Nyingma monasteries of Kham. Under Khyentsé Chökyi Lodrö's (1893–1959) sponsorship, a new set of printing blocks were carved for the ancient commentary. But in order to revive the *Gathering of Intentions*' long-lost commentarial tradition, the lamas had to do more than simply publish the physical text of the *Armor Against Darkness*. A long hiatus in the reading (*lung*) and explanation (*khrid*) lineages had resulted from the text's absence. In Tibetan Buddhism, every ritual system consists of three parts: the initiation, the reading, and the explanation. Each aspect has its distinct lineage, and all three lineages must be intact for a system to be considered vital. That is, there must be no gaps in the series of teacher-to-disciple transmissions that may be traced from the system's original teaching to the present day. And although no additional initiations are required, a reading and an explanation transmission are necessary for one's studies of the commentaries to be effective. Because the *Armor Against Darkness* had been lost for two hundred years, it could be neither read nor explained; both lineages were broken.

The solution to this problem came when another master from Katok, the great meditator Khenpo Ngakchung (1879–1941), experienced a vision (*dag snang*) of Nupchen Sangyé Yeshé, the author of the *Armor Against Darkness* himself. In this vision, Nupchen granted Khenpo Ngakchung the complete lineages anew, bestowing on him both the reading and the explanation transmissions. Thus inspired, Khenpo Ngakchung added to his visionary transmissions by composing a meditation manual (*bsnyen yig*) for the practice of the system's generation stage. From him, the teachings began to spread throughout Kham. The excitement that followed is palpable in the colophon to this manual:

> The master of the absolutely perfect teachings, the pervasive lord [Katok] Situ Rinpoché, Shedrup Chökyi Gyatso, widely propagated Dampa [Deshek] Rinpoché's commentarial outline of the *Gathering of Intentions*, as well as an annotated copy of the *Gathering of Intentions* from the oral traditions of former generations. I, at this monastic center [of Katok], obtained an authorization

> from him when he told me that, because there were far too many versions of the root text of the *Gathering of Intentions* that is a medicine for learning and study, I should, with a commitment to continuing the teachings on the *Gathering of Intentions*, establish a single [version] in terms of its general meaning, one that accords with the majority of explanations of this tantra. Subsequently, the supreme emanation of Pelyul, [the third] Penor Rinpoché, also encouraged me, requesting an explanation of the tantra, because, in consideration of the study center of Pelyul, [he thought] it vitally important to include [in the curriculum] an explanatory commentary to the *Gathering of Intentions*. Then later, Katok Chaktsa Tülku Rinpoché urgently requested that I explain the daily practice for the *Gathering of Intentions* and that I raise the point of the principal means for performing the propitiation during the cultivation of the generation phase. And then, Gojo Choktrül Shedrup Gyatso wanted to establish a retreat center for [practicing] the two, *Gathering of Intentions* and *Māyājāla*. Not wanting to refuse these many repeated exhortations, this ordinary follower of the great Katokpa Situ Chökyi Gyatso, [named] Dorjé Tekchok Tsel, or the Buddhist monk Tsültrim Gyatso [i.e., Khenpo Ngakchung], wrote this in his own place, the meditation hut of Jönpa Lung. By this [act], may the embers of the teachings of the triad of sutra, illusion, and mind of the early translations be rekindled.[25]

One person who received the newly revived lineages from Situ Rinpoché and Khenpo Ngakchung was yet a third Katokpa—Khenpo Nüden. At the request of Situ Rinpoché, the second Penor Rinpoché, and others, Nüden began work on a massive new subcommentary. He based it primarily upon the *Armor Against Darkness*, supplemented by Dampa's *Summary of the Gathering of Intentions* and the other early notes collected by Situ Rinpoché. This was a huge undertaking that required some five years of research, and numerous obstacles are said to have impeded Nüden in his writing. Some even began to think that the protectoress, Ekajaṭī, must have been blocking the project, because a sufficient amount of time had not passed since the *Armor Against Darkness* had been discovered—the time had not "ripened" yet.[26] Finally, the second Penor Rinpoché, just before his death, sent a last gift of encouragement, an ancient ritual dagger, symbolically meant to cut through the obstructions Nüden was experiencing. After this, it is said, the writing progressed more easily, and on the thirteenth day of the eighth Tibetan month in 1952, it was complete.

We may now return to the event with which this story began: the reenactment of the *Gathering of Intentions*' original teaching atop Mount Malaya. It was up to Nüden to teach his massive four-volume subcommentary.[27] To do so would require several months of uninterrupted time,[28] and no such opportunity arose until 1959. The young third Penor Rinpoché agreed to sponsor Nüden's transmission. Before beginning, Nüden set strict requirements concerning where and to whom he would teach. At the top of a mountain overlooking Pelyul monastery, a hermitage was built just for the occasion and named Fortress of Vajra-Garuda Rock. Only five students would be allowed: Penor Rinpoché, Tupzang Rinpoché, Zhechen Gangshar, Pelyul Khenpo Göndrup,[29] and Pelyul Dzongnang Rinpoché Jampel Lodrö (1930–1987).[30] The initiation was not granted, since all five students had already received it several times.[31] The teaching lasted four months.

In the colophon to his subcommentary, Khenpo Nüden describes the mountain above Pelyul where he taught as "the second forested site of Malaya."[32] He thus likened his revival of the *Gathering of Intentions*' commentarial tradition to Vajrapāṇi's original teaching on Mount Malaya in Śri Laṅka. Accordingly, his requirement that only five students join him mirrored the five excellent ones in the Malaya myth. Tupzang Rinpoché confirms that this was a conscious effort on Khenpo Nüden's part to establish a connection (*rten 'brel*) between the two events. In this reenactment, Nüden was Vajrapāṇi and Penor Rinpoché was the Lord of Laṅka. Just as the Lord of Laṅka puts Vajrapāṇi's words into writing with lapis ink upon gold at the end of the original teaching, Nüden presented Penor Rinpoché with his own handwritten manuscript of the subcommentary at the end of the four months. In establishing these connections with the original teaching myth, Nüden was returning to the source, tapping into the power of the *Gathering of Intentions*' mythic first teaching.

Not long after he transmitted his opus on the *Gathering of Intentions*, Khenpo Nüden died, and Penor Rinpoché soon fled Kham for south

India.[33] During his time in exile, Penor Rinpoché granted the initiation several times. Before he passed away, he made sure to transmit the entire tradition to his successors. Khenpo Nüden's teaching in eastern Tibet was the last in a series of efforts to revive the waning *Gathering of Intentions* tradition. They all shared a single strategy: an attempt to return to the source of the *Gathering of Intentions*' vitality, to reach back to its origin. Gyatrül Rinpoché, in his Spoken Teachings festival, returned the Nyingma pantheon home to the mandala of the Gathered Great Assembly, the "original" mandala that offered early Tibetans an elaborate organization scheme for all of tantra; Khenpo Ngakchung revived the lineage through a visionary encounter with Nupchen Sangyé Yeshé; Khenpo Nüden reenacted the myth of Vajrapāṇi's original teaching. Each attempt hearkened back to the *Gathering of Intentions*' origins. Each teacher in his own way revived the tradition by tapping into the power that was believed to lie at its source.

INTO EXILE

When Penor Rinpoché fled Tibet, he carried with him his treasured copy of Nüden's subcommentary, written in the author's own hand. However, he left behind the only recently rediscovered *Armor Against Darkness*, and once more, the work was lost.[34] Twenty years later, as Dudjom Rinpoché turned to the task of compiling his new *Expanded Spoken Teachings*, he began to search for a copy of Nupchen's famous commentary. Several times, he sent people to look in Tibet, but they always returned empty-handed. He knew that on the basis of the manuscript found at Tashi Lhünpo, a new set of printing blocks had been carved. Now he learned that, unfortunately, only a few prints had been made before the Chinese invasion, during which the blocks were apparently destroyed. Finally, word arrived of a single copy that had survived the Chinese desecrations, having been secreted away by Tsering Lama of Pelyul monastery.[35] In 1983, Dudjom Rinpoché sent Kunzang Lama, himself formerly of Pelyul, to fetch the text from Kham.[36]

Kunzang Lama obtained the book, along with what he described as about 100 kilograms of additional missing works, and assembled them in Lhasa. There he made contact with a group of nineteen Tibetans who were planning to make the illegal trek across the Himalaya to Nepal. He arranged to pay for their transportation to the border and to have them met on the Nepalese side by an associate who would then guide them down into Kathmandu. In return, they would each carry a volume or two of the rare books.

One morning in early December, the twenty Tibetans—nineteen escapees plus Kunzang Lama—climbed aboard a truck driven by two sympathetic drivers from Xinjiang Province and began the trip to Puhrang, on the Nepalese border. As they passed into each new region, the drivers changed the license plates so as not to drawn attention to the truck. This trick, combined with their good mechanical abilities, got them all safely to Puhrang in thirteen days.

There, the group pretended to be pilgrims en route to the holy Mount Kailash. A few days later, at 2:30 a.m., they were dropped at the side of a road to start the next leg of their journey. They walked through the night, and as morning came, they were still within sight of a Chinese checkpoint. It must have been too far away across the long snowy plain, for the Chinese did not come out to chase them, and the party hurried on. At last, around 4:00 the following afternoon, they reached the top of Tingkar pass, at an altitude of about 18,600 feet. At every kilometer along the border, the Chinese had set up concrete blocks saying "Nepal-China," even at the top of this remote pass.

Here too were piled sticks marking the local spirit's abode, where others had burned incense and hung offering flags. The group was cold and exhausted, so they resigned themselves to breaking from propriety and using the sticks to build a fire for tea. After this short rest, they continued until dark. One old monk had lagged behind all day, so they found a dry cave to wait in until he caught up. Awakening to their first morning in Nepal, they descended into the village of Tingkar, where Kunzang Lama's Nepalese contact, Sonam Dorjé, had been waiting for ten days. They all rested for a day before Kunzang Lama started back alone to Lhasa, so as to fly out legitimately on his visa. He left the group under the care of his friend.

After Kunzang left, however, a misunderstanding over money erupted between the Tibetans and Sonam Dorjé. Each Tibetan was supposed to pay Sonam three hundred rupees, but they had assumed this would be Nepalese rupees, and Sonam Dorjé was insisting on Indian currency, worth about twice as much. (Kunzang Lama notes that Sonam was correct that this had indeed been the agreement.) Tempers flared, and Sonam Dorjé left them in exasperation. Now without a guide, the Tibetans started on their own toward Kathmandu, but they did not get far before they were stopped by a Nepalese border patrol, who decided to force them back over the border. Back through Tingkar village and on up toward the border the Tibetans were led, becoming increasingly agitated. One old man in the group, who had already suffered considerably at the hands of the Chinese army, was especially scared. His sister tried to calm him down, but he finally panicked. In a fit of terror, he threw down his bags and flung himself into a freezing river, drowning almost immediately. The text he had been carrying was the *Armor Against Darkness*.

The sister took the text with her, and they continued up the pass. But near the top the Nepalese police suddenly stopped. Telling the Tibetans to go on and return to their own country, they turned around and went back down into Nepal. The Tibetans stood there for a while, wondering what to do. Eventually they decided to ignore the police and enter Nepal once more. The sister left her brother's heavy volumes in the care of Tingkar's village chief, one Patam Singh, and the group made their way to Kathmandu, this time without trouble.

All the books had made it except for the *Gathering of Intentions* commentary. The next year, Kunzang Lama paid Sonam Dorjé another 3,000 rupees to return to Tingkar village for the *Armor Against Darkness*. The trip was attempted but failed. The season was over, and they had to wait yet another year to get up to the village. Finally, in 1985, Kunzang Lama himself decided to go, along with Sonam Dorjé and a monk. They started from Delhi, traveling through Uttar Pradesh to Pitharagal on the Nepal border, where there was a customs checkpoint but no immigration station, then onward to Tingkar. After paying still more money to the "self-sacrificing" guardian of the text, Patam Singh, they retrieved their prize at last. During the two-year interim, the chieftain had offered it to the local (Gelukpa) lama. Fortunately, he had not appreciated the obscure Nyingmapa text and returned it to Patam Singh. The three returned triumphant to Delhi, to present the text to Dudjom Rinpoché.[37] Today, the elusive *Armor Against*

Darkness can be found in volumes 50 and 51 of Dudjom Rinpoché's *Expanded Spoken Teachings* collection.

The *Gathering of Intentions*' incongruous fate was due in large part to the nature of its own project. Its demise as a system that was commonly taught and practiced was an inevitable consequence of its very success. Its original purpose was to provide tenth-century Tibetans with a comprehensive set of interwoven strategies for organizing tantra. Once this structure had been adopted as the dominant paradigm of the Nyingma School, the unwieldy *Gathering of Intentions* had little more to offer. There were other, more succinct tantras for any number of specific practices. Before long, the *Gathering of Intentions*' commentaries were no longer read and its rituals no longer performed. If a tantric system's vitality is judged on whether its rituals are being practiced and its doctrines taught, the *Gathering of Intentions* is largely extinct. (Precisely such a perception was what spurred the early twentieth-century efforts to revive the waning tradition in eastern Tibet.) Yet in other, less visible ways, its influence continues as strongly as ever.

The Nyingma School as we know it today is united by an unconscious obedience to the *Gathering of Intentions*. Today's Nyingmapa may follow any of a vast array of treasure-based ritual systems, but they all have one canon in common: the Spoken Teachings. Of the three principal works (Sutra, Tantra, and Mind Class), the *Gathering of Intentions* is the least known, yet it has wielded the greatest influence over the *structure* of the Spoken Teachings, and thereby of the Nyingma School. Many of the structures fundamental to Nyingma identity and self-understanding derive directly from this tantra. Today, when the Nyingma School presents itself, whether ritually through the Spoken Teachings festival, mythically through the Mount Malaya myth, ontologically through the three transmissions (*brgyud gsum*), or doctrinally through the nine vehicles, it is always in terms received from the *Gathering of Intentions*.

This chapter has suggested that the *Gathering of Intentions* operates within the Gathered Great Assembly festival in the background, organizing the festival's proceedings; that its own particular rituals are not used is irrelevant to its larger role. This ritual function parallels the

Gathering of Intentions' role in early Tibet, providing an architecture for organizing all the other tantric ritual systems. And this correspondence suggests a further parallel regarding the *Gathering of Intentions*' incongruous place within today's Nyingma School: its invisibility may be related to its behind-the-scenes role within the festival.

In the festival, the *Gathering of Intentions*' concealment is intrinsic to its role as the principal organizing force. Today, the *Gathering of Intentions* is no longer read or practiced as a vital ritual system, yet it operates by defining the structures through which the Nyingmapa see and understand their own school. Perhaps only when this distinction is made—that the *Gathering of Intentions* continues to function through its pervasive structures and not through its particular rituals or texts—can its fate be fully comprehended.

There are several possible explanations why, after the thirteenth century, the *Gathering of Intentions* began to slip into disuse—the rise of treasure revelation, the continuing ritual innovations within the tantric classes of Mahāyoga and Atiyoga, the lack of a Sanskrit original. However, these explanations all miss a crucial point, because they assume the *Gathering of Intentions* operates on the same level—in the same dimension—as other tantric systems. In the festival, as in early Tibet, the *Gathering of Intentions* works to organize all the other tantras rather than compete with them. Today it functions through its structures, schemas that have come to pervade the entire Nyingma School, and this is precisely why it has slipped into disuse according to the normative criteria used to judge a system's vitality.

The *Gathering of Intentions*' influence is rarely apparent because its role is so diffuse. Through the eyes of the Nyingmapa, the *Gathering of Intentions*' organizational strategies have become so ubiquitous, repeated in so many other places throughout the tradition, that for them to have a single origin in the *Gathering of Intentions* is no longer conceivable. They are so pervasive that those working through them can rarely gain a perspective on them; to try to do so would be like the eye looking for itself, to use Nupchen's original metaphor.[38]

APPENDIX

THE FOUR ROOT TANTRAS OF ANUYOGA

The fundamental tantras of the Anuyoga class are known as the "four root sutras" and are typically listed as follows:

1. *Gathering of Intentions*
2. *Gathering of All Knowledge*
3. *Play of the Charnel Ground Cuckoo*
4. *Majestic Wisdom's Wheel of Lightning.*

This foursome is in fact a reduction of a possibly earlier fivefold collection cited by the eleventh-century Gö Khukpa Lhetsé in his polemical treatise, *Refutation of False Mantra*: "The *Gathering of Intentions*, the *Gathering of All Knowledge*, and the Five Dharmas of the King (*rgyal po'i chos lnga*) are fakes because they were written by Dorjé Pelgi Drakpa."[1] Just a few years later, also in the eleventh century, a similar set of "five sutras" came under attack, this time in the *Official Decree* (*Bka' shog*) of Zhiwa Ö.[2] In his list of corrupt (*'dres ma*) works, Zhiwa Ö repeated Gö Khukpa's earlier claim that the *Gathering of All Knowledge* and its circle of texts—together called the five sutras—were authored by Dorjé Pelgi Drakpa. Zhiwa Ö further dismissed all the relevant commentaries that stemmed from the early Zur clan.

Unfortunately, neither Gö Khukpa nor Zhiwa Ö specified which texts they intended as the "five dharmas of the king" or the "five sutras."

For this we must rely on the much later Nyingma apologist Sokdokpa (1552–1624), who explains that these five works corresponded to the four root sutras listed above, plus the *Great Precept on Mind Sutra* (*Sems lung chen mo'i mdo*). Evidently the latter was eventually discarded, and the remaining four were codified as the root sutras of Anuyoga. Today, the *Great Precept on Mind* appears not in the Anuyoga section of the *Collected Tantras of the Ancients* but under Atiyoga.

Various attempts have been made to organize the four Anuyoga tantras into groups. Perhaps the earliest was by Dampa Deshek. According to his system, within Anuyoga, seven early sutras (*mdo snga ma bdun*) are to be distinguished from seven later ones (*phyi ma bdun*). These are listed as follows:[3]

Seven early sutras:[4]
1. *Sky of Reality Treasury* (*Chos nyid nam mkha' mdzod kyi mdo*)
2. *Nectar Arising* (*Bdud brtsi 'byung ba'i mdo*)
3. *Gathering of All Correct Knowledge* (*Kun 'dus rig pa yang dag gi mdo*)
4. *Great Precept on Mind Great Perfection Sutra* (*Sems lung chen mo rdzogs chen gyi mdo*)
5. *Rosary of Majestic Lightning Mahāmāyā Sutra* (*Rngam pa glog phreng sgyu 'phrul gyi mdo*)
6. *Play of the Cuckoo Kīla Sutra* (*Khu byug rol pa phur pa'i mdo*)
7. *Trancending the World* (*'Jig rten 'das pa'i mdo*).

Seven later sutras:
1. *King of Initiations* (*Dbang bskur rgyal po'i rgyud*)
2. *Six Vidyādharas* (*Rig 'dzin drug gi mdo*)
3. *Supreme Samādhi* (*Ting 'dzin mchog gi mdo*)
4. *Joining the Secret Door* (*Gsang sgo 'brel ba'i mdo*)
5. *Not Straying from the Vajra* (*Rdo rje ma gol ba'i mdo*)
6. *Heaping Lamps* (*Sgron ma brtsegs pa'i mdo*)
7. *General Gathering of Intentions of All Tathāgatas* (*Spyi mdo sangs rgyas tham cad kyi dgongs pa 'dus pa'i mdo*).

Both lists include works that were later classified as Mahāyoga or Atiyoga. It seems that in the late twelfth century, when Dampa Deshek was writing, the classification of the Nyingma tantras as exclusively Mahāyoga, Anuyoga, or Atiyoga had yet to be settled definitively.

A more recent scheme for organizing the Anuyoga canon is offered by Dudjom Rinpoché in *The Nyingma School of Tibetan Buddhism*, where the following list is provided:[5]

1. The Four Root Sutras (*rtsa ba'i mdo bzhi*)
    a. *Gathering of All Knowledge*
    b. *Magnificent Thunderbolts*
    c. *Compendium of Intentions*
    d. *Play of the Charnel Ground Cuckoo*
2. The Six Tantras for Clarifying the Six Limits (*mtha' drug gsal bar byed pa'i rgyud drug*)
    a. *Dwelling in the Greatness of Samantabhadra Tantra* (*Kun tu bzang po che ba rang la gnas pa'i rgyud*)
    b. *King of Initiations* (*Dbang bskur rgyal po*)
    c. *Supreme Samādhi* (*Ting 'dzin mchog*)
    d. *Seven Appropriatenesses* (*Skabs sbyor bdun pa*)
    e. *True Purpose of Effort* (*Brtson pa don bden*)
    f. *Samaya Array* (*Dam tshig bkod pa*)
3. The Twelve Rare Tantras (*dkon rgyud bcu gnyis*)
    a. *Tantra of the Peaceful Gods* (*Zhi ba lha rgyud*)
    b. *Tantra of the Peaceful Gods of Reality* (*Chos nyid zhi ba'i lha rgyud*)
    c. *Great Tantra of the Wrathful Gods* (*Khro bo'i lha rgyud chen mo*)
    d. *Great Realization Tantra of the Wrathful Gods* (*Khro bo'i lha rgyud rtogs pa chen po*)
    e. *Scattering of Great Compassion* (*Thug rje chen po'i gtor gyud*)
    f. *Great Tantra of the Assembly of Secret Yoga* (*Rnal 'byor sang ba'i tshogs rgyud chen po*)
    g. *The Gloriously Blazing Wrathful Woman* (*Dpal 'bar khro mo*)
    h. *Red Rakta Tantra* (*Rak+ta dmar gyi rgyud*)
    i. *Blazing Tantra That Pacifies the Fire God* (*Me lha zhi bar gyur ba 'bar ba'i rgyud*)
    j. Vajra Tomb: A Wrathful Fire Offering (*Khro bo'i sbyin bsregs rdo rje'i dur mo*)

k. *Great Hūṃkara* (*Hūṃ mdzad chen mo*)
l. *Great Secret Moon* (*Zla gsang chen mo*)
4. The Seventy Literary Scriptures (*lung gi yi ge bdun cu*)
(It is unclear which tantras Dudjom refers to with this last heading.)

Given the many differences between Dampa Deshek's list and Dudjom's, the contents of the Anuyoga section have been unclear over the centuries. Even Jikmé Lingpa's late-eighteenth-century list exhibits significant differences from Dudjom Rinpoché's.[6] Nonetheless, the four root sutras represent a stable core found in all lists, from the twelfth century to the present. What follows is a discussion of the three root sutras other than the *Gathering of Intentions*, one at a time, each discussed in terms of "position in corpus and authorship," "internal structure," and "primary points of later tradition."

GATHERING OF ALL KNOWLEDGE

This is the root tantra (*rtsa rgyud*) for the entire Anuyoga class. The work consists of thirty-seven chapters. Each discusses a different aspect of the ritual system being presented. Generally speaking, the earlier chapters (1–9) introduce the conceptual framework for the system, including theoretical discussions of how the practitioner will progress along the path to enlightenment, the vows taken, and the philosophical views cultivated. Then the remaining chapters (10–37) present the various rituals that might be required by the practitioner, culminating in the elaborate initiation ceremony for which Anuyoga became famous in later centuries.

Position in Corpus and Authorship

The better-known *Gathering of Intentions* is often held to be the Anuyoga root tantra, but technically speaking it is the explanatory tantra to the *Gathering of All Knowledge*. Historically, the two works were clearly related. The *Gathering of All Knowledge* may even have been written first. It is shorter (at 276 folio sides), more condensed, and covers many of the same topics as the sprawling and more systematic *Gathering of Intentions*. While there are no commentaries on the *Gathering of All Knowledge*, the *Gathering of Intentions* and its commentary, the *Armor Against Darkness* by Nupchen Sangyé Yeshé, accomplish a similar function. Indeed, there are indications that the tantric system outlined in the *Gathering of Intentions* preexisted the work.[7]

Despite its present role as the root tantra of Anuyoga, there is no indication that the work's author(s) regarded it as such, nor even as an exclusively Anuyoga work. Rather, its author(s) seem to have considered it a work that spanned all three inner yogas, Mahāyoga, Anuyoga, and Atiyoga. (See, for example, 531.3, where the yoga of the Great Perfection is mentioned.) There is, however, evidence of a sexual yoga that includes elements unique to the perfection stage practices. (See in particular chapter 12, "On Accomplishing the Secret Union.") The presence of such elements may explain in part why this work was later classified as Anuyoga.

As the root tantra of Anuyoga, the *Gathering of All Knowledge* also heads the so-called "four root sutras of Anuyoga." Of these, the *Gathering of All Knowledge* and the *Gathering of Intentions* have a particularly close relationship, while the *Lightning of Majestic Wisdom* and the *Play of the Charnel Ground Cuckoo* may have been independent texts that were worked into the early Sutra Initiation tradition at a later time. (The evidence for this theory is discussed in the sections on these two tantras below.)

The question of authorship of the *Gathering of All Knowledge* remains unclear. The work may have emerged from the same international circle of Buddhist masters—from India, Nepal, Brusha, and Tibet—who were responsible for the *Gathering of Intentions*.

Internal Structure

The *Gathering of All Knowledge* is taught by Samantabhadra-Vajrasattva in his wrathful *heruka* form (Dpal Kun tu bzang po Rdo rje sems dpa' He ru ka) and in sexual union with his consort, Samantabhadrī (Kun tu bzang mo). More commonly known as Supreme Heruka (Che mchog; see 531.4), in this work he is also referred to by the title Lord of the Supreme Secret (Gsang ba mchog gi bdag pa). The sutra is taught to the Assembly of the Great Gathering (*'dus pa chen po'i tshogs*). While at first glance the name of the audience sounds generic, it may be significant that it closely resembles the name of the main Anuyoga mandala in the Spoken Teachings tradition, the Gathered Great Assembly.

The text does not adhere to any particular structure. There is, however, a loose progression from the laying of a theoretical groundwork in chapters 1–9 to rituals of worldly benefit in chapters 10, 13, and 17 (e.g., resurrecting zombies, traveling swiftly, prolonging one's life, and clairvoyance). Then, after the instructions on constructing the mandala in chapter 14, the work moves into the rituals used for spiritual ends, with the initiation coming near the end. But this structure is only loosely followed, and exceptions are easy to find.

Primary Points for Later Traditions

Chapter 1 is the longest chapter of the work. From the point of view of the later tradition, it is also one of the most important. It introduces the reader to the philosophical view and the conceptual apparatus for the ritual system. In particular, a number of lists are presented that are key to the later commentarial literature on the Anuyoga tradition. The first list consists of the three yogas, of the cause, the conditions, and fruition (see 372–83). The yoga of the cause seeks to understand the error (*'khrul pa gcig shes*) that shapes our basic state. The yoga of the conditions focuses on the nature of consciousness, whereby one progresses along the path to enlightenment. The yoga of fruition is the unmistaken enlightened state, called the "Great Perfection" (*rdzogs pa chen po*). Nupchen uses these three yogas to open the introduction to his *Armor of Darkness* commentary on the *Gathering of Intentions*.[8]

The discussion of the yoga of fruition includes several other lists that are important to the later exegetical tradition. In particular, four of the five yogas that are developed in the *Gathering of Intentions* appear, though they are buried in a longer list of eleven yogas (see 382.1–3). These five yogas as they normally appear are the yoga of aspiration, the yoga of opening the great lineage, the yoga of the great encouragement, the yoga of attaining the great prophecy, and the yoga of perfecting the great dynamism. All but the third, the yoga of the great encouragement, are present. Nowhere are the five yogas discussed in detail, but they are clearly intended as a tantric alternative to the five paths famous from the *prajnāpāramitā* literature. For example, during the *prajnāpāramitā's* second path, the path of joining (*sbyor lam*), one grows accustomed to the realization of emptiness until direct perception of reality is attained in the path of seeing (*mthong lam*). Here, during the yoga of opening the great lineage, one "abides in the great vehicle and develops strength through devotion" until "by seeing phenomena as they are, one receives encouragement" in the yoga of the great encouragement.[9] Apart from the slight changes in vocabulary, the gist remains the same and little else is added; the five yogas remain largely theoretical and are not tied directly to any specific tantric ritual practices.

Also included in the discussion of the yoga of fruition are the twelve "ways of arising," or ways tantra was taught in the world (see 380.5–7). These also appear in the *Gathering of Intentions*, where they give structure to the work as a whole. They are, however, listed differently in the two works. In the final volume of his commentary, Khenpo Nüden attempts to reconcile the two ways of listing them.[10]

Immediately following the Buddha's explanation of the three yogas is that of the ten levels (*sa bcu*). Like the five yogas mentioned above, this is a tantric re-presentation of a doctrinal set famous from the sutras, and again the discussion remains general. Chapter 1 ends with several further doctrinal lists that were less important to the later tradition.

The lists discussed in this opening chapter of the *Gathering of All Knowledge* became the building blocks for the system that is worked out more systematically in the *Gathering of Intentions*. In today's Nyingma School's educational program, these lists are all that remains of this system, preserved and studied as part of the *Three Vows* by Ngari Paṇchen.

A couple of other sections were also of particular importance for the later tradition. The Charnel Ground Mandala of the Supreme Secret (*dur khrod gsang ba mchog gi dkyil 'khor*) described in chapter 14 came to be used as the uncommon wrathful mandala of the Gathered Great Assembly.[11] There are two forms of the Gathered Great Assembly, the common and the uncommon, used in some initiation ceremonies for the Mahāyoga and the Anuyoga initiations respectively. (Though under the influence of the Mindröling tradition, the ceremony was later simplified so that only the common mandala was used for both sets of initiations.) Each mandala form has nine ascending levels, with both a peaceful and a wrathful mandala at its central and highest level.

Finally, the initiation ritual described in chapter 36 has all the basic elements used later in the so-called "Sutra Initiation" (*mdo dbang*) ceremony. This ceremony grants initiation into any or all of the nine levels of the Gathered Great Assembly mandala. It is divided into four streams of initiations, which are presented at the beginning of chapter 36. The first stream corresponds to the first six vehicles (through Yoga tantra), while the second, third, and fourth streams correspond to Mahāyoga, Anuyoga, and Atiyoga. These four streams are then further divided into the 36 root initiations, as was common in the later Sutra Initiation system. No mention is made of the last subdivision of these 36 into 831, as was common in the later tradition.

PLAY OF THE CHARNEL GROUND CUCKOO

The *Play of the Charnel Ground Cuckoo* is the shortest of the four root sutras of Anuyoga and the least cited in later literature. It focuses on the wrathful deity Vajrakīlaya and seems to have figured prominently in the traditions surrounding that deity, quite apart from its role within the four sutras. It is possible that the text initially existed as a Vajrakīlaya work and was only later revised and brought into the four sutras fold.[12] Of the four sutras, it demonstrates a particularly close connection to *Wisdom's Magificent Thunderbolts.*

Position in Corpus and Authorship

The *Play of the Charnel Ground Cuckoo* and *Wisdom's Magificent Thunderbolts* are similar in their narrative settings. Both works also have final chapters that were appended subsequent to their initial composition. These additional chapters both use the word "supplementary" (*phyi ma*) in their title. In the *Play of the Cuckoo*, the final chapter 14 is titled "A Presentation of Supplementary Topics" (*don phyi ma rim par bkod pa*). Moreover, in both works the final chapters open with explanations of their respective titles and use similar language in doing so.[13] These chapters may well have been written by a single author.

The final chapter of the *Play of the Cuckoo* exhibits a particularly strong concern for its own legitimacy and future welfare.[14] The same chapter also makes extensive reference to the King Dza narrative of the Vajrayāna's original appearance in the world. This narrative is an important element in the *Gathering of Intentions*. Taken together, all of the above facts indicate that this final chapter (and perhaps elements of the opening chapter) was added in order to tie the work to the four sutras, and thus to lend cohesion and legitimacy to the group as a whole.

The *Play of the Cuckoo* may have had a significant role in other Buddhist circles before and after it was brought into the four sutras' fold. The work is unique among the four for the strength of its focus on Vajrakīlaya, seen especially in chapters 7 and 8.

Perhaps reflecting the work's double role, a *Play of the Cuckoo* (*Khu byug rol ba*) appears twice in the eleventh-century King Zhiwa Ö's list of specious works, once as one of the apocryphal four sutras and once as one of the "Kīlaya tantras."[15] That Vajrakīlaya had some influence on the early Sutra Initiation tradition is also suggested by Lochen Dharmaśrī.[16]

Internal Structure

The narrative setting for the *Play of the Cuckoo* is the Mandala of the Supreme Secret (*gsang ba mchog gi dkyil 'khor*). The teacher is the Lord of the Supreme Secret (Gsang ba mchog gi bdag po), and the audience seems to vary between chapters. At first, the recipient is Samantabhadra, who is simply another aspect of the Lord of the Supreme Secret. In chapter 14, the audience is referred to as the "assembly of the gathered entourage" (*'dus pa'i 'khor tshogs*). In all of these ways—setting, teacher, and audience—the work is like *Wisdom's Magificent Thunderbolts*.[17] In chapter 2, however, there is yet another audience, the "general retinue" (*'khor mang po rnams*), that is not shared by the latter work.

Chapter 1 describes how the teacher of the tantra, the Lord of the Supreme Secret, is aroused by his consort, Samantabhadrī (Kun tu bzang mo), who sings songs to encourage him to teach. In thus awakening, the lord passes through several stages of *samādhi*, hence the title of the chapter. Chapter 2 discusses the nonconceptual mind of awakening (*bodhicitta*). Chapter 3 contains descriptions of the mandalas for each of the five families, ending with some brief instructions on granting a series of six initiations. Chapter 4 discusses the mandalas as they should be visualized, and chapter 5 describes the *mudrās* and mantras to be performed. Chapter 6 is a presentation of which type of being is appropriate for taming each of the six realms. Thus, the animals are to be tamed by the lion, the gods by Indra, and humans by a wheel-turning (*cakravartin*) king. As noted above, chapter 7 begins the section in which the practices for Vajrakīlaya are taught. The chapter describes the appearance of Vajrakīlaya's body and realm and how he destroys the evil demons (*dregs pa can*). Chapter 8 outlines the deity's wrathful mandala. Then chapters 9 through 13 contain teachings on various topics, as indicated in their titles, all with Vajrakīlaya as their focus. Finally, chapter 14 is the appended chapter, which ties the work to the four sutras of Anuyoga. A new audience for this chapter is made explicit in the first line; it is the "assembly of the gathered entourage" (*'dus pa'i 'khor tshogs rnams*), the standard audience for the four sutras group.

Primary Points for Later Traditions

Of the four sutras of Anuyoga, the *Play of the Cuckoo* is the least cited in later Sutra Initiation literature, and its contents have the least in common with the later tradition. The few relevant points that do appear are all in the final, fourteenth chapter. The audience for this chapter is introduced as the "assembly of the gathered entourage," which closely resembles the name for the audiences in the *Gathering of All Knowledge* and the *Gathering of Intentions*, and thus also the name of the main mandala in the later Sutra Initiation tradition, the Gathered Great Assembly. Also in the fourteenth chapter is a version of the King Dza myth, echoing a similar myth in the *Gathering of Intentions*. Notably, there is no mention of the elaborate initiation ceremony that is characteristic of the Sutra Initiation tradition.

WISDOM'S MAGNIFICENT THUNDERBOLTS

Wisdom's Magnificent Thunderbolts' final chapter also seems to have been added at a later date, probably to tie it more strongly to the four sutras group. In this and other ways, *Wisdom's Magnificent Thunderbolts* resembles the *Play of the Charnel Grounds Cuckoo.*

Position in Corpus and Authorship

Wisdom's Magnificent Thunderbolts is sometimes referred to as an "explanatory tantra,"[18] presumably to the Anuyoga root tantra, the *Gathering of All Knowledge*. This would be in addition to the famous *Gathering of Intentions*, which is more commonly considered the explanatory tantra.

It is unclear who the author was, but it is almost certain that there were more than one; the final chapter appears to have been composed after the rest of the text. This is made all but explicit by the chapter's title ("Setting Forth Some Supplementary Secrets"), but even more telling is the table of contents that appears in chapter 3. This summary of the topics covered in the following chapters stops with the penultimate chapter, 16, implying that chapter 17 had not yet been written.

Internal Structure

Wisdom's Magnificent Thunderbolts is taught by the Lord of the Supreme Secret, who is also called Samantabhadra in the work's opening lines. The lord's main interlocutor is another emanation of Samantabhadra, the Lion of Speech (*Smra ba'i seng ge*), who heads a larger audience often referred to as the "assembly of the gathered entourage" (*'dus pa'i 'khor tshogs*). The narrative setting for the teaching is the Mandala of the Supreme Secret (*gsang ba mchog gi dkyil 'khor*).

Chapter 1 introduces the teacher Samantabhadra. He appears in the company of the forty-two peaceful and the fifty-eight wrathful deities famous from the Māyājāla tantras. The chapter ends with Samantabhadra resting in sexual union with his consort, Samantabhadrī. In chapter 2, Samantabhadrī exhorts the buddha to manifest for the benefit of sentient beings. He gradually arises, and finally his own Lion of Speech emanation exhorts the Lord of the Supreme Secret to teach.

Thus the teaching proper beings with chapter 3, which introduces the ten topics to be discussed in the chapters that follow. They are not addressed in any detail but provide the structure for the rest of the text, so that this chapter serves as a sort of table of contents. The ten topics are: generating bodhicitta, the mandalas, the mudrās, the fourfold propitiation and accomplishment (*bsnyen grub bzhi*), the *siddhis*, the vows, asceticisms, taming the demons, the four activities, and urging perseverence (*brnag pa nan tur*). These are covered in chapters 4 through 16, which leaves chapter 17 conspicuously out of the main body of the text.

Chapter 4 describes the mind of enlightenment from an ultimate point of view. Next the standard three types of mandalas are introduced: the abstract "natural mandala," the visualized "*samādhi* mandala," and the physically constructed "reflection mandala." Chapter 5 describes the natural mandala (*rang bzhin gyi dkyil 'khor*). The first half interprets the various deities in the mandala in terms of *abhidharma* categories such as the five aggregates, the elements, and the sense bases. The second half describes the architecture of the mandala in more conventional terms. Chapter 6 tells how to visualize mandala by means of the three *samādhis* (*bsgoms pa'i, bskyed pa'i, lhag pa'i ting nge 'dzin*), and chapter 7 provides the ritual procedures for constructing a physical model of the mandala. The contents of the remaining ten chapters are relatively predictable given their titles; most focus on a variety of rituals. Finally, in chapter 17 the important initiation ceremony is discussed, and there is an extensive rendition of the buddha's subjugation of Rudra.

Primary Points for Later Traditions

The final chapter of *Wisdom's Majestic Thunderbolts* was written some time after its initial composition. This supplement was almost certainly made to strengthen the link between this work and the four sutras set. Thus it is not surprising to find many of the points that were important to the later tradition in this final chapter. The elements included in this chapter might reveal how the four sutras tradition as a whole was perceived, that is, which elements were deemed crucial to the tradition.

Apparently of foremost importance was the elaborate initiation ceremony. The thirty-six main initiations that are the basis for the ceremony are listed in the final chapter. They are divided into four sets, or "streams": ten outer initiations, eleven inner, thirteen accomplishment, and two secret. All this terminology is standard in the exegetical literature of the later Sutra Initiation tradition.

The other section that is cited regularly in the later literature is in chapter 5, on the "natural mandala" (*rang bzhin gyi dkyil 'khor*). The later Sutra Initiation ceremony used two main mandalas in a variety of ways, depending on which liturgical tradition was being followed. These came to be called the "uncommon" and the "common" mandalas of the Great Gathered Assembly. Each included, in turn, both a peaceful and a wrathful mandala. The uncommon peaceful mandala comes directly from this fifth chapter of *Wisdom's Magnificent Thunderbolts*, and the common peaceful mandala is also related to it, though more indirectly.[19] This mandala described in the second half of chapter 5 is home to the forty-two peaceful deities, which are likely drawn from the Māyājāla corpus of tantras in Mahāyoga.

GREAT PRECEPT ON MIND SUTRA

The *Great Precept on Mind* is the anomaly. In his critique of the Nyingma tantras, Gö Khukpa treats it separately. Then in the later literature, the "five sutras" are reduced to four,[20] with the *Great Precept on Mind* excluded. But even more important, this text uses few or none of the terms that are standard in the other four sutras. All this pushes it to the periphery of the group. [21]

The four sutras that came to be codified as such thus share much in common. They use unique terminologies and categories, a complex initiation ceremony, and similar mandalas. Generally speaking, they work to develop a doctrinal system for discussing tantra that is parallel to ones for sutra.

EARLY COMMENTARIES

If we accept the *Gathering of Intentions* as the composition of Dharmabodhi and friends around the middle of the ninth century, then the other three sutras were probably not translated by those claimed in their colophons, all of whom date from one hundred years earlier. The tradition holds that Nupchen was a disciple of Padmasambhava, which is unlikely, if not impossible, given his dates. There is a consistent desire in the later tradition to collapse age-of-fragmentation (and later) developments into the royal dynastic period. Thus the claims made in the Mkhyen brtse edition of the *Collected Tantras of the Ancients*, that Padmasambhava and Vairocana translated the *Gathering of All Knowledge* and Vimalamitra and Chokru Lui Gyeltsen translated *Wisdom's Magificent Thunderbolts*, are doubtful.[22] Who actually translated these works must remain undecided for the time being, though given the history of the *Gathering of Intentions*, it is quite possible that they were all originally written in Tibetan.

It is possible, however, that in its day the doctrinal system common to the four sutras enjoyed some renown throughout northern India, Nepal, and Tibet. The sheer number of well-known figures associated with it is a first indication. The fact that Dharmabodhi's *Condensed Meaning* is not cited by Nupchen may be evidence that other commentarial lineages were active from an early date, though it could also indicate that it is a later Tibetan apocryphon. But even more revealing is a discussion by Khenpo Nüden at the end of his exhaustive commentary. In writing this work, Nüden had access to all the related materials that Katok Situ Chökyi Gyamtso had gathered during his travels through central and eastern Tibet in the early twentieth century. By analyzing these sometimes quite ancient manuscripts, Nüden names four distinct commentarial traditions that already existed in tenth-century Tibet before they were gathered by the Zurs in the eleventh century:

> Regarding this, at the end of Dampa [Deshek]'s handwritten notes (*phyag mchan*) it says, "Lharjé Zur strove for the sake of all at the *Great Commentary*, which was the text for the three lords, Da, Len, and Khyé.[23] Then later, he authentically received it from Gongbuwa and Shangpa. And after that, [Dampa] Deshek received it in both ways from Lharjé, and from this excellence, I the round one (*ldom po*) received it." Thus when the Lord of the Guhyakas, Dropukpa, first received it in earnest from Da, Len, and Khyé, it was mainly in the system of the Great Commentary, the *Armor Against Darkness*. Later, when he received it from Gongbuwa and Shangpa, it was mainly in the system of the *Lung bstan skor*.[24] After that, the Omniscient Dampa Deshek received it from

> Lharjé Mar and Tsangpa in both systems. And then that excellent lord of dharma passed it on to Tsangtön Dorjé Gyeltsen. . . .
>
> After the annotated text revealed by Panchen Situ Rinpoché at Daklha Gampo, it says, "The intermediate[25] notes of Lharjé Dropukpa, Datsha, and Horpo have been preserved for some time by the discussions of Da, Len, and Yangkhyé. They have been looked over by the Drugu Bendé, Üpa Jobum, who gave his approving recommendation. May they continue for the welfare of beings."[26]
>
> Also, at the end of yet another recently discovered[27] ancient annotated text, it says that of the four different commentaries on the great sutra, Gartön Zangpo followed the system of the great scholar Sthiramati when he taught Rongzom Paṇḍita. And from the latter, it was received by Ruyong Rinchen Bar. Then it passed to Dakdra Dromtön Tengpo, who is said to have produced a newly annotated edition.[28]

Thus we can identify three of the "four different commentaries" as those by Sthiramati (taught to Rongzom), Nupchen, and King Dza (the purported author of the *Prophetic Commentary*). We cannot know for sure what the fourth one was—probably the *Condensed Meaning* of Dharmabodhi.

The Sthiramati commentaries, like the *Condensed Meaning*, are found together in the Peking edition of the *Bstan 'gyur*.[29] I have only examined one (the *Skabs 'grel bye brag rnam par bshad pa*). It is almost certainly a Tibetan composition, falsely attributed to the Indian Yogācāra author. It does appear to be an early work, however, since it is a short text (much like the *Condensed Meaning*) and makes little use of the elaborate exegetical apparatus that developed in later years. Beyond its Tibetan use of language, one clue that something may be amiss with its Sthiramati attribution is the presence of a quotation from Déwa Seldzé, who was supposed to have been the student of Sthiramati.[30]

It is unfortunate that the *Prophetic Commentary* attributed to King Dza is no longer extant. It is cited regularly throughout the Sutra Initiation tradition and was clearly an influential work from an early date.

Nupchen's "Great Commentary," the *Armor Against Darkness*, was by far the longest commentary on the *Sutra*, filling two volumes. He purportedly wrote it on the basis of his studies with Che Tsenkyé in Brusha.

He also completed a meditation retreat at Tselchen Nyuki Dorjé Drombu, which appears to have been around Drak Yongdzong, above his birthplace in Drak valley. This became the main pilgrimage place for accomplishing the *Compendium* system. Nupchen's *Armor Against Darkness* remains crucial to understand the obscure language and complicated doctrinal systems of the *Compendium*.

NOTES

INTRODUCTION

1. Here and throughout this study, I have opted to use the reconstructed title **Guhyagarbha* for the tantric scripture that goes by the Tibetan title *Gsang ba'i snying po*, in spite of Sanderson's important observation that the reconstruction **Guhyagarhba* is quite likely mistaken and should instead read **Guhyakośa* (Alexis Sanderson, "Pious Plagiarism: Evidence of the Dependence of the Buddhist Yoginītantras on Śaiva Scriptural Sources," unpublished seminar paper [Leiden, 1995], 8 n. 12). Given how well known the former title is, however, and the likelihood that many readers will be more familiar with contemporary scholarship on Tibetan rather than Indian Buddhism, I have chosen to follow popular tradition.
2. See Donald S. Lopez, Jr., *Elaborations on Emptiness* (Princeton: Princeton University Press, 1996), 15–45.
3. More precisely, it might better be called the explanatory tantra to the root tantra proper, namely the *Gathering of All Knowledge Sutra* (*Kun 'dus rig pa'i mdo*). In fact, there are four "root sutras" of the Anuyoga class. For summaries of them as a group, see the appendix.
4. L. Austine Waddell, *Tibetan Buddhism, with Its Mystic Cults, Symbolism and Mythology* (New York: Dover, 1972 [1895]), 58.
5. Waddell, *Tibetan Buddhism*, 73.
6. Helmut Hoffmann, *Religions of Tibet*, trans. Edward Fitzgerald (London: Allen & Unwin, 1961), 50–65 and 166–67.

7. Geoffrey Samuel, *Civilized Shamans: Buddhism in Tibetan Societies* (Washington, DC: Smithsonian Institution Press, 1993), 12.
8. Samuel, *Civilized Shamans*, 10.
9. Samuel, *Civilized Shamans*, 273.
10. For Samuel's definition of his terms, see *Civilized Shamans*, 9–10.
11. And to clarify, my argument here does not preclude the idea that some Tibetans were of a more visionary sort that functioned outside of large monastic institutions. Although tantric Buddhism has been deeply woven into the fabric of elite monastic Buddhism from its earliest days, at its fringes, it also inspired and interacted with a variety of more marginal types. Thus, while we should attend to the hermeneutical nuances that surround and often dilute the transgressive and anti-establishment rhetoric in the tantras, we should not overlook the less theological realities that sometimes played out in actual lived history, the groups and individuals who (rightly or wrongly) took the tantras at their word.
12. On the Mahāyoga side of the Spoken Teachings, see in particular Gyurme Dorje, "The *Guhyagarbhatantra* and Its XIVth Century Tibetan Commentary, *phyogs bcu mun sel*" (Ph.D. diss., University of London, SOAS, 1987); Robert Mayer, *A Scripture of the Ancient Tantra Collection, The* Phur-pa bcu-gnyis (Oxford: Kiscadale Publications, 1996); Cathy Cantwell and Robert Mayer, *The Kīlaya Nirvāṇa Tantra and the Vajra Wrath Tantra: Two Texts from the Ancient Tantra Collection* (Vienna: Verlag der Österreichischen Akademie der Wissenschaften, 2007); Jamgön Mipham, *Luminous Essence: A Guide to the Guhyagarbha Tantra*, trans. The Dharmacakra Translation Committee (Ithaca, NY: Snow Lion, 2009); Dodrupchen Jigme Tenpa'i Nyima, *Key to the Precious Treasury*, trans. Lama Chönam and Sangye Khandro (Ithaca, NY: Snow Lion, 2010; Lama Chönam and Sangye Khandro, *The Guhyagarbha Tantra: Secret Essence Definitive Nature Just As It Is* (Ithaca, NY: Snow Lion, 2011). On the Atiyoga side, see Longchenpa, *You Are the Eyes of the World*, trans. K. Lipman and M. Peterson (Novato, CA: Lotsawa, 1987); Samten Karmay, *The Great Perfection* (Leiden: Brill, 1988); Eva K. Neumaier-Dargyay, *The Sovereign All-Creating Mind, the Motherly Buddha* (Albany: State University of New York Press, 1992); Chögyal Namkhai Norbu and Adriano Clement, *The Supreme Source* (Ithaca, NY: Snow Lion, 1999); Sam van Schaik, "The Early Days of the Great Perfection," *Journal of the International Association of Buddhist Studies* 27, no. 1 (2004). Perhaps not surprisingly, given its relative invisibility within today's Nyingma circles, far less has been published on Anuyoga. Gyurme Dorje, "The rNying-ma Interpretation of Commitment and Vow," *The Buddhist Forum*, vol. 2, ed. Tadeusz

Skorupski (London: School for Oriental and African Studies, 1991), presents in passing the *Gathering of Intentions*' system of tantric vows. Rolf A. Stein, *Etude du monde chinois: institutions et concepts* (Paris: *Annuaire du College de France*, 1972, 1973, and 1974), refers to the work's influential myth of the buddhas' subjugation of Rudra. And on the same myth, see too Matthew T. Kapstein, *The Tibetan Assimilation of Buddhism* (Oxford: Oxford University Press, 2000), 163–77, and Jacob P. Dalton, *Taming of the Demons: Violence and Liberation in Tibetan Buddhism* (New Haven: Yale University Press, 2011). Kapstein, *The Tibetan Assimilation of Buddhism*, 97–105, also notes the influence of the *Gathering of Intentions*' nine vehicles system on the second Karmapa Karma Pakshi (1204–1283). Finally, Samten Karmay (*The Arrow and the Spindle: Studies in History, Myth, Rituals and Beliefs in Tibet* [Kathmandu: Mandala Book Point, 1998], 76–93) mentions the *Gathering of Intentions* in his article on the mythical figure of King Dza. Special note should also be made of Jann Ronis's valuable unpublished dissertation on the interplay between the Spoken Teachings and the Treasure Teachings at Katok monastery; see Jann M. Ronis, "Celibacy, Revelations, and Reincarnated Lamas: Contestation and Synthesis in the Growth of Monasticism at Katok Monastery from the Seventeenth Through Nineteenth Centuries" (Ph.D. diss., University of Virginia, 2009).

13. On this period and its significance in the early Tibetan assimilation of Buddhism, see Dalton, *Taming of the Demons*, 44–76. Matthew Kapstein ("Review of *The Taming of the Demons: Violence and Liberation in Tibetan Buddhism*," *Harvard Journal of Asiatic Studies* 73, no. 1 [2013]) has called attention to the uncertainty surrounding the dates of this text, suggesting that the *Gathering of Intentions* might date from the eleventh century, that is, some two hundred years later. I agree that the issue is impossible to resolve with absolute certainty. However, there are a couple of reasons to assume an earlier date.

    First, when we examine the state of tantric ritual development reflected in the *Gathering of Intentions* and its circle of four "root tantras of the Anuyoga class," the tradition's claim of an earlier date is lent some credibility. The initiation ceremony, for example, culminates in the secret initiation (*guhyābhiṣekha*) and goes no further, that is, it makes no mention of the wisdom-gnosis (*prajñājñāna*) and fourth initiations that became normative sometime around the ninth or the turn of the tenth century, respectively. However, the *Gathering of Intentions* does not in fact make reference to its own initiation system. Chapter 13 contains a discussion of initiation, but only at a general level. Chapter 31 includes an account of the buddha's inititation of Rudra and his horde into the mandala, which, while somewhat detailed, does not include a list of the specific initiations granted. To find a clear reference to the Sutra Initiation system proper, one must look to the other three root tantras of the so-called Anuyoga class; see especially chapter 36 of the *Gathering of All Knowledge Sutra* and chapter 17 of *Wisdom's Magnificent Thunderbolts*. References to the system's "four streams" (*chu bo bzhi*) also occur in the *Armor Against Darkness*, where (notably) Nupchen attempts to bring the system into line with what must have been the increasingly normative scheme of four initiations that is well known today (i.e., vase, secret, wisdom-gnosis, and fourth). Thus in chapter 13, Nupchen claims that "These four streams of initiations [of the *Gathering of Intentions* system] are also called the outer initiations of benefit, the *bodhicitta* initiation, wisdom through gnosis, and great bliss" (*Mun pa'i go cha*, vol. 50, 159.6–7). And again in chapter 31, he mixes several initiation schemes when explaining that some of Rudra's horde received "the outer initiations of benefit," some "the five inner initiations of ability (*nang gi nus pa'i dbang lnga*)," and others "the secret initiation, the initiation of the dissolving *tiklé*," while a fourth group received "the knowledge-wisdom initiation" and a fifth "the initiation that thoroughly stabilizes the great bliss." Nupchen's attempt here to align the three initiation systems of the **Guhyagarbha*, the *Gathering of Intentions*, and the later fourfold scheme makes some (theological, if not historical) sense and is quite skillful, implying that the normative four initiations line up with the vehicles of Yoga, Mahāyoga, Anuyoga, and Atiyoga. Nonetheless, it is also clearly contrived. This may well reflect the fact that some time had passed since the *Gathering of Intentions*' original composition, and Nupchen was striving to keep the system up to date. If this explanation is correct, it also encourages the idea that Nupchen was not responsible for composing the *Gathering of Intentions*. His reference to the fourth initiation of "thoroughly stabilizing the great bliss" might also suggest a date for his *Armor Against Darkness* of around the late ninth century; on the relatively late appearance of the fourth initiation in canonical tantric literature, see Harunaga Isaacson, "Tantric Buddhism in India (from c. A.D. 800 to c. A.D. 1200)," *Buddhismus in Geschichte und Gegenwart* (Hamburg: Internal publication of Hamburg University, 2010).

In any case, the ritual forms of the *Gathering of Intentions* and its supporting circle of tantras reflect a ninth-century period of development. And the *Gathering of Intentions* references, explicitly or implicitly, at least three late eighth-century Mahāyoga tantras, namely the *Guhyasamāja*, the **Guhyagarbha*, and the *Buddhasamāyoga*. (For one possible reference to the *Guhyasamāja*, see *Dgongs pa 'dus pa'i mdo*, 185 [translated in Dalton, *Taming of the Demons*, 176], and for the **Guhyagarbha*, see *Dgongs pa 'dus pa'i mdo*, 69.1–6. For a possible case of textual borrowing from the *Sarvabuddhasamāyoga*, compare *Dgongs pa 'dus pa'i mdo*, 163–66 [translated in Dalton, *Taming of the Demons*, 165–67] with *Sarvabuddhasamāyoga*, 156a.3–158b.5. For Nupchen's references to the **Guhyagarbha*, *Guhyasamāja*, as well as the *Samājottara*, see *Mun pa'i go cha*, vol. 50, 245–46.) Yet there is no indication of any awareness on the part of the *Gathering of Intentions*' authors of any later Yoginī tantras such as the *Cakrasaṃvara* and *Hevajra*. The work therefore reflects a similar literary milieu to that of the tantric texts from Dunhuang, i.e., a generally prior to the later dispensation (*phyi dar*) world. (As noted above, the *Armor Against Darkness*'s references to the normative set of four inititations suggest a somewhat later date for this work than that of its root text, the *Gathering of Intentions*. The *Armor Against Darkness*'s reference to the *Samājottara* is similarly remarkable and, like its references to the four initiations, place it in a different class from the tantric texts preserved at Dunhuang, which to my knowledge generally evince no awareness of either the four initiations or the *Samājottara*. One is left with an impression of a work that pre-dates the later dispensation but postdates the collapse of the empire, when the imperially sponsored importation of tantric materials ended. In other words, the *Armor Against Darkness* looks exactly as it should, given that it is supposed to be authored by a Tibetan master of the late ninth or early tenth century who made multiple trips to India and had his own contacts with the latest tantric writings of the period.)

Still more significantly, the *Gathering of Intentions*—usually under its alternate title, the *Scripture for Accomplishing Yoga* (*Rnal 'byor grub pa'i lung*)—is by far the most frequently cited text in Nupchen's other major work, the *Lamp for the Eyes in Contemplation*. (The *Gathering of All Knowledge* [the official root tantra to which the *Gathering of Intentions* is the explanatory tantra] is also cited regularly in the *Lamp for the Eyes*.) This means that if we were to move the *Gathering of Intentions*' dates forward to the eleventh century, we would similarly have to shift the dates of Nupchen's commentary, the *Armor Against Darkness*, and *Lamp for the Eyes*. Given the kinds of sources cited and concerns reflected in the *Lamp*, an eleventh-century or even later date for this work seems highly unlikely. In short, while we must leave the question somewhat open, there is, at least in my view, enough evidence to accept provisionally a ninth-century date for the *Gathering of Intentions*.

14. Such an idea, to render multiple Buddhist traditions in architecture, is not unique; one need only think of Samyé monastery's three stories that are held to embody the architectural styles of Tibet, Nepal, and China, or in later times, the nine-storied Gyantse stupa in central Tibet.
15. On this period, see especially Ronald M. Davidson, *Tibetan Renaissance* (New York: Columbia University Press, 2005).

1. ORIGINS: MYTH AND HISTORY

1. For an English translation of the *Sarvatathāgata-tattvasaṃgraha*'s narrative account of these five stages, the *pañcābhisaṃbodhi*, see Rolf Giebel, *Two Esoteric Sutras* (Berkeley: Numata Center for Buddhist Translation and Research, 2001), 23–25.
2. Ronald M. Davidson, *Indian Esoteric Buddhism: A Social History of the Tantric Movement* (New York: Columbia University Press, 2002), 148, has also noted the dominance of these two tantric myths; see also Ronald M. Davidson, "Reflections on the Maheśvara Subjugation Myth: Indic Materials, Sa-skya-pa Apologetics, and the Birth of Heruka," *The Journal of the International Association of Buddhist Studies* 14, no. 2 (1991): 199.
3. A complete translation of the *Gathering of Intentions*' Rudra-taming myth is appended to Jacob Dalton, *Taming of the Demons: Violence and Liberation in Tibetan Buddhism* (New Haven: Yale University Press, 2011).
4. Later Nyingmapa writers on the Spoken Teachings lineages often make the claim that only the Anuyoga tantras were transmitted on Mount Malaya, while the Mahāyoga tantras were received by King Dza and Atiyoga was received by Garap Dorjé, directly from Vajrasattva. This view even appears in some other Nyingma tantras, which for this reason, I would suggest, likely date from after the tenth century. (Chapter 5 of the *Kun tu bzang po ye shes gsal bar ston pa'i thabs kyi lam mchog 'dus pa'i rgyud* is cited as such a work by Lochen Dharmaśrī in his *Spyi don*, 38.4–5.) Such a partitioning of Mahāyoga, Anuyoga, and Atiyoga into three distinct lineages can only have taken hold after the *Gathering of Intentions* had been classified as Anuyoga only. (For more on these categories, see chapters 2 and 3 of the present study.) This was not, however, the intention of the *Gathering of Intentions*' authors; according to them, all three classes of teachings were transmitted together at Mount Malaya (via the symbolic transmission) and to King Dza (via the hearing transmission). This made

King Dza the source to which all human tantric lineages should be traced. (Note that there is no mention of Garap Dorjé in the *Gathering of Intentions*, though he does appear in Nupchen Sangyé Yeshé's *Bstam gtan mig sgron*, 191.4.)

5. *Dgongs pa 'dus pa'i mdo*, 617.3–4.
6. On Nupchen's dates, see Roberto Vitali, *The Kingdoms of Gu.ge Pu.hrang* (Dharamsala, India: Tho.ling gtsug.lag.khang lo.gcig.stong 'khor.ba'i rjes. dran.mdzad sgo'i go.sgrig tshogs.chung, 1996), 546–47.
7. On the fourfold structure of Nupchen's *Lamp*, see Jacob Dalton and Sam van Schaik, "Lighting the Lamp: An Examination of the Structure of the Bsam gtan mig sgron," *Acta Orientalia* 64 (2003).
8. Here I am assuming that Nupchen wrote his *Armor Against Darkness* sometime after his repeated trips to India and Nepal, but before he penned his *Lamp for the Eyes in Contemplation* (which regularly cites the *Gathering of Intentions*). According to his early auto/biography, the *Great Seal of Nup* (*Gnubs kyi rgya bo che*, 736.3–4), Nupchen composed his *Lamp for the Eyes* in order to purify the negative karma he accumulated during the Tibetan aristocracy's second revolt (*khengs log*) against the imperial family in 904 C.E. On the auto/biographical status of the *Great Seal of Nup*, see Jacob P. Dalton, "Preliminary Remarks on a Newly Discovered Biography of Gnubs chen sangs rgyas ye shes," in *Himalayan Passages: Tibetan and Newar Studies in Honor of Hubert Decleer*, ed. Benjamin Bogin and Andrew Quintman (Somerville, MA: Wisdom, 2014); on Nupchen's involvements in black magic, see Dalton, *Taming of the Demons*, 50–52; and on dating the second revolt, see Vitali, *The Kingdoms of Gu.ge Pu.hrang*, 547.
9. The early twentieth-century scholar Berthold Laufer has identified Brusha as "Little Pulu" in Chinese, "Belur" in Arabic, and the country of Buruso/Gilgit (see Berthold Laufer, "Die Bru-ža sprache und die historische stellung des Padmasambhava," *T'oung Pao* 9 [1908]: 2–4), while Geza Uray has added his agreement, noting that these identifications are borne out by Chinese sources (see Geza Uray, "The Old Tibetan Sources of the History of Central Asia up to 751 A.D.: A Survey," in *Prolegomena to the Sources on the History of Pre-Islamic Central Asia*, ed. J. Harmatta [Budapest: Akadémiai Kiadó, 1979], 283). In the same article, Laufer (6–8) examines the *Gathering of Intentions*' title in its Brusha and Sanskrit versions. Note that Little Pulu should be distinguished from Great Pulu, which is equivalent to Baltistan. On the early history of these two places, see also Luciano Petech, *The Kingdom of Ladakh*, Serie Orientale, vol. 51 (Rome: Istituto italiano per il Medio ed Estremo Oriente, 1977), 9–10.

10. D. Lorimer was the first Western scholar to note the existence of Burushaski, while working as a British agent in the region in the late nineteenth century. His three-volume study (*The Burushaski Language*, 3 vols. [Oslo: H. Aschehoug, 1935–38]), includes several translations of Burushaski folktales, as well as a grammar and a dictionary.
11. A. H. Dani and V. M. Masson, *History of Civilization in Central Asia*, vol. 4 (Paris: Unesco, 1992), 222–23.
12. Dan Martin, "'Ol-mo-lung-ring, the Original Holy Place," *Tibet Journal* 88, no. 1 (1995): 5.
13. Uray, "The Old Tibetan Sources," 282. See also Christopher Beckwith, *The Tibetan Empire in Central Asia* (Princeton: Princeton University Press, 1987), 116; Brandon Dotson, *The Old Tibetan Annals: An Annotated Translation of Tibet's First History* (Vienna: Verlag der Österreichischen Akademie der Wissenschaften, 2009), 120–21.
14. Beckwith, *The Tibetan Empire in Central Asia*, 163.
15. See Vitali, *The Kingdoms of Gu.ge Pu.hrang*, 166. Later sources also attest to continuing Tibetan involvements in Brusha well into the ninth century. Sonam Tsemo's twelfth-century *Door for Entry Into the Dharma* describes the role Brusha played in an 836 C.E. movement to develop the Buddhist traditions of western Tibet.
16. See Katok Dampa Deshek's *Rdo rje'i tha ram 'byed pa'i lde'u mig*, in *Rnying ma bka' ma rgyas pa*, vol. 52, 209.
17. Martin, "'Ol-mo-lung-ring," 58 and Samten Karmay, *The Arrow and the Spindle: Studies in History, Myth, Rituals and Beliefs in Tibet* (Kathmandu: Mandala Book Point, 1998), 119.
18. See Karmay, *The Arrow and the Spindle*, 32, and *Sngags log sun 'byin*, 'Gos khug pa lhas btsas, in Chag lo tsā ba et al., *Sngags log sun 'byin gyi skor* (Thimphu, Bhutan: Kunsang Tobgyel, 1979), 22.2–3.
19. When Khenpo Nüden, in his twentieth-century commentary on the *Gathering of Intentions*, explains the tantra's colophon, he divides it, so it states that first Dharmabodhi and Che Tsenkyé translated the *Gathering of Intentions* from Sanskrit into Burushaski, and then Dhanarakśita and Che Tsenkyé translated it from Burushaski into Tibetan. It is likely that a need for a Sanskrit original motivated this extrapolation, though Nüden was most likely following the lead of earlier commentators on this translation story; as Nüden points out in his own colophon, almost everything in his commentary was culled from earlier sources.
20. Rolf A. Stein, *Etude du monde chinois: institutions et concepts*, in *Annuaire du*

College de France (Paris: College de France, 1972), 502 (my translation from the French).

21. Another explanation offered by one contemporary Tibetan informant was that the translators—and Che Tsenkyé in particular—may have "gone native" during their time in Brusha, so much so that they no longer saw certain Burushaski words as non-Tibetan.
22. The earliest extant version of this story appears in Dampa Deshek's *Legs bshad nyi ma'i snang ba*, 48.3–4, a source notably written during the contentious years of the later dispensation period. Most subsequent commentators follow this storyline, though Dudjom Rinpoché has the team eventually returning to Brusha to complete the project; see Dudjom Rinpoche, *The Nyingma School of Tibetan Buddhism*, trans. Gyurme Dorje (Boston: Wisdom), 489.
23. More specifically, certain aspects of Rudra's past lives can be seen in the presentation of "the vehicle of the magical display manifesting" (*cho 'phrul mngon par 'byung ba'i theg pa*), while the nine mistaken views held by Rudra's followers appear also in chapter 25, where they structure the buddhas' discussions.
24. In fact, we can further break chapter 25 into its first half, which is an "action" part with Burushaski, and its second half (called the "Sutra of Decisively Cutting Off the Discussion on Taming by Means of Coercion and Violence"), which is doctrinal and lacks Burushaski.
25. Writing about the popularity of demon-taming narratives in early medieval India, and in the *Sarvatathāgata-tattvasaṃgraha* in particular, Davidson, *Indian Esoteric Buddhism*, 151, observes that "The snappiness of the dialogue employed in the scriptures suggests that the Maheśvara subjugation myth has been much influenced by Indian storytellers who continue to travel around, alone or in small troupes, and describe mythic combat using painted pictures on cloth hung behind them." Perhaps in the *Gathering of Intentions*' Burushaski narrative core we might detect a similarly popular telling.
26. Here I am thinking of the other three of the "four root sutras" of the Anuyoga class, and in particular of the "root tantra," the *Gathering of All Knowledge*. The latter covers many of the same topics as the longer and more systematic *Gathering of Intentions*, especially in its first chapter, which outlines the three yogas with which Nupchen opens his introduction to *Armor Against Darkness*, as well as several other doctrinal lists central to the *Gathering of Intentions*. Similar mandalas are described in

the *Gathering of All Knowledge*'s fourteenth chapter and the initiation ceremony in chapter 36, the latter complete with the "four streams" (*dbang gi chu bo bzhi*) that structure the later Sutra Initiation ceremony. The other two of the "four root sutras" seem somewhat less closely related to the *Gathering of Intentions*. Both the *Play of the Charnel Ground Cuckoo* and *Wisdom's Magnificent Thunderbolts* may have been tied into the group after their original composition, by means of their appended final chapters. Thus the former's fourteenth chapter refers to both King Dza and the audience called the "Assembly of the Gathered Entourage" (*'dus pa'i 'khor tshogs*), both central elements of the *Gathering of Intentions*. Similarly, the latter's seventeenth chapter (on "Setting Forth Some Supplementary Secrets"), which is not even mentioned in the work's "table of contents" found in chapter 3, refers to the four streams of the Sutra Initiation. This said, there is other evidence that these two tantras really may have grown out of the same original ritual milieu; whether any of the four is based on an Indic original is another question.

27. Davidson, *Tibetan Renaissance*, 150.
28. Paul Harrison, "Mediums and Messages: Reflections on the Production of Mahāyāna Sūtras," *Eastern Buddhist* 35, no. 1 (2003): 142.
29. *Spyi don*, 53.5–54.2.
30. On this basic tripartite structure, see Joel Tatelman, *The Glorious Deeds of Purna* (Richmond, England: Curzon, 2000), 4–10. On the links between the Rudra myth and normative Buddhist narrative literature, see Jacob P. Dalton, "Sometimes Love Don't Feel Like It Should: Redemptive Violence in Tantric Buddhism," in *Sins and Sinners: Perspectives from Asian Religions*, ed. Phyllis Granoff and Koichi Shinohara (Leiden: Brill, 2012).
31. Compare *Dgongs pa 'dus pa'i mdo*, 163–66 (translated in Dalton, *Taming of the Demons*, 165–67) to *Sarvabuddhasamāyoga*, 156a.3–159b.4. Note also the many close parallels between the Rudra narrative and the popular Tibetan retellings of the *Rāmayāṇa*; see J.W. de Jong, *The Story of Rāma in Tibet* (Stuttgart: Franz Steiner Verlag Wiesbaden GMBH, 1989).
32. Lin Li-kouang, "Puṇyodaya (na-t'i), un propagateur du tantrisme en chine et au camodge à l'époque de hiuan-tsang," *Journal Asiatique* (Paris) 227 (1935): 84n (my translation from the French).
33. The canonical passages that refer to the king are generally quite short. One of the longest is found in the *Śrī-tattvapradīpa-tantra*, 142b.1–3. See also *Śri-Sahajānandapradīpam-nāma-pañjikā*, 165a.5.
34. The literature on the King Dza myth exhibits some confusion about whether the king received the tantras 112 years or 28 years later. This

is likely due to the similarily between the Tibetan words for "eight" and "one hundred"—*brgyad* and *brgya*. Perhaps the *Gathering of Intentions* itself may be blamed for the confusion, as therein the number appears as a strange mixture of the two readings (*Dgongs pa 'dus pa'i mdo*, 347.3: *lo brgyad dang bcu gnyis*). Nupchen in his commentary uses 28 years (*Mun pa'i go cha*, vol. 50, 14.4: *lo nyi shu rtsa brgyad*). Given the above quotation from Butön, however, it may be that 112 was the earlier Indian number that was later misread by Nupchen and others, though Butön himself also has it as 28 (*Yo ga gru gzings*, 59a.6: *lo nyi shu rtsa brgyad*).

35. *Yo ga gru gzings*, 59a.4–5. For an English translation and discussion of the wider context of this passage, see Karmay, *The Arrow and the Spindle*, 81.
36. Butön does raise the question of the king's proper name, as the King Tsa that appears in this early version of the myth does not match the name King Indrabhūti that is common in the later tantras, with which he is more familiar. Unfortunately, Butön could not locate the **Śrī-samvarodāya-uttaratantra* that purportedly contained the above passage, so he settles on the name Indrabhūti as the more likely historical original, pointing to the next earliest (and extant) source, Jñānamitra's eighth-century commentary to the *Prajñāpāramitānayaśatapaṇcāśataka*, for justification; see *Prajñāpāramitānayaśatapaṇcāśatakaṭikā*, 272b7ff. (For two English translations of the relevant passage, see Davidson, "Indian Esoteric Buddhism," 242–43, and Christian Wedemeyer, *Making Sense of Tantric Buddhism: History, Semiology, and Transgression in the Indian Traditions* [New York: Columbia University Press, 2013], 84. Both scholars include valuable discussions of the legends surrounding Indrabhūti.) Dampa Deshek, a twelfth-century Nyingmapa writer, has Indrabhūti as King Dza's son and first disciple; see his *Legs bshad nyi ma'i snang ba*, 47.6. And the *Sayings of Wa* similarly mentions both kings, i.e., Dharma-Rāja (Ra' dza'), a king of India, and King Indrabhūti of Oḍḍiyāna.
37. Regarding this obviously spurious identification, Karmay, *The Arrow and the Spindle*, 78, writes that "It is fairly certain that King Tsa was known to the author to be connected with the tantric tradition and therefore the reason for identifying him with King Trisong Detsen may have been an effort on the part of the author to glorify the latter's patronage of Buddhism in Tibet." As Karmay also observes in the same article, Pelliot tibétain 1038 similarly identifies the demon (*gnod sbyin*) Dza as one of three progenitors of the first Tibetan king.
38. Yoshiro Imaeda, *Histoire Du Cycle de La Naissance et de La Mort* (Genève; Paris: Libraire Droz, 1981), 305–6, and Karmay, *The Arrow and the Spindle*, 285.

39. *Dgongs pa 'dus pa'i mdo*, 13.4 and 34.5. M. Monier-Williams, *Sanskrit-English Dictionary* (Oxford: Oxford University Press, 1899), 288, glosses *kuñjara* as, "anything pre-eminent in its kind (generally in compound, e.g. *rāja-kuñjara*, 'an eminent king')."
40. *Dgongs pa 'dus pa'i mdo*, 347.4. Note that Dharmaśrī (*Spyi don*, 35.2) names King Dza's father as the king of Zahor in eastern India, King *Utajāna (*za ho ra'i rgyal po u ta dzā na*).
41. The *Gathering of Intentions*' myth appears in the *Pillar Testament*, the *Collected Precepts on Maṇi*, the *Padma Chronicles* (there as Kuñjararāja), and the *Bai ro 'dra 'bag*, as well as in Longchenpa's *Sgrub mtha' mdzod*, the *Klong chen chos 'byung*, the *Mdo sde gdams ngag*, and many others. Per K. Sørensen, *The Mirror Illuminating the Royal Genealogies: Tibetan Buddhist Historiography: An Annotated Translation of the XIVth Century Tibetan Chronicle: rGyal-rabs gsal-ba'i me-long* (Wiesbaden: Harrassowitz Verlag, 1994), 535, discusses some later Tibetan critiques of the myth.
42. See Dalton, *Taming of the Demons*, 226 n. 1. For the later retellings, see Pasang Wangdu and Hildegard Diemberger, *dBa' bzhed: The Royal Narrative Concerning the Bringing of the Buddha's Doctrine to Tibet* (Wien: Verlag der Österreichischen Akademie der Wissenschaften, 2000), 24, and *Bka' chems ka khol ma*, 90–95.
43. Note that the Dunhuang manuscript IOL Tib J 711 includes a similar narrative in which the monk in question achieves a series of seven *samādhis* rather than dreams; for a translation of the relevant passage, see Dalton, *Taming of the Demons*, 62.
44. *Bka' chems ka khol ma*, 94–95.
45. See, for example, Dampa Deshek's *Dgongs 'dus kyi bsdus don*, 62–71.
46. See *Dgongs 'dus kyi bsdus don*, 70.5.
47. The three vehicles referred to here are in fact three sets of three vehicles, known as "the vehicle leading to the source," "the vehicle of awareness through asceticism," and "the vehicle of overpowering means." For more on this triad, see chapter 2 of the present study.
48. I.e., the third set of three vehicles listed in the previous note. As explained below, this third set corresponds to the inner yogas of Mahāyoga, Anuyoga, and Atiyoga. Later writers such as Dharmaśrī (*Spyi don*, 28.2) and Nüden (*Rnal 'byor nyi ma gsal bar byed pa*, vol. 53, 77.2–4) insisted that King Dza must be asking about all six of the tantric vehicles, but this is clearly not the case in the *Gathering of Intentions*, nor in Nupchen's early commentary.
49. *Dgongs pa 'dus pa'i mdo*, 13.3–14.3.

50. The *Gathering of Intentions* lists the ways of arising with slight variations in several places. Chapter 2 (*Dgongs pa 'dus pa'i mdo*, 14.5–15.2) lists them as follows: i) clearing any ignorant longings (ch. 6), ii) establishing the lamp (chs. 7–8), iii) finding certainty (9–14), iv) ascertaining the heart of enlightenment (ch. 15), v) definitively explaining the intention (16–19), vi) descending [to enact] the methods of disciplining (chs. 19–31; i.e., the Rudra-subjugation myth), vii) appearance through empowering (32–35), viii) proclamation of the lineage (36–38), ix) enacting whatever purposes (chs. 39–42), x) teaching the great prophesies (ch. 43), xi) severing the karmic continuum (ch. 44), xii) a complete discussion of the intention (chs. 45–75). These twelve may be based on a similar set found in the root tantra, *Gathering of All Knowledge*, 380.5–7. Though the two lists are quite different, Khenpo Nüden, at the end of his commentary, argues that they can be read as equivalents; see *Rnal 'byor nyi ma gsal bar byed pa*, vol. 56, 697.6–700.1. Nüden, apparently working off some early notes in his possession, also aligns the *Gathering of Intentions*' twelve ways of arising with the twelve deeds of the Buddha (*mdzad pa bcu gnyis*), in a reading that is thought provoking, if somewhat forced. If we accept that the *Gathering of Intentions*' authors intended such a correspondence, then the work's entire structure could be seen as a tantric reading of the twelve deeds.
51. *Dgongs pa 'dus pa'i mdo*, 16.3–5.
52. *Mun pa'i go cha*, vol. 50, 57.3–5. Note that Nupchen's wording here makes it quite clear that he, at least, was concerned to legitimate the tantric teachings by tying them to the historical Buddha through prophecy.
53. Names provided by *Mun pa'i go cha*, vol. 50, 46.6–47.1.
54. *Dgongs pa 'dus pa'i mdo*, 344.7–345.1.
55. *Dgongs pa 'dus pa'i mdo*, 347.3–5. According to the list of the twelve arisings provided above, chapter 43, which contains this prophecy, itself constitutes an entire way of arising, implying that merely by prophesying Secret Mantra, the Buddha was already introducing it into the world.
56. The somewhat unusual fact that the *Gathering of Intentions* has two settings receives much discussion in the commentaries. The first setting, in which the Buddha makes his prophecy, is called "the setting of the transmission prophecy" (*lung bstan brgyud pa'i gleng gzhi*), while the teaching atop Mount Malaya is called "the setting in which the blessings arise" (*byin rlabs 'byung ba'i gleng gzhi*). Nupchen discusses both at length in the introduction to his commentary, *Mun pa'i go cha*, vol. 50, 6–27.
57. *Dgongs pa 'dus pa'i mdo*, 17.5–7. Here we may be seeing evidence of the anxiety expressed by the Buddhist community over the absence of

the Buddha, discussed by Paul M. Harrison, "Buddhānusmṛti in the Pratyutpanna-Buddha-Saṃmukhāvasthita-Samādhi-Sūtra," *Journal of Indian Philosophy* 6 (1978): 37.

58. Nupchen refers to this second of the three transmissions as the *rig 'dzin rig pas brgyud* (*Mun pa'i go cha*, vol. 51, 16.6).
59. Dampa Deshek was clearly aware of the Dza myth's full details; see his *Legs bshad nyi ma'i snang ba*, 47.5, and he was likely repeating the myth as it was told in the early Zur tradition. (The twelfth-century Zur master Dropukpa is cited on this story by Gö Lotsawa in the *Blue Annals*; see George N. Roerich, *The Blue Annals* [Delhi: Motilal Banarsidass, 1976 (1949)], 158–59.) King Dza is also mentioned in another of the four "root sutras" (or tantras) of Anuyoga, the *Dur khrod khu byug rol pa'i rgyud ces bya ba theg pa chen po'i mdo*, 315.6. There, in a long prophecy, Vajrapāṇi is told that "For he who will have gathered the accumulations and be named King Dza, these [textual] compilations of yours will be activated to appear as holy scriptures."
60. *Spyi don*, 35.1–2.
61. *Spyi don*, 37.1.
62. Janet Gyatso, "The Logic of Legitimation in the Tibetan Treasure Tradition," *History of Religions* 33, no. 2 (1993): 112–13, discusses the later Nyingmapa use of the three transmissions to explain their treasure tradition.
63. Many would point to the Rudra myth found in Orgyen Lingpa's fourteenth-century *Padma Chronicles* as the most popular telling, but this version is itself based on the *Gathering of Intentions'* much earlier version.
64. David M. Knipe, "Night of the Growing Dead," in *Criminal Gods and Demon Devotees*, ed. Alf Hiltebeitel (Albany: State University of New York Press, 1989), 138. The edited volume in which this article is contained provides a good introduction into the variety of demon-taming myths and rituals in India, many of which derive from Vedic sources. On early Buddhism's involvements in demons and demon taming from an early point, see also Robert DeCaroli, *Haunting the Buddha: Indian Religions and the Formation of Buddhism* (New York: Oxford University Press, 2004).
65. A. B. Keith, *The Religion and Philosophy of the Veda and Upaniṣads* (Cambridge, MA: Harvard University Press, 1925), 147.
66. Mahadev Chakravarti, *The Concept of Rudra-Śiva Through the Ages* (Delhi: Motilal Banarsidass, 1986), 9.
67. As Chakravarti, *The Concept of Rudra-Śiva*, 20, observes, it also contains the earliest reference to Rudra as the Maheśvara ("Great God"), an epithet also used in some early Buddhist taming myths such as that of the *Sarvatathāgata-tattvasaṃgraha*.

68. Victor Mair, "Śāriputra Defeats the Six Heterodox Masters: Oral-Visual Aspects of an Illustrated Transformation Scroll (P4524)," *Asia Major* (3rd Series) 8, no. 2 (1995): 51–52, has written on the Indian precedents for the story of Śariputra's subjugation of the demon Raudrākṣa that appears in the early fifth-century *Xianyu jing*, a Chinese collection of Buddhist tales. A surprising number of the myth's key elements were in place by this early date. Already Raudrākṣa was a powerful magician and leader of a band of local heretics who required taming before a site could be claimed for a new Buddhist monastery. Several Dunhuang murals depict the tale, all dating from the Northern Zhou to early Tang periods; see Wu Hung, "What Is *Bianxiang*?—On the Relationship Between Dunhuang Art and Dunhuang Literature," *Harvard Journal of Asiatic Studies* 52, no. 1 (1992).
69. Though as Maheśvara's fury increases, he eventually displays his form as Mahāraudra.
70. Davidson, "Reflections on the Maheśvara Subjugation Myth," 203, identifies the *Guhyendutilaka* as the next step after the STTS in this process, which was in turn followed by the **Guhyagarbha-tattvaviniścaya* (where the myth was expanded into a full chapter) and many other tantras. The **Guhyagarbha* rendition, along with Longchenpa's commentary, was first translated by Gyurme Dorje, "The *Guhyagarbhatantra* and Its XIVth Century Tibetan Commentary, *phyogs bcu mun sel*" (Ph.D. diss., University of London, SOAS, 1987) and more recently by Lama Chönam and Sangye Khandro, *The Guhyagarbha Tantra: Secret Essence Definitive Nature Just As It Is* (Ithaca, NY: Snow Lion, 2011). A number of studies have been made of the development of the Rudra myth; see in particular Stein, *Etude du monde chinois* (1972–74), and, "La soumission de Rudra et autres contes tantriques," *Journal Asiatique* 283, no. 1 (1995); Nobumi Iyanaga, "Récits de la soumission de Maheśvara par Trailokyavijaya, d'après les sources chinoises et japonaises," *Tantric and Taoist Studies in Honour of R. A. Stein* (Mélanges Chinois et Bouddhiques Vol. XXII), ed. Michel Strickmann (Bruxelles: Institut Belge des Hautes Études Chinoises, 1985); Davidson, "Reflections on the Maheśvara Subjugation Myth"; Matthew T. Kapstein, "Samantabhadra and Rudra: Innate Enlightenment and Radical Evil in Tibetan Rnying-ma-pa Buddhism," in *Discourse and Practice*, ed. Frank E. Reynolds and David Tracy (Albany: State University of New York Press, 1992).
71. It may be significant that some Indian sources identify Meru and Malaya; see for example the *Mahābhārata* (Pratap Chandra Roy, *The Mahabharata of Krishna-Dwaipayana Vyasa*, 12 vols. [Calcutta: Oriental Publishing Company, 1962–63]: vol. 11, 27). In Tibet too, Khenpo Nüden makes a similar

identification (see *Rnal 'byor nyi ma gsal bar byed pa*, vol. 53, 770.1). The precise location of Mount Malaya depends on which textual system one consults. It has also been obfuscated by the existence of Pullira Malaya, one of India's main *piṭha* sites listed in a number of other tantras. Some scholars (e.g., Nundolal Dey, *The Geographical Dictionary of Ancient and Medieval India* [Delhi: Oriental Books Corporation, 1971 (1927)], 132, and Davidson, *Indian Esoteric Buddhism*, 209) have suggested that Pullira Malaya was a Buddhist name for the Agastya Malai, located at the southernmost end of the western Ghats, and so have placed Mount Malaya in the same location.

To do so, however, contradicts the later Tibetan tradition. Lochen Dharmaśrī, in his late seventeenth-century work (*Spyi don*, 32.3–5), identified the place as follows: "To the southeast of Jambuling, near Bengal, there is a small island previously held by demons known as 'the land of Laṅka.' . . . Later this place was held by the lion (*singha*) leader, and for this reason nowadays it is known as Singhala. . . . Malaya is at the center of the island, which is like four petals of a lotus. In the local tongue it is called Sumanakūṭa." (See too Dudjom Rinpoche, *The Nyingma School of Tibetan Buddhism*, 455, where the author locates Mount Malaya in Sri Lanka.) The Tibetan tradition's claim is supported by the fact that even today the central province of Sri Lanka is called Malaya, and Adam's Peak, otherwise known as Sumanakūṭa, is found in this province.

72. Rāvaṇa also plays a recurring role in the Rudra-taming myth itself. Rāvaṇa is of course best known from the famous epic, the *Rāmāyaṇa* (which did enjoy some popularity in early Tibet; see de Jong, *The Story of Rāma in Tibet*), and to Tibetans in particular from the *Blazing Flames Tantra*, another key early source for Tibetan Buddhist mythological themes (see Stein, *Etude du monde chinois* [1972], 501). Rāvaṇa's role in the *Blazing Flames Tantra* has been recounted by both Giuseppe Tucci, *Tibetan Painted Scrolls*, 3 vols. (Rome: Libreria dello Stato, 1949), 218, and Stein, *Etude du monde chinois* (1974), 516. Tucci has noted that the transliteration of the ten-headed demon ('Dar sha 'gri ba, for the Sanskrit Daśagrīva) and many other names in the *Blazing Flames Tantra* myth mirror those found in the Dunhuang manuscripts. Though this particular name for the Lord of Laṅka is absent in the *Gathering of Intentions* itself, Nupchen uses a similar one in his commentary. His spelling, however (*Mgrin bcu*—see *Mun pa'i go cha*, vol. 50, 14.4 and 29.5), does not match that of the *Blazing Flames*. Thus these two canonical works, the *Blazing Flames* and

the *Gathering of Intentions*, may not have been directly related at their inception, although in later centuries they were woven together in many mythic, ritual, and iconographic settings, perhaps most famously in the fourteenth-century *Bka' thang* literature of Orgyen Lingpa; Stein, *Etude du monde chinois* (1974), 517, points out that the 'Dar sha 'gri ba spelling resurfaced once more in the *Lha 'dre bka' thang* section in particular. It is also perhaps significant that Vajrapāṇi (a major figure in both *Blazing Flames* and the *Gathering of Intentions*), Dud gsol ma (from the *Blazing Flames Tantra*), and Legs ldan Nag po (who is none other than Rudra after he has been tamed in the *Gathering of Intentions*) all appear together in a late thirteenth-century depiction of the protector, Gur gyi Mgon po; on this iconographic trio, see Amy Heller, "Notes on the Symbol of the Scorpion in Tibet," in *Les habitants du Toit du monde*, ed. Samten Karmay and Philippe Sagant (Nanterre: Société d'ethnologie, 1997), 286. Finally, Stein viewed Rāvaṇa as a key figure in the early Bönpo legends. Given that Stein also saw Bönpo influences in the *Gathering of Intentions* (via the person of Chetsenkyé) and that Tucci saw Bönpo influences in the *Blazing Flames Tantra*, one should consider the extent to which early Buddhist-Bon distinctions were blurred, particularly in the arena of myth.

73. On Sri Lanka as a center for tantric Buddhism, see Roger Jackson, "A Tantric Echo in Sinhalese Theravāda: *Pirit* Ritual, the Book of *Paritta* and the *Jinapañjaraya*," *Journal of the Rare Buddhist Texts Research Project* 18 (1994); Lokesh Chandra, "The Contacts of Abhayagiri of Sri Lanka with Indonesia in the Eighth Century," in *Cultural Horizons of India*, vol. 4, ed. Lokesh Chandra (New Delhi: International Academy of Indian Culture and Aditya Prakashan, 1995); Jeffrey R. Sundberg, "The Wilderness Monks of the Abhayagirivihāra and the Origins of Sino-Javanese Esoteric Buddhism," *Bijdragen tot de Taal-, Land- en Volkenkunde* 160, no. 1 (2004); Jeffrey R. Sundberg and Rolf Giebel, "The Life of the Tang Court Monk Vajrabodhi as Chronicled by Lü Xiang: South Indian and Śrī Laṅkān Antecedents to the Arrival of the Buddhist Vajrayāna in Eighth-Century Java and China," *Pacific World Journal* 3, no. 13 (2011); Wedemeyer, *Making Sense of Tantric Buddhism*, 179.

74. Étienne Lamotte, *Saṃdhinirmocana sūtra, l'explication des mystères texte tibétain* (Louvain: Bureaux du Recueil, Bibliothèque de l'Université, 1988), 133–34. The same two chronicles (*Dīpavaṃsa*, ch. 1–2; *Mahāvaṃsa*, ch. 1) also tell of three visits that Śākyamuni pays to the island. On his first two visits, the Buddha tames and converts the *nāga*s of Laṅka, and on the

third he goes with 500 monks to stay atop Mount Sumanakūṭa, where he leaves his footprint on a rock (see Lamotte, *Saṃdhinirmocana sūtra*, 135).

75. See Samuel Beal, *Buddhist Records of the Western World* (New Delhi: Munshiram Manoharlal Publishers, 1983 [1884]), lxxii–llxxvi and II, 235–53. The Sri Lankan legends may have been pertinent for the *Gathering of Intentions*' authors for another reason: by the eighth century, principal control of Mount Sumanakūṭa had fallen to the Śaivas of Sri Lanka. The famous footprint was claimed as a print of Śiva, and new legends began to spread of the Sri Lankan king being converted once again, this time from Buddhism to Śaivism (see William Skeen, *Adam's Peak: Legendary, Traditional, and Historic Notices of the Samanala and Srī-pāda* [New Delhi: Asian Educational Services, 1997 (1870)], 35–36).
76. For a summary of the narrative, see Dalton, *Taming of the Demons*, 19–22, and for the complete English translation, see appendix A to the same study.
77. Dalton, *Taming of the Demons*, 163.
78. *Dgongs pa 'dus pa'i mdo*, 353.1–354.1. Bracketed additions largely based on Nupchen's *Mun pa'i go cha*, vol. 50, 516.3–4.
79. *Dgongs pa 'dus pa'i mdo*, 172. 4.
80. The *Gathering of Intentions*' position vis-à-vis this triad of Mahāyoga, Anuyoga, and Atiyoga is a complex issue that will be treated in chapter 2 of the present study.
81. *Dgongs pa 'dus pa'i mdo*, 233.6–234.1. The five yogas are as follows: the yoga of aspiration (*'dun pa'i sems pa'i rnal 'byor*), the yoga of opening the great lineage (*rigs chen 'byed pa*), the yoga of the great encouragement (*dbugs chen 'byin pa*), the yoga of attaining the great prophecy (*lung chen thob pa*), the yoga of perfecting the great dynamism (*rtsal chen rdzogs pa*). The number of yogas can be expanded, for practitioners of high, middling, or low capacity, to five, ten, or forty. The whole system is most extensively worked out in chapter 61, where all forty yogas are presented according to their correspondence to the ten levels. Dharmaśrī's *Spyi don*, 146–48, lists several conflicting opinions on how the various initiations correspond to the five yogas.
82. Listed as follows: i) *'gyur ba ma nges pa'i sa*, ii) *brten pa gzhi'i sa*, iii) *gal chen sbyong ba'i sa*, iv) *bslab pa rgyun gyi sa*, v) *bsod nams rten gyi sa*, vi) *brten pas khyad par du 'gro ba'i sa*, vii) *'bras bu skye ba'i sa*, viii) *gnas pa mi 'gyur ba'i sa*, ix) *brdal ba chos nyid*, x) *rdzogs pa ci chibs kyi sa*. The correspondence between levels and yogas is also found in chapter 61, *Dgongs pa 'dus pa'i mdo*, 471. These levels and the yogas also appear in the other four root

sutras of Anuyoga. In the root tantra, the *Gathering of All Knowledge*, for example, they are listed at the end of chapter 1.

83. *Mun pa'i go cha*, vol. 50, 255.4–5.
84. See *Dgongs pa 'dus pa'i mdo*, 77.1–78.1, combined with Dampa's explanation of the passage in his *Rdo rje'i tha ram 'byed pa'i lde'u mig*, 238.2–3.
85. Compared to some of the *Gathering of Intentions*' other doctrines, these two sets of paths and levels seem to have had relatively little influence upon the wider Tibetan tradition (compared to its Rudra myth, three transmissions, nine vehicles, Tshogs chen 'dus pa festival, and so forth), yet for many of the tradition's present-day scholars, they constitute the entirety of what is known about the *Gathering of Intentions*. In today's Nyingma monastic colleges (*bshad grwa*), these ten levels and five yogas are taught in the context of the *Three Vows* by Ngari Paṇchen. One graduate of the Nyingma Institute in Bylakuppe, South India, told me that the impression left upon him was of a strange system bearing no resemblance to the rest of Nyingma doctrine. Today's rote study of these levels and paths (*sa lam*) categories amounts to a strangely empty tribute to a text whose true influences upon the Nyingma School have been largely forgotten.
86. Chapter 4 of this study addresses the details of the initiation ceremony.
87. See Dharmaśrī's *Spyi don*, 139.3. Dharmaśrī notes an opening prayer from an unspecified initiation ritual manual (*dbang chog*) that links the precedent initiations to the subsequent initiations: "Just as the great beings of the highest level made offerings and requests to the Buddha Vajradhāra" (*Spyi don*, 141.6).
88. *Mun pa'i go cha*, vol. 50, 158. The *Sarvatathāgata-tattvasaṃgraha* and the *Guhyasamāja* tradition tell a similar story of the Buddha's enlightenment in terms of various consecrations; see Alex Wayman and Ferdinand D. Lessing, trans., *Mkhas grub rje's Fundamentals of the Buddhist Tantras* (Delhi: Motilal Banarsidass, 1978), 35–39.
89. The maṇḍala's structure is described in *Dgongs pa 'dus pa'i mdo*, 554.4–7.
90. See *Mun pa'i go cha*, vol. 51, 451.4 and 453.1, where Nupchen points this out.
91. *Mun pa'i go cha*, vol. 50, 287.5–288.2.
92. *Dgongs pa 'dus pa'i mdo*, 192.1–2. The awkward-sounding translation, "in the time of that temporality" (*de'i tshe de'i dus na*) may require some explanation: this phrase is found throughout the Rudra-taming myth, and Nupchen makes much of it in his *Armor Against Darkness* commentary, repeatedly drawing attention to the fact that the entire story takes place in the fourth time that is beyond yet inseparable from the ordinary times

of past, present, and future. I have chosen to translate it in the way I have in order to reflect Nupchen's reading.

93. *Mun pa'i go cha*, vol. 50, 287.3–4.
94. *Mun pa'i go cha*, vol. 50, 288.3.
95. *Mun pa'i go cha*, vol. 50, 288.2–3. I have taken some liberties with my translation, in order to clarify the meaning. The Tibetan reads as follows: *de dag ni thog ma dang tha ma med par smos pa las 'dir 'das pa'i dus btul ba dang / gsang ba 'byung ba dang gsungs pa'i lo rgyus smos pa dus 'dir yang 'byung ste / de dag dus gcig pa.*
96. It may be no coincidence that the *Gathering of Intentions*' original recipient, the Lord of Lanka, is also included within Rudra's horde at the time that the horde is subjugated and taught the tantra. In this sense, every time Secret Mantra arises, the recipient is also a demon being violently subjugated by a wrathful *heruka* atop Mount Malaya.

2. THE *GATHERING OF INTENTIONS* IN EARLY TIBETAN TANTRA

1. For more on Nupchen's role during this period, see Jacob Dalton, *Taming of the Demons: Violence and Liberation in Tibetan Buddhism* (New Haven: Yale University Press, 2011), 49–54. The other major early Tibetan exegete of the tantras to have received some recent scholarly attention is Ba/Nyen Pelyang, on whom, see Kammie Takahashi, "Rituals and Philosophical Speculation in the *Rdo rje sems dpa'i zhus lan*," in *Esoteric Buddhism at Dunhuang: Rites and Teachings for This Life and Beyond*, ed. Matthew T. Kapstein and S. van Schaik (Leiden: Brill, 2010), and "Contribution, Attribution, and Selective Lineal Amnesia in the Case of Mahāyogin dPal dbyangs," *Revue d'Etudes Tibétaines* 32 (2015).
2. On Nupchen's dates, see Roberto Vitali, *The Kingdoms of Gu.ge Pu.hrang* (Dharamsala, India: Tho.ling gtsug.lag.khang lo.gcig.stong 'khor.ba'i rjes. dran.mdzad sgo'i go.sgrig tshogs.chung, 1996), 546–47.
3. For more on Nupchen's role in the later Nyingmapa imagination, see Jacob Dalton, "Preliminary Remarks on a Newly Discovered Biography of Gnubs chen sangs rgyas ye shes," in *Himalayan Passages: Tibetan and Newar Studies in Honor of Hubert Decleer*, ed. Benjamin Bogin and Andrew Quintman (Somerville, MA: Wisdom, 2014).
4. On Nupchen's stated purpose for composing the *Lamp*, see Jacob Dalton and Sam van Schaik, "Lighting the Lamp: An Examination of the Structure of the Bsam gtan mig sgron," *Acta Orientalia* 64 (2003).

5. For several examples, see Jacob Dalton, "A Crisis of Doxography: How Tibetans Organized Tantra During the 8th–12th Centuries," *Journal of the International Association of Buddhist Studies* 28, no. 1 (2005): 147–51.
6. For discussion of this "natural" vehicle, see *Compendium of Intentions*, 349.1–350.7. Khenpo Nüden (*Rnal 'byor nyi ma gsal bar byed pa*, vol. 54, 464.6–476.5) explains that this vehicle functions simultaneously on five levels, listed in order of increasing subtlety. First, because all things come from the five physical elements, the buddhas are arising all the time as whatever is wanted. Second, space provides the opening for everything else; earth gives a firm ground for beings and plants; water is pliant, clear, constantly flowing, and quenching; fire is warm, bright, and rising upward; wind is unobstructed, unabiding, formless, powerful, and scattering. Third, each element brings beings to enlightenment: space is the all-pervading opening for appearance and emptiness; earth is everywhere in the sphere of Mahāyāna; water is pure calm abiding; fire is insight; wind scatters the objects of consciousness. Fourth, these five elements can also be experienced as the five primordial buddhas. And fifth, the final characteristic that is most useful in all five elements: nothing is really happening, so everything is already enlightened.
7. For the relevant passage, see *Dgongs pa 'dus pa' mdo*, 351.1–352.6. The Tibetan for the three vehicles discussed in this paragraph is: *kun 'byung 'dren pa' theg pa; dka' thub rig byed theg pa; dbang bsgyur thabs kyi theg pa.*
8. Samten Karmay, *The Arrow and the Spindle: Studies in History, Myth, Rituals and Beliefs in Tibet* (Kathmandu: Mandala Book Point, 1998), 148, and Sam van Schaik, "The Early Days of the Great Perfection," *Journal of the International Association of Buddhist Studies* 27, no. 1 (2004): 187–89, raise the issue of when exactly Atiyoga became an independent vehicle. Nupchen refers to it as a vehicle in his *Lamp for the Eyes in Contemplation*, but van Schaik argues that such references are "haphazard" and that Nupchen's earlier presentation of the nine "vehicles" in his *Armor Against Darkness* does not refer to Atiyoga as a vehicle at all (see earlytibet.com/2011/08/03/early-dzogchen-iv/). The latter point is not entirely true, as seen, for example, in *Mun pa'i go cha*, vol. 50, 135.1, where Nupchen refers to the "nine vehicles"; vol. 51, 6.4, where he refers to "the vehicle of Atiyoga pith instructions"; and vol. 51, 158.4, where he explains that the Great Perfection's "illumination of suchness within awareness is not an object [of meditation] for other vehicles." Such references indicate that Atiyoga was well on its way to becoming a vehicle by the mid-to-late ninth century. We may also observe, contra van Schaik and Karmay, that even

some Tibetan Buddhists working at Dunhuang did see the nine vehicles as vehicles; see for example Pelliot tibétain 322, 4–5: "Having opened his nine eyes, his wrathful gaze has the aspect of displaying the distinctions between the nine vehicles." The very fact that Atiyoga appears in the nine-vehicle schemes alongside the well-known *vehicles* of the Śrāvakas, Pratyekabuddhas, and Bodhisattvas seems to reflect a willingness on the part of many early Tibetans (and perhaps Indians) to see it as a vehicle. The gradual overall shift that took place over the course of the ninth century, from the Great Perfection as a ritual stage or interpretive register still tied to Mahāyoga to the Great Perfection/Atiyoga as its own vehicle with a distinct approach, reflected the development of a new rhetorical (and perhaps practical) space within early Tibetan Buddhist discourse, and in this sense the question of when the Great Perfection/Atiyoga became a vehicle is an important one. However, by the end of the ninth century, the issue is more how remarkably inchoate the concept of a tantric "vehicle" still was. The *Gathering of Intentions* and Nupchen's *Armor Against Darkness* demonstrate extraordinarily flexible (if not ill-thought-out) notions of "vehicles" in their treatments of Mahāyoga, Anuyoga, and Atiyoga as simultaneously distinct and intimately connected (vis-à-vis the three aspects of "Secret Mantra") vehicles.

9. See *Rdo rje'i tha ram 'byed pa' lde'u mig*, 238.2, for proof that Dam pa bde gshegs considered the *Gathering of Intentions* a work of Anuyoga, and the offhandedness of his remark implies he is repeating an already well-established classification.
10. Nor, for that matter, does the root tantra of Anuyoga, the *Gathering of All Knowledge*; see, for example, 67a.4, where the yoga of the Great Perfection is mentioned.
11. *Dgongs pa 'dus pa'i mdo*, 135.1.
12. This key Tibetan term for the highest class of Buddhist tantras is almost always reconstructed as *Anuttarayoga, but this appears to be a mistake; see Harunaga Isaacson, "Tantric Buddhism in India (from c. A.D. 800 to c. A.D. 1200)," in *Buddhismus in Geschichte und Gegenwart* (Hamburg: Internal publication of Hamburg University, 2010), and Dalton, "A Crisis of Doxography," 152 n. 84, 160–61. The actual term seen most commonly in the Sanskrit sources that is rendered into Tibetan as *Rnal 'byor bla na med pa* is Yoganiruttara.
13. *Sdom gsum rab dbye*, as transliterated in Sakya Pandita Kun dga' rgyal mtshan, *A Clear Differentiation of The Three Codes*, trans. Jared Douglas Rhoton (Albany: State University of New York Press, 2002), 309.

14. See van Schaik, "The Early Days of the Great Perfection," and for a summary of his findings, see 92.
15. Here I do not mean to overlook the fact that certain key Mahāyoga tantras had previously been considered Yoga tantras, e.g. the famous *Guhyasamāja Tantra*, which appeared among both the eighteen Vajroṣṇīṣa (Yoga) tantras and the eighteen Māyājāla (Mahāyoga) tantras. Some of these tantras that were upgraded may have had their contents updated too (the *Guhyasamāja*), others may not have (the *Śrī-Paramādya* and the *Nāmasaṃgīti*). Nonetheless, even those whose contents remained largely unchanged between classifications were subjected to new interpretations that brought them more into line with the Mahāyoga exegetical perspective. Thus the *Nāmasaṃgīti*, for example, has extant commentaries written in both Yoga and Mahāyoga styles; see Ronald M. Davidson, "The Litany of Names of Mañjuśrī," *Mélanges chinois et bouddhiques* 20 (1981): 15.
16. From the sacramental procedures of early Mahāyoga (late eighth c.) and the dying processes of the *Guhyasamāja*'s later interpreters (ninth and tenth c.) to the subtle-body systems of the *Hevajra* (tenth c.) and the visionary procedures of the *Kālacakra* (eleventh c.), all these practices were to be performed within the context of the perfection stage.
17. Added on the basis of *Rnal 'byor nyi ma gsal bar byed pa*, vol. 54, 487.6.
18. *Mun pa'i go cha*, vol. 50, 509.5–510.4. This does not appear to be one of the ten levels of the *Gathering of Intentions*' ritual system, but it is the name for the fifth of the five yogas in that system (*rtsal chen rdzogs pa'i rnal 'byor*). In his *General Exposition* (*Spyi don*, 16), Lochen Dharmaśrī explains that this fifth yoga is equivalent to the eighth to tenth levels, which might imply that Mahāyoga is supposed to result in the eighth level, Anuyoga in the ninth, and Atiyoga in the tenth.
19. Most famously seen in the *Pith Instructional Garland of Views*, attributed to Padmasambhava; see Dalton, "A Crisis of Doxography," 132–34.
20. Nupchen's *Armor Against Darkness* makes no mention of any particular connection between the *Gathering of Intentions* and the class of Anuyoga tantras. His *Lamp for the Eyes in Contemplation* includes sections on Mahāyoga and Atiyoga, but no Anuyoga, despite the fact that the same work's two most-cited sources are the *Gathering of Intentions* and the *Gathering of All Knowledge* (cited twenty-five times under the title *Rnal 'byor grub pa'i lung*, and twenty-three times under the title *Rdo rje bkod pa*, respectively).
21. *Mun pa'i go cha*, vol. 50, 510.4–511.3.

22. Namkhai Norbu, *Sbas pa'i rgum chung, The Small Collection of Hidden Precepts: A Study of an Ancient Manuscript on Dzogchen from Tun-huang* (Arcidosso, Italy: Shang-Shung Edizioni, 1984), 32–33.
23. *Dgongs pa 'dus pa'i mdo*, 414.5–7.
24. *Rnal 'byor nyi ma gsal bar byed pa*, vol. 55, 157.5–6.
25. In Dalton, *Taming of the Demons*, 275 n. 194, I neglected to edit out an old note suggesting that Nupchen himself interprets another passage "in terms of subtle body practices." In fact, this is not the case, and Nupchen has little to say about the passage in question.
26. Here I am thinking more of the *Hevajra*-style up-and-down movement of winds through an elaborate system of channels. My statement here excludes, of course, the fairly advanced circulations of the breath that appear in the *Guhyasamāja*-related materials, some of which date from the late eighth or ninth centuries (on which, see Christian K. Wedemeyer, *Āryadeva's* Lamp That Integrates the Practices *(*Caryāmelāpakapradīpa*)* (New York: The American Institute of Buddhist Studies, 2007), 88–95 and 175–205.
27. On this period, see Jacob Dalton, "The Development of Perfection: The Interiorization of Buddhist Ritual in the Eighth and Ninth Centuries," *Journal of Indian Philosophy* 32, no. 1 (2004), or better yet, Harunaga Isaacson, "Observations on the Development of the Ritual of Initiation (*Abhiṣeka*) in the Higher Buddhist Tantric Systems," in *Hindu and Buddhist Initiations in India and Nepal*, ed. Astrid Zotter and Christof Zotter (Wiesbaden, Germany: Harrassowitz Verlag).
28. For more on the Sutra Initation system, see chapter 4.
29. *Bstam gtan mig sgron*, 222.5–6. This line ends a highly significant passage for the study of the history of subtle body practice, as it appears to reflect a period of innovation that predates the compilation of the tenth-century *Hevajra Tantra* and other canonical sources that describe the techniques more explicitly. For a complete translation and discussion of the relevant passages in the *Lamp*, see my forthcoming book on tantric ritual manuals from Dunhuang.
30. *Dgongs pa 'dus pa' mdo*, 440.3–4.
31. Approximately the same lines appear in today's *Kun byed rgyal po*, 36a.5–6. It is also cited in the seventh chapter (on the Great Perfection) of Nupchen's *Bstam gtan mig sgron*, 295.3–4, where it is both attributed to the same *Great Sky of Vajrasattva* and accompanied by a similar comment; compare the present lines (*tha snyad tsam du grol zhes kyang bya ste/ de la bcings pa'i chos ma dmigs pa'i phyir ro*) to those in the *Lamp for the Eyes in*

Contemplation (rtog dpyod las 'das pa la bcings pa nyid ma dmigs pa'i phyir tha snyad tsam du grol zhes bya'o). This parallel increases the likelihood that the two works were indeed written by the same author. While it remains difficult, given the paucity of sources from tenth-century central Tibet, to prove conclusively that the *Armor Against Darkness* was written by the same author as the *Lamp for the Eyes in Contemplation*, the case is helped by the fact that the next earliest major author whose works survive, Katok Dampa Deshek, lists the *Armor Against Darkness* in his *Mdo phran khog dbub*, 6.

32. *Mun pa'i go cha*, vol. 50, 511.4–512.6.
33. *Mun pa'i go cha*, vol. 51, 48.4.
34. David Germano, "Architecture and Absence in the Secret Tantric History of the Great Perfection," *Journal of the International Association of Buddhist Studies* 17, no. 2 (1994): 209.
35. Germano, "Architecture and Absence," 223.
36. Van Schaik, "The Early Days of the Great Perfection," 170–75.
37. Dalton, "The Development of Perfection," 17–21.
38. *Mun pa'i go cha*, vol. 51, 38.3–6. Nupchen's discussion of the gradual approach begins on vol. 51, 25.3, and of the immediate on 38.4.
39. *Dgongs pa 'dus pa'i mdo*, 409.1–2.
40. *Mun pa'i go cha*, vol. 51, 25.6–26.3. See also Nüden's *Rnal 'byor nyi ma gsal bar byed pa*, vol. 55, 119.2–121.1. Nüden cites a closely related passage from the *Gathering of All Knowledge*, 403.5–7; see *Rnal 'byor nyi ma gsal bar byed pa*, vol. 55, 121.2–4. Having withdrawn from the afflicted mind, the passage says, "One blocks the cracks and openings and destroys the empty house piece by piece, whereupon the king's treasury is opened." If we read the empty house as the foundation consciousness, we might interpret the passage to mean that this eighth consciousness eventually collapses to reveal the mind of enlightenment. (The latter lines are corrupt in the Mtshams brag edition of the *Rnying ma rgyud 'bum*; compare both *Rnal 'byor nyi ma gsal bar byed pa* and the Sde dge edition of the Tibetan canon; see Hakuju Ui et al., eds., *A Complete Catalogue of the Tibetan Buddhis Canons [Bka'-'gyur and Bstan-'gyur]* [Sendai: Tōhoku Imperial University, 1934], 831, 27b.6–7.)
41. *Mun pa'i go cha*, vol. 51, 53.2.
42. *Mun pa'i go cha*, vol. 51, 58.3.
43. As cited by David F. Germano and William S. Waldron, "A Comparison of *Ālaya-vijñāna* in Yogācāra and Dzogchen," in *Buddhist Thought and Applied Psychological Research: Transcending the Boundaries*, ed. D. K. Nauriyal, M. S. Drummond, and Y. B. Lal (London and New York: Routledge, 2006), 46.

44. *Mun pa'i go cha*, vol. 51, 59.2–5. The crucial term Nupchen uses here—"the genuine foundation of unification"—does appear in at least three closely related Dunhuang manuscripts (Pelliot tibétain 654, IOL Tib J 681, and IOL Tib J 708) that contain what seem to be merely sutra-based discussions of the foundation consciousness. There, it appears as one of two kinds of *ālaya*: "the genuine foundation of the ground" (*gzhi don gyi kun gzhi*) and "the genuine foundation of unification (*sbyor ba'i don gyi kun gzhi*). Pelliot tibétain 654, 1 v. 5 even identifies the "root consciousness" (*rtsa ba'i rnam par shes pa*) as another word for the foundation conscousness, which is of some interest because Nupchen and the *Gathering of Intentions* use the same metaphor of the root to describe the awakened foundation. In this way too, Nupchen's account of Atiyoga appears to share much with the kinds of exoteric discussions of Buddhist meditation that were typical in Tibet in his day.
45. A similar view appears to have been held by at least some Tibetan *tāntrika*s of the age of fragmentation. A short Dunhuang ritual text based on the *Sarvatathāgata-tattvasaṃgraha*, for example, in listing the possible outcomes of a certain meditation, includes the following intriguing line: "If one [cultivates like that] for seven months to a year, the foundation consciousness will come to touch the *dharmadhātu*" (IOL Tib J 447/3, r28.9–10: *zla ba bdun tsam 'am lo gcig tsam gyis ni kun gzhi rnam par shes pa chos kyi dbyings la reg par 'gyur te*). In some ways, Nupchen's position here is similar to that of the third Karmapa, Rangjung Dorje (1284–1339), who some four centuries later would advocate an enlightened "foundation" (*kun gzhi*) distinct from the mundane "foundation consciousness" of the Yogācāra; see Klaus-Dieter Mathes, *A Direct Path to the Buddha Within* (Somerville: Wisdom, 2008), 57. David Higgins has noted that the Nupchen-attributed commentary to the Great Perfection Mind Class (*sems sde*) tantra, the *Rtse mo byung rgyal*, which is found in the *Greatly Expanded Spoken Teachings*, "clearly identifies this [ultimate] *kun gzhi* [i.e., *ālaya*] as a ninth consciousness that is distinct from the *ālayavijñāna*," which is termed "the ninth genuine all-ground that is the ground itself" (*gzhi don gyi kun gzhi dgu pa*); David Higgins, *The Philosophical Foundations of Classical Rdzogs chen in Tibet: Investigating the Distinction Between Dualistic Mind* (sems) *and Primordial Knowing* (ye shes) (Vienna: Arbeitskreis für Tibetische und Buddhistische Studien Universität Wien 2013), 179 [my additions]. However, despite the significance of the foundation in some of Nupchen's writings, the *Armor Against Darkness* foremost, the term plays only a slight role in his somewhat later *Lamp for the Eyes in Meditation*.

46. *Mun pa'i go cha*, vol. 51, 26.6–27.1.
47. According to an alternate scheme, Nupchen adds, one might fall into a particular meditative state, ranging from those of heretics, the *dhyānas*, up through the lower vehicles of the Śrāvakas, the Pratyekabuddhas, and the Vijñānavādins (see *Mun pa'i go cha*, vol. 51, 28.1–6).
48. *Mun pa'i go cha*, vol. 51, 30.4–6.
49. *Mun pa'i go cha*, vol. 51, 34.1–3.
50. *Dgongs 'dus kyi bsdus don*, 146.2.
51. *Mun pa'i go cha*, vol. 51, 35.3–4.
52. *Rnal 'byor nyi ma gsal bar byed pa*, vol. 55, 136.6 and 137.3–5, provides alternative interpretations of the same five signs.
53. *Mun pa'i go cha*, vol. 51, 37.1.
54. *Mun pa'i go cha*, vol. 50, 513.4–6.
55. *Mun pa'i go cha*, vol. 51, 158.4–5.
56. Elsewhere, David Germano, "The Funerary Transformation of the Great Perfection (*Rdzogs chen*)," *Journal of the International Association of Tibetan Studies* 1 (2005): 3, distinguishes between the early "pristine" and the later "funerary" brands of the Great Perfection. While Nupchen's writings support such a distinction in the ways outlined above, his account of Atiyoga in chapter 55 includes an extended discussion of the dying process, the bardo, and rebirth (see *Mun pa'i go cha*, vol. 51, 112–35). A few pages later (vol. 51, 118.6–119.3), Nupchen emphasizes the importance of yogins preparing for death by practicing the "dying *samādhi*" (*'chi ka'i ting nge 'dzin*). Intriguingly, he also mentions that the relevant "pith instructions on dying" (*'chi ka'i man ngag*) "should be understood from the mouth of one's lama" (compare too Nupchen's summary of Mahāyoga practice in *Bstam gtan mig sgron*, 26.1, where he refers to the *'da' ka'i man ngag*). Nupchen, at least, was already associating such "funerary" theories and practices with Mahāyoga and the Great Perfection in the late ninth century. The *Gathering of Intentions* and Nupchen's use of the eight consciousnesses to structure their explanations of Great Perfection meditation similarly anticipates the later Seminal Heart discussions, a point explicitly recognized by *Rnal 'byor nyi ma gsal bar byed pa*, vol. 55, 189.2–3.
57. On Buddhaguhya's account of these two earliest tantric classes, see Dalton, "A Crisis of Doxography," 121–24.

3. THE SPOKEN TEACHINGS

1. *Mdo dbang brgyud pa'i rnam thar*, 185.6.

2. See Zurham Śākya Jungné's roughly fourteenth-century *Gtad rgya lnga'i go don gyi brjed byang gi 'grel pa*, 165.2, and, probably based on that, the parallel passage in Lochen Dharmaśrī's *Spyi don*, 67.6. On dating the former work, see Jacob Dalton, "Lost and Found: A Fourteenth-Century Discussion of Then-Available Sources on gNubs chen sangs rgyas ye shes," *Bulletin of Tibetology (Special Issue, Nyingma Studies)* 50, no. 1 (2014): 39–53.
3. Ronald M. Davidson, *Tibetan Renaissance* (New York: Columbia University Press, 2005), 213.
4. For more on treasure revelation in the Nyingma School, see Janet Gyatso, "The Logic of Legitimation in the Tibetan Treasure Tradition," *History of Religions* 33, no. 2 (1993): 97–134, and Robert Mayer, "Scriptural Revelation in India and Tibet: Indian Precursors of the gTer-ma Tradition," *Tibetan Studies: Proceedings of the 6th Seminar of the International Association for Tibetan Studies Fagernes 1992*, vol. 2, ed. Per Kvaerne (Oslo: Institute for Comparative Research in Human Culture, 1994).
5. The *All-Creating King* is traditionally held to be foremost among the Mind Class tantras. David F. Germano, "Architecture and Absence in the Secret Tantric History of the Great Perfection," *Journal of the International Association of Buddhist Studies* 17, no. 2 (1994): 235, has observed that it could not have been composed before the late tenth century, but whether it was composed before, during, or after Zurché's lifetime remains unclear. Given that it is condemned as apocryphal by King Jangchup Ö of western Tibet in his famous late-eleventh-century edict (see Samten Karmay, *The Arrow and the Spindle: Studies in History, Myth, Rituals and Beliefs in Tibet* [Kathmandu: Mandala Book Point, 1998], 17–40) and that the edict claims that it was composed at Khro gangs in Upper Nyang (precisely where the early Zurs were active), it is quite possible that the early Zurs were involved with the work at some point early in its existence. On Jangchup Ö's claim, see too Christopher Wilkinson, "The *Mi nub rgyal mtshan Nam mkha' che* and *the Mahā Ākāśa Kārikās: Origins and Authenticity*," *Revue d'Etudes Tibétaines* 24 (2012): 33.
6. *Spyi don*, 67.4–6. See also the earlier but similar passage in Zurham's *Gtad rgya lnga'i go don gyi brjed byang gi 'grel pa*, 165.5.
7. This is not to say that the Zurs were not otherwise involved in treasure revelations. In Jacob Dalton, "Preliminary Remarks on a Newly Discovered Biography of Gnubs chen sangs rgyas ye shes," in *Himalayan Passages: Tibetan and Newar Studies in Honor of Hubert Decleer*, ed. Benjamin E. Bogin and Andrew Quintman (Somerville, MA: Wisdom, 2014), I suggest that they may have taken a particular interest in the treasures of Gya Zhang-

trom (supposedly concealed by Nupchen), a treasure revealer who lived and worked in close proximity to the stronghold of the early Zur.

8. Such disagreements *might* have been behind Lharjé Yangkhyé's criticisms of Rongzom Paṇḍita (see Dudjom Rinpoche, *The Nyingma School of Tibetan Buddhism*, trans. Gyurme Dorje [Boston: Wisdom, 1991], 708). As we shall see below, Lharjé Yangkhyé appears to have been associated with the early Zurs.
9. Karmay, *The Arrow and the Spindle*, 30 and 38.
10. See, for example, *Mdo dbang brgyud pa'i rnam thar*, 229–31 and 237.
11. One particularly well-documented example is the case of Drokmi Lotsawa, who (with Zurché's financial help) paid 500 ounces of gold to the Indian Gayadhara so that the latter would never transmit the *Path and Result* teachings to any other Tibetan; see Cyrus Stearns, *Luminous Lives* (Boston: Wisdom, 2001), 93 and Davidson, *Tibetan Renaissance*, 165–69.
12. On the composition of the *All-Creating King*, see Samten Karmay, *The Great Perfection* (Leiden: Brill, 1988), 207, and Germano, "Architecture and Absence," 235–36. On the **Guhyagarbha*, see Davidson, *Tibetan Renaissance*, 153, and on the *Gathering of Intentions*, see chapter 1 of the present study.
13. One exception is *Zurchungpa's Testament*, a translation of which has recently been published (Dilgo Khyentse Rinpoche, *Zurchungpa's Testament*, trans. The Padmakara Translation Group [Ithaca, NY: Snow Lion, 2006]), but there is little of historical value in this short and largely doctrinal work. Biographies of all three Zur patriarchs are included in the *Mdo dbang brgyud pa'i rnam thar*, 185–253, but they focus primarily on the miraculous doings of these three figures and say little about their writings or the contents of their teachings. On the "way of the Zur" (*zur lugs*) more generally, we have the relatively late *Zur lugs gsang snying yig cha'i skor* and Nathaniel D. Garson, "Context and Philosophy in the Mahāyoga System of rNying-ma Tantra" (Ph.D. diss., University of Virginia, 2004).
14. *Mdo dbang brgyud pa'i rnam thar*, 201.6.
15. Here I am following the 1996 biography, *Rgyal ba kaḥ thog pa'i lo rgyus mdor bsdus*. Dudjom, *The Nyingma School of Tibetan Buddhism*, provides the slightly different spelling for Dampa's father's name: *Sga rigs gtsang pa Dpal sgra*.
16. There is some confusion among the sources regarding Dampa's relationship to Pakmo Drüpa, the great student of Gampopa. *Rgyal ba kaḥ thog pa'i lo rgyus mdor bsdus*, 20, concludes that "In some earlier histories Pakmo Drüpa is said to be [Dampa's] maternal cousin. However, on this point I take as the authoritative source the *Grub mchog rjes dran*, a biography

by Dampa Rinpoché's direct disciple, Gelong Dingpopa." Dingpopa's early biography has Dampa and Pakmo Drüpa as brothers, but Pakmo's own biographies do not bear this out. It was perhaps for this reason that later sources (including Dudjom, *The Nyingma School of Tibetan Buddhism*, 689) downgraded the relationship to cousins. (My thanks to Jann Ronis for his views on this point. Ronis's forthcoming monograph on the history of Katok monastery will add much to my own sketchy notes on Dampa and his legacy.)

17. Katok monastery would eventually become a Nyingma institution, but Dampa studied widely, even for his day, and he appears to have held Cakrasaṃvara particularly close. This is not surprising given his Kagyu ties to both Pakmo Drüpa and the first Karmapa, Düsum Khyenpa.
18. *Rgyal ba kaḥ thog pa'i lo rgyus mdor bsdus*, 21. Around this time, the Mi nyag (Tanguts) were under attack from all sides, from the Tibetans, the Chinese, and (ultimately) the Mongols. On the Mi nyag (or Xi xia) dynasty, see Elliot Sperling, "Miscellaneous Remarks on the Lineage of Byang La-stod," partial version published in *Zhongguo Zangxue*, special issue (1992).
19. *Dam pa bde gshegs kyi rnam thar bsdus pa*, 9b.6–10a.1; see also *Rgyal ba kaḥ thog pa'i lo rgyus mdor bsdus*, 22. For other Nyingma teachings he received from his teacher Jangchup Sengé, see *Dam pa bde gshegs kyi rnam thar bsdus pa*, 8b.5–9a.5.
20. In his *Thob yig gang+ga'i chu rgyun*, the Fifth Dalai Lama claims that Dampa also studied directly under Zur Śākya Sengé himself. He may have contended this because Dampa so often cites Śākya Sengé's oral teachings (*Lha rje sgro phug pa'i zhal nas . . .*) as the final arbiter on various points of controversy. However, if the commonly held dates for the two lamas are accepted (1074–1134 for Śākya Sengé and 1122–1192 for Dampa), a direct relationship seems unlikely, particularly given that Dampa supposedly spent his youth studying in Kham. The Great Fifth's suggestion also contradicts the lineage traced by Dampa himself (*Legs bshad nyi ma'i snang ba*, 49.5), in which he states that he studied under Dropukpa's two students, Lharjé Mar and Tsangpa. Lharjé Mar may be the same as Dzamtön, though only because both are said to be Dampa's main teacher for the *Gathering of Intentions*. Dampa's other teacher, whom he calls only Tsangpa, could be Tsangpa Jitön, who is named as one of Dropukpa's disciples in Dudjom, *The Nyingma School of Tibetan Buddhism*, 649. But neither Lharjé Mar/Dzamtön nor Tsangpa appears in Pema Trinlé's *Biographies for the Sutra Initiation Lineage*. In fact, the Katok tradition is completely omit-

ted from this much later work, as discussed in more detail in chapter 5 of the present study.

21. *Rgyal ba kaḥ thog pa'i lo rgyus mdor bsdus*, 23. The Kagyu School's own lists of Düsum Khyenpo's students, however, would disagree with this assessment. (My thanks to Andrew Quintman for this information.)
22. *Rgyal ba kaḥ thog pa'i lo rgyus mdor bsdus*, 25.
23. *Dam pa bde gshegs kyi rnam thar bsdus pa*, 16b.5–17a.1.
24. *Rgyal ba kaḥ thog pa'i lo rgyus mdor bsdus*, 26.
25. On Dampa's teaching and writing activities relating to the *Gathering of Intentions* system, see *Dam pa bde gshegs kyi rnam thar bsdus pa*, 20b.4–21b.2.
26. The first four of these five works are collected in volume 52 of Dudjom Rinpoché's *Rnying ma bka' ma rgyas pa*, while the fifth, Dampa's *Outline of the Vehicles*, resurfaced more recently, appearing as an independent publication (along with a commentary by Katokpa Yeshé Gyeltsen).
27. T. Griffith Foulk, "Myth, Ritual, and Monastic Practice in Sung Ch'an Buddhism," *Religion and Society in T'ang and Sung China*, ed. P. B. Ebrey and P. N. Gregory (Honolulu: University of Hawai'i Press, 1993), 86.
28. Here I have tentatively corrected Dampa's transcription of the second, third, and fourth names in his lineage; he has In tra pu tri, NA ga pu tri, and Gu hya pu tri (*Legs bshad nyi ma'i snang ba*, 47.6–48.1). The later tradition has Kukkurāja closer to King Dza. See, for example, Dudjom, *The Nyingma School of Tibetan Buddhism*, 460, who is following Dharmaśrī's *General Exposition*. In fact, much of the Indian section of Dampa's lineage was changed in the later tradition. One suspects the influence here of other accounts.
29. Nup Yeshé Gyatso taught Gya Lodrö Jangchup, who taught in turn Tokar Namkha. The latter's teaching career was divided into three phases. Early in life he taught the *Gathering of Intentions* to four brothers from Lhodrak, in mid-life he taught Zhu Sönam Śākya, and in late life he taught Zurché. Zurché taught Zurchung, who taught his "four pillars and eight beams" but especially Zur Śākya Sengé (a.k.a. Dropukpa). Regarding the names of the four brothers taught by Tokar early in life, Dampa writes only, "Nanam Zhangyön, and so forth," but Pema Trinlé (*Mdo dbang brgyud pa'i rnam thar*, 185) provides the full list: Nanam Zhangyön, Shang kyi Tongtsap Pakpa Gyatso, Nanam gi Garchung Tsültrim Zangpo, Uyukpa Yar Selwe Jangchup. However, Pema Trinlé divides not Tokar's but his teacher's, Gya Lodrö Jangchup, career into three periods, so it is the latter who teaches the four brothers. As in Dampa's account, Pema Trinlé places the four brothers in the early period, but then puts Tokar in the middle,

and Zhu Sönam Śākya, the king of Lower Nyang, in the later period. This bumps Zurché off the list, and instead he studies under the latter Zhu Sönam Śākya.

30. Here Nup Yeshé Gyatso teaches Khulungpa Nanam Tsültrim Jangchup (the Khulungpa added from Pema Trinlé's *Mdo dbang brgyud pa'i rnam thar*, 254.2), who in turn transmits to Geshé Marchung Lhodrakpa. The latter also receives teachings from Zurchung, though according to Pema Trinlé (254.4) these were limited to Great Perfection Mind Class transmissions (*sems phyogs rgyud sde*). Dampa then tells a short story in which one Lharjé Shangchungpa Darma Sönam (called Shangnak Langza Sönam Dar by Pema Trinlé (254.3) and Langtön Darma Sönam of Shang Lhapu by Gö Lotsawa (George N. Roerich, *The Blue Annals* [Delhi: Motilal Banarsidass, 1976 (1949)], 126) meets Marchung, who is lying ill at an old monastery. Shangpa nurses him back to health, for which he receives the *Gathering of Intentions* according to the exegetical tradition of the *Prophetic Commentary* (*'Grel pa lung bstan ma*, a.k.a. *Lung bstan gyi skor*), along with some Mind Class teachings. Then Shangpa passes these on to Zur Śākya Sengé.
31. The first genre includes the major commentaries such as *Armor Against Darkness* and *Prophetic Commentary*, the full title of which is *'Grel pa lung bstan ye shes snang ba rgyan*. Five other commentaries are also listed: *Dka' spyod*, *Gser gzong*, *Lcags 'grol ba*, *Rgya mdud 'grel*, *Rnam bshad chen po*. I have only been able to identify the author of the last of these, which Dharmaśrī (*Spyi don*, 51) says is Hūṃkara. The second genre is structural analyses, of which there are seven (see *Mdo phran khog dbub*, 6.5–7.1). Most are attributed to the Indian master Dharmabodhi, along with two to King Dza: *Greater Condensed Meaning* (*Don bsdus che ba*) by King Dza, *Lesser Condensed Meaning* (*Don bsdus chung ba*) by Dharmabodhi, *Byung tshul bsdus pa* by King Dza, *Tshul gsal byed*, *Me long gsal byed* by Dharmabodhi, *Skol mdo rgyas bsdus*, which Dharmaśrī (*Spyi don*, 51) attributes to Dharmabodhi, *Man ngag spyi gcod*. A large number of the works Dampa lists are attributed to Dharmabodhi, whose importance to the early tradition is indicated by the fact that Dampa sometimes refers to him simply by the title, "the master" (*slob dpon*; see, for example, *Legs bshad nyi ma'i snang ba*, 27.4). Some of the Dharmabodhi works Dampa mentions have recently resurfaced, appended to the back of the *Len Manual*. The third genre consists of outlines (*sa gcod*), of which only one is mentioned, the *Gser gzong*; the last of the four kinds of general theoretical commentaries are those works that clear up any problems; here again, only one is cited, the *Pe re ka rtsa 'grel*.

32. *Mdo phran khog dbub*, 7.4–5. "Vows" is actually missing from the list but is provided later, on 8.5. Nine works focus on the issue of view: *Gding chen bcu pa, De kho na nyid dris lan lnga bcu pa, Gegs sel brgyad pa, Lam rim stod, Mdo bsres*, alternatively titled *Me long bstan pa* (Dampa later [9.2] ascribes this to Dharmabodhi), *Me long gsum pa, Byung tshul snying po, Mtshan nyid gsal sgron, Mdo bzhi'i bye brag*. Dampa lists four texts concerned with the ritual practices for the *Gathering of Intentions*: *Spyod pa bsdus pa'i sgron ma, Bsnyen bkur gsal byed, Mdo sde dri med, Bla ma'i rim pa*. Seven are listed on the arrangement of the mandala: *Rang bzhin dkyil 'khor bstan pa, Dal gsum pa, Rin chen phreng ba'i stod, Dal bdun pa, Thig don bskul ba, Lung gi rdo rje las rim, Dal gyi mngon rtogs*. Eight are listed on the stages of initiation: *Rin chen phreng ba'i smad, Rna rgyud rdo rje zam pa, Dbang gi lde'u mig, Dbang don bsdus pa, Dbang don rgyas pa, Dbang don rgya cher bshad pa, Dbang gi man ngag gsang ba* (heavily cited by Dharmaśrī, who [on *Spyi don*, 21.2] seems to say it is by Déwa Seldzé), *Sa tha dang dbang gi rim pa*. Five are listed on the vows: *Dam tshig gcan 'phrang chen mo, Rgyun bshags chen mo, Dam tshig spyi khrus bshags pa, Dam tshig gi gter, Khrus lung rgyal mtshan*. Six are listed on the mundane (*thun mong*) accomplishments and four on the supramundane accomplishments: *Tshe grub, Pra, Ro langs, Rkang mgyogs, Mngon shes, Gzungs ma 'gugs pa*. And *Lam rim chen po* by Déwa Seldzé, *Mdo bsres* by Dharmabodhi, *Skabs 'grel* by Sthiramati, *Rgyu rta lam rtsa(l) 'grel* by King Dza. It is hard to believe the first six were independent texts; they do not sound like titles, and they are not cited elsewhere in the *Gathering of Intentions* literature. They may have been oral instructions or perhaps abbreviated sets of notes. *Mdo bsres* also appeared under the "view" heading. Finally, the *Skabs 'grel* is discussed in appendix 2 as one of the few extant works attributed to an Indian author. Five are listed on the activities: *Ye shes mtshon chen* by Déwa Seldzé, *Ro bsregs bcu bzhi* by Vimalamitra, *Mdo yi dngos po gnyis pa* also by Vimalamitra, *Dpe chung rang gnas, Drag po 'dus byed*. Three are listed on *samādhi* with signs and eleven on *samādhi* without signs: *Zhi khro rtogs pa lha rgyud kyi man ngag* by Vimalamitra, *Khro bo las phreng* by Hūṃkara, *Bsam gtan cho ga'i sgron ma* by *The Gathering of Intentions* scholar Dharmabodhi. And *Thugs kyi sgron ma, Sems don byed pa, Rig pa'i sgron ma, Ljong shing, Le lag gsum pa, Bsam gtan rig pa'i nyi ma, Gsam gtan mig sgron rtsa 'grel, Bsam gtan me long snang ba, Bsam gtan spu gri snang ba, Bdud rtsi lung gi bsam gtan, Bsam gtan sgron ma*.
33. See n. 20 above.
34. Lharjé was a title much used by the early Zurs and their circle, and Zurchung was usually called Lharjé Dé.

35. See both *Mdo dbang brgyud pa'i rnam thar*, 231–32, and *Spyi don*, 75.6. He also appears in Dudjom's history as a critic of Rongzom Chökyi Zangpo (Dudjom, *The Nyingma School of Tibetan Buddhism*, 708; see also n. 8 above). Yangkhyé's relationship to Rongzom may also mean he received the commentarial lineage of Sthīramati, since Rongzom is said to have received this transmission from his childhood teacher, Gartön Zangpo (see *Rnal 'byor nyi ma gsal bar byed pa*, vol. 56, 704.3).
36. Roerich, *The Blue Annals*, 160.
37. Dampa likely derived this concept of the incidental from chapter 68 of the *Gathering of Intentions*, though Kawa Peltsek's late-eighth or early ninth-century *Lta ba rim par bshad pa*, 424b.2, already mentions the category.
38. For a discussion of this assimilation, see Bryan J. Cuevas, *The Hidden History of The Tibetan Book of the Dead* (New York: Oxford University Press, 2003), 63–67.
39. *Theg pa spyi bcings rtsa 'grel*, 7. On this scheme, see also Karmay, *The Great Perfection*, 152–163; Matthew T. Kapstein, *The Tibetan Assimilation of Buddhism* (Oxford: Oxford University Press, 2000), 104; Jacob Dalton, "A Crisis of Doxography: How Tibetans Organized Tantra During the 8th–12th Centuries," *Journal of the International Association of Buddhist Studies* 28, no. 1 (2005): 128–30.
40. Dampa analyzes each vehicle in terms of seven aspects: how to begin, view, *samādhi*, practice, ethical conduct, path duration, result. These would reappear in the later initiation liturgies.
41. *Theg pa spyi bcings rtsa 'grel*, 31–32.
42. The commentaries following this system include: Longchenpa's *Dispelling the Darkness from the Ten Directions* (see Gyurme Dorje, "The *Guhyagarbhatantra* and Its XIVth Century Tibetan Commentary" [Ph.D. diss. University of London, SOAS, 1987], 982–97), Yungtön's *Gsal byed me long*, 432–36, and Dharmaśrī's *Gsang bdag dgongs rgyan*, 326–28. In Dudjom, *The Nyingma School of Tibetan Buddhism*, 62–69, where we find a parallel discussion, the "great sutra" is in fact *Gathering of Intentions*.
43. Compare Vilāsavajra's early presentation to that of Padmasambhava's *Pith Instructional Garland of Views*, the whole of which is devoted to **Guhyagarbha*'s thirteenth chapter and which includes more of the terms used in the later tradition (and by the *Gathering of Intentions*) to discuss the mundane views, including the materialists.
44. *Gsang ba snying po'i 'grel pa spar khab*, 556.2–4.
45. Yungtön opts for the former model, Dharmaśrī for the latter. Longchenpa does not mention Anuyoga, though perhaps say he opts for the former

model because he divides Mahāyoga into father and mother tantras (and Anuyoga is sometimes described as equivalent to the mother tantras).

46. Nupchen may (very obliquely) refer to the same **Guhyagarbha* passage in *Mun pa'i go cha*, vol. 51, 428.3–5, and if so, he too drops Anuyoga from his discussion. In his subcommentary, *Rnal 'byor nyi ma gsal bar byed pa*, vol. 56, 257, Nüdon adds it in with Atiyoga.
47. *Rtsa rgyud gsang ba'i snying po'i 'grel pa nyi ma snying po*, vol. 2, 237.5–238.1. Italics added.
48. *Rtsa rgyud gsang ba'i snying po'i 'grel pa nyi ma snying po*, vol. 2, 602.1.
49. *Rtsa rgyud gsang ba'i snying po'i 'grel pa nyi ma snying po*, vol. 2, 602.5–603.1.
50. *Theg pa spyi bcings rtsa 'grel*, 152.
51. Kapstein, *The Tibetan Assimilation of Buddhism*, 242 n. 53, notes the influence the *Gathering of Intentions* exerted upon the second Karmapa, Karma Pakshi. The latter grew up around the Katok educational system, and given the *Gathering of Intentions*' prominence there, "We may say summarily that Karma Pakshi's view of the general architecture of the path is derived from the *Mdo dgongs-pa 'dus-pa* (The Sūtra Gathering All Intentions) and other fundamental works of the anuyoga" (Kapstein, *The Tibetan Assimilation of Buddhism*, 105).
52. As translated by Jann Michael Ronis, "Celibacy, Revelations, and Reincarnated Lamas: Contestation and Synthesis in the Growth of Monasticism at Katok Monastery from the Seventeenth Through Nineteenth Centuries" (Ph.D. diss., University of Virginia, 2009), 14. "Illusion" (*sgyu*) and "tantra" (*rgyud*) are used interchangeably in this triad. The former simply refers to the larger Māyājāla tantras within which the **Guhyagarbha Tantra* is included. Also in the sixteenth century, the Katokpa master Sönam Gyeltsen (b. 1466–1540) composed another famous nine vehicles study entitled *Thoroughly Illuminating Sun Rays, Clarifying the Intended Meaning of the Vehicles of Sutra and Mantra*. He cites so heavily from Dampa's *Outline of the Vehicles* that his study can be viewed as another commentary on that earlier work. Sönam Gyeltsen was also known for introducing the Spoken Teachings into Sikkim and Bhutan, and in this way Dampa's teachings spread throughout the Himalayan region (*Rgyal ba kaḥ thog pa'i lo rgyus mdor bsdus*, 73–75). For more on this master, see Frank-Karl Ehrhard, "Kaḥ thog pa Bsod nams rgyal mtshan (1466–1540) and His Activities in Sikkim and Bhutan," *Bulletin of Tibetology* 39, no. 2 (2003).
53. Although the first three Zur patriarchs may not have been directly involved in formulating the *Collected Tantras of the Ancients*, there is considerable evidence that later members of their clan played pivotal roles.

The fourteenth-century Zur Zangpo Pel is said to have produced a particularly early edition (see Dudjom, *The Nyingma School of Tibetan Buddhism*, 669), and Robert Mayer suggests that Künpang Drakgyel, working at the Zur stronghold of Ukpalung, compiled a "proto-" edition, "perhaps sometime between the 11th and the 13th centuries" (though he notes that Ehrhard dates him somewhat later, to the thirteenth or fourteenth century); Mayer, *A Scripture of the Ancient Tantra Collection, The* Phur-pa bcu-gnyis (Oxford: Kiscadale, 1996), 223–24. Finally, Matthew Kapstein, "The *Sun of the Heart* and the *Bai-ro-rgyud-'bum*," *Revue d'Etudes Tibétaines* 15 (2008): 283–84, has suggested that the *Collected Tantras of Vairo[cana]*, an early collection of Great Perfection writings that may have functioned as a kind of precursor to the *Collected Tantras of the Ancients*, was also associated with the Zur. For a survey of the early history of the *Collected Tantras of the Ancient*, see Mayer, *A Scripture of the Ancient Tantra Collection*, 223–32.

54. Writing about the *Collected Tantras of the Ancients*, but primarily referring to the Spoken Teachings portions of those collections by implication, Cantwell and Mayer recognize the same crucial relationship when they write, "In a very broad sense, they serve as the measure and model for the new *gter ma* revelation, which in general should not deviate too much from the NGB in style and contents" (Cathy Cantwell and Robert Mayer, *The Kīlaya Nirvāṇa Tantra and the Vajra Wrath Tantra: Two Texts from the Ancient Tantra Collection* [Vienna: Verlag der Österreichischen Akademie der Wissenschaften, 2007], 1).
55. Jonathan Z. Smith, *Imagining Religion: From Babylon to Jonestown* (Chicago: University of Chicago Press, 1982), 48.

4. THE RISE OF THE SUTRA INITIATION

1. Donald S. Lopez, Jr., *The Madman's Middle Way: Reflections on Reality of the Tibetan Monk Gendun Chopel* (Chicago: University of Chicago Press, 2006), 9, relates a telling story in which the early twentieth-century Gelukpa monk Gendün Chömpel is caught silently reading his portion amid the cacophony of one such ceremony.
2. The manuscripts from Dunhuang include, for example, one almost-complete copy of the *Guhyasamāja Tantra*, with copious commentarial notes, and not all of the sutras were written for meritorious reasons alone. I do not mean to suggest there was some edenic time in the past when monks read their sutras (or tantras) only for the content; even in early India, many recited or copied sutras for their apotropaic or merit-making

qualities. Nonetheless, the study of canonical works and their contents does seem to have decreased over the centuries in Tibet. Lopez observes that during "the period of the *śāstras*," an "admittedly rather amorphous" period of late Indian Mahāyāna, "the sūtras, which seem at first to have been recited and worshipped, became the object also of scholastic reflection" (Donald S. Lopez, Jr., ed., *Curators of the Buddha: The Study of Buddhism Under Colonialism* [Chicago: University of Chicago Press, 1995], 24).

3. The system's mandala, called the Gathered Great Assembly, is said to be second in size only to the *Lung rdo rje bkod pa*, which is the *Gathering of Intentions*' treasure equivalent, revealed by Chögyur Lingpa (1829–1870). Dudjom, *The Nyingma School of Tibetan Buddhism*, 847 tells us that the *Lung rdo rje bkod pa* was first received by Chögyur Lingpa in his past life as Nup Yönten Gyatso, from his teacher, Nupchen Sangyé Yeshé, a story that further attested to this *terma*'s ties to the *Gathering of Intentions.*
4. Other presentations of the Rudra/Maheśvara myth and the nine vehicles circulated in early Tibet. The Dunhuang manuscripts, for example, include both; for a Rudra myth, see IOL Tib J 419/5, and for a version of the nine vehicles that closely resembles that of the *Gathering of Intentions*, see IOL Tib J 644 (translated in Jacob Dalton, "A Crisis of Doxography: How Tibetans Organized Tantra During the 8th–12th Centuries," *Journal of the International Association of Buddhist Studies* 28, no. 1 [2005]: 115–81). The presence of these and other renditions would have helped the *Gathering of Intentions*' versions to gain broad acceptance. Nonetheless, within the Nyingma School of the later dispensation period, the *Gathering of Intentions* clearly served as the standard source for both the myth and the doxography.
5. On the discovery of the **Guhyagarbha*, see Ronald M. Davidson, *Tibetan Renaissance* (New York: Columbia University Press, 2005), 404 n. 112.
6. See, for example, Gyurme Dorje, "The *Guhyagarbhatantra* and Its XIVth Century Tibetan Commentary, *phyogs bcu mun sel*" (Ph.D. diss., University of London, SOAS, 1987), 835, where Longchenpa reads the third and fourth initiations into the **Guhyagarbha*'s initiation system.
7. There seems to be some confusion in the sources regarding the transmissions within the Len clan. Taking as my starting point Pema Trinlé's *Mdo dbang brgyud pa'i rnam thar*, 257–58, and *Rgya mtsho'i 'jug mngogs*, vol. 41, 23.5, here and below I note the more significant differences between the lineages traced by still two other sources, Sokdokpa Lodrö Gyeltsen's *Shel gyi me long*, 370.2–374.5 and Lochen Dharmaśrī's *Spyi don*, 55–114. Already Zurchung had taught Len Śākya Zangpo (one the "four pillars"

of his disciples) and Len Nyatselwa Śākya Jangchup. The latter, together with Gartön Zungé, transmitted the *Gathering of Intentions* to Sektön Dorjé Gyeltsen, who then taught Lenben Dorjé Ö. He, in turn, taught several students, including his own son, Len Tsöndru, as well as Len Sönam Gyelpo and Lharjé Lhabum. (Dharmaśrī's *Spyi don*, 88.5–89.5 mentions only the first two, writing that Lhabum received it later from Len Sönam Gyelpo. Lhabum does appear in Dharmaśrī's *Spyi don*, 91.2, as the father, and in Sokdokpa's *Shel gyi me long*, 374.4, as the teacher, of the important Lentön Sönam Gönpo, which would seem to be a way of abbreviating the lineage.) The son, Len Tsöndru, was famous for having built the seat monastery of Zhikpo Dütsi in Zé Tangkya (as noted by both Sokdokpa in *Shel gyi me long*, 374.2, and Dharmaśrī in *Spyi don*, 88.6). On Zhikpo Dütsi and this site, see Dudjom Rinpoche, *The Nyingma School of Tibetan Buddhism*, trans. Gyurme Dorje (Boston: Wisdom, 1991), 656. Next, Lharjé Lhabum and Len Sönam Gyelpo passed the lineage on to Len Pelden Chökyi Sengé, who then gave it to Lentön Sangyé Pel. (Dharmaśrī, *Spyi don*, 90.3, points out that the lineage can be traced from Len Sönam Gyelpo to Len Chökyi Sengé either through Lhabum or directly.) Lentön Sangyé Pel seems to have consolidated several of the lines that had proliferated up to that point, receiving the tradition according to the Len, Zur, Se, and Zhang systems (see *Mdo dbang brgyud pa'i rnam thar*, 259.4). As Dharmaśrī (*Spyi don*, 91.3) points out, the latter Zhang system refers to a seal of entrustment (*gtad rgya*) lineage that Pema Trinlé (*Mdo dbang brgyud pa'i rnam thar*, 260.3) traces from Len Dorjé Ö to Nyitön Sangyé Bum to one Zhangtön Künga Bum, after whom Pema Trinlé drops it. The Se system may be related somehow to the Atiyoga tradition of the same name that was connected to the Northern Treasures and based near Gyangkhar Wené. On this lineage, see the *Thob yig gang+ga'i chu rgyun* by the Fifth Dalai Lama.

8. This manual has recently resurfaced in the *Bka' ma rgyas pa shin tu rgyas pa* collection (see *Bka' ma rgyas pa shin tu rgyas pa* 1, vols. 61–62, or *Bka' ma rgyas pa shin tu rgyas pa* 3, vols. 22–23). For a summary of its contents, see Jacob Dalton, "Lost and Found: A Fourteenth-Century Discussion of Then-Available Sources on gNubs chen sangs rgyas ye shes," *Bulletin of Tibetology (Special Issue, Nyingma Studies)* 50, no. 1 (2014): 39–53. As the latter suggests, the new manual is in fact a two-volume collection of ritual materials, the compilation of which should probably be attributed to the fourteenth-century master Zurham Śākya Jungné. The original core of the *Len Manual*—the part most likely written by Lentön himself—is probably best represented by the first text in the collection. One might hazard

an approximate date for this original manual as follows: Lentön taught Drölmawa, in a meeting supposed to have taken place around 1318 (as can be deduced by combining two passages in the *Mdo dbang brgyud pa'i rnam thar*, 263.1 and 266.2). It seems safe to assume that Lentön had written his initiation manual before this, which might put his composition around 1300. According to Dharmaśrī's *Spyi don*, 91.6–92.1, Len Sönam Gönpo was also an accomplished treasure revealer, who discovered a scroll in Pehar Ling at Samyé and entrusted it to Menlung Üpa. This Menlungpa (who should not be confused with the later and better known teacher of Pema Trinlé and the Great Fifth) is the Menlungpa Śākya Ö of Dudjom, *The Nyingma School of Tibetan Buddhism*, 686. He was the student of Kyitön Chökyi Sengé, who studied directly under Dropukpa. This suggests that all these Len figures must have followed in quick succession, since in other lineages only two generations span all of them.

9. He also passed it to Lama Nyangtön Pel Dorjé. Sokdokpa (*Shel gyi me long*, 374.3) says this Nyangtön (whom he calls Nyangtön Sherap Pel) received it directly from Len Tsöndru. He then passed it to Rong Gyong Khangpa Zitön Śākya Zangpo, who then passed it to Drölmawa. Because he organizes his lineage into monks vs. mantrikas, Sokdokpa is particularly unclear on how the Len family relates. For Drölmawa's birth and death dates, see *Mdo dbang brgyud pa'i rnam thar*, 261.7 and 266.3 respectively. Drölmawa was also one of Zur Jampa Sengé's two main students, the other being Yungtönpa Dorjé Pel (1284–1365), another notable member of the Len clan who wrote an authoritative commentary on the **Guhyagarbha* according to the Zur exegetical tradition and who, under the third Karmapa, was a major figure in the fourteenth-century Great Perfection Seminal Heart tradition. He also received the *Gathering of Intentions* transmission from Zur Jampa Sengé, who stood at the end of a completely different "seal of entrustment" line that is quickly traced by Pema Trinlé as follows: the line started from Dropukpa and passed through Zur Nakpo, Amé Sherap, Lachen Relpuwa, Metön Gönpo, Khepa Sechenpo, Druptop Lhünpel, Bendé Wangchuk Gyeltsen, to Zur Jampa Sengé (see *Mdo dbang brgyud pa'i rnam thar*, 253.1–5). A seal of entrustment is generally required to become an official lineage holder, but Pema Trinlé seems to have named this section of the lineage after the text from which he drew it, Yungtön's manual for the Sutra Initiation, the *Gtad rgya gsang mtshan ma'i dbang chog* (which I have not located). Yungtön, like Drölmawa, ultimately passed his lineage to Zurham.

10. This work I date as follows: since Drölmawa (1294–1375) and Yungtönpa Dorjé Pel (1284–1365) taught Zurham, we can place the latter figure in the last half of the fourteenth century, with his student, Nyelwa, writing around the late fourteenth, or perhaps early fifteenth, century.
11. It was used by both Sokdokpa and his associates as well as the Northern Treasures Evam Chogar community, despite the close ties maintained between the Sokdokpa faction and the Katok tradition, so close that the former were often assumed to have followed Katok's *River of Honey* manual, when in fact they based themselves on the *Jewel Rosary*. This is explained in Pema Trinlé's *Rgya mtsho'i 'jug mngogs*, vol. 42, 8.3–4. The *Jewel Rosary* also later served as the basis for Pema Trinlé's seventeenth-century manual, the *Entry Point Into the Ocean of Mandalas*.
12. The author Moktön Dorjé Pelzangpo's teacher, was none other than Yeshé Gyeltsen (author of the commentary to Dampa Deshek's *Outline of the Vehicles*). Khenpo Jamyang of Katok gives Yeshé Gyeltsen's birth date as 1395 (see *Rgyal ba kaḥ thog pa'i lo rgyus mdor bsdus*, 51). On this basis I am assuming that Moktön was active during the late fifteenth century.
13. There are indications that some lineage holders may have only granted initiation up to the level appropriate to their disciples' particular abilities (see discussions on this in *Spyi don*, 148–53 and 241), but it appears that initiation into all nine vehicles, in some form or other, was the norm. On a related point, Dharmaśrī admits that of course most recipients of these initiations will not actually be established in the high levels of realization necessary for truly mastering every vehicle; for ordinary disciples, the best one can hope for is that the initiations "arrange the karmic conditions for ensuring what will [only later] be attained" (*Spyi don*, 154.3).
14. Each of the four streams of initiation is then divided and subdivided as follows:10 outer initiations are further divided into 108 coarse branch initiations. Similarly, eleven inner (Mahāyoga) initiations are subdivided into 606. Then 13 accomplishment initiations subdivide into 115, and two secret initiations remain unelaborated as two. In all, there are 36 initiations that subdivide into 831 coarse branches. These are all listed and discussed by Dharmaśrī in *Spyi don*, 217–38, though the 36 primary divisions appear already in chapter 36 of the *Gathering of All Knowledge*.
15. This correspondence was assumed by several of my informants and can be seen clearly spelled out in a passage from what looks to be an early commentary, the *Rgya mdud 'grel*, cited by Dharmaśrī on *Spyi don*, 187.4.
16. Dharmaśrī discusses the sources for these mandalas in his *Spyi don*, 186–88. Of the two uncommon mandalas, the wrathful mandala is the Supreme

Mandala of the Secret Charnel Grounds (*dur khrod gsang ba mchog gi dkyil 'khor*) that is explained in the root tantra of the Anuyoga class, the *Gathering of All Knowledge Sutra*, specifically in chapter 14, "On the System for the Accomplishment of the Gathered Great Assembly" (*Tshogs chen 'dus pa'i bsgrubs lugs kyi le'u*). What looks like the same mandala is also partly described in several other chapters of the *Gathering of All Knowledge Sutra*, chapters 16, 18, 22, and 23. The uncommon peaceful mandala derives from chapter 5 of *Wisdom's Magnificent Thunderbolts*. Dharmaśrī does not provide the precise chapter involved in this peaceful form, so I assume it to be chapter 5 on the basis of my own study. For a discussion of *Wisdom's Magnificent Thunderbolts*, which is another of the four root sutras of Anuyoga, see the appendix. Regarding the common mandalas, the wrathful is taken from the ninth chapter of *Gathering of the Herukas Tantra* and the peaceful from the same mandala in the *Wisdom's Magnificent Thunderbolts*, then both are combined with certain aspects of the wrathful and peaceful mandalas described in the *'Dren pa'i las byang che le*. The latter work is apparently the short text found in the *Glan chog*, 370.5–374.4. It is attributed to the Indian master Déwa Seldzé, and according to Dharmaśrī was extracted from a tantra entitled *Vairocana's Seminal Essence: The King of Initiations Tantra* (on this claim, see *Spyi don*, 134.6–135.1; see also *Spyi don*, 21.1, where Dharmaśrī refers to the *'Dren pa'i las byang* and several other works with the title *Kalba dum bu'i rgyud*).

17. That both names refer to the same person is made clear in the colophon to the *Consecration Ritual Notes* ascribed to him (*Las tho rab gnas*, 410.2). The name Déwa Seldzé seems to have become more commonly used in later literature, for example throughout the works of Lochen Dharmaśrī.
18. Déwa Seldzé's writings on the ritual systems of the *Gathering of Intentions* were organized into three sets of six texts each, and for this reason they became known as the "Pith Instructions of the Eighteen in Three Sixes" (*Man ngag drug gsum bco brgyad*). The first of these three sets, entitled the "Six Chapters on the Hidden Initiation" (*Gab pa'i dbang le*), consisted of the six chapters Déwa Seldzé extracted from another tantra. The second and third sets are expressly stated to be Déwa Seldzé compositions. Nupchen labeled these the "Six Required Sādhanas" (*Dgos pa'i sgrub thabs drug*) and the "Six Kinds of Required Equipment" (*Dgos pa'i cha rkyen drug*). The eighteen texts are all clearly laid out by Nupchen in his *Root of the Seal of Entrustment for the Initiation* (*Dbang gi gtad rgya'i rtsa ba*), which is then quoted by Dharmaśrī in his *Spyi don*, 20.3–6. Many, if not all, of these works have recently resurfaced in the *Len Manual* collection; see for

example the *Dbang don bsdus* (*Glan chog* 61, 388.2–389.4), *Dbang don rnam par 'byed pa* (389.4–396.1), *Dbang don rgya cher 'byed pa* (396.2–396.5), *Las tho rab gnas* (405.1–410.2). When the *Las tho rab gnas* is compared to several passages quoted from it by Dharmaśrī, they are in perfect agreement. It is difficult to say with certainty how much of a hand Nupchen had in the composition of these works. For the purposes of this study, I have accepted the tradition's attribution of them to Déwa Seldzé. In any case, Nupchen likely made certain changes in collecting, editing, and possibly translating these works. In fact, the colophon to the *Dbang gi thig gdab* tells us that it was written by Ācārya Selwé Gyen and Jowo Sangyé, i.e., none other than Nupchen. Other short texts on the initiation rites that are attributed to Nupchen also appear in the same *Len Manual* collection, on which see Dalton, "Lost and Found."

19. This figure and his writings are the focus of chapter 6 of the present study.
20. Dharmaśrī (*Spyi don*, 245) mentions several practice lists (*las tho*) he came across during his own research, including those by Lharjé Gar (Dampa Deshek's teacher), Gö Tsilungpa, Lharjé Khün, Lharjé Śākya Gön, and Lentön Sönam Gönpo, and various ones from the Kyi system (Skyi lugs) as well as the practice manual (*phyag bzhes*) of Len chenpo Dorjé Ö (a.k.a. Lenben Dorjé Ö). To my knowledge, none of these is extant.
21. On dating this manual, see n. 8 above.
22. A comment by Dharmaśrī makes it appear that the tantra system may have been more commonly used than the pith instructions system. In *Spyi don*, 242.2–4, Dharmaśrī seems to describe a separate, and somewhat marginal, lineage for the early pith instructions system: "In accordance with the intention of Déwa Seldzé's *Las tho*, the initiation of the fully complete sutra was received by Lopön Amé from the four: the father of So Pelden, Len Gyekhawa, Yutön Chögön, and Che Jamsé. Then he granted to So Pelden, he to Roktön Künga Döndrup, and he to Yungtön Dorjé Pel in the palace of Nyedo. Then he granted it to Jang Sotön Śākya Pel, and so on."
23. Drölmawa marked a crucial point in the lineage, for it was after him that the three distinct lines (of Drölmawa's son, Zurham, and Zurmo) diverged, reuniting only three centuries later in the two brothers of Mindröling, Terdak Lingpa and Lochen Dharmaśrī. Here, in the construction of ritual manuals, we are seeing additional evidence that something unusual happened after Drölmawa.
24. *Spyi don*, 109.2–5.

25. *Mdo dbang brgyud pa'i rnam thar*, 269.5–6. See also *Rgya mtsho'i 'jug mngogs*, vol. 41, 13.5–14.1, where Pema Trinlé argues the same point. Although the new branch mandalas are thus usually attributed to Zurham, there is some evidence to suggest that they may have been added a little earlier. Dharmaśrī cites a passage by Yungtön Dorjé Pel (1284–1375) in which Yungtön appears to be defending precisely such a change in the ritual format: "According to some who do not understand our methods, we admit that the individual mandalas for both sutra and tantra were not clearly present [in the earlier tradition], but then, bringing together the inner initiations and the accomplishment initiations within the Gathered Great Assembly mandala, we simply imputed [the rest]" (*Spyi don*, 241.3–4). Unfortunately Dharmaśrī does not include Yungtön's response to such criticism. Yungtön was one of Zurham's two main teachers for the Sūtra tradition. That he is already referring to criticisms of using branch mandalas for all nine vehicles may indicate that this innovation, which is generally ascribed to Zurham, began one generation earlier. Yungtön's admission "that the individual mandalas are not clearly present" in the earlier materials suggests that he was writing during the very earliest days of the new branch mandalas, when they had not yet gained broad acceptance. No matter who was first responsible for the change, it can likely be dated to around the last half of the fourteenth century.
26. *Las tho rab gnas*, 406.5–6. Note that Ubhayā tantra, usually the fifth vehicle, is often excluded in the Sutra Initiation tradition, which allowed the gods and humans vehicle to be included as the first vehicle while still keeping a total of nine. This meant that including a branch mandala for Kriyā and Yoga was in effect having a mandala for each of the outer tantric vehicles. If we can believe the attribution of the *Consecration Ritual Notes* to the ninth-century Indian master Déwa Seldzé, it is interesting to consider whether a Sutra Initiation ceremony with a set of nine vehicles that included gods and humans but not Ubhayā might have predated the compilation of the *Gathering of Intentions*. (Déwa Seldzé is supposed to have taught Dharmabodhi, who may have been involved in composing the *Gathering of Intentions*.) If true, this would lend further credence to the idea that the *Gathering of Intentions* and its circle of "root sutras" had at least one foot in a genuinely early and possibly Indian ritual system.
27. This option is outlined in the Déwa Seldzé texts found in the Glan Manual. Déwa Seldzé does not refer to the two forms of the Gathered Great Assembly Mandala as "common" and "uncommon," but as the "mandala from the *Las byang chen po*" and the "mandala of the Supreme Secret" (*gsang*

ba mchog gi dkyil 'khor; see *Glan chog*, 404.6 and 405.3). In the long passage translated above, Dharmaśrī wrote that the common mandala first appeared in the *Amazing Practice Manual*, one of the six chapters extracted by Déwa Seldzé, which explains Déwa Seldzé's name for this mandala. The the uncommon mandala is also known as the "Supreme Mandala of the Secret Charnel Grounds" (*dur khrod gsang ba mchog gi dkyil 'khor*), and this is certainly the name to which Déwa Seldzé is referring in the passage here.

28. Unfortunately the identity of these two figures remains obscure to me.
29. As noted above (ch. 3, n. 52), "illusion" (*sgyu*) and "tantra" (*rgyud*) are used interchangeably in this triad, with "illusion" refering to the *Māyājāla* corpus in general.
30. *Rgyal ba kaḥ thog pa'i lo rgyus mdor bsdus*, 64–65.
31. In this way, the Sutra Initiation during this period might be seen as a kind of one-stop shop, not unlike the *Bari Gyatsa* in the New Schools tradition, a single system that offered all of the most important initiations of the Nyingma Spoken Teachings tradition.

5. DORJÉ DRAK AND THE FORMATION OF A NEW LINEAGE

1. Though I am emphasizing the work Pema Trinlé put into the *Gathering of Intentions* tradition, much of his attention was of course also given to organizing the ritual texts of the Northern Treasures, as observed by Martin Boord, *The Cult of the Deity Vajrakīlaya* (Tring, UK: The Institute of Buddhist Studies, 1993), 30.
2. I take this date from the Tibetan Buddhist Resource Center's website (www.tbrc.org). The site also suggests a date of death of 1625, but that is probably too late given that Ngagi Wangpo (b. 1580) was his reincarnation.
3. That the lineage was broken between the two brothers and Pema Trinlé is reflected in the fact that, when Pema Trinlé eventually rebuilt his community's Spoken Teachings lineage, he was forced to exclude the intervening two figures of Ngagi Wangpo and his father, Tashi Topgyel, even though they were central to the community's main Northern Treasures lineage.
4. For the following analysis I have relied primarily on Pema Trinlé's *Biographies for the Sutra Initiation Lineage*. An abbreviated lineage also appears in his initiation ritual manual, *Entry Point Into the Ocean*. The two sources are almost entirely in agreement, though a few minor differences occur. The *Biographies for the Sutra Initiation Lineage* was written later, so the

differences can perhaps be attributed to further discoveries made by Pema Trinlé in the meantime. If so, the *Biographies* may be a slightly more accurate reflection of his research.

5. As will be explained below, Katokpa Moktön Dorjé Pelzangpo (*Sbrang rtsi'i chu rgyun*, 63–68) traces the line through Zurmo. Sokdokpa (*Shel gyi me long*, 370–80) follows the lineage of the son, without even mentioning the other two lineages passing through Zurham and Zurmo (though he does refer to Zurham by name in another context; see *Shel gyi me long*, 375.4, where he discusses a Great Perfection Mind Class lineage in accordance with Zurham's earlier arrangement). To find a discussion of all three lineages, one must look to Lochen Dharmaśrī (whose writings form the focus of chapter 6). This difference in attitude between Pema Trinlé and Dharmaśrī regarding the other lineages is significant. Although both were close allies of the Fifth Dalai Lama, it appears that Pema Trinlé was more focused on excluding the other Nyingma lineages and Dharmaśrī was more inclusive. Perhaps due to its completeness, Dharmaśrī's account is the one reproduced (nearly verbatim) in Dudjom Rinpoché's *The Nyingma School of Tibetan Buddhism*, trans. Gyurme Dorje (Boston: Wisdom, 1991).
6. *Mdo dbang brgyud pa'i rnam thar*, 269.4–5.
7. See *Mdo dbang brgyud pa'i rnam thar*, 299.6. On Black Excellence (Legs ldan nag po) being the subjugated form of Rudra, see Jacob Dalton, *Taming of the Demons: Violence and Liberation in Tibetan Buddhism* (New Haven: Yale University Press, 2011), 204.
8. See *Mdo dbang brgyud pa'i rnam thar*, 382.2–3.
9. See Dudjom, *The Nyingma School of Tibetan Buddhism*, 718, on this section of the lineage. Following the death of Gongra Lochen, Menlungpa was nominated by the Fifth Dalai Lama as the new teacher at the monastery of Tsang Gongra. Menlungpa was then responsible for transmitting the *Collected Tantras of the Ancients* to the Dalai Lama. See Franz-Karl Ehrhard, "Recently Discovered Manuscripts of the *rNying ma rgyud 'bum* from Nepal," *Tibetan Studies: Proceedings of the 7th Seminar of the International Association for Tibetan Studies*, ed. Helmut Krasser et al. (Vienna: Verlag der Österreichischen Akademie der Wissenschaften, 1997), 1n.
10. *Mdo dbang brgyud pa'i rnam thar*, 386.4–387.1.
11. *Rgya mtsho'i 'jug mngogs*, vol. 43, 635.4–5.
12. *Mdo dbang brgyud pa'i rnam thar*, 413.1–6.
13. I remain unclear about what is happening here. Possibly this is Menlungpa telling Pema Trinlé what his own secret name is, before giving Pema Trinlé his name.

14. *Mdo dbang brgyud pa'i rnam thar*, 413.6–415.1.
15. *Rgya mtsho'i 'jug mngogs*, vol. 43, 636.1–637.2.
16. See Dudjom, *The Nyingma School of Tibetan Buddhism*, 821.
17. *Rgya mtsho'i 'jug mngogs*, vol. 41, 12.2–5.
18. Zurmo gave her transmission to Zurtön Śākya Shenyen, from whom it passed to Dra'o Chöbum, a Katok master who also inherited Katok's own tradition, traced straight back to Dampa Deshek. After him, the lineage soon fell to the master Moktön Dorjé Pelzangpo, who wrote the ritual manual entitled the *River of Honey* (discussed in chapter 4). For Moktön's description of the lineage, see *Sbrang rtsi'i chu rgyun*, vol. 64, 63–68.
19. Sokdokpa (*Shel gyi me long*, 380.4–5) traces the line of the son from Drölchen to Namdingpa Namkha Dorjé, to Khedrup Shami Dorgyel, then to Jetsun Yudruk Dorjé, who taught Sokdokpa, who then passed it to Gongra Lochen. The latter figure also appears in Pema Trinlé's own lineage biographies as the teacher of Dreshongpa. Gongra also taught Dreshongpa's student, Menlungpa, in accordance with the Katok System; see *Mdo dbang brgyud pa'i rnam thar*, 396.1.
20. It is possible that Ngari Paṇchen and Lekden Dorjé considered themselves part of a lineage that passed through Zurham. As already noted, Pema Trinlé claims to have availed himself of some handwritten notes on the Sutra Initiation by Ngari Paṇchen. Whether this is true, and how exactly Ngari Paṇchen himself conceived of his place in the Sutra Initiation ineages, remains unclear. In any case, after the Northern Treasures community was forcibly evicted from its home, the Sutra Initiation lineage was lost.
21. The Fifth Dalai Lama had appointed the third Yölmowa regent of Dorjé Drak in the period following Ngagi Wangpo's death. In this role, the Yölmowa Tendzin Norbu oversaw the identification of Pema Trinlé as the next incarnation of Gödemchen. Shortly after fulfilling this responsibility, the Yölmowa died in 1644, when Pema Trinlé was only four years old. The fourth Yolmo Tülku, Zilnön Wangyel Dorjé, was seven years younger than Pema Trinlé and had relatively little to do with Dorjé Drak. More will be said of this figure below. On the influential line of Yolmo Tülkus, see Ehrhard, "Recently Discovered Manuscripts," and Benjamin E. Bogin, *The Illuminated Life of the Great Yolmowa* (Chicago: Serindia, 2013).
22. *Mdo dbang brgyud pa'i rnam thar*, 424.4–6.
23. *Mdo dbang brgyud pa'i rnam thar*, 424.4. It is not certain that the Desi made this claim. It appears at the end of the "printer's colophon," so here I

assume that it was made by Sangyé Gyatso, since it was he who requested and commissioned the carving of the blocks.

24. The same verses appear in the identical printer's colophons (*par byang*) of both the *Mdo dbang brgyud pa'i rnam thar*, 421.2–424.6, and the *Rgya mtsho'i 'jug mngogs*, vol. 43, 637.4–643.2.
25. *Mdo dbang brgyud pa'i rnam thar*, 422.1–423.1, or *Rgya mtsho'i 'jug mngogs*, vol. 43, 639.1–3.
26. *Mdo dbang brgyud pa'i rnam thar*, 424.2–4, or *Rgya mtsho'i 'jug mngogs*, vol. 43, 642.1–4.
27. Sönam Gyatso was subsequently recognized as the third in this new incarnation line, with his two previous incarnations retrospectively named the First and Second Dalai Lamas.
28. Samten Karmay, *The Arrow and the Spindle: Studies in History, Myth, Rituals and Beliefs in Tibet* (Kathmandu: Mandala Book Point, 1998), 509.
29. *Gu bkra'i chos 'byung*, 448: "The great treasure [revealer, Zhikpo Lingpa] himself, along with Sokdokpa Lodrö Gyeltsen and Gongra Lochen, were known as the Nang-Sok-Gong trio. During their lifetimes, all the Nyingma spoken teachings and treasures spread widely. These have remained without deterioration even up to the present day, thanks to the kindness of the great treasure [revealer, Zhikpo Lingpa]. However, the precious omniscient Fifth did not like this Nang-Sok-Gong trio." For more on the controversy, see E. Gene Smith, *Among Tibetan Texts: History and Literature of the Himalayan Plateau* (Boston: Wisdom, 2004), and Matthew Akester, "The 'Vajra Temple' of gTer ston Zhig po gling pa and the Politics of Flood Control in 16th Century lHa sa," *Tibet Journal* 26, no. 1 (2001): 14–15 n. 22–23.
30. *Byang pa'i rnam thar*, 457.4–5. On Zhikpo Lingpa, see Per K. Sørensen and Guntram Hazod, *Rulers on the Celestial Plain: Ecclesiastic and Secular Hegemony in Medieval Tibet. A Study of Tshal Gung-thang* (Vienna: Verlag der Österreichischen Akademie der Wissenschaften, 2007), esp. 516–26; Matthew Akester, "The 'Vajra Temple'" and "Khyung tshang brag: The 'Black Demon Peering' at lHa sa," *Tibet Journal* 26, no. 1 (2001): 25–34.
31. On Sokdokpa's ritual performances and his relationship with the Tsang kings, see James Gentry, "Representation of Efficay: The Ritual Expulsion of Mongol Armies in the Consolidation and Expansion of the Tsang," in *Tibetan Ritual*, ed. José I. Cabezón (Oxford: Oxford University Press, 2010), esp. 146–52, and Dalton, *Taming of the Demons*, 133–36.
32. Dudjom, *The Nyingma School of Tibetan Buddhism*, 783 (with transcribed names adjusted to match my own system). I have seen no mention,

however, that Lekden Dorjé played any role in the climactic episode when (in Dudjom Rinpoché's words), "the entire monastic community of their seminary became a wandering encampment, as a result of the depredations of Zhingshakpa, the governor of Tsang."

33. *Byang pa'i rnam thar*, 458.5–6. The final comparisons are likely references to the tale of Sundarī, in which heretics persuade the brahmin girl to say she had slept with the *tathāgata*, and the standard biographies of Padmasambhava, which typically end the master's visit with accusations by the royal ministers.
34. This family had enjoyed great successes in the preceding years. According to Leonard van der Kuijp ("Notes Appropos of the Transmission of the Sarvadurgatipariśodhanatantra in Tibet," *Studien zur Indologie und Iranisk* 16, no. 7 [1992], 113), prior to 1466, Jang Ngamring had been a see of Bodong Paṇchen. This appears to have changed during the lifetime of Namgyel Draksang (1395–1475), whose son (according to Götsangpa Natsok Rangdröl's *Phyogs thams cad las rnam par rgyal ba'i rnam thar*, 31b.4–5), the Jangdak Namkha [Tsewang] Dorjé, then oversaw the expansion of his family's rule from Latö Jang over the Lho region. Götsangpa expresses his opinion, following Tsangnyön himself, it seems (see also *Rje btsun gtsang pa he ru ka'i thun mong gi rnam thar*, 11b.4–7), that this was an unjust annexation. According to the Fifth Dalai Lama, this Namkha Dorjé had three sons. The middle son became a monk, while the ambitious younger son, Künga Lekpa, appears to have usurped the elder's (Namkha Rinchen) position as the family head. "The youngest became lord of the whole of Lho and Jang and became famous as a terrible hero," writes the Great Fifth (Giuseppe Tucci, *Tibetan Painted Scrolls*, 3 vols. [Rome: Libreria dello Stato, 1949], 632). However, considerable confusion surrounds these events. Lhatsun Rinchen Namgyel (*Grub thob gtsang pa smyon pa'i rnam thar*, 53.2–3), for example, names just two sons (Namkha Lekpa and Künga Lekpa), and Cyrus Stearns, *King of the Empty Plain: The Tibetan Iron-Bridge Builder Tangtong Gyalpo* (Ithaca, NY: Snow Lion, 2007), 583 n. 1136, has the former as king. Worse still, the Fifth goes on to write that both the eldest and youngest brothers were fathers to Tashi Topgyel, but most sources have the eldest, Namkha Rinchen, as the real father, while Franz-Karl Ehrhard, "The Mnga' bdag Family and the Tradition of Rig 'dzin zhig po gling pa (1524–1583) in Sikkim," *Bulletin of Tibetology* 41, no. 2 (2005): 15, has Namkha Tsewang Dorjé as his father. Clearly more work is required to sort through the differing opinions. In his *Chronicles* (see Tucci, *Tibetan Painted Scrolls*, and, for a full translation, Zahiruddin

Ahmad, *A History of Tibet by the Fifth Dalai Lama of Tibet* [Bloomington: Indiana University Press, 1995]), the Fifth writes that all three sons of Namkha Dorjé were fathers to Tashi Topgyel, but in his *Byang pa'i rnam thar*, 462.4, he recognizes that the middle brother, being a monk, could not have been. Given the allegiances of the period, it is also noteworthy that the mother of Tashi Topgyel, named Chökyong Dzomchen, was from the governing family of Lhasa (see Kun bzang nges don klong yangs' *Nor bu do sal*, 139b.3). Also, Tucci appears to have mistaken Tashi Topgyel Wangpö De as two names when it is only one.

35. The Dalai Lama goes on to explain that "If the conditions were not in order, he would be born into a family of ministers to that ruling family, as a son of the Jang Khangsar in a rooster or monkey year. In that [latter] case, before the son would be born, the father would die, [but] if he were born into the ruling family, he would enjoy a long relationship with his father" (*Byang pa'i rnam thar*, 465.3–4).
36. See Tucci, *Tibetan Painted Scrolls*, 631–41. On this family, see also Luciano Petech, *Central Tibet and the Mongols: The Yüan-Sa-skya Period of Tibetan History* (Rome: Istituto Italiano per il Medio ed Estremo Oriente, 1990), 53 n. 60; Elliot E. Sperling, "Miscellaneous Remarks on the Lineage of Byang La-stod," *China Tibetology*, special issue (1992): 272–77; Per K. Sørensen, *The Mirror Illuminating the Royal Genealogies: Tibetan Buddhist Historiography: An Annotated Translation of the XIVth Century Tibetan Chronicle: rGyal-rabs gsal-ba'i me-long* (Wiesbaden: Harrassowitz Verlag, 1994), 33 n. 92.
37. *Byang pa'i rnam thar*, 465.5–466.3.
38. Such an explanation would entail that Lekden Dorjé's decision was not made until Tashi Topgyel was already in his late teens, for Tashi Topgyel was born in 1550 and Zhingshakpa Karma Tseten did not take Samdruptsé until 1565. In other words, any disagreement with the Tsang court could not have taken place until 1566 at the earliest. An alternative explanation might be that the Fifth Dalai Lama in the above passage was referring to a later move by the Tsang kings—possibly even by Karma Tenkyong Wangpo (1606–1642)—to take control of the Northern Treasures line retroactively. This would mean that the Dalai Lama was not referring here to the problems encountered by Lekden Dorjé at all.
39. See *Byang pa'i rnam thar*, 479.1.
40. Tseten Dorjé is referring here to the Jang Lord's family roots in Minyak, which is located in the eastern Tibetan region of Kham.

41. *Bdud 'joms rgyal rabs*, 493.2–5. On the ten fields and liberation rites in general, see Dalton, *Taming of the Demons*, 87, and on the role of Rāhula in such violent practices, see Per K. Sørensen and Guntram Hazod, *Civilization at the Foot of Mount Sham-po: The Royal House of lHa Bug-pa-can and the History of g.Ya'-bzang* (Vienna: Verlag der Österreichischen Akademie der Wissenschaften, 2000), 167–73.
42. *Byang pa'i rnam thar*, 468.6–469.1. The prophecy is said to appear in Ngari Paṇchen's *Rikdzin Yongdu*.
43. *Byang pa'i rnam thar*, 469.3–5.
44. *Byang pa'i rnam thar*, 484.2–3. See also the *Dar mdo rdo rje brag*, 5–6, which claims that Tashi Topgyel traveled to Dartsedo and established the small temple that would eventually become the Dorjé Drak monastery there.
45. This is almost certainly the Katok Khenpo Gtsang pa Padma Rgyal mtshan, who is discussed in the *Rgyal ba kaḥ thog pa'i lo rgyus mdor bsdus*, 79–81. The same pages also refer to a student of his, one Hor po Tshe rgyal, or Rgyal thang pa Ston pa seng ge, who appears in our passage as Wönpo Tsegyel. The reference to Lang Darma would have been seen as insulting because it is the name of the supposedly demonic king who caused the early Tibetan empire to collapse, plunging Tibet into its so-called age of fragmentation.
46. *Byang pa'i rnam thar*, 497.2–498.1.
47. *Rgya mtsho'i 'jug mngogs*, vol. 41, 13.4–5.
48. *Rgya mtsho'i 'jug mngogs*, vol. 41, 108.6–109.2. The details of Pema Trinlé's arrangements are quite technical, and dicussion of them would certainly lead away from our present focus on lineage. For this reason, a survey of the various systems of initiation ritual is left for the next chapter.
49. Guru Tashi (*Gu bkra'i chos 'byung*, 448) points out a similar resignation by the Fifth Dalai Lama, when he is forced to trace his *Bka' brgyad bde gshegs 'dus pa* lineage (received from Terdak Lingpa) through Zhikpo Lingpa.

6. THE MINDRÖLING TRADITION

1. Kurtis Schaeffer, "Ritual, Festival and Authority Under the Fifth Dalai Lama," in *Power, Politics, and the Reinvention of Tradition: Tibet in the Seventeenth and Eighteenth Centuries*, ed. Bryan J. Cuevas and Kurtis R. Schaeffer (Leiden: Brill), 194. Schaeffer's paper provides several illuminating examples of what I am calling Sangyé Gyatso's "bureaucratization" of the Ganden Podrang. See also Christoph Cüppers, "Registers and Account Books of the dGa'ldan Pho-brang Government," in *The Paṇḍita and the Siddha:*

Tibetan Studies in Honour of E. Gene Smith, ed. Ramon Prats (Dharamsala, India: Amnye Machen Institute, 2007), 12–15.

2. As noted by Kurtis Schaeffer, "The Fifth Dalai Lama Ngawang Lopsang Gyatso," in *The Dalai Lamas: A Visual History*, ed. Martin Brauen (Chicago: Serindia, 2005), 70–74, the Fifth Dalai Lama composed an entire text on the seating arrangements for the Mönlam Chenmo. Schaeffer observes how, in this text, the Dalai Lama establishes the monks of his own monastery, Drepung, as the "elders" of the *saṅgha* and positions them at the top of his seating hierarchy.
3. Luciano Petech, *Central Tibet and the Mongols: The Yüan-Sa-skya Period of Tibetan History* (Rome: Istituto Italiano per il Medio ed Estremo Oriente, 1990), 120.
4. Hugh E. Richardson, *Ceremonies of the Lhasa Year* (London: Serindia, 1993), 7.
5. For a recent study of another large-scale ritual created during this same period at Mindröling, but based on Terdak Lingpa's treasure, see Richard J. Kohn, *Lord of the Dance: The Mani Rimdu Festival in Tibet and Nepal* (Albany: State University of New York Press, 2001). While Terdak Lingpa's treasures have certainly spread since the early eighteenth century, his reformulation of the Spoken Teachings remains far more influential in today's Nyingma School.
6. Kohn, *Lord of the Dance*, 11 and 49. The new Ganden Podrang government went to some efforts to create their own public ritualized dance traditions (*'chams*), based on those of the Lang Pakmodrüpa; see Olaf Czaja, *Medieval Rule in Tibet: The Rlangs Clan and the Political and Religious History of the Ruling House of Phag mo gru pa* (Wien: Verlag der Österreichischen Akademie der Wissenschaften, 2013), 23. The Fifth Dalai Lama even composed his own treatise on ritual dance, translated and analyzed by René de Nebesky-Wojkowitz in *Tibetan Religious Dances: Tibetan Text and Annotated Translation of the 'Chams Yig*, ed. Christoph von Fürer-Haimendorf (The Hague: Mouton, 1976).
7. More recently a "greatly expanded" collection (*Bka' ma shin tu rgyas pa*) in 133 volumes was compiled at Katok, with the final version published in 2009.
8. Later generations supplemented these basic manuals with *rgyun mkhyer*, *bla brgyud gsol 'debs*, and the like. It also seems that, at times, the Mindröling family chose not to compose certain manuals when earlier ones already existed, written by particularly famous lamas.
9. See *Rnying ma bka' ma rgyas pa*, vol. *zha*.

10. Dudjom Rinpoche, *The Nyingma School of Tibetan Buddhism*, trans. Gyurme Dorje (Boston: Wisdom, 1991), 732. I have replaced the translation of the *Gathering of Intentions*' title to match that used in the present study.
11. The five relevant volumes are known collectively as Dharmaśrī's *Sources About the Gathering of Intentions* (*'Dus pa mdo skor gyi yig cha*), and almost all the texts therein focus on the system's ritual tradition (see *Lo chen gsung 'bum*, vols. 9–13; see also *Rnying ma bka' ma rgyas pa*, vols. 14–16). The first volume contains two texts dealing with the mandala rituals. The second volume contains four works: the *'Dus pa mdo'i sgrub khog rin chen 'od kyi snang ba* discusses the ritual procedures of the *sādhana* according to the four ritual stages of propitiation and accomplishment (*bsnyen sgrub kyi yan lag bzhi*). This is a large-scale *sādhana*, to be performed by an assembly of monks, not the sort an individual might perform on a daily basis. The *sādhana* is accompanied by a second work that serves as an appendix to both the *sādhana* and the mandala ritual manual in the first volume. The remaining two texts are performance lists (*tho*) for the initiation and the blessing (*dngos grub len*) ceremonies respectively. Volume 3 contains the initiation ritual manual (*dbang chog*) followed by a short description of the ritual cards (*tsakli*) needed for the initiations. Volume four consists of seven texts. The first, the *General Exposition*, is a more general study of the *Gathering of Intentions* and its history and thus a major work not focused exclusively on ritual. The remaining six texts are relatively short works on how to draw the mandala (*thig tshon gi bya ba*), the ritual dances, and the musical accompaniments (*rol mo*). Finally, volume 5 contains three works on the offerings ceremonies, including the manual for the fire sacrifice (*sbyin sreg*).
12. E. Gene Smith, *Among Tibetan Texts: History and Literature of the Himalayan Plateau* (Boston: Wisdom, 2001), 20–22.
13. *Spyi don*, 133.6–134.2.
14. Thus in fact Dharmaśrī is making a three-part distinction among the lineage of the basic tantra itself, which was first taught atop Mount Malaya and received by King Dza; the "fully complete four streams" consisting of the other eight vehicles that were first gathered in the person of Garap Dorjé; and the fully complete practice tradition, which was first assembled by Déwa Seldzé around the mid-ninth century. (None of these origins is historically verifiable.) Part of the problem is the tension between the *Gathering of Intentions*' original claim to include Atiyoga, which would therefore first have appeared in the world atop Mount Malaya along with all the inner tantras (i.e., Mahā-Anu-Ati), and the later tradition's claim that Atiyoga originated later, during the lifetime of Garap Dorjé.

15. *Spyi don*, 132.1–132.5. Having in this way dismissed the idea that Garap Dorjé might have been the first to hold the fully complete practice tradition of the Sutra Initiation, Dharmaśrī turns to the possibility that Nupchen might have made it up. He outlines the following faulty line of reasoning: Déwa Seldzé does not appear in any of the individual lineages for the other eight vehicles. However, Nupchen does figure in all the lineages. Therefore, Nupchen must have been the first human to hold all the individual lineages, as well as the fully complete practice tradition. The flaw here, as Dharmaśrī points out, is that although Déwa Seldzé does not appear in the later lists for the individual lineages, that does not mean that he did not hold all of those lineages. Many persons may hold a single lineage, but only one of them finally will be chosen for inclusion in the later lists.
16. See, for example, *Spyi don*, 185.6 and 245.1.
17. These are said to have first appeared in the six chapters extracted by Déwa Seldzé.
18. For a summary of how Dharmaśrī divided the coarse branches among the vehicles, see *Spyi don*, 220–21. There is considerable overlap among the first three vehicles, so that the seventh coarse branch, the name initiation (*ming dbang*), is granted twice, once during the gods and humans vehicle and again in the *śrāvaka* vehicle. Such repeats happen twenty-seven times, and four "additional" (*lhag por*) initiations are added, so that by the end of these six vehicles the 108 coarse branches have in practice grown to 139 in number (on this, see *Spyi don*, 239.3).
19. See *Rdo rje'i them skas*, 6.6.
20. *Rdo rje'i them skas*, 63.6–64.1. This passage confirms that the individual coarse branch initiations are distinguished only for the fully complete or pith instructions system, whereas the tantra system restricts itself to the more general thirty-six "root initiations." This is borne out upon examination of Dharmaśrī's manual itself. In the section where the ten outer initiations are granted according to the tantra system (which begins on *Rdo rje'i them skas*, 327.2), Dharmaśrī makes no mention of the coarse branch initiations. Rather, each of the ten root initiations is granted as a single initiation. Abbreviated in this way, several initiations do not even use the empowering substances (*dbang rdzas*) and are granted instead through a brief visualization and a prayer.
21. *Rdo rje'i them skas*, 7.1–2.
22. *Spyi don*, 243.6–244.1.
23. *Rdo rje'i them skas*, 7.1–2.

24. See *Rdo rje'i them skas*, 491.3–503.6. These initiations strongly resemble the secret initiation, the wisdom gnosis initiation, and the fourth initiation common to all Yoganiruttara tantras.
25. *Spyi don*, 244.5.6. After these final secret initiations, the whole ceremony ends with a long-life initiation (*tshe dbang*) and, if appropriate, the conferral of the seal of entrustment.
26. *Spyi don*, 241.3–6. The *Len Manual* was unusual for only describing the initiations of the first three initiation streams, leaving the initiations for Atiyoga secret. In the manual as it is today, the secret stream is found in an appendix added by Zurham himself (see *Glan chog*, vol. 61, 788–833), at the end of which Zurham insists that he wrote it, "in accordance with [what was taught by] Lenchen Śākya Gönpo Pelden Chöseng and Zurben Chöjé Jampa Sengé" (*Glan chog*, vol. 61, 810.2). This is probably why someone might see no evidence for the Atiyoga initiations in the *Len Manual*.
27. For these dates, see *Rdo rje'i them skas*, 567.4–5, and *Spyi don*, 259.2–3.
28. Terdak Lingpa's biological son was the second Mindröling throne holder and would have been only five years old in 1691.
29. *Spyi don*, 124.4–125.2.
30. "The second time, the Sutra Initiation was bestowed to the excellent lord lama's son and relatives and to Öchok Tülku [Cetön Ngawang Künzang Rangdröl], Tangdrok Tülku [Künzang Lekdrup], Bönlung Tülku, and so on, and the last time to [Peling] Sungtrül Ngawang Künzang Dorjé (1680–1723), Yönpo Tülku, Khampa Tülku, Nawo Dungyü, Rongpa Dzokchen Tülku, and so forth" (*Spyi don*, 127.1–3; bracketed additions are culled from colophon of the *Rdo rje'i them skas*, 566.6–567.1). The colophon to Dharmaśrī's manual adds a few more names, including Dokham Gojo Lama Namdröl Zangpo, Pel Lama Yeshé, and Dorjé Gön.
31. On the reasons for the Dzungars' Tibetan expedition, see Luciano Petech, *China and Tibet in the Early XVIIIth Century* (Leiden: Brill, 1972), 32–33.
32. Petech, *China and Tibet in the Early XVIIIth Century*, 53–54.
33. Smith, *Among Tibetan Texts*, 19.

7. RETURNS TO THE ORIGIN

1. There are six "mother" monasteries in the Nyingma School: two in central Tibet—Dorjé Drak and Mindröling—and four in Kham—Katok, Pelyul, Dzokchen, and Zhechen. Except for Katok, all were founded in the one hundred years between 1632 (Dorjé Drak) and 1735 (Zhechen), and even Katok was "re-founded" in 1656.

2. On the Nyarong war, see Yudru Tsomu, "Local Aspirations and National Constraints: A Case Study of Nyarong Gonpo Namgyel and His Rise to Power in Kham (1836–1865)" (Ph.D. diss., Harvard University, 2006). On the rise of Kham in the nineteenth century more generally, see Alexander P. Gardner, "The Twenty-five Great Sites of Khams: Religious Geography, Revelation, and Nonsectarianism in Nineteenth-Century Eastern Tibet" (Ph.D. diss., University of Michigan, 2006); Jann Michael Ronis, "Celibacy, Revelations, and Reincarnated Lamas: Contestation and Synthesis in the Growth of Monasticism at Katok Monastery from the Seventeenth Through Nineteenth Centuries" (Ph.D. diss., University of Virginia, 2009), "Powerful Women of Degé: Reassessing the Reign of Tsewang Lhamo (d. 1812)," *Revue d'Etudes Tibétaines* 22 (2011): 61–82, "Deeds of the Dergé King," in *Sources of Tibetan Tradition*, ed. Matthew Kapstein, Kurtis Schaeffer, and Gray Tuttle (New York: Columbia University Press, 2013), 607–13, and "The Prolific Preceptor: Si tu paṇ chen's Career as Ordination Master in Khams and Its Effect on Sectarian Relations in Sde dge," *Journal of the International Association of Tibetan Studies* 7 (2013): 49–85.
3. For the Sakya School, they created the *Compendium of Tantric Systems* and the *Compendium of Sādhanas*; for the Kagyu, the *Treasury of Kagyu Mantra*; and for the Nyingma and Bon, the *Treasury of Precious Treasures* and the *Treasury of Oral Instructions*. In addition, Jamgön Kongtrül compiled his encyclopedic *Treasury of Knowledge*, a far-ranging history of Tibetan Buddhism (all of which has now been translated and published by Snow Lion). On the compilation of Kongtrül's five treasuries, see Gardner, "The Twenty-five Great Sites of Khams," 251–61.
4. E. Gene Smith, *Among Tibetan Texts: History and Literature of the Himalayan Plateau* (Boston: Wisdom, 2001), 229 (with my phoneticizations). The Nyingmapa of the nineteenth century emphasized the differences between their own scholastic curriculum and that of the Gelukpa. These differences were certainly real, but the trend toward standardization was still apparent, and by the time Jamgön Mipham Gyatso (1846–1912) composed his elegant commentaries, it was undeniable. On this figure, see John Pettit, *Mipham's Beacon of Certainty* (Boston: Wisdom, 1999); Smith, *Among Tibetan Texts*, 227–33; Karma Phuntsho, *Mipham's Dialectics and the Debates on Emptiness* (London and New York: Routledge Curzon, 2005); Douglas Duckworth, *Jamgon Mipam: His Life and Teachings* (Boston: Shambala, 2011).
5. Jamgön Kongtrül's selection of texts to include in his *Treasury of Precious Treasures* in particular led to some controversy, most famously his

decision to exclude the revelations of the well-connected Rikdzin Nyima Drakpa (1647–1710); see Dan Martin, "The Emergence of Bon and the Tibetan Polemical Tradition" (Ph.D. diss., Indiana University, 1991), 173–81; Bryan J. Cuevas, *The Hidden History of The Tibetan Book of the Dead* (New York: Oxford University Press, 2003), 179–90; *Gu bkra'i chos 'byung*, 829–55.

6. For a list of the thirteen tantras included, see Lama Tsering Jampal Zangpo, *Garland of Immortal Wish-Fulfilling Trees*, trans. Sangye Khandro (Ithaca: Snow Lion, 1988), 97. For an account of Getsé's invitation and of his project to reestablish the Spoken Teachings in Kham more generally, see Ronis, "Celibacy, Revelations, and Reincarnated Lamas," 188–211.
7. As quoted and translated by Ronis, "Celibacy, Revelations, and Reincarnated Lamas," 197–98. As Ronis (p. 209) further observes, Getsé even seems to have accepted the earlier critiques of his own Katok-based Sutra Initiation tradition for having become overly complicated.
8. For a discussion of Getsé's motivations in this regard, see Ronis, "Celibacy, Revelations, and Reincarnated Lamas," 199–201. Getsé was in part responding to Gelukpa criticisms of the Nyingma School for its lack of a coherent institutional structure. The nineteenth-century eastern Tibetan movement against local village lamas and toward ethics and institutional monasticism has also been discussed by Smith, *Among Tibetan Texts*, 23, and Jacob Dalton, *Taming of the Demons: Violence and Liberation in Tibetan Buddhism* (New Haven: Yale University Press, 2011), 150–51.
9. My thanks to Jann Ronis for generously providing this reference. Ronis is preparing what will surely be a valuable study of this new index, which includes a history of the various editions of the Spoken Teachings.
10. This according to Tupten Pelzang Rinpoché (henceforth Tupzang Rinpoché), an expert on the Spoken Teachings, in a series of interviews conducted at Pelyul monastery in May and June, 2001.
11. Zangpo, *Garland of Immortal Wish-Fulfilling Trees*, 96–97.
12. On this Pelyul xylographic edition in twenty volumes, see Gyurme Dorje, "The *Guhyagarbhatantra* and Its XIVth Century Tibetan Commentary, *phyogs bcu mun sel*" (Ph.D. diss., University of London, SOAS, 1987), 167 n. 175, where he cites an interview with Dudjom Rinpoché. According to him, the *Sung kama* edition (in 14 volumes) that appears in the Public Law 480–funded collection is in large part based on these two nineteenth-century editions. The Pelyul edition was then supplemented by Dudjom Rinpoché in the 1980s to make the *Expanded Spoken Teachings of the Nyingma School* collection (in 57 volumes), also found in the PL480. More recently, a further "greatly expanded" (*shin tu rgyas pa*) edition has

been published in 133 volumes. The latter was compiled with the inspiration of Khenpo Münsel (1916–1993) and overseen by Katok Khenpo Jamyang, a scholar who passed away in 1999.

13. Dudjom Rinpoche, *The Nyingma School of Tibetan Buddhism*, trans. Gyurme Dorje. (Boston: Wisdom, 1991), 738.
14. Zangpo, *Garland of Immortal Wish-Fulfilling Trees*, 97.
15. At Zhechen in Kathmandu a "great accomplishment" (*sgrub chen*) is performed, but this requires the *sādhana* practice to continue unbroken throughout each night, so at most other places it is not done. A more literal translation of what I am calling a "festival" (*sgrub mchod*) is an "accomplishment ritual." The term *sgrub mchog* is used by Dudjom Rinpoché when he refers to the festival in question his *Bdud 'joms rgyal rabs*, 410. Jacob P. Dalton, "The Uses of the *Dgongs pa 'dus pa'i mdo* in the Development of the Rnying-ma School of Tibetan Buddhism" (Ph.D. diss., University of Michigan, 2002), appendix 6, contains a brief description of this festival as it was performed on two recent occasions, at Namdroling monastery in June 2000 and at Pelyul monastery in June 2001.
16. At Zhechen in Kham it begins on the twenty-seventh day of the third month, running for seven days, while at Zhechen in Kathmandu it runs for ten days, beginning on the tenth day of the first month every year. And at Katok it is performed from the third to the fifteenth of the first month. The dates for Zhechen and Katok in Kham are based on oral communication from Moktsa Tülku, May 14, 2001. The dates for Zhechen in Kathmandu were communicated to me by Matthieu Ricard, January 29, 2000. Other Nyingma monasteries throughout India also perform the festival, including the Mindröling branch in Dehra Dun and, in the ninth month, Ringu Tülku's monastery, where, I was told, only the Gathered Great Assembly mandala is accomplished because of limited resources.
17. Penor Rinpoché, at the Sutra Initiation he granted in October 1999, referred to the *Gathering of Intentions* as "the mother of all the teachings."
18. His arrival is dated in his *Gangs ljongs dbus gtsang gnas bskor lam yig nor bu zla shel gyi se mo do*, 418.
19. The following story, except where otherwise noted, was told to me three times during my research—first by Kunzang Lama of Namdroling (in an interview conducted on October 21, 1999), then by Rikdzin Pema of Zhechen in Kathmandu (on September 8, 2000), and finally by Tupzang Rinpoché of Pelyul in Kham (on May 29, 2001). Except on those points noted, the three versions were generally in agreement.

20. Khenpo Nüden refers to her advice as a "prophecy" (*lung bstan*) in the colophon to his subcommentary (*Rnal 'byor nyi ma gsal bar byed pa*, vol. 56, 714: *gtsang bkra shis lhun por dpal ldan sngags kyi srung mas brda lung dang mthun par mdo 'grel mun pa'i go cha phyag tu son pa)*. The use of this term indicates that the discovery might be understood as a kind of treasure revelation. Tupzang Rinpoché also used the term "prophecy" in telling this story.
21. Some who told me this story describe this light entering through a high window to shine down upon the text, but most described it as a more mysterious light (possibly rainbow colored) shimmering around the text. For an account of a similar light revealing the location of a treasure (i.e., *gter ma*), see Janet Gyatso, "The Logic of Legitimation in the Tibetan Treasure Tradition," *History of Religions* 33, no. 2 (1993): 124, where Rikdzin Gödem's revelations are described.
22. It seems that Dharmaśrī possessed a copy of the *Armor Against Darkness*, as he cites it regularly in his *General Exposition*.
23. This part of the story was related to me by Rikdzin Pema of Zhechen.
24. On these further discoveries, see *Rnal 'byor nyi ma gsal bar byed pa*, vol. 56, 702.4–704.6.
25. *Bsnyen yig legs bshad skya reng dang po'i snang ba*, 490.4–491.5.
26. This interpretation was suggested to me by Kunzang Lama of Namdroling monastery in Bylakuppe, India.
27. The following story of Nüden's teaching is based primarily on a series of interviews conducted with Tupzang Rinpoché in May 2001. I heard the story several other times, but only Tupzang Rinpoché's was a firsthand account.
28. Whenever the *Gathering of Intentions* is transmitted, certain rituals are required in the morning and the evening of each day. These are described in the *'Chad thabs zin bris nyung ngu rnam gsal* by Jamyang Chökyi Lodrö ('Jam dbyangs blo gros rgya mtsho, *Spyi mdo dgongs 'dus kyi 'chad thabs zin bris nyung ngu rnam gsal, Bka' ma shin tu rgyas pa 1*, vol. 52, 321–34).
29. A major student of Nüden's and a teacher of both Penor Rinpoché and Tupzang Rinpoché. He left Tibet in the same party with Penor Rinpoché but was shot dead en route by the Chinese.
30. Also a teacher of Penor Rinpoché.
31. Tupzang Rinpoché had received it in the Katok tradition (using the *River of Honey* initiation manual) twice from the Katok Khenpo Jorden, who also gave the same initiation to Nüden, as well as Penor Rinpoché and Dongnang Rinpoché. Tupzang Rinpoché received it in the Mindröling tradition from Penor Rinpoché. He also received the reading transmissions for the

Dorjé Drak and Nyelwa Delek initiation manuals from Khenpo Jamyang of Katok, who himself probably received them from Khenpo Jorden. Penor Rinpoché also received the initiation in the Dorjé Drak tradition, though I have not determined from whom.

32. *Rnal 'byor nyi ma gsal bar byed pa*, vol. 56, 713.5.
33. The blocks for Nüden's commentary are said to have been hidden at Muksang monastery by the fourth Karma Kuchen, according to Tupzang Rinpoché, who showed me a print made from these same blocks. The new version found in Dudjom Rinpoché's *Bka' ma rgyas pa* collection fills four volumes, but the older edition from the Muksang blocks is only two volumes. I have not seen these older Nüden blocks myself.
34. Penor Rinpoché's decision certainly made sense, given that Nüden's commentary incorporates word-for-word the entirety of the *Gathering of Intentions* itself and the *Armor Against Darkness*. The trouble was that, although Nüden marked every word from the root text, it was impossible to tell which are his own words and which are Nupchen's.
35. Tsering Lama is also the author of a famous history of Pelyul, an English translation of which has been published by Zangpo, *A Garland of Immortal Wish-Fulfilling Trees*.
36. The following story comes from two interviews with Kunzang Lama (conducted October 21, 1999, and June 13, 2000). Gene Smith confirmed the story, as he was working with Dudjom Rinpoché on saving rare Tibetan books at that time.
37. A final obstacle arose when they found that a single page had somehow been left in Kham, but Kunzang Lama was easily able to retrieve it on his next trip to Tibet.
38. *Mun pa'i go cha*, vol. 51, 56.1.

APPENDIX

1. *Sog bzlog gsung 'bum*, Vol. 1, 481.3. Nyangrel Nyimé Özer tells us that Dorjé Pelgi Drakpa was an important teacher of Nupchen Sangyé Yeshé (*Nyang ral chos 'byung*, 435). If true, Gö Khukpa's claim that the *Gathering of All Knowledge* and the *Gathering of Intentions* were written by Nupchen's Tibetan teacher might mean that Nupchen fabricated his trip to Brusha, and that in composing his *Armor Against Darkness* he was simply commenting on his own teacher's apocryphal work. Gö Khukpa's accusation may be read another way, so that in blaming Dorjé Pelgi Drakpa, Gö was actually directing his attack at the student, trying to discredit Nupchen.

Whatever the case may be, it is clear that Nupchen was a lightning rod for both positive and negative polemics in later histories and treatises.

2. On this work, see Samten Karmay, *The Great Perfection* (Leiden: Brill, 1998), 17–40, where Karmay dates the *Bka' shog* to 1092.
3. *Theg pa spyi bcings rtsa 'grel*, 113.
4. My translations of the titles listed here and below were done "on the fly," without any knowledge of most of the works in question. In other words, they are not trustworthy.
5. Dudjom Rinpoche, *The Nyingma School of Tibetan Buddhism*, trans. Gyurme Dorje (Boston: Wisdom, 1991), 289.
6. *Snga 'gyur rgyud 'bum rin po che'i rtogs par brjod pa*, 388.
7. For more on this subject, see chapter 3.
8. *Mun pa'i go cha*, vol. 50, 8.1.
9. *Mun pa'i go cha*, vol. 50, 39.5–40.1.
10. *Rnal 'byor nyi ma gsal bar byed pa*, vol. 56, 697.5.
11. For a discussion of the mandalas, see Dharmaśrī's *Spyi don*, 186.
12. Cathy Cantwell and Robert Mayer, *Early Tibetan Documents on Phur pa from Dunhuang* (Vienna: Verlag der Österreichischen Akademie der Wissenschaften, 2008), 80, note a parallel between ITJ331/3 and the received tantra.
13. Compare for example *Wisdom's Magnificent Thunderbolts*, 169.7, with *Dur khrod khu byug rol pa'i rgyud ces bya ba theg pa chen po'i mdo*, 297.7.
14. See especially 315–20.
15. See Samten Karmay, *The Arrow and the Spindle: Studies in History, Myth, Rituals and Beliefs in Tibet* (Kathmandu: Mandala Book Point, 1998), 33. Zhi-ba 'Od also lists a "*Bshad rgyud* of *Khu byug rol ba*."
16. *Spyi don*, 50.6–51.2.
17. Further evidence of a link between the two works may be a passage that appears at the beginning of the eighth chapter of the Khyentse edition of the *Play of the Charnel Ground Cuckoo*: "From the Charnel Grounds and the Magnificent Thunderbolts" (vol. *da*, 585.6: *dud khrod dang ni ngam 'glog nas*). However, if this line is referring to the two titles, it misspells them, and the same passage in the Mtshams 'brag edition reads very differently (see 268.1).
18. See *Spyi don*, 1–260, 158.3, and 191.4.
19. On the textual derivations of the Gathered Great Assembly mandalas, see *Spyi don*, 186–187.
20. See Dudjom, *The Nyingma School of Tibetan Buddhism*, 289. In his *Brief Structural Analysis of the Sutra*, Dampa provides a list of the writings on the

Compendium that were circulating in his day. The last text listed is titled the *Mdo bzhi'i bye brag*, apparently a discussion of the differences between the four sutras. This is useful for hazarding a guess on when the four sutras were settled as such. Given that Zhiwa Ö's *Decree* refers to them as the "five sutras" in 1092, and here, sometime around 1161 (the date for the founding of the Katok *bshad grwa*), they appear as four, we can tentatively suggest that the four fundamental tantras of anuyoga were consolidated as a set in the early twelfth century. Also, Pema Trinlé mentions (*Mdo dbang brgyud pa'i rnam thar*, 189.2) that Zurché, who was active in the eleventh century, studied them as five sutras. The fact that even within the Zur tradition there was a shift from five to four also suggests it was not the case that the Zurs were following a four-sutra tradition even as Zhiwa Ö referred to a five-sutra tradition.

21. Yet further evidence that the fifth "sutra," the *Sems lung chen mo*, should not be included in this circle of texts is its different presentation of the nine vehicles in which Mahāyoga, Anuyoga, and Atiyoga are subdivisions of Yoga tantra. This system mirrors the presentation in the *Pith Instructional Garland of Views* that is often pointed to as a forerunner to the nine-vehicles system.
22. *Play of the Charnel Ground Cuckoo* has no colophon. The unreliability of these attributions is further accentuated by the fact that other editions of the *Rgyud 'bum* disagree. For example, in the Degé, the translators given for the *Compedium of Knowledge* are Vimalamitra and Klu'i Rgyal mtshan instead of Mkhyen brtse's Padmasambhava and Vairocana. Mtshams 'brag gives no translator.
23. According to *Mdo dbang brgyud pa'i rnam thar*, 247, these are the three from whom Dropukpa received it. This means that the Lharjé Zur mentioned here is probably Dropukpa, a.k.a. Zur Śākya Sengé.
24. It appears that this was the lineage offshoot associated with the Marpa family, mentioned in *Mdo dbang brgyud pa'i rnam thar*, 254. See chapter 4 for a more extensive discussion of this section of the lineage.
25. I.e., not of the early period of Sthiramati, Dharmabodhi, Nupchen, etc. and not of the later tradition. Pema Trinlé uses this term (*bar skabs*) to refer to a different period, namely that between the Nup clan and Dropukpa; see *Mdo dbang brgyud pa'i rnam thar*, 255.1.
26. This seems to mean that the annotated text being quoted here from Daklha Gampo and by Üpa Jobum (an attribution confirmed by *Rnal 'byor nyi ma gsal bar byed pa*, vol. 55, 417.5) was based upon three sets of notes—by Zur Śākya Sengé, Datsa, and Horpo respectively—all from the

"intermediate" period of the *Sutra*'s history. (Yangkhyé appears elsewhere in Nüden as Lharjé Yangkhyé.)

27. All by Situ Rinpoché, apparently.
28. *Rnal 'byor nyi ma gsal bar byed pa*, vol. 56, 702.4–704.6. The last line implies that this set of notes being discussed was written by the last in the sequence just traced, Dakdra Dromtön Tengpo. So far this makes three manuscripts discovered by Situ Rinpoché: one by Dampa, one by Üpa Jobum, and one by Dromtön Tengpo.
29. Including the *Condensed Meaning*, these *Sutra*-related works fill folios 597b8–644a8. The three attributed to Sthiramati are (in the Peking edition of the Tibetan canon; see Daisetz Teitaro Suzuki, *The Tibetan Tripitika: Peking Edition* [Tokyo-Kyoto: Tibetan Tripitika Research Institute, 1957]): 4752, *Skabs 'grel bye brag rnam par bshad pa*; 4753, *Byang chub sems kyi ljon shing*; 4754, *Rgyan dam pa sna tshogs rim par phye ba bkod pa* (trans. Klu'i rgyal mtshan).
30. See *Skabs 'grel bye brag tu bshad pa*, 31.

GLOSSARY

accomplishment initiation stream of renown	*sgrub dbang grags pa'i chu bo*
All-Creating King	*Kun byed rgyal po*
Amé Sherap	A mes shes rab
Armor Against Darkness	*Mun pa'i go cha*
Ati Tenpé Gyeltsen	A ti bstan pa'i rgyal mtshan, third Rdzogs chen rin po che
Ba Rakṣi	Rba Rak shi
Bam Mipam Gönpo	Bam Mi pham mgon po
Bari Gyatsa	*Ba ri brgya rtsa*
Bendé Wangchuk Gyeltsen	Ban de Dbang phyug rgyal mtshan
Bendom Dorjé Gyeltsen	Ban ldom Rdo rje rgyal mtshan
Biographies for the Sutra Initiation Lineage	*Mdo dbang brgyud pa'i rnam thar*
Blazing Flames Tantra	*Me lce 'bar ba'i rgyud*
Bodong Paṇchen	Bo dong pan chen
Bönlung Tülku	Bon lung sprul sku
Brief Structural Analysis of the Sutra	*Mdo phran khog dbub*
Chak Lotsawa Chöjé Pel	Chag lo tsA wa Chos rje dpal
Che Jamsé	Lce Byams sras
Chogyur Lingpa	Mchog 'gyur gling pa
Chöjé Jampa Bum	Chos rje Byams pa 'bum
Chokru Lui Gyeltsen	Cog ru Klu'i rgyal mtshan

Chökyong Dzomchen	Chos skyong 'dzom chen
Chongyé	'Phyong rgyas
Collected Intentions of the Guru	*Bla ma dgongs 'dus*
Collected Precepts on Maṇi	*Ma ni bka' 'bum*
Compendium of Sādhanas	*Sgrub thabs kun btus*
Compendium of Tantric Systems	*Rgyud sde kun btus*
Consecration Ritual Notes	*Las tho rab gnas*
Crystal Mirror	*Shel gyi me long*
Da/Zhang Datik	Zla/Zhang Mda' tig
Dakdra Dromtön Tengpo	Bdag 'dra 'Brom ston 'theng po
Daklha Gampo	Dwags lha sgam po
Dampa Deshek	*See* Katok Dampa Deshek
Dartsedo	Dar rtse mdo
Da Sengé Pel	Mda' Seng ge dpal
Datsha	Mda' tsha
Dawning of the Sun of Good Explanation	*Legs bshad nyi ma'i snang ba*
Degé	Sde dge
Dési Sangyé Gyatso	Sde srid Sangs rgyas rgya mtsho
Déwa Seldzé (a.k.a. Selwé Gyen)	Bde ba gsal mdzad
Dilgo Khyentsé Rinpoché	Ldil mgo Mkhyen brtse rin po che
Dingpopa	*See* Gelong Dingpopa
Dispelling the Darkness from the Ten Directions	*Phyogs bcu mun sel*
Dokham Gojo Lama Namdröl Zangpo	Mdo khams Go 'jo bla ma rnam grol bzang po
Dongpo Könchok Rinchen	Sdong po Dkon mchog rin cen
Dorjé Dudjom Gökyi Demtruchen	Rdo rje bdud 'joms Rgod kyi ldem phru can (*see* Gödemchen)
Dorjé Dudjom Tsel (secret name given to Pema Trinlé)	Rdo rje bdud 'joms rtsal
Dorjé Gön	Rdo rje mgon
Dorjé Tekchok Tsel	Rdo rje theg mchog rtsal
Drak Yongdzong	Sgrags yongs rdzong
Dra'o Chöbum	Bra'o Chos 'bum
Drepung	'Bras spungs
Drikung Peldzin Nyi'o Zangpo	'Bri gung Dpal 'dzin Nyi 'od bzang po
Drölchen Sangyé Rinchen (Gyeltsen Pelzangpo)	Sgrol chen Sangs rgyas rin chen rgyal mtshan dpal bzang po
Drölmawa Drotön Samdrup Dorjé	'Bro ston Bsam grub rdo rje

Dropukpa	Sgro phug pa
Drotön Pelden Drak	Gro ston Dpal ldan grags
Drugu Bendé Üpa Jobum	Gru gu ban de Dbus pa Jo 'bum
Druptop Lhünpel	Grub stob Lhun dpal
Düsum Khyenpa	Dus gsum mkhyen pa
Dzamtön Drowé Gönpo	'Dzam ston 'gro ba'i mgon po
Dzokchen	Rdzogs chen
Dzokchen Gyelsé Zhenpen Tayé	Rdzogs chen rgyal sras gzhan phan mtha' yas
Dzokchenpa Namkha Drukdra	Rdzogs chen pa Nam mkha' 'brug sgra
Dzokchen Rinpoché	*See* Ati Tenpé Gyeltsen
Dzongnang Rinpoché Jampel Lodrö	Rdzong nang rin po che 'Jam dpal blo gros
Entry Point Into the Ocean	*Rgya mtsho'i 'jug mngogs*
Evam Chokar	E wam lcog sgar
Expanded Spoken Teachings of the Nyingma School	*Rnying ma bka' ma rgyas pa*
Explanation of the Views in Stages	*Lta ba rim par bshad pa*
Fortress of Vajra-Garuda Rock	Rdo rje'i khyung brag gi rdzong
Ga (clan)	Sga
Gampopa	Sgam po pa Bsod nams rin chen
Ganden Podrang	Dga' ldan pho 'brang
Garap Dorjé	Dga' rab rdo rje
Garland of Views: A Pith Instruction	*Man ngag lta ba'i 'phreng ba*
Gartön Zangpo	Gar ston bzang po
Gartön Zungé	Mgar ston Zung nge
Gathered Great Assembly	Tshogs chen 'dus pa
Gathering of All Knowledge Sutra	*Kun 'dus rig pa'i mdo*
Gathering of Intentions Sutra	*Dgongs pa 'dus pa'i mdo*
Gathering of the Herukas Tantra	*He ru ka 'dus pa'i rgyud*
Gelong Dingpopa	Dge slong Lding po pa
General Exposition	*Spyi don*
Geshé Marchung Lhodrakpa	Dge shes Mar chung Lho brag pa
Getsé	*See* Katok Getsé
Gewa Pel	Dge ba 'phel
Gödemchen	Rgod ldem can
Gojo Choktrül Shedrup Gyatso	Go 'jo mchog sprul Bshad sgrub rgya mtsho
Gö Khukpa (Lhetsé)	'Gos khug pa lhas btsas

Golden Awl	*Gser gzong*
Gö Lotsawa	'Gos Lo tsa ba
Gongbuwa	Gong bu ba
Gongra Lochen Zhenpen Dorjé	Gong ra lo chen Gzhan phan rdo rje
Götsangpa Natsok Rangdröl	Rgod tshang pa Sna tshogs rang grol
Gö Tsikungpa	'Gos Rtsi khung pa
Gö Tsilungpa	'Gos Rtsis lung pa
Greatly Expanded Spoken Teachings	*Bka' ma shin tu rgyas pa*
Great Precept on Mind Sutra	*Sems lung chen mo*
Great Seal of Nup	*Gnubs kyi rgya bo che*
Great Sky of Vajrasattva	*Rdo rje sems dpa' nam mkha' che*
Gya Lodrö Jangchup	Rgya Blo gros byang chub
Gyangkhar Wené	Rgyang mkhar dben gnas
Gyatrül Padma Dongak Tendzin	Rgya sprul Padma mdo sngags bstan 'dzin
Gyatrül Rinpoché	Rgya sprul rin po che
Gyelwa Yungtönpa	Rgyal ba G.yung ston pa (*see* Yungtönpa Dorjé Pel)
Illuminating Mirror	*Gsal byed me long*
Illuminating the Sun of Yoga	*Rnal 'byor nyi ma gsal bar byed pa*
inner initiation stream of arising	*nang dbang 'byung ba'i chu bo*
Jamgön Kongtrül	'Jam mgon kong sprul
Jamgön Mipham Gyatso	'Jam mgon mi pham rgya mtsho
Jampa Namdak	Byams pa rnam dag
Jamyang Chökyi Lodrö	'Jam dbyangs chos kyi blo gros
Jamyang Khyentsé Wangpo	'Jam dbyangs mkhyen brtse'i dbang po
Jamyang Rinchen Gyeltsen	'Jam dbyangs rin chen rgyal mtshan
Jangchup Ö	Byang chub 'od
Jangchup Sengé	Byang chub seng ge
Jangdak Namkha Tsewang Dorjé	Byang bdag Nam mkha' tshe dbang rdo rje
Jang Khangsar	Byang khang gsar
Jang Ngamring	Byang ngam ring
Jang Sotön Śākya Pel	Byang So ston Shākya dpal
Jewel Rosary	*Rin chen phreng ba*
Jikmé Lingpa	'Jigs med gling pa
Jönpa Lung	Ljon pa lung
Jowo Lharjé	Jo bo Lha rje
Kam Lotsawa	Kam Lo tsā ba

Karma Kuchen	Ka rma sku chen
Karma Pakshi	Karma Pak+shi
Karma Tenkyong Wangpo	Karma bstan skyong dbang po
Karma Wangdruk Tsel	Karma Dbang drug rtsal
Katok	Kaḥ thog
Katok Chaktsa Tülku Rinpoché	Kaḥ thog Phyag tsha sprul sku rin po che
Katok Dampa Deshek	Kaḥ thog Dam pa bde gshegs
Katok Getsé	Kaḥ thog dge rtse
Katok Situ Chökyi Gyamtso	Kaḥ thog si tu Chos kyi rgya mtsho
Kawa Peltsek	Ska ba dpal brtsegs
Key for Opening the Vajra Lock	*Rdo rje'i tha ram 'byed pa'i lde' mig*
Khampa Tülku	Khams pa sprul sku
Khang Śākya Zangpo	Khang Shākya bzang po
Kharchu	Mkhar chu
Khedrup Shami Dorgyel	Mkhas grub Sha mi rdo rgyal
Khenpo Göndrup	Mkhan po Mgon sgrub
Khenpo Jamyang	Mkhan po 'Jam dbyangs
Khenpo Jorden	Mkhan po Sbyor ldan
Khenpo Münsel	Mkhan po Mun sel (a.k.a. Tshul khrims rgya mtsho)
Khenpo Ngakchung	Mkhan po Ngag chung
Khenpo Nüden	Mkhan po Nus ldan (legs bshad 'byor ldan)
Khepa Sechenpo	Mkhas pa Sres chen po
Khulungpa Nanam Tsültrim Jangchup	Khu lung pa Sna nam Tshul khrim byang chub
Khyé/Khyen	Khyed/Khyen
Khyentsé Chökyi Lodrö	Mkhyen brtse Chos kyi blo gros
Khyüngchenri	Khyung chen ri
The King of Initiations Tantra	*Rnam par snang mdzad thig le dbang bskur ba rgyal po'i rgyud*
Künga Lekpa	Kun dga' legs pa
Künga Lhamdzé	Kun dga' lha mdzes
Künpang Lhawang Dorjé	Kun spangs lha dbang rdo rje
Kyitön Chökyi Sengé	Skyi-ston Chos-kyi Seng-ge
Kyitön Tsering Wangpo	Skyi ston Tshe ring dbang po
Kyotön Śākya Yeshé	Skyo ston Shākya ye shes
Lachen Relpuwa	Bla chen Ral phu ba

Lama Nyangtön Pel Dorjé	Bla ma Nyang ston dpal rdo rje
Lamp for the Eyes in Contemplation	*Bsam gtan mig sgron*
Langdro Tülku Tsewang Gyelpo	Lang 'gro sprul sku Tshe dbang rgyal po
Langtön Darma Sönam	Lang ston Dar ma bsod nams
Latö Jang	La stod Byang
Lekden (Dudjom) Dorjé	Legs ldan (bdud 'joms) rdo rje
Lekpa Pelzang	Legs pa dpal bzang
Lenben Dorjé Ö (a.k.a. Len Chenpo)	Glan ban Rdo rje 'od
Len Chenpo Dorjé Ö (a.k.a. Lenben Dorjé Ö)	Glan chen po Rdo rje 'od
Len Dorjé Ö	Glan Rdo rje 'od
Len Gyekhawa	Glan Sgyed kha ba
Len Manual	*Glan chog*
Len Nyatselwa Śākya Jangchup	Glan Nya rtsal ba Shākya byang chub
Len Pelden Chökyi Sengé	Glan Dpal ldan chos kyi seng ge
Len Śākya Zangpo	Glan Shākya bzang po
Len Sönam Gyelpo	Glan Bsod nams rgyal po
Len the Great, Śākya Gönpo Pelden Chöseng	Glan chen Shākya mgon po dpal ldan chos seng
Lentön Sangyé Pel	Glan ston Sangs rgyas dpal
Lentön Sönam Gönpo	Glan ston Bsod nams mgon po
Len Tsöndrü	Glan Brtson grus
Lhachen Dreshongpa Chögyel Dorjé	Lha chen Bres gshongs pa Chos rgyal rdo rje
Lharjé Dé	Lha rje Bde
Lharjé Gar	Lha rje 'Gar
Lharjé Khün	Lha rje 'Khun
Lharjé Lhabum	Lha rje Lha 'bum
Lharjé Mar	Lha rje Smar (= Dzamtön?)
Lharjé Śākya Gön	Lha rje Shāka mgon
Lharjé Shangchungpa Darma Sönam	Lha rje Shangs chung ba Dar ma bsod nam
Lharjé Yangkhyé	Lha rje Yang khyed
Lhatsun Rinchen Namgyel	Lha btsun rin chen rnam rgyal
Lhodrak	Lho brag
Longchenpa	Klong chen pa
Lopön Amé	Slob dpon A me
Lopön Dorjé Pel	Slob dpon Rdo rje dpal

Lower Nyang	Nyang smad
Lozang Chökyi Gyeltsen (First Paṇchen Lama)	Blo bzang chos kyi rgyal mtshan
Marchung Sherap Ö	Mar chung shes rab 'od
Marpa Tromgyel	Mar pa Khrom rgyal
Marpa Yönten Jangchup	Mar pa Yon tan byang chub
Menlungpa Lochok Dorjé	Sman lung pa Blo mchog rdo rje
Menlungpa Śākya Ö	Men lung pa Shākya 'Od
Menlung Üpa	Sman lung Dbus pa
Metön Gönpo	Me ston Mgon po
Mind Class	*sems sde*
Mindröling	Smin grol gling
Minyak Tsashing	Mi nyag Rtsa shing
Moktön Dorjé Pelzangpo	Rmog ston Rdo rje dpal bzang po
Moktsa Tülku	Rmog rtsa sprul sku
Mönlam Chenmo	Smon lam chen mo
Muksang	Rmugs sangs
Namdingpa Namkha Dorjé	Gnam sdings pa Nam mkha' rdo rje
Namkha Gyeltsen	Nam mkha' rgyal mtshan
Namkha Rinchen	Nam mkha' rin chen
Nanam gi Garchung Tsültrim Zangpo	Sna nam gyi Gar chung Tshul khrims bzang po
Nanam Tsültrim Jangchup	Sna nam Tshul khrims byang chub
Nanam Zhangyön	Sna nam Zhang yon
Nangtsé chieftain	Snang rtse Sde pa
Nawo Dungyü	Rna bo gdung brgyud
New Treasure of Choling	*Mchog gling gter gsar*
Ngagi Wangpo	Ngag gi dbang po
Ngari Paṇchen Pema Wangyel	Mnga' ris paN chen Padma dbang rgyal
Ngawang Lozang Gyatso (Fifth Dalai Lama)	Ngag dbang blo bzang rgya mtsho
Ngok Yönten Chok	Rngog Yon tan mchog
nonsectarian movement	Ris med
Northern Treasures	Byang gter
Nup Yeshé Gyatso	Gnubs Ye shes rgya mtsho
Nup Yönten Gyatso	Gnubs Yon tan rgya mtsho
Nyangrel Nyimé Özer	Nyang ral nyi ma'i 'od zer
Nyangtön Pel Dorjé	Nyang ston Dpal rdo rje

Nyangtön Sherap Pel	Nyang ston Shes rab dpal
Nyari Gyatön	Nya ri Rgya ston
Nyedo	Snye mdo
Nyelwa Delek	Dmyal ba bde legs
Nyitön Sangyé Bum	Nyi ston Sangs rgyas 'bum
Öchok Tülku Cetön Ngawang Künzang Rangdröl	'Od mchog sprul sku Lce ston ngag dbang kun bzang rang grol
Orgyen Lingpa	O rgyan gling pa
Ornamental Appearance of Wisdom: A Commentary on the Sūtra	*Mdo 'grel ye shes snang ba rgyan*
Ornament to the Lord of the Guhyakas' Intention	*Gsang bdag dgongs rgyan*
outer initiation stream of tantra	*phyi dbang rgyud kyi chu bo*
Outline of the Vehicles	*Theg pa spyi bcings*
Padma Chronicles	*Padma bka' thang*
Pakmo Drüpa Dorjé Gyelpo	Phag mo gru pa Rdo rje rgyal po
Paṇchen Lama	Paṇ chen Bla ma
Pehar Ling	Pe har gling
Pelgyi Chökor	Dpal gyi chos 'khor
Peling Sungtrül Ngawang Künzang Dorjé	Pad gling gsung sprul Ngag dbang kun bzang rdo rje
Pel Lama Yeshé	Dpal bla ma ye shes
Pelri Densawa	Dpal ri gdan sa ba
Pelyul	Dpal yul
Pema Gyurmé Gyatso	Padma 'gyur med rgya mtsho
Pema Trinlé	Padma 'phrin las
Perfection of Wisdom Sūtra in 150 Lines	*Prajñāpāramitānayaśatapañcāśataka*
Pillar Testament	*Bka' chems ka khol ma*
Play of the Charnel Ground Cuckoo	*Dur khrod khu byug rol pa*
Pön Gelu	Dpon Dge lu
Powo	Spo bo
Prophetic Commentary	*'Grel pa lung bstan ma*
Pure Crystal Mirror: Guidelines for Clarifying Regulations and Prohibitions in Twenty-One [Chapters]	*Blang dor gsal bar ston pa'i drang thig dwangs shel me long nyer gcig pa*
Purification of All Negative Rebirths	*Sarvadurgatipariśodhana*
Ra Lotsawa	Rwa Lo tsā ba
Rapjampa Chakpa Chöpel	Rab 'byam pa Chags pa chos 'phel

Rechungpa	Ras chung pa
Refutation of False Mantra	*Sngags log sun 'byin*
Rikdzin Yongdu	*Rig 'dzin yongs 'dus*
Ringül Tülku	Ri mgul sprul sku
Rinpung	Rin spungs
River of Honey	*Sbrang rtsi'i chu rgyun*
Roktön Künga Döndrup	Rog ston Kun dga' don grub
Rolang Dewa	Ro langs bde ba
Rong Gyong Khangpa Zitön Śākya Zangpo	Rong gyong khang pa Gzi ston shākya bzang po
Rongpa Dzokchen Tülku	Rong pa Rdzogs chen sprul sku
Rongzom Chökyi Zangpo	Rong zom chos kyi bzang po
Ruyong Rinchen Bar	Ru yong Rin chen 'bar
Śākya Sengé	Shākya seng ge
Samdruptsé	Bsam 'grub rtse
Samyé	Bsam yas
Sangdak Trinlé Lhündrup	Gsang bdag 'Phrin las lhun sgrub
Sangyé Gyatso	*See* Dési Sangyé Gyatso
Sayings of Wa	*Dba' bzhed*
Scriptural Vajra Array	*Lung rdo rje bkod pa*
seal of entrustment	*Gtad rgya*
secret initiation stream of perfection	*gsang dbang rdzogs pa'i chu bo*
Sektön Dorjé Gyeltsen	Sreg ston Rdo rje rgyal mtshan
Selwé Gyen (a.k.a. Déwa Seldzé)	Gsal ba'i rgyan
Seminal Heart	Snying thig
Seminal Heart of the Great Expanse	Klong chen snying thig
Shang kyi Tongtsap Pakpa Gyatso	Shangs kyi stong tshab 'Phags pa rgya mtsho
Shang Lhapu	Shangs lha phu
Shangnak Langza Sönam Dar	Shangs nag Lang za bsod nams dar
Shangpa	Shangs pa
Sherap Sengé	Shes rab seng ge
Situ Rinpoché Shedrup Chökyi Gyatso	Si tu Rin po che Bshad sgrub chos kyi rgya mtsho
Sokdokpa Lodrö Gyeltsen	Sog bzlog pa Blo gros rgyal mtshan
Sönam Gyatso (a.k.a. Third Dalai Lama)	Bsod nam gya mtsho
Sönam Gyeltsen	Bsod nams rgyal mtshan

Sönam Tsemo	Bsod rnam rtse mo
So Pelden	So Dpal ldan
Summary of the Gathering of Intentions	*Dgongs 'dus kyi bsdus don*
Tai Situ Jangchup Gyeltsen	Ta'i si tu Byang chub rgyal mtshan
Taktsé	Stag rtse
Tangdrok Tülku Künzang Lekdrup	Thang 'brog sprul sku Kun bzang legs grub
Tashi Lhünpo	Bkra shis lhun po
Tashi Topgyel Wangpö De	Bkra shis stobs rgyal dbang po'i sde
Terdak Lingpa Rikdzin Gyurmé Dorjé	Gter bdag gling pa Rig 'dzin 'gyur med rdo rje
Thoroughly Illuminating Sun Rays, Clarifying the Intended Meaning of the Vehicles of Sutra and Mantra	*Mdo sngags theg pa'i dgongs don gsal byed nyi 'od rab gsal*
Three Vows	*Sdom gsum*
Tokar Namkha	Tho gar nam mkha'
Treasury of Kagyu Mantra	*Bka' brgyud sngags mdzod*
Treasury of Knowledge	*Shes bya kun khyab*
Treasury of Oral Instructions	*Gdams ngag mdzod*
Treasury of Precious Treasures	Rin chen gter mdzod
Tsang Gongra	Gtsang Gong ra
Tsangmo Rinchen Gyen	Gtsang mo Rin chen rgyan
Tsangnyön Heruka	Gtsang smyon He ru ka
Tsangpa	Rtsang pa
Tsangpa (Jitön?)	Rtsang pa Byi ston
Tsangpa Peldrak	Gtsang pa Dpal grags
Tsangpa Rapjampa	Gtsang pa Rab 'byams pa
Tsangpo (river)	Gtsang po
(Chöjé) Tsangtön Dorjé Gyeltsen	(Chos rje) gtsang ston Rdo rje rgyal mtshan
Tselchen Nyuki Dorjé Drombu	Rtsal chen nyug gi rdo rje sgrom bu
Tsering Lama Jampel Zangpo	Tshe ring bla ma 'jam dpal zang po
Tsewang Norbu	Tshe dbang nor bu
Tsuglak Pelgé	Gtsug lag dpal dge
Tsültrim Gyatso	Tshul khrims rgya mtsho
Tupten Pelzang Rinpoché	Thub bstan dpal bzang rin po che
Tupzang Rinpoché	*See* Tupten Pelzang Rinpoché
Ukpalung	'Ug pa lung

Upper Nyang	Nyang stod
Uyukpa Yar Selwe Jangchup	'U yug pa Dbyar gsal ba'i byang chub
Vajra Staircase	*Rdo rje'i them skas*
Wisdom's Magnificent Thunderbolts	*Ye shes rngam glog*
Wönpo Tsegyel	Dbon po tshe rgyal
Yardrok	Yar 'brog
Yeshé Gyeltsen	Ye shes rgyal mtshan
Yidzin Wangmo	Yid 'dzin dbang mo
Yölmowa Tendzin Norbu (a.k.a. Third Yolmo Tülku)	Yol mo ba Bstan 'dzin nor bu
Yönpo Tülku	Yon po sprul sku
Yudruk Dorjé	G.yu drug rdo rje (also G.yu 'brug rdo rje)
Yungtönpa Dorjé Pel	G.yung ston pa Rdo rje dpal
Yutön Chögön	G.yu ston Chos mgon
Zé Tangkya	Bzad Thang skya (or Gzang Thang skya)
Zhamarpa Chökyi Wangchuk	Zhwa dmar pa Chos kyi dbang phyug
Zhangtön Künga Bum	Zhang ston Kun dga' 'bum
Zhechen Gangshar	Zhe chen Gang shar
Zhikpo Dütsi	Zhig po bdud rtsi
Zhikpo Lingpa	Zhig-po Gling-pa
Zhingshakpa Karma Tseten	Zhing shag pa Karma tshe brtan
Zhingshakpa Tseten Dorjé	Zhing shag pa Tshe brtan rdo rje
Zhu Sönam Śākya	Zhu Bsod nams shākya
Zilnön Wangyel Dorjé	Zil gnon dbang rgyal rdo rje
Zurben Chöjé Jampa Sengé	Zur ban Cho rje byams pa seng ge
Zurham Śākya Jungné	Zur ham Shākya 'byung gnas
Zur Jampa Sengé	Zur Byams pa seng ge
Zurmo Gendün Bum	Zur mo Dge 'dun 'bum
Zur Nakpo	Zur Nag po
Zur Śākya Sengé	Zur Shākya seng+ge
Zurtön Śākya Shenyen	Zur ston ShAkya bshes gnyen

BIBLIOGRAPHY

SANSKRIT AND TIBETAN SOURCES

Bdud 'joms chos 'byung. Bdud 'joms 'jigs bral ye shes rdo rje. Chengdu: Si khron mi rigs dpe skrun khang, 1996.

Bdud 'joms rgyal rabs. Bdud 'joms 'jigs bral ye shes rdo rje. *Gangs can bod chen po'i rgyal rabs 'dus gsal du bkod pa sngon med dwangs shel 'phrul gyi me long*. Delhi: Konchog Lhadrepa, 1994.

Bka' chems ka khol ma. Lanzhou: Kan su'u mi rigs dpe skrun khang, 1989.

Bka' ma shin tu rgyas pa 1. Various authorship. The 110-volume *Bka' ma rgyas pa shin tu rgyas pa* collection held by the Tibetan Buddhist Resource Center in Cambridge, MA. No publication information available.

Bka' ma shin tu rgyas pa 2. Various authorship. The 120-volume *Bka' ma rgyas pa shin tu rgyas pa* collection held by David Germano of the University of Virginia and by the Tibetan Buddhist Resource Center in Cambridge, MA. No publication information available.

Bka' ma shin tu rgyas pa 3. Various authorship. Full title: *sNga 'gyur bka' ma shin tu rgyas pa*, 133 vols. Chengdu: Si khron mi rigs dpe skrun khang, 2009.

Bsam gtan mig sgron. Gnubs chen sangs rgyas ye shes. *Rnal 'byor mig gi bsam gtan*. Leh, Ladakh: S. W. Tashigangpa, 1974.

Bsnyen yig legs bshad skya reng dang po'i snang ba. Mkhan po Ngag chung. *Bka' ma shin tu rgyas pa 1*, vol. *zi*, 335–491.

Byang pa'i rnam thar. Ngag dbang blo bzang rgya mtsho, Dalai Lama V. *Byang pa rig 'dzin chen po ngag gi dbang po'i rnam par thar pa ngo mtshar bkod pa rgya mtsho*. In *Bka' ma mdo dbang gi bla ma brgyud pa'i rnam thar and Rig 'dzin ngag gi dbang po'i rnam thar*, 427–553. Leh: S. W. Tashigangpa, 1972.

'Chad thabs zin bris nyung ngu rnam gsal. 'Jam dbyangs blo gros rgya mtsho. *Spyi mdo dgongs 'dus kyi 'chad thabs zin bris nyung ngu rnam gsal. Bka' ma shin tu rgyas pa 1*, vol. 52, 321–34.

Dam pa bde gshegs kyi rnam thar bsdus pa grub mchog rjes dran. Lding po pa. No publication information. (TBRC RID: W26096)

Dar mdo rdo rje brag. Gzen dkar sprul sku Thub bstan nyi ma. Dar *mdo rdo rje brag dgon pa bskyar gso'i zhal 'debs zhu yig*. Kanding: Dar mdo rdo rje brag dgon pa, 1994.

Dgongs 'dus kyi bsdus don. Dam pa bde gshegs. *Spyi mdo dgongs 'dus kyi bsdus don padma dkar po'i phreng ba*. In *Rnying ma bka' ma rgyas pa*, vol. 52, 61–206.

Dgongs pa 'dus pa'i mdo. Full title: *De bzhin gshegs pa thams cad kyi thugs gsang ba'i ye shes; don gyi snying po rdo rje bkod pa'i rgyud; rnal 'byor grub pa'i lung; kun 'dus rig pa'i mdo; theg pa chen po mngon par rtogs pa; chos kyi rnam grangs rnam par bkod pa zhes bya ba'i mdo*. In *Rnying ma'i rgyud 'bum*, vol. 16, 2–617.

Dur khrod khu byug rol pa'i rgyud ces bya ba theg pa chen po'i mdo. In *Rnying ma'i rgyud 'bum*, vol. 15, 213–321.

'Dus pa mdo'i sgrub khog rin chen 'od kyi snang ba. Lo chen Dharmaśrī. In *Lo chen gsung 'bum*, vol. 10, 1–170. (Also found in *Rnying ma bka' ma rgyas pa*, vol. 14, 507–657.)

Gangs ljongs dbus gtsang gnas bskor lam yig nor bu zla shel gyi se mo do. Kaḥ thog si tu Chos kyi rgya mtsho. Tashijong, Palampur, H.P.: Sungrab Nyamso Gyunphel Parkhang, 1972.

Glan chog. Glan ston Bsod nams mgon po. *'Dus pa chen po mdo'i sgrub khrigs bzhin dbang byang lag len*. In *Bka' ma shin tu rgyas pa 1*, vols. 60–61.

Gnubs kyi rgya bo che. *Sangs rgyas ye shes rin po che'i lo rgyus gnubs kyi bka' shog chen mo*. Attributed to Gnubs chen Sangs rgyas ye shes. In *Bka' ma shin tu rgyas pa 3*, vol. 42, pp. 693–746. Chengdu: Kaḥ thog mkhan po 'jam dbyangs, 1999.

Grub thob gtsang pa smyon pa'i rnam thar dad pa'i spu slong g.yo ba. Lha btsun rin chen rnam rgyal. In S.W. Tashi gang pa, ed., *Bde mchog mkha' 'gro snyan rgyud (Ras chung snyan rgyud): Two manuscript collections of texts from the yig cha of gTsang-smyon He-ru-ka*, vol 1. Sman rtsis shes rig spendzod, vol. 11. Leh, Ladakh, 1971.

Gsal byed me long. G.yung ston. *Dpal gsang ba'i snying po'i rgyud gsal byed me long*. In *Rnying ma bka ma rgyas pa*, vol. 28, 5–589.

Gsang ba snying po'i 'grel pa spar khab. Vilāsavajra. In *Rnying ma bka' ma rgyas pa*, vol. 23, 389–619.

Gsang bdag dgongs rgyan. Lochen Dharmaśrī. *Dpal gsang ba'i snying po de kho na nyid nges pa'i rgyud kyi 'grel pa gsang bdag dgongs rgyan*. In *Rnying ma bka ma rgyas pa*, vol. 32, 5–461.

Gtad rgya lnga'i go don gyi brjed byang gi 'grel pa. Zur haṃ shākya 'byung gnas. In

Bka' ma shin tu rgyas pa 3, vol. 23, 106–80 (= *Bka' ma shin tu rgyas pa 1*, vol. 61, 438a.4 to 481a.3).

Gu bkra'i chos 'byung. Gu ru bkra shis. Beijing: Krung go'i bod kyi shes rig dpe skrun khang, 1990.

Khrag' 'thung rtsa 'chams kyi brjed byang kun bzang rnam par rtsen pa'i rol mo. Lo chen Dharmaśrī. In *Lo chen gsung 'bum*, vol. 12, 413–505.

Kun byed rgyal po. Full title: *Chos thams cad rdzogs pa chen po byang chub kyi sems kun byed rgyal po*. Sde dge edition of the Tibetan canon; see Hakuju Ui et al., eds., *A Complete Catalogue of the Tibetan Buddhist Canons (Bkaḥ-ḥgyur and Bstan-ḥgyur)*. Sendai: Tōhoku Imperial University, 1934, 828. Bka' 'gyur, *rgyud 'bum ka*, ff. 1b.1–86a.7.

Kun 'dus rig pa'i mdo; rnal 'byor bsgrub pa'i rgyud ces bya ba theg pa chen po'i mdo. In *Rnying ma'i rgyud 'bum*, vol. 15, 321–672.

Las tho rab gnas. Bde ba gsal mdzad. In *Len Manual* 61, 405–10.

Legs bshad nyi ma'i snang ba. Dam pa bde gshegs. *'Dus pa mdo'i khog dbub legs bshad nyi ma'i snang ba*. (Sometimes referred to as *Yang khog dbub*.) In *Rnying ma bka' ma rgyas pa*, 52, 13–59.

Lo chen gsung 'bum. Lo chen Dharmaśrī. Collected Works of Smin-gling Lo chen Dharmaśrī. 18 vols. Dehra Dun: D. G. Khocchen Trulku, 1975.

Lta ba rim par bshad pa. Ska ba dpal brtsegs. Peking edition of the Tibetan canon; see Daisetz Teitaro Suzuki, *The Tibetan Tripitika: Peking Edition*. Tokyo-Kyoto: Tibetan Tripitika Research Institute, 1957, 4728.

Man ngag lta ba'i phreng ba. Padmasambhava. In *Rnying ma bka' ma rgyas pa*, vol. 23, 159–75.

Mchod gar gyi brjed byang mchod sprin rnam par spro ba'i rol mo. Lo chen Dharmaśrī. In *Lo chen gsung 'bum*, vol. 12, 507–37.

Mdo dbang brgyud pa'i rnam thar. Padma 'phrin las, Rdo rje brag rig 'dzin II. *'Dus pa mdo dbang gi bla ma brgyud pa'i rnam thar ngo mtshar dad pa'i phreng ba*. In *Bka' ma mdo dbang gi bla ma brgyud pa'i rnam thar and Rig 'dzin ngag gi dbang po'i rnam thar*, 1–425. Leh, Ladakh: S. W. Tashigangpa, 1972.

Mdo phran khog dbub. Kaḥ thog Dam pa bde gshegs. In *Rnying ma bka' ma rgyas pa*, vol. 52, 5–11.

Mdo sngags theg pa'i dgongs don gsal byed nyi 'od rab gsal. Kaḥ thog pa Bsod nams rgyal mtshan. Publication information unknown.

Mun pa'i go cha. Gnubs chen Sangs rgyas ye shes. *Sangs rgyas thams cad kyi dgongs pa 'dus pa mdo'i dka' 'grel mun pa'i go cha lde mig gsal byed rnal 'byor nyi ma*. In *Rnying ma bka' ma rgyas pa*, vols. 50–51.

Nor bu'i do sal. Kun bzang nges don klong yangs. *Bod du byung ba'i gsang sngags snga' 'gyur gyis bstan 'dzin skyes mchog rim byon gyi rnam thar nor bu'i do sal*. Dalhousie, H.P., India: Damchoe Sangpo, 1976.

Nyang ral chos 'byung. Nyang ral nyi ma 'od zer. *Chos 'byung me tog snying po sbrang rtsi'i bcud*. Vol. 5 of the series entitled *Gangs can rig mdzod*. Lhasa: Bod ljongs mi dmangs dpe skrun khang, 1988.

Phyogs thams cad las rnam par rgyal ba'i rnam thar. Rgod tshang pa Sna tshogs rang grol. *Gtsang smyon he ru ka phyogs thams cad las rnam par rgyal ba'i rnam thar rdo rje theg pa'i gsal byed nyi ma'i snying po*. No publication information. (TBRC RID: W4CZ1247)

Prajñāpāramitānayaśatapañcāśatakaṭikā. Sde dge edition of the Tibetan canon; see Hakuju Ui et al., eds., *A Complete Catalogue of the Tibetan Buddhist Canons (Bkaḥ-ḥgyur and Bstan-ḥgyur)*. Sendai: Tōhoku Imperial University, 1934, 2647. Bstan 'gyur. *rgyud ju*, 272b.7–294a.5.

Rdo rje'i tha ram 'byed pa'i lde'u mig. Dam pa bde gshegs. *'Dus pa mdo'i dka' 'grel rdo rje'i tha ram 'byed pa'i lde'u mig*. In *Rnying ma bka' ma rgyas pa*, vol. 52, 207–78.

Rdo rje'i them skas. Lo chen Dharmaśrī. *Rgyud dang man ngag gi lugs gcig tu dril ba'i dbang chog rdo rje'i them skas*. In *Lo chen gsung 'bum*, vol. 11, 1–569. (Also found in *Rnying ma bka' ma rgyas pa*, vol. 16, 5–685.)

Rgya mtsho'i 'jug mngogs. Padma 'phrin las, Rdo rje brag rig 'dzin II. *'Dus pa mdo'i dbang gi cho ga khrigs su byas pa dkyil 'khor rgya mtsho'i 'jug mngogs*. In *Rnying ma bka' ma rgyas pa*, vols. 41–43.

Rgyal ba kaḥ thog pa'i lo rgyus mdor bsdus. 'Jam dbyangs rgyal mtshan. Chengdu: Si khron mi rigs dpe skrun khang, 1996.

Rin chen phreng ba. Dmyal ba bde legs. *'Dus pa chen po mdo'i dbang chog rin chen phreng ba*. In *Bka' ma shin tu rgyas pa 1*, vol. 63. (Also in *Bka' ma shin tu rgyas pa 2*, vol. 92.)

Rje btsun gtsang pa he ru ka'i thun mong gi rnam thar yon tan gyi gangs ri la dad pa'i seng+ge rnam par rtse ba. Dngos grub dpal 'bar. No publication information. (TBRC RID: W2CZ6647.)

Rnal 'byor nyi ma gsal bar byed pa. Mkhan po Nus ldan rdo rje. *Dpal spyi mdo dgongs pa'dus pa'i 'grel pa rnal 'byor nyi ma gsal bar byed pa'i legs bshad gzi ldan 'char kha'i 'od snang*. In *Rnying ma bka' ma rgyas pa*, vols. 53–56.

Rnying ma bka' ma rgyas pa. 56 vols. Various authorship. Bdud 'joms 'jigs bral ye shes rdo rje, ed. Kalimpong, W.B.: Dubjang Lama, 1982.

Rnying ma'i rgyud 'bum. Rdo rje thogs med, ed., *The Mtshams brag Edition of the Rñing ma rgyud 'bum*. 46 vols. Thimphu, Bhutan: National Library, Royal Government of Bhutan, 1982.

Rtsa rgyud gsang ba'i snying po'i 'grel pa nyi ma snying po. Kaḥ thog si tu Chos kyi rgya mtsho. In *Bka' ma shin tu rgyas pa 1*, vols. 48–49.

Sahajānandapradīpam-nāma-pañjikā. Sde dge edition of the Tibetan canon; see Hakuju Ui et al., eds., *A Complete Catalogue of the Tibetan Buddhist Canons*

(Bkaḥ-ḥgyur and Bstan-ḥgyur). Sendai: Tōhoku Imperial University, 1934, 1202. Bka' 'gyur, *rgyud 'bum ja*, ff. 160a1–208b1.

Sarvabuddhasamāyoga. Sde dge edition of the Tibetan canon; see Hakuju Ui et al., eds., *A Complete Catalogue of the Tibetan Buddhist Canons (Bkaḥ-ḥgyur and Bstan-ḥgyur)*. Sendai: Tōhoku Imperial University, 1934, 366. Bka' 'gyur, *rgyud 'bum ka*, ff. 151b.1–193a.6.

Sbrang rtsi'i chu rgyun. Rmog ston Rdo rje dpal bzang po. *Mdo dbang khams lugs su grags pa sbrang rtsi'i chu rgyun*. In *Bka' ma shin tu rgyas pa 1*, vols. 64–66. In *Bka' ma shin tu rgyas pa 2*, vols. 25–28.

Sems lung chen mo'i mdo gsang ba spyi rgyud. In 'Jam dbyangs mkhyen brtse, ed., *The Gting skyes Edition of the Rñing ma rgyud 'bum*. 36 vols. Thimphu, Bhutan: National Library, Royal Government of Bhutan, 1973. Vol. *ga*, 130–63.

Shel gyi me long. Sog bzlog pa Blo gros rgyal mtshan. *Dam pa'i chos lung a nu yo ga gtso bor ston pa/ 'dus pa mdo'i dbang bskur ba'i bca' thabs lag len rab tu gsal ba shel gyi me long*. In *Sog bzlog gsung 'bum*, vol. 2, 311–83.

Skabs 'grel bye brag tu bshad pa. Sthiramati. In *Bka' ma shin tu rgyas pa 2*, vol. 95, 5–38.

Sngags log sun 'byin. 'Gos khug pa lhas btsas. In Chag lo tsā ba et al., *Sngags log sun 'byin gyi skor*. Thimphu, Bhutan: Kunsang Tobgyel, 1979.

Snga 'gyur rgyud 'bum rin po che'i rtogs pa brjod. 'Jigs med gling pa. Ngagyur Nyingmay Sungrab Series, vol. 31.

Sog bzlog bgyis tshul gyi lo rgyus. Sog bzlog pa Blo gros rgyal mtshan. In *Sog bzlog gsung 'bum*, vol. 1, 203–59.

Sog bzlog gsung 'bum. Sog bzlog pa Blo gros rgyal mtshan. 2 vols. New Delhi: Sanje Dorji, 1975.

Spyi don. Lo chen Dharmaśrī. *'Dus pa'i mdo dbang spyi don rgyud lung man ngag gi gnad gsal byed sgron me*. In *Lo chen gsung 'bum*, vol. 12, 1–260. (Also found in *Rnying ma bka' ma rgyas pa*, vol. 14, 5–345.)

Śri-tattvapradīpa-mahāyogīni-tantrarāja: Sde dge edition of the Tibetan canon; see Hakuju Ui et al., eds., *A Complete Catalogue of the Tibetan Buddhist Canons (Bkaḥ-ḥgyur and Bstan-ḥgyur)*. Sendai: Tōhoku Imperial University, 1934, 423. Bka'-'gyur, rgyud-'bum nga. ff. 136–42.

Theg pa spyi bcings rtsa 'grel. Dam pa bde gshegs. With commentary by Ye shes rgyal mtshan. Chengdu: Si khron mi rigs dpe skrun khang, 1997.

Thob yig gang+ga'i chu rgyun. Ngag dbang blo bzang rgya mtsho, Dalai Lama V. *Zab pa dang rgya che ba'i dam pa'i chos kyi thob yig gang+ga'i chu rgyun*. In *Rgyal dbang lnga pa chen po'i gsum 'bum*. 25 vols. Dharamsala, India: Nam gsal sgron ma, 2007. Vols. 1–4.

Tshogs chen 'dus pa'i dkyil 'khor gyi cho ga dri med 'od kyi phreng ba. Lo chen Dharmaśrī. In *Rnying ma bka' ma rgyas pa*, vol. 14, 459–505.

Tshogs chen 'dus pa'i sgrub thabs dngogs grub char 'bebs. Lo chen Dharmaśrī. In *Rnying ma bka' ma rgyas pa*, vol. 14, 349–443.

Ye shes rngam glog. *Ye shes rngam pa glog gi 'khor lo zhes bya ba theg pa chen po'i mdo*. In *Rnying ma'i rgyud 'bum*, vol. 15, 2–212.

Yo ga gru gzings. Bu ston rin chen grub. Full title: *Rnal 'byor rgyud gyi mtshor 'jug pa'i gru gzings*. In *Collected Works of Bu ston*, vol. 11 (*da*), 1a–92a. Lhasa: Zhol par khang, 2000.

Zur lugs gsang snying yig cha'i skor. Zur 'tsho btsun pa dkon mchog tshul khrims. 4 vols. Dalhousie, India: Damchoe Sangpo, 1980.

WESTERN LANGUAGE SOURCES

Ahmad, Zahiruddin. *A History of Tibet by the Fifth Dalai Lama of Tibet*. Bloomington: Indiana University Press, 1995.

Akester, Matthew. "The 'Vajra Temple' of gTer ston Zhig po gling pa and the Politics of Flood Control in Sixteenth-Century lHa sa." *Tibet Journal* 26, no. 1 (2001): 3–24.

—. "Khyung tshang brag: the 'Black Demon Peering' at lHa sa." *Tibet Journal* 26, no. 1 (2001): 25–34.

Beal, Samuel. *Buddhist Records of the Western World*. New Delhi: Munshiram Manoharlal Publishers, 1983 [1884].

Beckwith, Christopher L. *The Tibetan Empire in Central Asia*. Princeton: Princeton University Press, 1987.

Bogin, Benjamin E.. *The Illuminated Life of the Great Yolmowa*. Chicago: Serindia, 2013.

Boord, Martin. *The Cult of the Deity Vajrakīlaya*. Tring, UK: The Institute of Buddhist Studies, 1993.

Cantwell, Cathy and Robert Mayer. *The Kīlaya Nirvāṇa Tantra and the Vajra Wrath Tantra: Two Texts from the Ancient Tantra Collection*. Vienna: Verlag der Österreichischen Akademie der Wissenschaften, 2007.

—. *Early Tibetan Documents on Phur pa from Dunhuang*. Vienna: Verlag der Österreichischen Akademie der Wissenschaften, 2008.

Chakravarti, Mahadev. *The Concept of Rudra-Śiva Through the Ages*. Delhi: Motilal Banarsidass, 1986.

Chandra, Lokesh. "The Contacts of Abhayagiri of Sri Lanka with Indonesia in the Eighth Century." In *Cultural Horizons of India*, vol. 4, ed. Lokesh Chandra, 10–21. New Delhi: International Academy of Indian Culture and Aditya Prakashan, 1995.

Chönam, Lama and Sangye Khandro. *The Guhyagarbha Tantra: Secret Essence Definitive Nature Just As It Is*. Ithaca, NY: Snow Lion, 2011.

Cuevas, Bryan J. *The Hidden History of The Tibetan Book of the Dead*. New York: Oxford University Press, 2003.

Cüppers, Christoph. "Registers and Account Books of the dGa'ldan Pho-brang Government." In *The Paṇḍita and the Siddha: Tibetan Studies in Honour of E. Gene Smith*, ed. Ramon Prats, 12–15. Dharamsala, India: Amnye Machen Institute, 2007.

Czaja, Olaf. *Medieval Rule in Tibet: The Rlangs Clan and the Political and Religious History of the Ruling House of Phag mo gru pa*. Wien: Verlag der Österreichischen Akademie der Wissenschaften, 2013.

Dalton, Jacob. "The Uses of the *Dgongs pa 'dus pa'i mdo* in the Development of the Rnying-ma School of Tibetan Buddhism." Ph.D. diss., University of Michigan, 2002.

——. "The Development of Perfection: The Interiorization of Buddhist Ritual in the Eighth and Ninth Centuries." *Journal of Indian Philosophy* 32, no. 1 (2004): 1–30.

——. "A Crisis of Doxography: How Tibetans Organized Tantra During the 8th–12th Centuries." *Journal of the International Association of Buddhist Studies* 28, no. 1 (2005): 115–81.

——. *Taming of the Demons: Violence and Liberation in Tibetan Buddhism*. New Haven: Yale University Press, 2011.

——. "Sometimes Love Don't Feel Like It Should: Redemptive Violence in Tantric Buddhism." In *Sins and Sinners: Perspectives from Asian Religions*, ed. Phyllis Granoff and Koichi Shinohara, 295–308. Leiden: Brill, 2012.

——. "Preliminary Remarks on a Newly Discovered Biography of Gnubs chen sangs rgyas ye shes." In *Himalayan Passages: Tibetan and Newar Studies in Honor of Hubert Decleer*, ed. Benjamin E. Bogin and Andrew Quintman, 145–62. Somerville, MA: Wisdom, 2014.

——. "Lost and Found: A Fourteenth-Century Discussion of Then-Available Sources on gNubs chen sangs rgyas ye shes." *Bulletin of Tibetology (Special Issue, Nyingma Studies)* 50, no. 1 (2014): 39–53.

Dalton, Jacob and Sam van Schaik. "Lighting the Lamp: An Examination of the Structure of the Bsam gtan mig sgron." *Acta Orientalia* 64 (2003): 153–75.

Dani, A. H. and V. M. Masson. *History of Civilization in Central Asia*. 6 vols. Paris: UNESCO, 1992.

Davidson, Ronald M. "The Litany of Names of Mañjuśrī." *Mélanges chinois et bouddhiques* XX (1981): 1–69.

——. "Reflections on the Maheśvara Subjugation Myth: Indic Materials, Sa-skya-pa Apologetics, and the Birth of Heruka." *The Journal of the International Association of Buddhist Studies* 14, no. 2 (1991): 197–235.

——. *Indian Esoteric Buddhism: A Social History of the Tantric Movement*. New York: Columbia University Press, 2002.

——. *Tibetan Renaissance*. New York: Columbia University Press, 2005.

DeCaroli, Robert. *Haunting the Buddha: Indian Religions and the Formation of Buddhism*. New York: Oxford University Press, 2004.

de Jong, J. W. *The Story of Rāma in Tibet*. Stuttgart: Franz Steiner Verlag Wiesbaden GMBH, 1989.

Dey, Nundolal. *The Geographical Dictionary of Ancient and Medieval India*. Delhi: Oriental Books Corporation, 1971 [1927].

Dorje, Gyurme. "The *Guhyagarbhatantra* and Its XIVth Century Tibetan Commentary, *phyogs bcu mun sel*." Ph.D. diss., University of London, SOAS, 1987.

——. "The rNying-ma Interpretation of Commitment and Vow." In *The Buddhist Forum*, vol. 2, ed. Tadeusz Skoupski, 71–95. London: School for Oriental and African Studies, 1991.

Dotson, Brandon. *The Old Tibetan Annals: An Annotated Translation of Tibet's First History*. Vienna: Verlag der Österreichischen Akademie der Wissenschaften, 2009.

Duckworth, Douglas. *Jamgon Mipam: His Life and Teachings*. Boston: Shambala, 2011.

Dudjom Rinpoche. *The Nyingma School of Tibetan Buddhism*. Trans. Gyurme Dorje. Boston: Wisdom, 1991.

Ehrhard, Franz-Karl. "Recently Discovered Manuscripts of the *rNying ma rgyud 'bum* from Nepal." In *Tibetan Studies: Proceedings of the 7th Seminar of the International Association for Tibetan Studies*, ed. Helmut Krasser et al., 253–68. Vienna: Verlag der Österreichischen Akademie der Wissenschaften, 1997.

——. "Kaḥ thog pa Bsod nams rgyal mtshan (1466–1540) and His Activities in Sikkim and Bhutan." *Bulletin of Tibetology* 39, no. 2 (2003): 9–26.

——. "The Mnga' bdag Family and the Tradition of Rig 'dzin zhig po gling pa (1524–1583) in Sikkim." *Bulletin of Tibetology* 41, no. 2 (2005): 11–29.

Foulk, T. Griffith. "Myth, Ritual, and Monastic Practice in Sung Ch'an Buddhism." In *Religion and Society in T'ang and Sung China*, ed. P. B. Ebrey and P. N. Gregory, 147–208. Honolulu: University of Hawai'i Press, 1993.

Gardner, Alexander P. "The Twenty-five Great Sites of Khams: Religious Geography, Revelation, and Nonsectarianism in Nineteenth-Century Eastern Tibet." Ph.D. diss., University of Michigan, 2006.

Garson, Nathaniel D. "Context and Philosophy in the Mahāyoga System of rNying-ma Tantra." Ph.D. diss., University of Virginia, 2004.

Gentry, James. "Representation of Efficacy: The Ritual Expulsion of Mongol

Armies in the Consolidation and Expansion of the Tsang." In *Tibetan Ritual*, ed. José I. Cabezón, 131–63. Oxford: Oxford University Press, 2010.

Germano, David F. "Architecture and Absence in the Secret Tantric History of the Great Perfection." *Journal of the International Association of Buddhist Studies* 17, no. 2 (1994): 203–335.

——. "The Funerary Transformation of the Great Perfection (*Rdzogs chen*)." *Journal of the International Association of Tibetan Studies* 1 (2005): 1–54.

Germano, David F. and William S. Waldron. "A Comparison of *Ālaya-vijñāna* in Yogācāra and Dzogchen." In *Buddhist Thought and Applied Psychological Research: Transcending the Boundaries*, ed. D. K. Nauriyal, M. S. Drummond, and Y. B. Lal, 36–68. London and New York: Routledge, 2006.

Giebel, Rolf. *Two Esoteric Sutras*. Berkeley: Numata Center for Buddhist Translation and Research, 2001.

Gyatso, Janet. "The Logic of Legitimation in the Tibetan Treasure Tradition." *History of Religions* 33, no. 2 (1993): 97–134.

Harrison, Paul M. "Buddhānusmṛti in the Pratyutpanna-Buddha-Saṃmukhāvasthita-Samādhi-Sūtra." *Journal of Indian Philosophy* 6 (1978): 35–57.

——. 2003. "Mediums and Messages: Reflections on the Production of Mahāyāna Sūtras." *Eastern Buddhist* 35, no. 1: 115–51.

Heller, Amy. "Notes on the Symbol of the Scorpion in Tibet." In *Les habitants du Toit du monde*, ed. Samten Karmay and Philippe Sagant, 283–97. Nanterre: Société d'ethnologie, 1997.

Higgins, David. *The Philosophical Foundations of Classical Rdzogs chen in Tibet: Investigating the Distinction Between Dualistic Mind* (sems) *and Primordial Knowing* (ye shes). Vienna: Arbeitskreis für Tibetische und Buddhistische Studien Universität Wien, 2013.

Hiltebeitel, Alf, ed. *Criminal Golds and Demon Devotees*. Albany: State University of New York Press, 1989.

Hoffmann, Helmut. *Religions of Tibet*. Trans. Edward Fitzgerald. London: Allen & Unwin, 1961.

Imaeda, Yoshiro. *Histoire Du Cycle de La Naissance et de La Mort*. Genève; Paris: Libraire Droz, 1981.

——. "Un extrait tibétain du *Mañjuśrīmūlakalpa* dans les manuscrits de Touen-houang." *Nouvelles contributions aux études de Touen-houang, Hautes études orientales* (Genève) 17 (1987): 303–17.

Isaacson, Harunaga. "Tantric Buddhism in India (from c. A.D. 800 to c. A.D. 1200)." In *Buddhismus in Geschichte und Gegenwart*. Hamburg: Internal publication of Hamburg University, 2010.

—. "Observations on the Development of the Ritual of Initiation (*abhiṣeka*) in the Higher Buddhist Tantric Systems." In *Hindu and Buddhist Initiations in India and Nepal*, ed. Astrid Zotter and Christof Zotter, 261–79. Wiesbaden, Germany: Harrassowitz Verlag, 2010.

Iyanaga, Nobumi. "Récits de la soumission de Maheśvara par Trailokyavijaya, d'après les sources chinoises et japonaises." In *Tantric and Taoist Studies in Honour of R.A. Stein* 3, Mélanges Chinois et Bouddhiques vol. XXII, ed. Michel Strickmann. Bruxelles: Institut Belge des Hautes Études Chinoises, 1985.

Jackson, Roger R. "A Tantric Echo in Sinhalese Theravāda: *Pirit* Ritual, the Book of *Paritta* and the *Jinapañjaraya*." *Journal of the Rare Buddhist Texts Research Project* 18 (1994): 121–40.

Kapstein, Matthew T. "Samantabhadra and Rudra: Innate Enlightenment and Radical Evil in Tibetan Rnying-ma-pa Buddhism." In *Discourse and Practice*, ed. Frank E. Reynolds and David Tracy, 51–82. Albany: State University of New York Press, 1992.

—. *The Tibetan Assimilation of Buddhism*. Oxford: Oxford University Press, 2000.

—. "The *Sun of the Heart* and the *Bai-ro-rgyud-'bum*." *Revue d'Etudes Tibétaines* 15 (2008): 275–88.

—. "Just Where on Jambudvīpa Are We? New Geographical Knowledge and Old Cosmological Schemes in Eighteenth-Century Tibet." In *Forms of Knowledge in Early Modern South Asia*, ed. Sheldon Pollock, 291–310. Durham: Duke University Press, 2011.

—. "Review of *Taming of the Demons: Violence and Liberation in Tibetan Buddhism*." *Harvard Journal of Asiatic Studies* 73, no. 1 (2013): 177–84.

Karmay, Samten. *Treasury of Good Sayings: A Tibetan History of Bon*. London: Oxford University Press, 1972.

—. *The Great Perfection*. Leiden: Brill, 1988.

—. *The Arrow and the Spindle: Studies in History, Myth, Rituals and Beliefs in Tibet*. Kathmandu: Mandala Book Point, 1998.

Keith, A. B. *The Religion and Philosophy of the Veda and Upaniṣads*. Cambridge, MA: Harvard University Press, 1925.

Khyentse Rinpoche, Dilgo. *Zurchungpa's Testament*. Trans. The Padmakara Translation Group. Ithaca, NY: Snow Lion, 2006.

Knipe, David M. "Night of the Growing Dead." In *Criminal Gods and Demon Devotees*, ed. Alf Hiltebeitel, 123–56. Albany: State University of New York Press, 1989.

Kohn, Richard J. *Lord of the Dance: The Mani Rimdu Festival in Tibet and Nepal*. Albany: State University of New York Press, 2001.

Kun dga' rgyal mtshan, Sakya Pandita. *A Clear Differentiation of the Three Codes*. Trans. Jared Douglas Rhoton. Albany: State University of New York Press, 2002.

Lamotte, Étienne. *Saṃdhinirmocana sūtra, l'explication des mystères texte tibétain*. Louvain: Bureaux du Recueil, Bibliothèque de l'Université, 1935.

Laufer, Berthold. "Die Bru-ža sprache und die historische stellung des Padmasambhava." *T'oung Pao* 9 (1908): 1–46.

Li-Kouang, Lin. "Puṇyodaya (na-t'i), un propagateur du tantrisme en chine et au camodge à l'époque de hiuan-tsang." *Journal Asiatique* (Paris) 227 (1935): 83–100.

Longchenpa. *You Are the Eyes of the World*. Trans. K. Lipman and M. Peterson. Novato, CA: Lotsawa, 1987.

Lopez, Donald S., Jr., ed. *Curators of the Buddha: The Study of Buddhism Under Colonialism*. Chicago: University of Chicago Press, 1995.

——. *Elaborations on Emptiness: Uses of the Heart Sūtra*. Princeton: Princeton University Press, 1996.

——. *The Madman's Middle Way: Reflections on Reality of the Tibetan Monk Gendun Chopel*. Chicago: University of Chicago Press, 2006.

Lorimer, D.L.R. *The Burushaski Lanuage*. 3 vols. Oslo: H. Aschehoug, 1935–38.

Mair, Victor. "Śāriputra Defeats the Six Heterodox Masters: Oral-Visual Aspects of an Illustrated Transformation Scroll (P4524)." *Asia Major* (3rd Series) 8, no. 2 (1995): 1–53.

Martin, Dan. "The Emergence of Bon and the Tibetan Polemical Tradition." Ph.D. diss., Indiana University, 1991.

——. "'Ol-mo-lung-ring, the Original Holy Place." *Tibet Journal* 88, no. 1 (1995): 48–82.

Mathes, Klaus-Dieter. *A Direct Path to the Buddha Within*. Somerville, MA: Wisdom, 2008.

Mayer, Robert. "Scriptural Revelation in India and Tibet: Indian Precursors of the gTer-ma Tradition." In *Tibetan Studies: Proceedings of the 6th Seminar of the International Association for Tibetan Studies Fagernes 1992*, vol. 2, ed. Per Kvaerne, 533–44. Oslo: Institute for Comparative Research in Human Culture, 1994.

——. *A Scripture of the Ancient Tantra Collection, The* Phur-pa bcu-gnyis. Oxford: Kiscadale Publications, 1996.

Mipham, Jamgön. *Luminous Essence: A Guide to the Guhyagarbha Tantra*. Trans. The Dharmacakra Translation Committee. Ithaca, NY: Snow Lion, 2009.

Monier-Williams, M. *Sanskrit-English Dictionary*. Oxford: Oxford University Press, 1899.

de Nebesky-Wojkowitz, René. *Tibetan Religious Dances: Tibetan Text and Annotated Translation of the 'Chams Yig*. Ed. Christoph von Fürer-Haimendorf. The Hague: Mouton, 1976.

Neumaier-Dargyay, E. K. *The Sovereign All-Creating Mind, the Motherly Buddha*. Albany: State University of New York Press, 1992.

Norbu, [Chögyal] Namkhai. *Sbas pa'i rgum chung, The Small Collection of Hidden Precepts: A Study of An Ancient Manuscript on Dzogchen from Tun-huang*. Arcidosso, Italy: Shang-Shung Edizioni, 1984.

Norbu, Chögyal Namkhai and Adriano Clement. *The Supreme Source*. Ithaca, NY: Snow Lion, 1999.

Petech, Luciano. *China and Tibet in the Early XVIIIth Century*. Leiden: Brill, 1972.

—. *The Kingdom of Ladakh*. Serie Orientale, vol. 51. Rome: Istituto italiano per il Medio ed Estremo Oriente, 1977.

—. *Central Tibet and the Mongols: The Yüan-Sa-skya Period of Tibetan History*. Rome: Istituto Italiano per il Medio ed Estremo Oriente, 1990.

Pettit, John. *Mipham's Beacon of Certainty*. Boston: Wisdom, 1999.

Phuntsho, Karma. *Mipham's Dialectics and the Debates on Emptiness*. London and New York: Routledge Curzon, 2005.

Richardson, H. E. *Ceremonies of the Lhasa Year*. London: Serindia, 1993.

Roerich, George N. *The Blue Annals*. Delhi: Motilal Banarsidass, 1976 [1949].

Ronis, Jann Michael. "Celibacy, Revelations, and Reincarnated Lamas: Contestation and Synthesis in the Growth of Monasticism at Katok Monastery from the Seventeenth Through Nineteenth Centuries." Ph.D. diss., University of Virginia, 2009.

—. "Powerful Women of Degé: Reassessing the Reign of Tsewang Lhamo (d. 1812)." *Revue d'Etudes Tibétaines* 22 (2011): 61–82.

—. "Deeds of the Dergé King." In *Sources of Tibetan Tradition*, ed. Matthew Kapstein, Kurtis Schaeffer, and Gray Tuttle, 607–13. New York: Columbia University Press, 2013.

—. "The Prolific Preceptor: Si tu paṇ chen's Career as Ordination Master in Khams and Its Effect on Sectarian Relations in Sde dge." *Journal of the International Association of Tibetan Studies* 7 (2013): 49–85.

Roy, Pratap Chandra. *The Mahabharata of Krishna-Dwaipayana Vyasa*. 12 vols. Calcutta: Oriental Publishing Company, 1962–63.

Samuel, Geoffrey. *Civilized Shamans: Buddhism in Tibetan Societies*. Washington, DC: Smithsonian Institution Press, 1993.

Sanderson, Alexis. "Pious Plagiarism: Evidence of the Dependence of the Buddhist Yoginītantras on Śaiva Scriptural Sources." Leiden: Unpublished seminar paper, 1995.

Schaeffer, Kurtis R. "The Fifth Dalai Lama Ngawang Lopsang Gyatso." In *The Dalai Lamas: A Visual History*, ed. Martin Brauen, 64–91. Chicago: Serindia, 2005.

——. "Ritual, Festival and Authority Under the Fifth Dalai Lama." In *Power, Politics, and the Reinvention of Tradition: Tibet in the Seventeenth and Eighteenth Centuries*, ed. Bryan J. Cuevas and Kurtis R. Schaeffer. Leiden: Brill, 2006.

Skeen, William. *Adam's Peak: Legendary, Traditional, and Historic Notices of the Samanala and Srī-pāda*. New Delhi: Asian Educational Services, 1997 [1870].

Smith, E. Gene. *Among Tibetan Texts: History and Literature of the Himalayan Plateau*. Boston: Wisdom, 2001.

Smith, Jonathan Z. *Imagining Religion: From Babylon to Jonestown*. Chicago: Chicago University Press, 1982.

Sørensen, Per K. *The Mirror Illuminating the Royal Genealogies: Tibetan Buddhist Historiography: An Annotated Translation of the XIVth Century Tibetan Chronicle: rGyal-rabs gsal-ba'i me-long*. Wiesbaden: Harrassowitz Verlag, 1994.

Sørensen, Per K. and Guntram Hazod. *Civilization at the Foot of Mount Sham-po: The Royal House of lHa Bug-pa-can and the History of g.Ya'-bzang*. Vienna: Verlag der Österreichischen Akademie der Wissenschaften, 2000.

——. *Rulers on the Celestial Plain: Ecclesiastic and Secular Hegemony in Medieval Tibet. A Study of Tshal Gung-thang*. Vienna: Verlag der Österreichischen Akademie der Wissenschaften, 2007.

Sperling, Elliot E. "Miscellaneous Remarks on the Lineage of Byang La-stod." *China Tibetology*, special issue (1992): 272–77.

Stearns, Cyrus. *Luminous Lives*. Boston: Wisdom, 2001.

——. *King of the Empty Plain: The Tibetan Iron-Bridge Builder Tangtong Gyalpo*. Ithaca, NY: Snow Lion, 2007.

Stein, Rolf A. *Etude du monde chinois: institutions et concepts*. In *Annuaire du College de France*. Paris: College de France, 1972: 489–510, 1973: 457–70, 1974: 499–517.

——. "La soumission de Rudra et autres contes tantriques." *Journal Asiatique* 283, no. 1 (1995): 121–60.

Sundberg, Jeffrey R. "The Wilderness Monks of the Abhayagirivihāra and the Origins of Sino-Javanese Esoteric Buddhism." *Bijdragen tot de Taal-, Land- en Volkenkunde* 160, no. 1 (2004): 95–123.

Sundberg, Jeffrey and Rolf Giebel. "The Life of the Tang Court Monk Vajrabodhi as Chronicled by Lü Xiang: South Indian and Śrī Laṅkān Antecedents to the Arrival of the Buddhist Vajrayāna in Eighth-Century Java and China." *Pacific World Journal* 3, no. 13 (2011): 129–222.

Suzuki, Daisetz Teitaro. *The Tibetan Tripitika: Peking Edition*. Tokyo-Kyoto: Tibetan Tripitika Research Institute, 1957.

Takahashi, Kammie. "Rituals and Philosophical Speculation in the *Rdo rje sems dpa'i zhus lan*." In *Esoteric Buddhism at Dunhuang: Rites and Teachings for This Life and Beyond*, ed. Matthew T. Kapstein and S. van Schaik, 85–141. Leiden: Brill, 2010.

——. "Contribution, Attribution, and Selective Lineal Amnesia in the Case of Mahāyogin dPal dbyangs," *Revue d'Etudes Tibétaines* 32 (2015): 5-23.

Tatelman, Joel. *The Glorious Deeds of Purna*. Richmond, England: Curzon, 2000.

Tenpa'i Nyima, Dodrupchen Jigme. *Key to the Precious Treasury*. Trans. Lama Chönam and Sangye Khandro. Ithaca, NY: Snow Lion, 2010.

Tsomu, Yudru. "Local Aspirations and National Constraints: A Case Study of Nyarong Gonpo Namgyel and His Rise to Power in Kham (1836–1865)." Ph.D. diss., Harvard University, 2006.

Tucci, Giuseppe. *Tibetan Painted Scrolls*. 3 vols. Rome: Libreria dello Stato, 1949.

Ui, Hakuju, et al., eds. *A Complete Catalogue of the Tibetan Buddhist Canons (Bkaḥ-ḥgyur and Bstan-ḥgyur)*. Sendai: Tōhoku Imperial University, 1934.

Uray, Geza. "The Old Tibetan Sources of the History of Central Asia up to 751 A.D.: A Survey." In *Prolegomena to the Sources on the History of Pre-Islamic Central Asia*, ed. J. Harmatta, 275–304. Budapest: Adadémiai Kiadó, 1979.

van der Kuijp, Leonard W. J. "Notes Appropos of the Transmission of the Sarvadurgatipariśodhanatantra in Tibet." *Studien zur Indologie und Iranisk* 16, no. 7 (1992): 109–25.

van Schaik, Sam. "The Early Days of the Great Perfection." *Journal of the International Association of Buddhist Studies* 27, no. 1 (2004): 165–206.

Vitali, Roberto. *The Kingdoms of Gu.ge Pu.hrang*. Dharamsala, India: Tho.ling gtsug.lag.khang lo.gcig.stong 'khor.ba'i rjes.dran.mdzad sgo'i go.sgrig tshogs.chung, 1996.

Waddell, L. Austine. *Tibetan Buddhism, with Its Mystic Cults, Symbolism and Mythology*. New York: Dover, 1972 [1895].

Wangdu, Pasang and Hildegard Diemberger. *dBa' bzhed: The Royal Narrative Concerning the Bringing of the Buddha's Doctrine to Tibet*. Wien: Verlag der Österreichischen Akademie der Wissenschaften. 2000.

Wayman, Alex and Ferdinand D. Lessing, *Mkhas grub rje's Fundamentals of the Buddhist Tantras*. Delhi: Motilal Banarsidass, 1978.

Wedemeyer, Christian K. *Āryadeva's* Lamp That Integrates the Practices (Caryāmelāpakapradīpa*)*. New York: The American Institute of Buddhist Studies, 2007.

——. *Making Sense of Tantric Buddhism: History, Semiology, and Transgression in the Indian Traditions*. New York: Columbia University Press, 2013.

Wilkinson, Christopher. "The *Mi nub rgyal mtshan Nam mkha' che* and *the Mahā Ākāśa Kārikās: Origins and Authenticity.*" *Revue d'Etudes Tibétaines* 24 (2012): 21–80.

Wu Hung. "What Is *Bianxiang*?—On the Relationship Between Dunhuang Art and Dunhuang Literature." *Harvard Journal of Asiatic Studies* 52, no. 1 (1992): 111–92.

Zangpo, Lama Tsering Jampal. *Garland of Immortal Wish-Fulfilling Trees.* Trans. Sangye Khandro. Ithaca, NY: Snow Lion, 1988.

INDEX

accomplishment, signs of, 46, 58
accomplishment initiation stream of renown, 69, 108
aeons of the universe, 22–23, 33
afflicted mind (*kliṣṭa-manas*), 42, 43, 173
age of fragmentation (*sil bu'i dus*), xviii, 3, 4, 30, 49, 50, 55, 174, 198
All-Creating King, 49, 52, 176, 177
Altan Khan, 89
Amazing Practice Manual for Guiding (Déwa Seldzé), 110
Amitabha, xv
Anuyoga, xix, 24, 25, 33, 35, 36–40, 47, 49, 62, 63, 64, 68, 69, 70, 72, 73, 74, 104, 108, 132–48
Armor Against Darkness (Nupchen), 3, 15–16, 31, 35, 39, 40, 46, 47, 56, 58, 115, 124–28, 130–31, 136
Armor of Exhortation, 27, 28
Asaṅga, 43
Aṣṭasāhasrikā, 53
Atharvaveda, 20
Atiśa, xv, 54
Ati Tenpé Gyeltsen, 117
Atiyoga, xix, 1, 24, 25, 31, 33, 35, 36, 37, 40–47, 49, 56, 62, 63, 64, 67, 69, 70, 72, 73, 74, 75, 102, 103, 109, 110, 132, 133
avadāna, 9
Avalokiteśvara, xv, 100, 101
Bengal, 2, 10, 164
Biographies for the Sutra Initiation Lineage, 72, 192
Black Excellence, 81, 193
Blue Annals (Gö Lotsawa), 58
bodhicitta, 35, 38, 39, 142, 144, 152
Bodhisattvabhūmi (Asaṅga), 43
bodhisattva vehicle, 24, 32, 33
Bon/Bön tradition, 5, 13, 116, 165
Brahmā, 16, 23
branch initiations, 72. *See also* coarse branch initiations
branch mandalas (*yan lag gi dkyil 'khor*), 70, 71, 72, 73, 74, 80, 105, 106, 107, 111, 191
Brief Structural Analysis of the Sutra (Dampa), 55, 56, 57
Brusha, 1–6, 21, 155, 156, 157, 207
Buddha Śākyamuni, 2, 120. *See also* Śākyamuni
Burushaski, xviii, 3, 5, 6, 7, 9, 21, 156, 157
Butön, 10, 11, 159

Cakrasaṃvara, xiii, 53, 54, 153, 178
Capable Intelligence, 27, 28
channels and winds (*rtsa rlung*), 38, 39, 172. *See also* subtle body
Che Tsengyé, 3, 4, 147, 156, 157
Chongyé, 92, 93, 94

Cittamātra, 61. *See also* Vijñānavāda/Vijñanavādins
coarse branch initiations, 72, 106, 107, 188, 201
Collected Precepts on Maṇi, 12
Collected Tantras of the Ancients, 64, 118, 134, 146, 183–84, 193
common mandala, 70, 108, 139, 192
conceptualizations, 44–45
consciousnesses, eight, 42, 43, 175
Consecration Ritual (Déwa Seldzé), 72, 189, 191
continuous wheel (*'khor lo rgyun*), vehicle of, 32

Dalai Lamas, xv, 79, 82, 85, 86, 88, 89, 90, 92, 93, 97, 98, 100, 101, 112, 113. *See also* Fifth Dalai Lama; Fourteenth Dalai Lama
Dampa Deshek, 52–64, 67, 68, 74, 75, 118, 126, 134, 136, 146, 162
Davidson, Ronald, 7, 50
Dawning of the Sun of Good Explanation: A Structural Analysis of the Gathering of Intentions (Dampa), 55, 57
Degé, 116–19
Dési Sangyé Gyatso, 87, 97, 99, 100
Déwa Seldzé (Selwé Gyen), 70, 71, 72, 73, 104–5, 106, 109, 110, 147, 181, 189, 190, 191, 192, 200, 201
Dhanarakṣita, 3, 56
Dharmabodhi, 3, 156, 180, 181
dharmakāya buddha, 1, 14, 19
dharmas of the king, five, 133
Dharmaśrī, 9, 71, 102, 103–4, 105, 106, 107, 108, 109–11. *See also* Lochen Dharmaśrī
Dīpavaṃsa, 21
Dorjé Drak monastery, 78–96, 98, 99, 113, 124, 194, 198, 202
Dorjé Gyeltsen, 60, 62, 63
Dorjé Pelgyi Drakpa, 5
Dreshongpa, 82, 96
Drölchen Sangyé Rinchen Gyeltsen Pelzangpo, 80, 86
Drölmawa Drotön Samdrup Dorjé, 69, 71, 80, 86, 88
Dromtön, xv
Dudjom Rinpoché, 91, 93, 101, 119, 128, 130, 131, 134–35
Dunhuang, 11, 32, 34, 39, 153, 170, 174, 185
Düsum Khyenpa, 53, 178
Dzamtön Drowé Gönpo, 53, 55, 57, 68, 178
Dzokchen, monastery of, 117, 118–19, 202
Dzokchen Gyelsé Zhenpen Tayé, 101, 118, 119
Dzokchenpa Namkha Drukdra, 81
Dzungars, 113, 124, 202

early sutras, seven (*mdo snga ma bdun*), 134
eight consciousnesses, 43, 175
eighteen initiations of benefit, ability, and profundity (*phan nus zab dbang bco brgyad*), 75
Ekajaṭī, 124, 126
emanation, mechanics of, 1–3
enlightenment, vehicles to, 23, 24, 76
Evam Chokar, 79, 80, 83, 86, 87, 90, 91, 92
excellent ones, five (*dam pa lnga*), 13, 14, 15, 16, 17, 26, 27, 114, 127
Expanded Spoken Teachings of the Nyingma School, 101, 128, 131, 204
explanatory tantra, 13, 51, 136, 143, 149

Fa-Hsiang, 21
Fifth Dalai Lama, xxi, 81, 82, 85, 86, 87, 88, 89, 90, 91, 92, 93, 94, 96, 97, 99, 100, 102, 116
five buddha families (*tathāgata*, *vajra*, *ratna*, *padma*, and *karma*), 2, 14, 25
five dharmas of the king, 133
five excellent ones (*dam pa lnga*), 13, 14, 15, 16, 17, 26, 27, 114, 127
five meditative signs of accomplishment, 46. *See also* signs of accomplishment
five paths, xix, 24, 25
five signs (that one is nearing end), 45
five sutras, 133
five yogas, xix, 24, 166
Fortress of Vajra-Garuda Rock, 127
Foulk, Griffith, 55
foundation consciousness (*ālayavijñāna*), 43, 44, 173, 174
four root sutras. *See* four root tantras
four root tantras (of Anuyoga), 57, 133–40, 133–48, 157–58, 189

Fourteenth Dalai Lama, 114
fully complete sutra initiation (*Mdo youngs rdzogs kyi dbang*), 70, 73, 104, 105, 107

Ganden Podrang government, 88, 97, 98, 100, 199
Garap Dorjé, 56, 103, 104, 105, 154, 155, 200
Gartön Zungé, 68
Gathered Great Assembly (*Tshogs chen 'dus pa*) Mandala, xix, 25, 70, 71, 72, 73, 75, 106, 107, 108, 115, 116, 120–23, 128, 131–32
Gathering of All Knowledge, 133, 135–40, 142, 143, 146, 149, 152, 153, 157, 158, 161, 167, 170, 173, 189, 207
Gathering of Intentions Sutra (*Dgongs pa 'dus pa'i mdo*): decline/diminishment/demise of, xxii, 47, 67–68, 69, 74, 76, 131, 132; in early Tibetan tantra, 30–47; as fundamental to identity of Nyingma School, xxiii, 68; historical origins of, 3–9; as largely extinct, 131; length of, 5; as *locus classicus* of Nyingma School, 11, 19, 32; mystic origins of, Rudra myth, 19–26; mythic origins of, King Dza myth, 10–19; original purpose of, xviii, xxiii; overview of origins of, 1–3; pollution of, 88; power of, 29; as root tantra of Anuyoga class, xv; successes and failures of, 66–68; as touchstone, 115; translation of, xviii, 3, 4, 5, 7, 8, 9
Gelukpa, xvii, 89, 100, 124, 130, 184, 203, 204
Geluk School, xvi, xvii, 89, 99, 113
General Exposition (Dharmaśrī), 8, 102, 103, 110, 171, 200, 206
General Prophecy of Ratna [Lingpa], 89
generation stage (*utpattikrama*), 34, 35, 36, 37
Genghis Khan, xv
genuine foundation of unification (*sbyor ba don gyi kun gzhi*), 44, 174
Germano, David, 41
Gesar epic, 4
Getse Mahāpaṇḍita, 117, 118
Gewa Pel, 52, 53
Gilgit, 4
Gödemchen, 79, 90, 91, 194
Gö Khukpa Lhetse, 5, 133, 145, 207
Gö Lotsawa, 58, 162, 180
Gongpa Rabsel, 48
Gongra faction, 102
Gongra Lochen Zhenpen Dorjé, 81, 90, 94, 96, 193, 194, 195
gray texts, 7–8, 52
Great Perfection (Rdzogs chen), 31, 36, 37, 40–47, 51, 56, 138, 169, 170, 172
Great Perfection Mind Class, 58, 174, 175, 180, 193
Great Prayer Festival (*smon lam chen mo*), 99, 100
Great Precept on Mind Sutra (*Sems lung chen mo'i mdo*), 133, 145
Great Seal of Nup, 30
ground-and-path summaries (*sa lam*), 66
Guhyabodhi, 56
Guhyagarbha, xiii, 39, 48, 49, 51, 52, 58, 59, 60–61, 62, 63, 67, 68, 75, 101, 118, 149, 152, 153, 163, 183, 185, 187
Guhyasamāja, xiii, 39, 68, 153, 167, 171, 172, 184
Guru Tashi, 89
Gushi Khan, 89
Gyatrül Padma Dongak Tendzin, 119
Gyatrül Rinpoché, 119, 120, 128

Harrison, Paul, 8
Hayagrīva, 24, 123
hearing transmission of persons (*gang zag snyan brgyud*), 18
Hevajra, xiii, 39, 53,153, 171, 172
historical origins (of *Gathering of Intentions*), 3–9
History of How the Mongols Were Repelled (Sokdokpa), 90
Hoffman, Helmut, xvi
Hsuan-Tsang, 21
Hunza Valley, 4

incidental views, 59
Indic ritual system, role of behind composition of *Gathering of Intentions*, 7
Indrabhūti, 2, 10, 12, 159
Indrabodhi, 56

initiations: branch initiations, 72; coarse branch initiations, 72, 106, 107; eighteen initiations of benefit, ability, and profundity (*phan nus zab dbang bco brgyad*), 75; *Māyājāla* initiations, 110, 123; precedent initiations (*sngon byung*), 25; purposes of, 65; secret initiation (*guhyābhiṣeka*), 39; subsequent initiations (*rjes 'jug*), 25; Sutra Initiation. *See* Sutra Initiation (*mdo dbang*): ten outer initiations, 73, 106, 107
initiation streams (*dbang gi chu bo*), 69
inner heat (*gtum mo*) practices, 39–40
inner initiation stream of arising, 69, 107

Jamgön Kongtrül Lödro Tayé, 116, 117
Jampa Namdak, 53
Jamyang Khyentsé Wangpo, 116, 117
Jamyang Rinchen Gyeltsen, 81, 102
Jangchup Sengé, 53
Jangpa family, 91, 92
Jewel Rosary (Nyelwa), 69, 71, 74, 80, 86, 102, 188
Jikmé Lingpa, 103, 136
Jñānamitra, 12
Jowo Lharjé, 58

Kagyu School, xvi, 53, 54, 116
Kālacakra, 47, 171
Kam Lotsawa, 53
Kangyur, 65
Karmapa, 53, 54, 151, 174, 178,183, 187
Katok monastery/tradition/system, 53, 54, 57, 62, 63, 64, 67, 68, 69, 74–76, 86, 94–95, 96, 102, 109, 110, 117, 118
Katok Situ Chökyi Gyamtso, 124
Key for Opening the Vajra Lock: An Explanation of the Difficult Points in the Gathering of Intentions (Dampa), 55, 57
Kham, xxii, 48, 53, 54, 74, 89, 94, 110, 113, 116, 117, 118, 119, 120, 125, 127, 128
Kham System, 75, 86, 88
Khenpo Jamyang, 75
Khenpo Khyentsé Lodrö (Khenpo Nüden), 114
Khenpo Ngakchung, 125, 126, 128
Khenpo Nüden, 39, 57, 126, 127, 128
Khyentsé Chökyi Lodrö, 125

King Dza, 2, 3, 10–19, 21, 26, 28, 29, 56, 67, 104, 105
King Tsa, 11. *See also* King Dza
Kriyā, 32, 33, 47, 48, 61, 72, 191
Kukkura/Kukkurāja, 12, 56, 179
Künga Lhamdzé, 85
Kuñjara, 11, 14, 17
Kunzang Lama, 128, 129, 130, 205, 206, 207
Kyitön Tsering Wangpo, 81

Lamotte, Étienne, 21
Lamp for the Eyes in Contemplation (Nupchen), 3, 31, 39, 153, 155, 169, 171, 172, 173, 174
Lang Darma (Wui Dumten), 4, 198
Langdro Tülku Tsewang Gyelpo, 80
Laṅka, 10, 13, 17, 20, 21, 23, 26, 114, 127, 164
Laṅkāvatāra Sūtra, 20, 21, 53
Later Dispensation period, 47
later sutras, seven (*phyi ma bdun*), 134
Lekden Dudjom Dorjé, 79, 81, 87, 90, 91, 92, 96
Lekpa Pelzang, 80
Len clan, 68–69, 71
Len Manual (Lentön), 69, 71, 72, 106, 180, 186, 189, 190
Len System (*Glan lugs*), 69, 73, 74
Lentön Sönam Gönpo, 69, 71, 186, 187, 190
Lhachen Dreshongpa Chögyel Dorjé, 81, 82
Lharjé Mar, 57, 147, 178
Lharjé Yangkhyé, 58
Lhato Tori, 11, 12–13
Lightning of Majestic Wisdom, 136
lineage (*ch'an-tsung*), xiii, xiv, xxi, 2, 9, 19, 29, 50, 51, 54, 55–56, 58, 63, 65, 67, 68–69, 78, 79–82, 83, 84, 85, 86, 88, 90, 94, 96, 98, 102–103, 104, 105, 112, 119, 125, 126, 128
Lochen Dharmaśrī, xxii, 8, 18, 70, 98, 101–2, 113, 141. *See also* Dharmaśrī
Lord of Laṅka, 16, 17–18, 23, 27, 29, 114, 127, 164
Lozang Chökyi Gyeltsen, 124

magical display manifesting, vehicle of the (*cho 'phrul mngon par 'byung ba*), 32–33, 157
Mahā-Anu-Ati triad, 62, 106, 200
Mahākaruṇā, 23

Mahāvaṃsa, 21
Mahāyāna, 8, 24, 169, 185
Mahāyoga, xix, 1, 20, 24, 25, 31, 33, 34–36, 37, 38, 40, 47, 49, 51, 58, 61, 62, 63, 64, 67, 68, 69, 70, 72, 73, 74, 75, 102, 108, 109, 132
Maheśvara, 3, 10, 20
Mahottara Heruka, 70, 122
Majestic Wisdom's Wheel of Lightning, 132
mandala palace, xix, 70
mandalas, xix, 2, 14, 25–26, 35, 36, 38, 52, 57, 59, 69, 70, 72, 73, 74, 75, 76, 82, 101, 105, 106, 107, 109, 110, 111, 115, 117, 119, 120–21, 122, 123. *See also* branch mandalas (*yan lag gi dkyil 'khor*); Gathered Great Assembly (*Tshogs chen 'dus pa*) Mandala; root mandala (*rtsa ba'i dkyil 'khor*)
Maṇi Rimdu festival, 101
Mañjuśrīmūlakalpa Tantra, 11
Marpa clan of Lhodrak, 56
Māyā, 58
Māyājāla initiations, 110, 123
Māyājāla mandala, 122
meditation periods, 45
meditative signs of accomplishment, five, 46. *See also* signs of accomplishment
Menlungpa Lochok Dorjé, 81, 82, 83, 84, 85, 96
mental consciousness (*manovijnana*), 43
mental waverings, 44, 45
Mind Class Meanings of A (*sems sde a don*), 75, 110
Mindröling tradition, 97–113, 116, 117, 118, 119
Minyak Tsashing, 91
Mökton Dorjé Pelzangpo, 69, 74, 76, 88, 102, 109, 110
monastic debate manuals (*yig cha*), 66
Mount Kailash, 129
Mount Malaya, 10, 13, 17, 18, 20, 26, 27, 28, 29, 104, 105, 127, 131
Mount Meru, 2
Mount Sumeru, 20
mythic origins (of *Gathering of Intentions*): King Dza, 10–19; Rudra, 19–26

Nāgabodhi, 56
Namdroling monastery, 120, 205
Namkha Gyeltsen, 92
Nang-Sok-Gong/Nang-Zhik-Gong, 89, 90, 96, 102
Nangtsé faction, 89, 91, 92, 94, 95, 96
natural secret meaning/the natural, the secret meaning, 61, 62, 63
New Schools, xvi, 10, 34, 51, 55
New Treasure of Choling, xiii
Ngagi Wangpo, 79, 85, 86–87, 92, 94, 95, 96, 192, 194
Ngari Paṇchen Pema Wangyel, 79, 81, 86, 90, 91, 92, 93, 102, 167, 194
Ngawang Losang Gyatso, 82, 86
nine (sub)vehicles, 33
nine vehicles (of *Gathering of Intentions*), xviii–xix, 25, 32, 33, 36, 37, 57, 58, 59, 60, 62, 67, 69, 70, 73, 74, 76, 104, 131
nonsectarian movement (*ris med*), 116
Northern Treasures (*Byang gter*), 79, 81, 85, 86, 87, 90, 92, 94, 95, 96, 99, 102, 186, 192, 197
Nüden, 127. *See also* Khenpo Khyentsé Lodrö (Khenpo Nüden)
Nupchen Sangyé Yeshé, 3–4, 15, 24, 25, 26, 27–28, 29, 30–33, 35, 36, 38, 39, 40–41, 42–43, 44, 45, 46, 47, 51, 56, 70, 71, 80, 115, 124, 125, 128, 132, 136, 145
Nups/Nup clan, 54, 56
Nup Yeshé Gyatso, 56
Nup Yönten Gyatso, 56
Nyelwa Delek, 69, 71, 72, 74, 80, 86, 207
Nyingmapa, xvii, xviii, xxiii, 29, 50, 51, 89, 90, 95, 113
Nyingma School, xv, xvi, xvii, xviii, xxiii, 1, 3, 11, 19, 29, 31, 32, 33, 36, 37, 47, 49, 51, 52, 59, 64, 66, 67, 73, 74, 76, 77, 80, 89, 90, 96, 98, 100, 102, 108, 109, 113, 115–19, 122, 131, 132
The Nyingma School of Tibetan Buddhism, 134–35

obscurations, 44, 45
Oḍḍiyāna, 2, 10
Old Tibetan Annals, 4
Ornamental Appearance of Wisdom: A Commentary on the Sūtra, 18
outer initiations, ten, 73, 106, 107

outer initiation stream, 72, 106–7
Outline of the Vehicles (Dampa), 55, 58, 59, 63, 74, 179, 183, 188

Padma Gyurmé Gyatso, 113
Padmasambhava, xv, xvi, 54, 91, 145, 146, 171, 182
Pakmo Drüpa, 53, 54
Paṇchen Lama, xv, 124
Patam Singh, 130
Path and Result, 53
Pawo Tsuklak Trengwa, 64
Pelgyi Chökor, 53
Pelyul Dzongnang Rinpoché Jampel Lodrö, 127
Pelyul Khenpo Göndrup, 127
Pelyul monastery, 117, 118, 119, 120, 127, 128
Pema Gyalpo, 63
Pema Norbu Rinpoché, 114. *See also* Penor Rinpoché
Pema Trinlé, 72, 78, 79–88, 89, 90, 94, 95, 96, 98, 99, 102, 113
Penor Rinpoché, 121, 126, 127–28
perception (*dmigs pa*), 46
perfection stage (*niṣpannakrama* or *utpannakrama*), 35, 36, 37, 38, 39, 47, 67, 68, 108, 137, 171
Pillar Testament, 11, 12, 160
pith instructions system (*man ngag lugs*), 70, 71, 72, 103, 105, 106, 107, 108
Play of the Charnel Ground Cuckoo, 132, 136, 140–42
Podrang Zhiwa Ö, 5. *See also* Zhiwa Ö
poisons, three, 22, 23, 33
Polhané Sönam Topgye, 113
Pön Gelu, 54
Prabhāhasti, 56
practice tradition (*phyag bzhes*), 104, 105
Pratyekabuddhas, 33, 37
precedent initiations (*sngon byung*), 25
Prophetic Commentary (King Dza), 56, 57, 58
Pugyel empire, xviii, 49
Pure Crystal Mirror: Guidelines for Clarifying Regulations and Prohibitions in Twenty-One [Chapters], 97
Purification of All Negative Rebirths, 2

Ra Lotsawa, 53
Rāmāyaṇa, 21, 158, 164
Rāvaṇa, 16, 18, 20, 23, 26, 27, 114
Rechungpa, 53
Refutation of False Mantra (Gö Khukpa Lhetse), 132
religious ceremony, as political strategy, 98–101
Ṛgveda, 19, 20
Richardson, Hugh, 100
Rinchen Namgyal, 101
ritual cards (*tsakli*), 109
ritual manuals, xv, xvii, xx, xxi, 30, 49, 51, 75, 80, 81, 82, 85, 86, 88, 94, 95, 101, 104, 105, 109, 112, 121
River of Honey (Moktön), 69, 74, 76, 86, 88, 95, 102, 109
Rolang Dewa (Garap Dorjé), 56
rolled into one (*gcig tu dril ba*) system, 105, 111
root mandala (*rtsa ba'i dkyil 'khor*), 70, 72, 73, 74, 107. *See also* common root mandala; uncommon root mandala
root sutras, four, 133. *See also* four root tantras
root tantra (*rtsa rgyud*), xv, 13, 49, 51, 67, 68, 118, 135. *See also* four root tantras (of Anuyoga)
Rudra, 3, 5, 6, 7, 9, 10, 19–26, 27, 29, 67

Ṣaḍakṣarī, 101
sādhana, xiii, 51, 110
Śaivism, 20
Śākya Jungné, 48
Śākya Mudrā, 56
Śākyamuni, 13, 14, 16, 17, 24, 26, 70, 120
Sakya Paṇḍita, 34
Śākya Prabhā, 56
Sakya School, xvi, 116
Śākya Sengé, 56
Samādhirāja, 53
Samantabhadra, 70
Śambhala, 2
Saṃdhinirmocana, 53
Samdruptsé, 81, 88
Samuel, Geoffrey, xvi–xvii
Sangdak Trinlé Lhündrup, 102, 124

Sangyé Gyatso, 87, 97, 99, 100
Sarvabuddhasamāyoga, 9, 153, 158
Sarvatathāgata-tattvasaṃgraha, 2, 11, 20, 69, 167, 174
Sayings of Wa, 11
Schaeffer, Kurtis, 97
Scripture for Accomplishing Yoga (*Rnal 'byor grub pa'i lung*), 153
secret body, 38–39, 40, 46
secret initiation (*guhyābhiṣeka*), 39
secret initiation stream of perfection, 69, 108
Secret Mantra, 13, 15, 16, 17, 24, 26, 27, 28, 33, 34, 36, 42, 44, 46, 47, 92, 94
Seminal Essence of the Great Expanse, 116
Seminal Heart traditions, 46, 67
Seminal of the Heart of Great Expanse, xiii
seven early sutras (*mdo snga ma bdun*), 134
seven later sutras (*phyi ma bdun*), 134
sexual union, 35, 38, 39, 46
Shangpa, 58
Sherap Sengé, 53
Siddhārtha, 25
signs, five (that one is nearing end), 45
signs of accomplishment, 46, 58
Situ Rinpoché Shedrup Chökyi Gyatso, 124–25, 126
Śiva, 20
Śiva-Rudra cult, 20
six tantras, 57, 135
Smith, Gene, 116
Smith, J. Z., 64
Sokdokpa Lodrö Gyeltsen, 86, 88, 90, 94, 133
Sonam Dorjé, 129, 130
Sönam Gyatso, 89
Sönam Tsemo, 53
Songtsen Gampo, 11
Spoken Teachings (*bka' ma*), xvii, xviii, 31, 48–64, 67, 75–76, 79, 80, 87, 98, 99, 101–4, 109, 111–12, 117, 118, 131
Spoken Teachings festival (*sgrub mchod*), 120–23, 128
Śrāvakas, 33, 37, 70, 73
Śrī Heruka, 123
Sri Lanka, Buddhism in, 20–21
Śrī-saṃvarodaya-uttaratantra (*Dpal sdom pa'i 'byung ba'i rgyud phyi ma*), 10
Stein, R. A., 5
strategy of adoption and rejection (*'dor len bya tshul*), 105
subcommentary, by Nüden, 39, 57, 126, 127, 128
subsequent initiations (*rjes 'jug*), 25
subtle body techniques/practices, 38, 39, 40, 47, 67, 68
Sucandra, 2
Sudāya-jātaka, 9
Summary of the Gathering of Intentions (Dampa), 55, 57, 126
Sutra, Illusion, and Mind, 64, 75, 117, 126
Sutra, Tantra, and Mind Class, 33, 49, 131
sutra, tantra, and mind (*mdo rgyud sems gsum*), 33, 49
Sutra Initiation (*mdo dbang*), 25, 37, 39, 65–77, 79, 80, 83, 85, 87, 89, 94, 95, 96, 98, 102, 103, 104, 109, 111, 115, 137, 140, 142, 145, 152, 158, 191
Śvetāśvatara Upaniṣad, 20
symbolic transmission of *vidyādharas* (*rig 'dzin brda brgyud*), 17, 18, 27

Tai Situ Jangchup Gyeltsen, 100
taming myths, 19, 20, 21, 28, 67
tantras, six, 57, 135
tantra system (*rguyd lugs*), 70, 71, 103, 104, 105, 107, 108
tantric myth: reader as playing active role in, 29; reading of, 26–29
tantric ritual, secrecy of, xiv
Tashi Topgyel Wangpö De, 86, 91, 92, 93, 94, 96
tenets (*grub mtha'*), 44, 66
ten levels, xix, 24, 25, 58
ten outer initiations, 73, 106, 107
Terdak Lingpa Rikdzin Gyurmé Dorjé, 98, 99, 100, 101, 110, 111, 113, 118
Theravadin Buddhism, 20
thought transmission of the conquerors (*rgyal ba dgongs brgyud*), 13–14, 18
three doors, 41, 57, 61, 84, 96
three poisons, 22, 23, 33
three transmissions (*brgyud pa gsum*), 3, 17, 18, 21, 57, 115, 123, 131
Tibetan Book of the Dead, 59

transmissions, three (*brgyud pa gsum*), 3, 17, 18, 21, 57, 115, 123, 131, 162
treasure, xiii, xviii, 50, 51, 59, 67, 80, 100, 116, 131, 132
Treasure Teachings (*gter ma*), xvii, xviii, 31, 49
triad of sutra, tantra, and mind (*mdo rgyud sems gsum*), 33, 49
Trisong Detsen, xv, 11, 91
Tsangmo Rinchen Gyen, 53
Tsangpa Peldrak, 52
Tsering Lama Jampel Zangpo, 118, 128
Tsewang Norbu, 103
Tsongkhapa, 99
Tupzang Rinpoché, 127, 206
twelve ways of arising (*byung tshul bcu gnyis*), 15, 57

Ukpalung (The Valley of the Owls), 48, 52, 64, 81, 184
Ulkāmukha, 16
uncommon root mandala, 70, 72, 108, 192

Vajradhātu, 2, 69, 70, 72, 73, 75, 106
Vajra-Heruka, 24
Vajrakīlaya, 101, 123, 140–42
Vajrakumāra Bhurkuṃkūṭa, 24
Vajrapāṇi, 10, 11, 13, 14, 16, 17, 18, 20, 26, 27, 28, 29, 56, 105, 114, 127, 128
Vajrasattva, 9
Vajra Staircase: An Initiation Ritual Manual That Unifies the Systems of Tantra and Pith Instructions (Dharmaśrī), 103
Vajravidāraṇā, 72, 106
Vasudhāra, 30
vehicle for ascertaining the ultimate (*don dam nges pa'i theg pa*), 33
vehicle that extracts the source [of suffering], 33
Vijaya, 21
Vijñānavāda/Vijñanavādins, 43, 44. *See also* Cittamatra
Vilāsavajra, 61, 62
Vimalakīrti, 16
Vimalamitra, 54
Vimalaprabhā, 2

Waddell, L. Austine, xvi
way of Rong[zom] and Long[chenpa], 51
way of the Zur, 51
ways of arising, twelve (*byung tshul bcu gnyis*), 15, 17, 26, 57, 139, 160
Wisdom's Magnificent Thunderbolts, 140, 142–45
Wu Hsing, 10

Yajurveda, 20
Yamāntaka, 31, 123
Yeshé Gyeltsen, 63, 74
Yidzin Wangmo, 85, 93
Yogācāra doctrine, 46
Yoga tantra, 20, 69, 33, 34, 72, 73, 140, 209
Yolmo Tülku Tendzin Norbu, 87
Yudruk Dorjé, 88, 90, 94

Zhamarpa, 81
Zhang-zhung, 5
Zhechen Gangshar, 127
Zhikpo Lingpa, 89, 90, 91, 92, 95, 195, 198
Zhingshakpa Tseten Dorjé, 92, 93
Zhiwa Ö, 5, 132
Zurché (Zur the Elder), 48, 49, 51, 52, 54, 56, 58, 176, 177, 179, 180, 209
Zurchung (Zur the Younger) Sherap Drakpa, 48, 49, 51, 58, 177, 179, 180, 185
Zurham Śākya Jungné, 69, 71, 71–72, 73, 74, 76, 80, 86, 88, 106, 186, 187, 188, 190, 191, 193, 194, 202
Zurmo Gendün Bum, 80, 86, 190, 193, 194
Zurpoche Śākya Jungné. *See also* Zurché
Zur Śākya Sengé (Dropukpa), 48, 49, 53, 56, 58, 68, 146, 162, 178, 179, 187, 209
Zur Spoken Class (*bka' sde zur ba*), 49
Zur System, xxi, 72, 73, 80. *See also* Zurs/Zur tradition
Zurs/Zur tradition, 32, 33, 47, 48–52, 55, 56, 58, 59, 62, 64, 67, 68, 71, 75, 80

GPSR Authorized Representative: Easy Access System Europe, Mustamäe tee 50, 10621 Tallinn, Estonia, gpsr.requests@easproject.com

www.ingramcontent.com/pod-product-compliance
Lightning Source LLC
Chambersburg PA
CBHW022043290426
44109CB00014B/966
* 9 7 8 0 2 3 1 1 7 6 0 1 9 *